Power, Pedagogy and Praxis

CRITICAL ISSUES IN THE FUTURE OF LEARNING AND TEACHING

This series represents a forum for important issues that do and will affect how learning and teaching are thought about and practised. All educational venues and situations are undergoing change because of information and communications technology, globalization and paradigmatic shifts in determining what knowledge is valued. Our scope includes matters in primary, secondary and tertiary education as well as community-based informal circumstances. Important and significant differences between information and knowledge represent a departure from traditional educational offerings heightening the need for further and deeper understanding of the implications such opportunities have for influencing what happens in schools, colleges and universities around the globe. An inclusive approach helps attend to important current and future issues related to learners, teachers and the variety of cultures and venues in which educational efforts occur. We invite forward-looking contributions that reflect an international comparative perspective illustrating similarities and differences in situations, problems, solutions and outcomes.

Series Editors:

Michael Kompf - *Brock University, Canada* (michael.kompf@brocku.ca)

&

Pamela M Denicolo - *University of Reading, UK* (p.m.denicolo@reading.ac.uk)

Power, Pedagogy and Praxis

Social Justice in the Globalized Classroom

Shannon A. Moore
Brock University, Canada

Richard C. Mitchell
Brock University, Canada

SENSE PUBLISHERS
ROTTERDAM / TAIPEI

A C.I.P. record for this book is available from the Library of Congress.

ISBN 978-90-8790-490-6 (paperback)
ISBN 978-90-8790-491-3 (hardback)
ISBN 978-90-8790-492-0 (e-book)

Published by: Sense Publishers,
P.O. Box 21858, 3001 AW
Rotterdam, The Netherlands
http://www.sensepublishers.com

Printed on acid-free paper

Cover photo: Divino and the MASJES Program (http://www.brocku.ca/socialjustice/index.php)

TABLE OF CONTENTS

ACKNOWLEDGMENTS

We owe a debt of gratitude to many individuals who made this volume possible. The impetus for this text began through conversations with Professor Michael Kompf of Brock University, Canada, and his mentorship was pivotal. We also thank Michel Lokhorst of Sense Publishers for his editorial expertise, professionalism and endorsement. Particular thanks go as well to faculty, staff and students of the Masters of Social Justice and Equity Studies at Brock University for their permission to use the cover photograph which was originally created for that program. Finally, this anthology is dedicated to the memory and life's work of Professor Katarina Tomaševski (please see her biography for more information), and we are grateful to Ken Kehls for his contribution to the creation of an executive summary of her Global Report, *The State of the Right to Education Worldwide: Free or Fee?*

Shannon Moore and Richard Mitchell

RICHARD C. MITCHELL AND SHANNON A. MOORE

INTRODUCTION

Power, Pedagogy and Praxis – Towards Common Ground

Whether one sees the current wave of globalization as a new ideology obscuring trends that have always accompanied modernity's colonialist, capitalist expansions, or whether one sees something qualitatively novel, the dilemma for contemporary social scientists is the same – to make sense of what they observe (Weber 2002). This approach sets the tone for a text drawing upon both theory and empiricism with scholars from diverse critical and pedagogical discourses at various stages of their careers, and sadly, one of our number deceased since the work was undertaken in mid-2006 (see Tomaševski 2006b). The themes guiding us were various expressions of institutional, social, legal, political, and personal power, pedagogy and praxis, and clearly, each rests lightly upon highly contested terrain while tethering readers to the shifting ground of an emergent, new discourse (see Appadurai 1996; Apple, Kenway and Singh 2005; Bloch, Kennedy, Lightfoot and Weyenberg 2006; Burbules and Torres 2000; Crossley 2000; Malott 2008; Spring 2006; Stromquist 2000 for additional analyses). Throughout this chapter, our aim is to foster a critical dialogue about what social justice might mean in the context of the many pedagogical perspectives of the whole anthology. Although it is fair to say an exhaustive analysis is beyond the scope of this project, the text presumes to be global in content with individual scholars from Canada, the US, UK, and Europe predominant.

Similar to Foucault's attempt to historicize his ontological inquiries (1977), we too attempt to define some of the contours of this emergent discourse, not of the body/mind, but something nonetheless of the subjective experiences of teaching/learning for hundreds of millions of humans without essentializing (see also Besley and Peters 2008: 58; Osler and Vincent 2002). Kincheloe (2008) acknowledges that for critical pedagogues at this historical juncture, decisions must be taken about whether or not to continue to allow many people in North America, especially in non-white sub-cultures like Indigenous, African American, Latino/a, and Asian, not to mention around the world…

> …to look at what we do as basically a North American appropriation of a South American thing. In many ways the state of critical pedagogy right now in North America constitutes a few North Americans appropriating a Freirean pedagogy and taking it into a U.S. or Canadian context….they see critical pedagogy as primarily a North American white thing, and often times a white male thing (in Malott 2008: 158).

S.A. Moore and R.C. Mitchell (eds.), Power, Pedagogy and Praxis: Social Justice in the Globalized Classroom, 1–17.

With these insights in mind, Kincheloe further asserts that critical educators should work to convince various 'sub-cultures' that there is something to be gained by joining in common ethical and political purpose to create conditions that lead towards greater social justice, seeing critical pedagogues as allies in this project (see Giroux; McLaren and Jaramillo; Linds and Goulet; Wotherspoon this volume). At the same time, critical pedagogues must recall that their own traditions, history and theorizing have frequently drawn from diverse, non-white, often Indigenous and other cultural contexts. Theorizing in this way doesn't necessarily mean leading anything new, but as Kincheloe points out, most often involves humbly listening and standing alongside oppressed groups in solidarity.

As Canadian-based scholars and active researchers we also observe how United Nations metanarratives such as the Millennium Development Goals[1] (or MDGs 2000) and the Convention on the Rights of the Child (or CRC 1989) have de facto established a common pedagogical and conceptual ground towards social justice throughout the world. As editors, though, we were confronted with the challenge of advancing any one notion of social justice from a globalized perspective, but found concepts such as 'just society' (Clark 2006) important to define, again without essentializing through the narrowed lens of a minority worldview. While many scholars would scoff at UN narratives being emancipatory or anti-oppressive approaches, they nonetheless offer an adequate set of organizing principles to begin thinking about our themes in an age of economic, political and technological uncertainty – without utopian idealism (see particularly Giroux; McLaren and Jaramillo; Tomaševski this volume). Yearly collections of macro-statistics by UN agencies such as WHO and UNICEF, for example, show that while the total global population has doubled since 1960, one odious indicator of humanity's progress or lack thereof as represented by the daily under-five mortality rates for children has astonishingly almost halved (UNICEF 2007). We contend that something extraordinary is occurring particularly with regard to this fourth MDG that seems to have entirely escaped the panoptic eye of international media and intellectuals alike (see also Rosling's 2007 astute analysis). We would argue that 'universal' access to primary education is simply a continuation of this globalized development trend.

Assessing the largest of many oppressed 'groups', the United Nations Children's Fund (UNICEF 2006) promotes gender equality as the third MDG, and when this is achieved, they argue, benefits will be felt not just amongst women and girl children but in many other spheres from poverty and hunger reduction to global health and environmental sustainability. Yet, as Katarina Tomaševski's final international report (2006b) indicates, the often obscured globalized factors limiting access need to be exposed as 'the lie of international support for free education'. Tomaševski was renowned as the first UN Special Rapporteur to request that her mandate be discontinued on the basis that she could not fully address this as a fundamental right, but merely as an aspiration to be realized progressively and most saliently as one that was subject to the whims of 'available resources'. Findings from her unprecedented study put the human right to education back where it belongs using it as the yardstick to assess the role and influence of World Bank directors as the chief architects in the global design of education. In addition, she highlights budgetary imbalances between military and education at national levels, as well as discrimination on the basis of gender, which the richest players in the international community have repeatedly pledged to eliminate but have so far failed to do.

Indeed, while "education for all" is the second of the eight MDGs articulated by world society representatives in New York to open this decade (United Nations 2006), some laudable progress has been achieved but much is yet to be done (Mundy 2006, 2007; UNESCO 2007a, b). UNICEF's flagship yearly report "The State of the World's Children 2007" showed that in the long run, social justice initiatives within education and particularly those targeted towards women still hold out the best possibility that all other Millennium Goals may be reached.

As an additional outcome of these globalized ways of thinking and knowing, many observers now agree that access to primary education, at the very least, is a fundamental human rights issue (David 2002; see also O'Byrne's 2003 analysis; and Mundy this volume). Although many also disagree, they frequently reveal a shaky historical, legal, and political grasp of this evolution (for example Lindahl 2006: 6-7, 19). Lindahl (2006) dismisses "issues of access, equality, and gender" as "moot", and in an astounding lack of attention to detail he accuses China of not having ratified the Convention on the Rights of the Child when in truth the US and Somalia are the only nations left to commit to children's rights within and without education (UNICEF 2006). While observing this is a "complex question to answer", how Lindahl concludes educational concerns related to gender are moot is ill-defined, and at worst, appears discriminatory and sexist. In contrast, educational sociologist Stromquist (2000) takes a measured stance in her critical analysis of globalized educational trends particularly towards "gender [a]s an area where culture, power and structures intersect at full strength". She reviews macro- and micro-systemic perspectives within indigenous and student resistance movements, the World Bank, the World Social Forum, the World Economic Forum, and linkages between and amongst transnational corporations. She reconsiders the emerging educational entrepreneurialism in developed and developing world contexts with its "consequences of globalization on women... [and] the social construction of gender". She declares that due to neoliberal notions the state should reduce its intervention" within educational systems since "gender policies are being weakened" (2000: 133, 143-144; also Conway 2006 and this volume; Mundy 2002, 2006, 2007 and this volume).

SOCIAL JUSTICE WITHIN AND WITHOUT EDUCATION: POWER, PEDAGOGY AND PRAXIS

Many analysts are observing how this generation is the first ever with the capacity to eradicate hunger and extreme poverty while there are perhaps just as many who believe the 3.4 million 'residents' dwelling within Dhaka's Malek slum (or Kenya's Kibera where one third of Nairobi's residents struggle to survive) have no right to access any form of education. Addressing participants of the World Social

Forum in early 2007, UN-HABITAT Director Mrs. Anna Tibaijuka observed these dynamics, and that the Nairobi event was being held at a crucial time in human history with half the world's population now living within urban areas. This is a result of natural population growth, human mobility – including rural-urban and international migration – as well as the reclassification of rural areas. "It is therefore important to consider the challenges of urbanization as you discuss women and poverty and listen to testimonies of women". Mrs. Tibaijuka challenged participants to a greater appreciation of the hardships faced by these demographics of extreme poverty. "Slums pose serious challenges to…women and the girl child who bear the brunt of all this because of their disadvantaged position in society as proscribed by our cultures, traditions, values and belief systems" (UN-HABITAT 2007 electronic cite; also Conway's analysis this volume). Achieving equity in anyone's classroom or within their political and cultural systems is a foremost expression of social justice in this era since education has emerged as the cornerstone for establishing all other human rights (Mundy 2002; Tomaševski 2006a, b; this volume).

Although definitions of social justice vary in depth and breadth, equity and fairness are two of the most common concepts. From a US perspective, qualitative theorist Charmaz (2005: 508-513) emphasizes that "a social justice focus can sensitize us to look at both large collectivities and individual experiences in new ways". However, "not only are justice and injustice abstract concepts, but they are, moreover, *enacted processes*, made real through actions performed again and again". Thus, in most classrooms it is apparent there are pedagogical processes embedded within larger societal structures that run along a north/south divide – the development of trade and new technologies, for example, has benefited northern economies the most over centuries of colonialist exploitation. Clearly, most students in the industrialized regions of the globe are thus beneficiaries of the newest technologies. The current, rapid exchanges of new information in a "rhizomatic" fashion first described by psychoanalyst Carl Jung (1956), taken up in greater depth by philosophers Deleuze and Guattari (1987), and more recently by educators such as Allan and I'Anson (2004), Bloch, Kennedy, Lightfoot and Weyenberg (2006), Mitchell (2007), and Moore (2007) to describe theoretical development is only the latest example. This rhizome metaphor conceptualizes educational research in a fashion similar to Charmaz (2005: 507) who contends that social justice inquiries are where social scientists may fruitfully apply "constructive social critique and change through qualitative research".

Moreover, educational philosopher Clark (2006: 272) adroitly observes "in one sense we are all for social justice – it would be hard to imagine that anyone would be for social injustice". Fair enough, perhaps, yet one must frequently question this premise particularly when dimensions of religiosity, poverty, ethnicity, gender, ability, sexual identities, or abuses of educational power converge. Recalling Scraton (1997: 186), this convergence often concerns…

> …adult power…a power readily and systematically abused. It is a dangerous and debilitating power, capable of stunting the personal development and potential of even the most resilient children….What is so difficult for adults,

> as power-brokers, to accept is that the 'crisis' is not of childhood' but one of adultism.

While the CRC has been widely critiqued by social scientists for the universalized, general notions of childhood that shaped its negotiations from 1979-1989 (Mitchell 2005), such views are visible within legal discourses as well. Pupavac (1998), for one, is quite skeptical of underlying psychoanalytic theories within the CRC and their "protective view of childhood not part of the experience of most countries of the South . . . [the CRC] infantilises children from Southern nations" (in Steiner and Alston 2000: 517). Notwithstanding similar early concern, Burman (2001) has encouraged exploration of the linkages between women's and children's rights urging researchers to engage in a little "cultural and disciplinary tourism and experiment with ideas from outside western psychology", and to move away from more reified models of childhood and perhaps human rights (see also Burman 1995, 1996).

> As feminists and child-rights activists have rightly pointed out [Jackson, 1993], it would be ironic indeed if we dispensed with the notion of the individual as cultural baggage just at the very moment that women and children were beginning to acquire some hard-won rights there-by . . . we should [work alongside] . . . rights approaches . . . towards formulating more genuine interpersonal and intersubjective approaches to development and education (Burman 2001: 14–15; also Woodhead 1999, 2000; Wyness 1999 for similar views).

O'Byrne (2003) also observes that "within academic circles, children's rights are often discussed separately from human rights". A key problem with conceptualizing children's rights lies squarely with the multiple definitions of childhood "which of course differ across time and space". To address this apparent under-theorizing and the resultant lingering confusion about the CRC within childhood, educational, developmental, justice and health studies, Lenzer (2002) calls for "a reintegration of the isolated segments of the children's rights agenda within the framework of human rights" (207-208). In-so-far as children are human, they are subjects of "human rights standards, specifics of age are irrelevant", contends O'Byrne (2002: 374) in agreement.

The UN Millennium Development Goals echo the same principles found within the CRC, and the treaty remains unique within international law as the most ratified agreement in history. The CRC asserts the human rights of children in 192 states including the centrality of access to publicly funded education obliged in Articles 28 and 29. CRC Article 42 further obliges states to inform both children and adults of the treaty 'principles and provisions', and that this rights-based approach applies to all young people less than eighteen years of age throughout the world. Research by Mitchell (2005) comparing educational policies in two northern democracies also found that metanarratives such as the CRC straddle the modernist/postmodernist divide when applied according to local culture (see also Freeman 2007; Mitchell 2000, 2003). On the whole, the authors drawn upon to this point emphasize the necessity for a transdisciplinary appreciation of human rights education, and the subsequent exercise of political, institutional, and interpersonal power relations. We also contend that a transdisciplinary appreciation of UN metanarratives offers a new framework for reconceptualizing this exercise of power, and along with this, a new understanding of our increasing interdependencies within local, national, environmental and transnational pluralities (Mitchell 2007).

Nevertheless, such transparent, democratic, rights-based approaches where power is exercised with accountability in mind may be more easily achieved in theory than in practice. The suggestion here is to forge a way forward by understanding how such globalized discourses may be applied in the everyday lives of oppressed or marginalizaed young people. In this project, we find ourselves agreeing with Dutch feminist Sevenhuijsen (1999) who argues:

> Policy texts are sites of power…by establishing narrative conventions, authoritative repertoires of interpretation and frameworks of argumentation and communication, they confer power upon preferred modes of speaking and judging, and upon certain ways of expressing moral and political subjectivity (cited in Moss and Petrie 2002: 81).

Simply stated, no nation-state needs any more new laws or human rights agreements; instead all states and the power-players regulating the systems within them need to uphold existing commitments (Kienge-Kienge Intudi 2007). With this exercise of power in mind, we move to a discussion of transdisciplinarity as a congruent conceptual framework for understanding and applying rights-based relationships in the globalized classroom.

TRANSDISCIPLINARY STANDPOINT

Anglo-American ethnographers Canaan and Montgomery (2004) discuss the nuances confronting contemporary academic knowledge workers, and argue that an analytical framework locating students, staff, and institutions within both local and extra-local patterns of stratification…

> …in particular those being created by increasingly globalizing capital flows, production processes, and labor use – would clarify our theoretical understanding of empiricism in this growing field of study. Such analysis is of growing importance as the role of the university is undergoing profound transformations and students, faculty, and administrations might be operating with contradictory ideas about their own positions and about what higher education is and can be. We contend such an approach will clarify the theoretical significance of students' practices in particular educational contexts (740).

In a meta-analysis of literature looking at similar barriers, Theoharis (2004: 2) maintains the US system fails to educate too many students on the margins, and he offers one definition, not in universalized terms, "but in the realities of public school work, in that social justice means that these administrators and teachers advocate, lead and keep at the center of their practice and vision issues of race, class, gender, disability, sexual orientation, and other historically marginalizing conditions". His work results from an activist's need to create social justice in public education and to help enlarge the body of scholarship focused on equity issues.

As Mirchandani (2005: 86) shrewdly observes, after decades of interdisciplinary rumination on postmodernism isn't it high time to move "from the epistemological to the empirical"? Transcending disciplines and embedded binaries such as modernity/postmodernity or quantitative/qualitative is also the handiwork of critical social pedagogues. Thus, the editorial standpoint of this collection reflects the increasing complexity of young people's lives in both hemispheric contexts while cutting across and standing against the anti-child/anti-youth hegemonies noted by Giroux (2003), Giroux and Searls-Giroux (2004), McLaren and Farahmandpur (2001 a, b), Moss and Petrie (2002), Scraton (1997), Tomaševski (2006a, b) and other critical theorists in childhood and youth, cultural, human rights, [dis]ability, and pedagogical studies.

Lingard (2000) has also noted the disjuncture between the global economy and individual nation-states, with the latter seen as both complicating and mediating entities (see also Conway 2006; Crossley 2000; Escobar 2004; Fisher and Ponniah 2003; Mundy 2002 for additional analyses). This rupture may be more pronounced since power politics are still organized within the boundaries of nation-states, but to appreciate the new contours emerging within any one educational system, one must also reconceptualize how national, cross-national, post-national and supra-national politics are unfolding simultaneously through multilateral international organizations in a systemic complexity described by legal theorist Niklas Luhmann as "social autopoiesis" (1982, 1997). The World Bank, IMF, UN, UNESCO, and OECD, for example, play larger leadership roles in financing, research and policy development than many individual actors in the 50 poorest states exert on their own destinies (Conway 2006 and this volume; Mundy 2002, 2006, 2007 and this volume). Recalling the Foucauldian sense of relations of power, these dimensions are both discursive and political forces that disperse, circulate, produce and regulate relationships between students and pedagogues – social and political. We view the problems of creating social justice in anyone's classroom as those diverging from gender, ethnicity, religion, culture, poverty, sexual identity and physical ability.

The authors drawn upon thus far each in their own way foreground a fundamental tension we confronted as editors in our analysis of relevant literature. In the effort to avoid universalizing any one educational issue, we must first acknowledge the privileged positions we occupy as educators who would philosophize social justice when it is existentially reduced to life and death for so many beyond our borders. In line with Crossley (2000) and other contemporary educators, we take up some responsibility to uncover new theoretical and practice perspectives with our argument for a transdisciplinary approach to better understand the intersections amongst critical pedagogy, social justice and human rights. This stance starts with criticality towards theory, law, and policy, an assumption that education might also be emancipatory, and finally, that praxis is a minimum standard for entering any related discourse. Thus, we aim to move beyond the limitations of a single pedagogical lens by opening up a more organic episteme that coincidentally offers previously silenced actors opportunities to be heard (as Conway; Giroux; Linds and Goulet; Kellett and Ward; McLaren and Jaramillo; Moore, Mitchell and Melchior; and Smith argue in this volume).

Comprehensive responses to the question of how we might begin to address humanity's uneven "globality" (Schafer 2005) are emerging within cross-cultural dialogues that embrace transdisciplinary thinking within and through education (Freeman 2007; Mitchell 2007; Moore 2007; Tomaševski 2006a, b; Woodhead 1999). In line with Kincheloe's (2008) recent analysis, Nicolescu (1999: 4) articulates this vision most succinctly: "The emergence of a new culture, capable of contributing to the elimination of tensions menacing life on our planet will be impossible without a new type of education which takes into account all the dimensions of the human being". Change and permanent interrogation are focal points of transdisciplinarity, and through these lenses we also take the stance that human populations are being re-orientated towards interconnectedness and social justice (for example globalized humanitarian relief efforts during environmental disasters). These are, in fact, the core expressions for transforming disequilibrium and peace-building contend authors such as Moore (2004) and Nicolescu (2002).

To illustrate the need, when individual young people 'fall through the cracks' – a common Anglo-American euphemism describing early, preventable deaths through sexual and/or physical abuse, neglect or addiction – critics respond with a type of blame that includes myopic interventions directed at single professions. As Foucault has argued, disciplinary approaches such as this are modernist in their origin (Dahlberg Moss and Pence 1999; Mitchell 2005, 2007) whereas in this post- or late-modern moment the lived realities of young people in both northern and southern spaces are complex and pluralistic, pointing epistemologically even ontologically towards new interdependencies (Baumann 2005: 1090; Conway 2006; Luhmann 1997; Mitchell 2003, 2007; Moore 2007). Acknowledging Appadurai's (1996) seminal work illuminating similar themes, we nevertheless take up a different standpoint towards development of a congruent theoretical framework for this project (see also Tikly's 2001 and Crossley's 2000 trenchant contributions).

> Multidisciplinarity concerns studying a research topic not as just one discipline but in several at the same time...it brings a plus to the discipline in question [but this plus] is in exclusive service to this discipline…Interdisciplinarity concerns the transfer of methods from one discipline to another…like multidisciplinarity, interdisciplinarity overflows the disciplines, but its goal still remains within the framework of disciplinary research…transdisciplinarity concerns that which is between disciplines, across the different disciplines, and beyond all disciplines (Nicolescu 2002: 42-44).

Throughout this text, activists, researchers, scholars and pedagogues have been brought together in a transdisciplinary 'bricolage' (see Kincheloe and McLaren's 2005 discussion of this notion) to analyze what they contend social justice looks like from their vantage points. These discussions integrate critical, cultural, legal, pedagogical, sociological, psychological, physiological, medical, biological, social work, performance, [dis]ability, humanities, and Indigenous discourses. At the same time, each illuminates in their own way the growing need to transcend intellectual silos in order to offer a fresh look at how pedagogical practices with young people are being created and destroyed. Addressing this need also addresses the active, reflexive, critical demands of democratic forms of citizenship, and challenges pedagogues and pupils alike who view themselves being herded into narrow chutes of consumerism by the present generation of elders. Along with our own voices, each author adds their own call for a more radicalized, even revolutionary expression of democratic citizenship as Beck and Beck-Gernsheim (2002), Giroux (2003), and Stromquist (2000: 171) have previously articulated (also Connolly; Fancy and Spearey; Wotherspoon this volume).

In these ways, transdisciplinarity within educational contexts concerns emergent new thinking, new ways of accessing old ways of thinking, construction of new ways of knowing, and praxis in order to transcend tired, dichotomous critiques by recognizing multiple new sites and forms of knowledge creation. Somerville and Rapport (2000: 6-7) emphasize that transdisciplinary approaches to science, politics, education, and cultural studies of media and the arts sharply contrast multi- or even interdisciplinary methodologies, and are fundamentally associated with critique. In a description of peace research and education, for example, "Eckhardt (1974) spoke of 'breaking through disciplinary barriers, disobeying the rules of disciplinary etiquette.' In contrast to disciplinarity... transcendence is heretical. It is a generic rebel pushing beyond orthodoxy... the term connotes transformation". In this regard, "Michel Foucault, not Aristotle or Plato...is the paradigmatic figure of transdisciplinary studies". Transdisciplinarity is defined by Nicolescu (2002), Russell (2000) and others as moving beyond traditional epistemological expressions of scholarship–a way of knowing "that will be essential in the 21st and later centuries" (Koizumi 2001: 219).

Drawing upon a wide range of contributors during a 1999 Montreal symposium Visser (1999) describes this integrative, transdisciplinary view of education in the coming era:

- Learning is still an underdeveloped concept, but it is necessary for all humans to be able to adapt to continuous and ever-faster change in an increasingly complex world. Fundamental changes are urgently required in the way school systems throughout the world are organized that must include more holistic conceptualizations of schools themselves as only one part of a comprehensive learning environment.
- Learning is a transdisciplinary concept related to overarching concerns such as change and growth; community-based processes and development; complex, diverse, and emerging adaptive expressions; new

designs for systems of knowledge construction interacting with, and building upon, existing knowledge bases; lifelong learning at different levels of organizational complexity; neuroscience and lifespan cognitive development; the interconnections and distinctions between and among data, information, knowledge and wisdom; and new technologies for learning, languages, cognition, and meta-cognition. Efforts to transcend these currently separated views will acquire a transdisciplinary, integrative vision of learning.

- Learning has to do with the capacity to interact creatively and constructively with problems. In most of our current pedagogical practices throughout the minority and majority worlds such problems are often concealed or ignored altogether. In a similar manner to Freire (1970, 1999), learning therefore needs to be re-focused on problems, including their historical and epistemological contexts.

Thus, transdisciplinary research and scholarship generally create their own criteria and standards because of the unique, emergent qualities listed above, including a greater legitimization of knowledge creation by Indigenous stakeholders, and other more marginalized actors located in spaces outside the political confines of the 'corporate-academic-military-industrial' complex (McLaren and Jaramillo 2007 and this volume). As critical social pedagogues, we contend that transdisciplinarity is also the most cogent framework for approaching social justice praxis in order to achieve a progressive realization of the human right to education in all nation-states.

A GLOBALIZED CLASSROOM?

As highlighted, we have gained in this project from the posthumous research contribution by Dr. Katarina Tomaševski and her final study on the human right to education in 170 non-OECD states. Her commitment to uncovering the reasons for the collective global failure to uphold education as a basic human right reveal the pivotal shift from 'free' to 'fee' in many states, and the language of the free market led by the often insidious role of World Bank directors as architects in the globalized classroom. Primary education was Tomaševski's focus since the original rationales for declaring education as the birthright of all children remain unchanged in the present era. In this concern she echoes Spring (2004: 64-65) who concludes that the Bank is simply "extending the reach of colonialism" through its lending practices. The basis for her analysis and findings comes from exhaustive fieldwork that made it transparent how and why children in poor countries could not afford to go to primary school: Public education in name: legally *free* but really *for fee*. The rhetoric of international resolutions, declarations, and recommendations are churned out by parts of the international community while other parts erode the possibility of realizing this right to education for tens of millions. Any explanation of this simultaneous affirmation and denial of the right to education within the United Nations (UN) - an organization committed to human rights, loudly proclaiming then quietly betraying - is not easy to reconcile when the global division of labour keeps human rights in their place, and when challenges of exclusion are impeded by vehement denials and exhortations that *education is a human right*.

Singh, Kenway and Apple (2005: 1) decry the "relative dearth of education research" while at the same time identifying a zeitgeist for globalized knowledge and its mainly minority-world educational agenda including "a scaffold for considering the effects on education of [both] neoliberal and neoconservative globalisms". In response, this volume is empirically well anchored with Tomaševski's analysis of the rhizomatic flow of knowledge and resources from external structures, and resulting practices within individual classrooms located within both northern and southern hemispheres.

Tomaševski (2006b) charges that there is a lack of vocabulary relating to payments levied in public primary education *which should be free*, but the World Bank's term, "user or school fees", is the most widespread since many such charges originated from the Bank's policies. Thus, it transpires that "the cost of education can be prohibitively high and prevent poor children from enrolling or force them to drop out before completing schooling which is, in the laws of most countries, defined as compulsory." Tomaševski contends this problem is linked to the well-documented exemption of international institutions from the law. The first step toward eliminating the present global phenomenon of poverty-based exclusion, she maintains, is through the integration of governmental human rights obligations into domestic education policies and strategies. At the core is this fact: "Public funding for education necessitates acceptance of governments' powers to raise revenue through taxation and to prioritize the *right to education* in its budgetary allocations." It follows then that in cases where this is not financially viable, international cooperation should facilitate rather than hinder the universalization of education in one state at a time. When this omission hinders the birthright of every child to free, primary education Tomaševski (2006) advocates this be constructed, understood and denounced as a violation of fundamental human rights.

Most observers will recall how the World Bank was created as an integral dimension of post-World War II Bretton Woods agreements to avoid future world wars by international and multilateral institutions, and to ensure an open international trading system with global financial stability. Their loan strategies have gradually evolved from support of public infrastructure projects such as roads, railways, and power plants, to the provision of capital for other inputs necessary for development, namely the maintenance of educational and health services. The World Bank group comprises four agencies: the International Bank for Reconstruction and Development; the International Development Association; the International Finance Corporation; and the Multilateral Investment Guarantee Agency (see also Conway 2006; Mundy 2002; Weekes 2006). Nonetheless, the combined experience of vast populations of young people impacted by the Bank's 'development' projects within dozens of nation-states is found to be disturbingly discriminatory.

Tomaševski's report examined the laws, policies, and practices in the main regions of the world; documented the recognition or denial of the right to education according to region and sub-region; discerns why this is so; and highlights the impact of the educational model that was chosen or imposed within this free or for-fee dichotomy. If the first step towards finding a solution is to agree on the problem, global policymakers are a long way from solving the problem because key questions are avoided–particularly the nomenclature of access to education and the right to education where the former implicates the ability to pay and the latter is an entitlement. Also missing in the attempts to universalize primary education into a unified global strategy is what any recognition of human rights requires: the foundation of individual entitlements and corresponding public responsibilities. The omission of a governmental obligation to make education free and compulsory denies education as a human right—a sentiment corresponding to US policy, echoed by the World Bank (WB) and fundamentally unchallenged by global actors in both education and human rights.

Monitoring the state of the right to education world-wide should be a formal responsibility of UN human rights bodies and the United Nations Educational, Scientific, and Cultural Organization (UNESCO). As a critic of the UN Commission on Human Rights (Tomaševski 2006b) during her time Special Rapporteur on the Right to Education, she presided over the unprecedented abolition of her office on the grounds of the erosion of its credibility – perhaps a hopeful sign signaling some form of international, intergovernmental accountability. While Lindahl (2006: 7) reports "over 100 million young people do not go to school" and that two thirds of these are girls, the Paris-based UN Educational, Social and Cultural Organization (UNESCO) admits worldwide confusion exists over the numbers stemming largely from a lack of accurate data. Nevertheless, their estimates offer some pause for encouragement as these macro-statistics record the decreasing numbers:

> [B]etween 1999 and 2004, the worldwide total fell dramatically by almost 4% a year from abut 98 million to 77 million. The most dramatic reduction occurred in South and West Asia, where the number of out-of-school children was halved from around 31 million to 16 million. While encouraging, this progress must not lead to complacency as the actual number of out-of-school children may be higher than indicated by administrative data (UNESCO 2007: 2).

Tomaševski's rights-based approach allows educational relationships to be better appreciated as praxis of power. Within these numbers we find a hint of the magnitude of violations and how all human rights principles are conceptually and politically interconnected–gender equity, primary education, and the eradication of absolute poverty. Perhaps divergent and less strident views on the development work of the World Bank may exist, but Tomaševski (2006a, b, 2007) is unequivocal – WB directors and program managers are global educators embedded within the power relations impacting local pedagogy and praxis in 170 nations. A central tension within this hierarchal relationship is ideological since banks, by definition, are driven by economics not human rights. In fact, governments who export the service of education would have to invest billions in hard currency if primary education was without charge in all parts of the globe. As editors, we contend that the creation and dissemination of new educational knowledges can no longer stand on the tired legs of mediaeval academic and political structures, but must move beyond to embrace feminist, Indigenous and other marginalized epistemologies as new sources for planetary survival. While obstacles to making primary education free and compulsory for all children in all nations are perhaps enormous, surely they evaporate when compared to the hundreds of billions being squandered on the economics and madness of war.

NOTE

1 At the United Nations Millennium Summit in New York 6 to 8 September, 2000, the largest gathering of world leaders in history adopted Eight Millennium Development Goals to be achieved by 2015 including: MDG #1 – To Eradicate Extreme Poverty and Hunger; MDG #2 – To Achieve Universal Primary Education; MDG #3 – To promote Gender Equality and Empower Women; MDG #4 – To Reduce Child Mortality; MDG #5 – To Improve Maternal Health; MDG #6 – To Combat HIV/AIDS, Malaria and Other Diseases; MDG #7 – To Ensure Environmental Sustainability; and MDG #8 – To Develop a Global Partnership for Development.

REFERENCES

Allan, J., & I'Anson, J. (2004). Children's rights in school: Power, assemblies and assemblages. *The International Journal of Children's Rights, 12*(2), 123–138.

Appadurai, A. (1996). *Modernity at large: Cultural dimensions of globalization.* Minneapolis, MN: University of Minnesota Press.

Apple, M. W., Kenway, J., & Singh, M. (Eds.). (2005). *Globalizing education – Policies, pedagogies and politics.* New York: Peter Lang Publishing, Inc.

Bauman, Z. (2005). Afterthought: On writing; On writing sociology. In N. K. Denzin & Y. S. Lincoln (Eds.), *The Sage Handbook of Qualitative Research* (3rd ed., pp. 1089–1098). London: Sage Publications.

Beck, U., & Beck-Gernsheim, E. (2002). *Individualization – Institutionalized individualism and its social and political consequences.* London: Sage Publications Ltd.

Besley, T. A. C., & Peters, M. (2008). Subjectivity & truth – Foucault, educaion, and the culture of self. In *Counterpoints – Studies in the postmodern theory of education – Joe L. Kincheloe and Shirley R. Steinberg – General Editors – Vol. 303.* New York: Peter Lang Publishers.

Bloch, M. N., Kennedy, D., Lightfoot, T., & Weyenberg, D. (2006). *The child in the world/The world in the child – Education and the configuration of a universal, modern and globalized childhood.* New York: Palgrave/Macmillan.

Burbules, N. C., & Torres, C. A. (Eds.). (2000). *Globalization and education – Critical perspectives.* New York: Routledge.

Burman, E. (1995). Developing differences: Gender, childhood and economic development. *Children & Society, 9*(3), 121–142.

Burman, E. (1996). Local, global or globalised: Child development and international child rights legislation. *Childhood, 3*(1), 45–66.

Burman, E. (2001). Beyond the baby and the bathwater: Postdualistic developmental psychologies for diverse childhoods. *European Early Childhood Education Research Journal, 9*(1), 5–22.

Charmaz, K. (2005). Grounded Theory in the 21st Century: Applications for Advancing Social Justice Studies. In Norman K. Denzin and Yvonna S. Lincoln (Eds.), *The Sage Handbook of Qualitative Research* (3rd ed., pp. 507-536). London: Sage Publications.

Clark, J. (2006). Social justice education and schooling: Some philosophical issues. *British Journal of Educational Studies, 54*(3), 272–287.

Conway, J. (2006). *Praxis and politics: Knowledge production in social movements*. New York and London: Routledge.

Crossley, M. (2000). Bridging cultures and traditions in the reconceptualisation of comparative and international education. *Comparative Education, 36* (3), 319-332.

Dahlberg, G., Moss, P., & Pence, A. (1999). *Beyond quality in early childhood education and care – Postmodern perspectives*. London: Routledge/Falmer.

David, P. (2002). Implementing the rights of the child: Six reasons why the human rights of children remain a constant challenge. *International Review of Education, 48*(3–4), 259–263.

Deleuze, G., & Guattari, F. (1987). *A thousand plateaus*. Minneapolis, MN: University of Minnesota Press.

Devine, D. (2002). Children's citizenship and the structuring of adult-child relations in the primary school. *Childhood, 9*(3), 303–320.

Escobar, A. (2004). Beyond the third world: Imperial globality, global coloniality and anti-globalisation social movements. *Third World Quarterly, 25*(1), 207–230.

Fisher, W. F., & Ponniah, T. (2003). Introduction: The world social forum and the re-invention of democracy. In W. F. Fisher & T. Ponniah (Eds.), *Another world is possible: Popular alternatives to globalization at the world social forum* (pp. 1–20). London & New York: Zed Books.

Foucault, M. (1977). *Discipline and punish: The birth of the prison*. London: Penguin.

Freeman, M. (2007). Why it remains important to take children's rights seriously. *The International Journal of Children's Rights, 15*(1), 5–23.

Freire, P. (1970). *Pedagogy of the oppressed*. New York: Herder and Herder.

Freire, P. (1999). Education and community involvement. In M. Castells, R. Flecha, P. Freire, H. A. Giroux, D. Macedo, & P. Willis (Eds.), *Critical education in the new information age* (pp. 83–92). Boston: Rowman & Littlefield Publishers, Inc.

Giroux, H. (2003). *The abandoned generation – Democracy beyond the culture of fear*. New York: Palgrave Macmillan.

Giroux, H., & Searls Giroux, S. (2004). *Take back higher education – Race, youth and the crisis of democracy in the post-civil rights era*. New York: Palgrave Macmillan.

Jung, C. G. (1956). *1953–1979: The collected works of C.G. Jung – 20 Vols. Symbols of transformation, bollingen series XX* (R. F. C. Hull, Trans., H. Read, M. Fordham, G. Adler, & Wm. McGuire, Eds.). Princeton: Princeton University Press.

Kienge-Kienge Intudi, R. (2007). The application of the international convention on the rights of the child in Africa: When the law is tested by the reality. In A. Ang, I. Delens-Ravier, M. Delplace, C. Herman, D. Reynaert, V. Staelens, et al. (Eds.), *The UN children's rights convention: Theory meets practice. Proceedings of the International Interdisciplinary Conference on Children's Rights, 18–19 May 2006, Ghent, Belgium* (pp. 23–31). Mortsel, Belgium: Intersentia.

Kincheloe, J. (2008). The past, present, and future of critical pedagogy: With Joe Kincheloe. In C. S. Malott (Ed.), *A call to action – An introduction to education, philosophy, and native North America*. From *Counterpoints – Studies in the postmodern theory of education – Joe L. Kincheloe and Shirley R. Steinberg – General Editors – Vol. 324* (pp. 153–162). New York: Peter Lang Publishers.

Kincheloe, J. & McLaren, P. (2005). Rethinking Critical Theory and Qualitative Research. In Norman K. Denzin and Yvonna S. Lincoln (Eds.), *The Sage Handbook of Qualitative Research –* (3rd ed., pp. 303-342). London: Sage Publications.

Koizumi, H. (2001). Trans-disciplinarity. *Neuroendocrinology Letters*, 22, 219–221.

Lenzer, G. (2002). Children's studies and the human rights of children: Toward a unified approach. In K. Alaimo & B. Klug (Eds.), *Children as equals – Exploring the rights of the child* (pp. 207–225). Maryland, MD: University Press of America.

Lindahl, R. (2006). The right to education in a globalized world. *Journal of Studies in International Education, 10*(1), 5–26.

Lingard, B. (2000). It is and it isn't: Vernacular globalization, educational policy and restructuring. In Nicholas C. Burbules & Carlos A. Torres (Eds.), *Globalization and education – Critical perspectives* (pp. 79–108). New York: Routledge.

Luhmann, N. (1982). The world society as a social system. *International Journal of General Systems, 8*(2), 131–138.

Luhmann, N. (1997). Globalization or world society: how to conceive modern society? *International Review of Sociology, 7*(1), 67–79.

Malott, C. S. (Ed.). (2008). *A call to action – An introduction to education, philosophy, and native North America. Counterpoints – Studies in the postmodern theory of education – Joe L. Kincheloe and Shirley R. Steinberg – General Editors – Vol. 324.* New York: Peter Lang Publishers.

McCarthy, C., & Dimitriades, G. (2000). Globalizing pedagogies: Power, resentment and the re-narration of difference. In N. C. Burbules & C. A. Torres (Eds.), *Globalization and education – Critical perspectives* (pp. 187–204). New York: Routledge.

McLaren, P., & Farahmandpur, R. (2001a). Educational policy and the socialist imagination: Revolutionary citizenship as a pedagogy of resistance. *Educational Policy, 13*(3), 343–378.

McLaren, P., & Farahmandpur, R. (2001b). Teaching against globalization and the new imperialism: Toward a revolutionary pedagogy. *Journal of Teacher Education, 52*(2), 136–150.

McLaren, P. & Jaramillo, N. (2007) *Pedagogy and praxis in the age of empire: Towards a new humanism.* Rotterdam: Sense Publishers.

Mirchandani, R. (2005). Postmodernism and sociology: From the epistemological to the empirical. *Sociological Theory, 23*(1), 86–115.

Mitchell, R. C. (2000). Implementing children's rights in British Columbia using the population health framework. *The International Journal of Children's Rights, 8*(4), 333-349.

Mitchell, R. C. (2003). Ideological reflections on the DSM IV-R (or pay no attention to that man behind the curtain, Dorothy!). *Child and Youth Care Forum, 32*(5), 281–298.

Mitchell, R. C. (2005). Postmodern reflections on the UNCRC: Towards utilising Article 42 as an international compliance indicator. *The International Journal of Children's Rights, 13*(3), 315–331.

Mitchell, R. C. (2007). Towards a transdisciplinary model within child and youth rights education. In A. Ang, I. Delens-Ravier, M. Delplace, C. Herman, D. Reynaert, V. Staelens, et al. (Eds.), *The UN children's rights convention: Theory meets practice. Proceedings of the International Interdisciplinary Conference on Children's Rights, 18–19 May 2006, Ghent, Belgium* (pp. 181–200). Mortsel, Belgium: Intersentia.

Montgomery, L. M. & Canaan, J. E. (2004). Conceptualizing higher education students as social actors in a globalizing world: A special issue. *International Journal of Qualitative Studies in Education, 17*(6), 739–748.

Moore, S. A. (2004). Towards an integrated perspective: Restorative justice, cross-cultural counselling and school-based programming. In M. Honore France, M. C. Roderiguez, & Geoff G. Hett (Eds.), *Diversity, culture and counselling: A Canadian perspective* (pp. 347–355). Calgary, AB: Detselig.

Moore, S. A. (2007). Restorative justice. In R. B. Howe & K. Covell (Eds.), *A question of commitment: Children's rights in Canada* (pp. 179–208). Waterloo, ON: Wilfrid Laurier University.

Moss, P., & Petrie, P. (2002). *From children's services to children's spaces – Public policy, children and childhood.* London: Routledge/Falmer.

Mundy, K. (2002). Education in a reformed World Bank. *International Journal of Educational Development, 22*, 483–508.

Mundy, K. (2006). Education for all in the new development compact. *International Review of Education, 52*, 23–48.

Mundy, K. (2007). Education for all: Paradoxes and prospects. In D. P. Baker & A. W. Wiseman (Eds.), *Education for all: Global promises, national challenges.* Oxford, UK: Elsevier.

Nicolescu, B. (1999). *The transdisciplinary evolution of learning.* Paper presented to the *Symposium on Overcoming the Underdevelopment of Learning* held at the annual meeting of the American Educational Research Association, Montreal, Canada, April 19–23, 1999.

Nicolescu, B. (2002). *Manifesto of transdisciplinarity.* New York: State University of New York Press.

O'Byrne, D. J. (2003). *Human rights – An introduction.* London: Pearson Education.

Osler, A., & Vincent, K. (2002). *Citizenship and the challenge of global education*. Wiltshire, UK: Cromwell Press.

Pupavac, V. (1998). The infantilization of the south and the UN convention on the rights of the child. In H. J. Steiner & P. Alston (Eds.), *International human rights in context – Law, politics, morals* (pp. 517–518). New York: Oxford University Press.

Rosling, H. (2007). *Debunking third-world myths with the best statistics you'll ever see*. TED – Ideas WorthSpreading. Retrieved February 25, 2008, from http://www.ted.com/index.php/talks/view/id/92

Russell, W. (2000). *Forging new paths: Transdisciplinarity in Universities*. Wisenet – Australia's Women in Science Inquiry Network 53. Retrieved February 29, 2008, from http://www.wisenet-australia.org/issue53/contnt53.htm

Schafer, W. (2005). The uneven globality of children. *Journal of Social History, 38*(4), 1027–1039.

Scraton, P. (Ed.). (1997). *'Childhood' in 'crisis'?* London: Routledge.

Singh, M., Kenway, J., & Apple, M. (2005). Globalizing education: Perspectives from above and below. In M. Apple, J. K. Michael Singh (Eds.), *Globalizing education – Policies, pedagogies and politics* (pp. 1–29). New York: Peter Lang Publishing, Inc.

Somerville, M. A., & Rapport, D. J. (2000). *Transdisciplinarity: ReCreating integrated knowledge*. Oxford: EOLSS Publishers Co. Ltd.

Spring, J. (2004). *How educational ideologies are shaping global society – Intergovernmental organizations, NGOs, and the decline of the nation-state*. Mahwah, NJ: Laurence Erlbaum Associates, Publishers.

Stromquist, N. P. (2000). *Education in a globalized world: The connectivity of economic power, technology and knowledge*. New York: Rowman & Littlefield Publishers, Inc.

Sweeney, G. (2006). Tomaševski book review: A teaching aid on right to education. *Human Rights Features* (September 18–24), 9.

Theoharis, G. (2004). *The rough road to justice – A meta-analysis of the barriers to teaching and leading for social justice*. Paper presented at the University Council of Educational Administration, November 12–15, 2004. Kansas City, MO.

Tikly, L. (2001). Globalisation and education in the postcolonial world: towards a conceptual framework. *Comparative Education*, 37(2), 151-171.

Tomaševski, K. (1999). *Education is not yet a human right*. Talk by the Special Rapporteur to the UN Commission on Human Rights. Oxfam, London. Retrieved February 28, 2008, from http://www.katarinatomasevski.com/

Tomaševski, K. (2006a). *Human rights obligations in education worldwide*. Nijmegen, The Netherlands: Wolf Legal Publishers.

Tomaševski, K. (2006b). *The state of the right to education worldwide – Free or fee 2006 global report*. Retrieved February 29, 2008 from http://www.katarinatomasevski.com/

Tomaševski, K. (2007). Are we educating children as people with rights or just talking about it? In A. Ang, I. Delens-Ravier, M. Delplace, C. Herman, D. Reynaert, V. Staelens, et al. (Eds.), *The UN children's rights convention: Theory meets practice. Proceedings of the International Interdisciplinary Conference on Children's Rights, 18–19 May 2006, Ghent, Belgium* (pp. 165–180). Mortsel, Belgium: Intersentia.

United Nations. (1989). *Convention on the rights of the child*. New York: UN General Assembly.

United Nations Educational, Social and Cultural Organization. (2007a). Institute for statistics: The MDG report.Retrieved January 30, 2008, from http://www.uis.unesco.org/ev_en.php?ID=6941_201&ID2=DO_TOPIC

United Nations Educational, Social and Cultural Organization. (2007b). Institute for statistics: Out of school children: How many are there and who are they? Retrieved January 30, 2008, from http://www.uis.unesco.org/TEMPLATE/pdf/EducGeneral/OOSC-FAQ.pdf

United Nations Habitat–Shelter for All. (2007). *United Nations habitat hosts world social forum women's court in Nairobi*. Retrieved January 29, 2008, from http://www.unhabitat.org/content.asp?cid=4293&catid=5&typeid=6&subMenuId=0

United Nations International Children's Emergency Fund. (2006). *State of the world's children 2007*. New York: UNICEF. Retrieved February 29, 2008, from http://www.unicef.org/sowc/index_37436.html

United Nations Office of the High Commissioner for Human Rights. (1998). *United Nations decade for human rights education 1995–2004*. New York and Geneva: United Nations.

United Nations. (2006). *Millennium development goals report*. New York: United Nations. Retrieved February 29, 2008, from http://mdgs.un.org/unsd/mdg/Resources/Static/Products/Progress2006/MDGReport2006.pdf

Visser, J. (1999). *Overcoming the underdevelopment of learning: A transdisciplinary view*. Paper presented at the Symposium on Overcoming the Underdevelopment of Learning held at the annual meeting of the American Educational Research Association, Montreal, Canada April 19–23, 1999. Retrieved February 29, 2008, from http://www.eric.ed.gov/ERICWebPortal/custom/portlets/recordDetails/detailmini.jsp?_nfpb=true&_&ERICExtSearch_SearchValue_0=ED433361&ERICExtSearch_SearchType_0=eric_accno&accno=ED433361

Weber, M. (July 2002). Engaging globalization: Critical theory and global political change–Alternatives: Global, local, political. *Alternatives: Global, local, political*. Boulder, CO: Lynne Reinner Publishers. Retrieved March 1, 2008, from http://findarticles.com/p/articles/mi_go2624/is_200207/ai_n7087312

Weekes,R.(2002).*World Bank: Success or failure*. Retrieved February 29, 2008, from http://www.idebate.org/debatabase/topic_details.php?topicID=173

Woodhead, M. (1999). Reconstructing developmental psychology – Some first steps. *Children & Society*, *13*(1), 3–19.

Woodhead, M. (2000) "Children's rights and children's development: rethinking the paradigm". In E. Verhellen (Ed. 2000), pp. 113-127, *Understanding Children's Rights - Collected Papers presented at the 5th International Interdisciplinary Course on Children's Rights*. Belgium: University of Ghent.

Wyness, M. (1999). Childhood, agency and education reform. *Childhood*, *6*(3), 353–368.

KATARINA TOMAŠEVSKI

THE STATE OF THE RIGHT TO EDUCATION WORLDWIDE: FREE OR FEE?

2006 Global Report

EDITORS' NOTE

The following is a synopsis of former UN Special Rapporteur for Education Dr. Katarina Tomaševksi's 280-page final investigation of the global right to education, respectfully collated by Brock University Faculty of Education Doctoral Candidate Mr. Ken Kehls. Readers are encouraged to appreciate the breadth and depth of the study, as well as the fullness of findings and analysis of the original author, by accessing the entire report from her website at: http://www.katarinatomasevski.com/images/Global_Report.pdf.

PREFACE

In the following study, analysis and discussion of the ongoing and sanguine response by the international community to violations of the human right to education are provided with thorough statistical breakdowns from 170 countries where free public education is frequently unavailable to many children. Each regional sub-division is assessed according to whether a legal guarantee of free education exists, and whether charges are leveled. Twenty-two types of charges are then provided alongside the countries allowing such, including: supplementing inadequate public funding of schools (34 countries including China, Pakistan, Bosnia, Russia and the Philippines); registration, admission, or enrolment (19 countries, including Burma, Colombia, and Fiji); periodic payments during attendance (28 countries, including Indonesia, Nepal, South Africa and China); charges for tests or examinations (Burma, China, Indonesia, Kenya); school building and maintenance (13 countries including Bhutan, Laos and Fiji); teaching and learning materials, where "school textbooks are increasingly sold on the free market, but charges for books and other materials have been reported" (16 countries including Iran, Cambodia. and Ukraine); and fees for non-citizens (7 countries including Jordan and New Zealand).

Primary education is the focus of the report because the original reasons for declaring it a child's birthright remain unchanged. The incentive for the report is the fieldwork that made it apparent that children in poor countries could not go to primary school because it was unaffordable: Public education in name, legally free but really for-fee. The rhetoric of international resolutions, declarations, and recommendations are churned out by parts of the international community while other parts erode the possibility of realizing the right to education. Any explanation

S.A. Moore and R.C. Mitchell (eds.), Power, Pedagogy and Praxis: Social Justice in the Globalized Classroom, 19–53.

of this simultaneous affirmation and denial of the right to education within the United Nations (UN), an organization committed to human rights, loudly proclaiming then quietly betraying, is not easy to reconcile when the global division of labour keeps human rights in their place, and when challenges of exclusion are impeded by vehement denials that *education is a human right*.

The report examines the laws, policies, and practices in 170 countries, documents the recognition or denial of the right to education; discerns why this is so, and highlights the impact of the educational model that was chosen or imposed within this free or for-fee dichotomy. If the first step towards finding a solution is to agree on the problem, global policymakers are a long way from solving the problem because key questions are avoided–particularly the nomenclature of access to education and the right to education where the former implicates the ability to pay whereas the latter is an entitlement.

Missing in the attempts to universalize primary education into a unified global strategy is what human rights require: the foundation of individual entitlement and corresponding public responsibilities. The omission of a governmental obligation to make education free and compulsory denies education as a human right—a sentiment corresponding to US policy and echoed by the World Bank (WB), and unchallenged by global actors in education and human rights.

In order for primary education to be universalized for all children, it must be compulsory. To be compulsory, it has to be free. To be compulsory and free, it must be a government responsibility as demonstrated by what today's post-industrializing countries have been practicing for two decades. To make education compulsory and not make it free makes it an unworkable solution when access means the ability to pay. The need for a human rights challenge stems from the double standard whereby we apply to the poor a much lower standard than we would accept for ourselves.

Monitoring the state of the right to education world-wide should be a formal responsibility of UN human rights bodies and the United Nations Educational, Scientific, and Cultural Organization (UNESCO). As a critic of the UN Commission on Human Rights (Tomaševski 2005b) as Special Rapporteur on the right to education, its unprecedented abolition on the grounds of the erosion of its credibility may be a hopeful sign, signaling intergovernmental accountability.

INTRODUCTION

When the international community is called upon to furnish support in education in any areas in need around the world, the appeals usually go to the UN—specifically to the UNESCO, which, given its name, is formally recognized as the lead agency. However, despite calls for harmonization and alignment from multilateral organizations (Smith 2006), governments continue to receive conflicting advice (UNESCO 2006b: para. 7) from assorted consultant bodies: discrepancies in advice originating in the clashing global approaches to education. Within the 2 per cent of internationally funded education, much is used in financing parallel creditors' and donors' bureaucracies, generating an assortment of documentation unique to the requirement of each reporting body. This report advocates the rights-based approach, but acknowledges that this has been and is being excluded from the global design of education by the largest architects. Although UNESCO is formally committed to the right to education (UNESCO 2005: para. 26), many other global stakeholders are not–each stake is different with each definition of education incompatible. Private sectors not governed by public but private law treating education as a commercial service to be sold and purchased inevitably conflicts with education defined as a free public service and redefined as a fundamental human right. Development banks, for example, operate on a spreadsheet where education figures as expenditure to be decreased to diminish fiscal deficit which conflicts with the requirement of international human rights law to prioritize the right to education: the assurance of free and compulsory education for all children.

WHY DON'T WE HAVE A SINGLE GLOBAL STRATEGY FOR EDUCATION?

Free and compulsory education for all the world's children forms the backbone of international human rights law but does *not* shape global educational strategies. In formal policy-making, it is one-state-one-vote. In decision-making to finance such policies, it is one-dollar-one-vote. Global educational governance is determined by the purse of individual governments (for examples of controversies regarding the US influence on the UN as chief paymaster, see "America's war for hearts and minds: Mind your language," *The Economist*, 17 June 2006).

The ministry of foreign affairs may be supporting global declarations on the right of education, while its ministry of trade simultaneously negotiates increased exports on education, benefiting from the lack of educational opportunities in poor countries as worst case scenario. Critics are easily silenced by the profits generated for national educational institutions. The country's ministry of finance may support debt servicing which impedes free primary education in poor indebted countries while its gender ministry may, at the same time, lamenting the educational exclusion of girls which such debt servicing entails.

A country's ministry of finance may support debt servicing to creditor and donor governments which impedes free primary education in indebted countries. How much or how little of promised debt relief trickles down to education depends on the contractual small print, which describes the conditions of debt relief for each country and circumscribes the fate of education (see UNESCO 2002: 175). Countries seeking debt relief are required to comply with the six global prescriptions for education detailed in chronological order as indicated in Table 1.1.

Each of the poorest countries should report under the human rights treaties it is party to, submit due reports to the bilateral and multilateral donors, prepare a PRSP so as to qualify for debt relief, generate an EFA plan, notify its commitments under the GATS, and also prepare its strategy and reports on MDGs.

Table 1.1 From human rights law to MDGs: 6 Global Blueprints for Educators

Human Rights Law	1921/1948	International human rights law defines universal human rights obligations corresponding to the right to education, which prioritize each child's right to free and compulsory education	The existing network of human rights treaties obliges each state party to periodically report on its compliance with international obligations, comprising education; these reports furnish authoritative interpretations of the right t education and self-assessments of governmental performance
OECD/G8	1960/1975	Internationally, the OECD countries apply human rights law; externally, different policies guide bilateral and multilateral aid, and distinct conditions apply to bilateral and multilateral debt relief; policy coherence figures high on the agenda but the value of educational exports to poor countries dwarfs aid and debt relief	Numerous and diverse policies define the ends and means for bilateral and multilateral aid, with education routinely separated from human rights; extensive documentation by aid recipients is required by each donor; its conflicting external roles as donor, creditor and exporter of educational services are disjoined.
World Bank	1963	The largest provider of external funding for education, it pursues its own strategy, and is a gatekeeper in assessing countries' eligibility for development finance and debt relief.	There are 139 countries and territories to which the World Bank has provide loans to education in 1963-2006, and small grants have been provided to countries which qualified for debt relief; extensive documentation and literature describes the ends and means of its involvement in education.
EFA/UNESCO	1990	The Education for All (EFA) strategy pledged to universalize education in 1990 and again in 2000; it is based on the commitments of international agencies (UNESCO, UNDP, UNFPA, UNICEF, and the World Bank) and ministers of education; the EFA has remained with UNESCO, while global consensus was reached for lower standards embodied in the MDGs	Individual countries are expected to prepare national EFA Action Plans, which overlap with their MDG plans, the PRPSs, and their reports under human rights treaties; a biannual global monitoring report, prepared within UNESCO tracks progress in developing countries and countries in transition

WTO/GATS	1995	The GATS (General Agreement on Trade in Services) has formally institutionalized the sale or purchase of education; less than one third of WTO members have made commitments to liberalize trade in education services	Official documents generated by the secretariat and individual governments have clarified that education as a free public service (as a rule coinciding with compulsory education) remains governmental responsibility and is exempt from trade law
MDGs/UN	2000	A global consensus was forged around the Millennium Development Goals (MDGs) in 2000 by the heads of states or governments; they include primary school completion for all children by 2015	Individual countries are expected to prepare their own strategies, plans and progress reports; extensive documentation is generated by the United Nations to track global, regional, and country progress towards the MDGs

Countries not seeking but providing aid, members of the OECD—created in 1960, the OECD (Organization for Economic Cooperation and Development) is often dubbed 'the rich man's club' because its original membership was confined to Western and/or Northern developed industrialized countries—are bound by human rights law internally, and indeed, they ensure free and compulsory schooling for all children and young people. As the OECD works on G8 priorities, their individual and collective decisions on aid and/or debt relief are not founded on education as a human right: it merely happens to be a happy coincidence that they are able to afford the provision of free and compulsory education. Their varied and vague commitments to the MDGs or to the EFA are degraded so as to prioritize safeguards for their exports under WTO rules.

The global discord implicitly illustrated in Table 1.1's six parallel tracks routinely hinders rather than helps the poorest countries. Low revenues and high deficits inhibit increasing finance to make (or keep) education free. Human rights law mandates increased public investment in education but international financial institutions demand reduced fiscal deficit. Because this is a condition for accessing international development finance, human rights law is ignored. The consequence is that the possibility of a free education is converted to a for-fee education, the cost of which is transferred from governmental to family budgets.

The subsequently divergent pathways of the chronology illustrate that human rights law has binding precedence on all governments involved, yet is ignored as an analytical or organizational reference point in the development of collective strategies.

Having established the minimal definition of the right to education as a universal human right to free and compulsory education, the following Table 1.2 demonstrates the evasive language used in global political commitments. Reflecting underlying decisions not to use human rights law as guidance, it further highlights that it took fifteen years of Declarations to finally appropriate the wording of the Universal Declaration of Human Rights stating that education should be free and compulsory.

Table 1.2 International human rights law vs. Global Targets 1990-2005

International legal guarantees	*Global political commitments*
Universal Declaration of Human Rights (1948): Education shall be free, at least in the elementary and fundamental stages. Elementary education shall be compulsory.	
UNESCO Convention against Discrimination in Education (1960): The States Parties to this Convention shall undertake to formulate, develop and apply a national policy which,…will…in particular…make primary education free and compulsory.	
International Covenant on Economic, Social, and Cultural Rights (1966): Primary education shall be compulsory and free for all.	
Protocol of San Salvador to the American Convention on Human Rights (1988): The States Parties to this Protocol recognize that…primary education should be compulsory and accessible to all without cost.	
Convention on the Rights of the Child (1989): States Parties…shall, in particular…make primary education compulsory and available free for all.	
Charter on the Right and Welfare of the African Child (1990): States Parties to the present Charter…shall in particular: provide free and compulsory basic education.	*Jomtien Conference on Education for All* (1990): Every person—child, youth, and adult—shall be able to benefit from educational opportunities designed to meet their basis learning needs. Universal access to, and completion of, primary education (or whatever higher level of education is considered as "basic") by the year 2000.
(Revised) European Social Charter (1996): …Parties undertake, either directly or in cooperation with public and private organizations… to provide to children and young persons a free primary and secondary education as well as to encourage regular attendance in schools.	*Dakar World Education Forum* (2000): We re-affirm (…) that all children, young people and adults have the human right to benefit from an education that will meet their basic learning needs…Ensuring that by 2015 all children…have access to and complete free and compulsory education of good quality.

United Nations Millennium Development Goals (2000):
Ensure that, by 2015, children everywhere, boys and girls alike, will be able to complete a full course of primary schooling.
World Summit Outcome (2005):
We reaffirm our commitment to support developing country efforts to ensure that all children have access to and complete free and compulsory primary education of good quality.

Rhetorically offering much less than what is mandated by international human rights law, the implicit rule is then *silence* about this, and any other facet of the global discord following rhetorical partnerships that obscures underlying conflicts between incompatible concepts. This incompatibility inhibits coherent educational policy, openly flouts human rights protection to which most governments are formally committed, and undermines the rule of law by disregarding inconvenient parts of that law and supplanting it with arbitrariness. Global targets have been agreed upon and flouted precisely because there is no single or effective set of rules for making them and against breaking them.

In the absence of global rules regarding accountability, today's entitlements in public education are based on country-code lottery: considerable for those lucky to be born in a wealthy country, absent for those with no such luck. There is no coherent check between external policy priorities of creditor and donor countries, and their internal educational policies. It is taken for granted that OECD countries ensure primary education for 96 per cent of their children; in Latin America and East Asia, 94 per cent. In education, this is defined as universal coverage, despite the fact that 100 per cent is required to meet the definition "universal." Educational statistics accept that one in ten children is out of school because UNESCO determines education universal when it reaches 90 per cent (UNESCO/UNICEF 2005). If education is not universal in the wealthy parts of the world, is it surprising that strategies elaborated for the poor promise even less?

HOW AND WHY THE EXISTING GLOBAL TARGETS NULLIFY HUMAN RIGHTS?

Quite a few governments which subscribed in 2000 to the most broadly accepted set of global targets (the MDGs) have changed in the six years after they were adopted. Most will be out of office fifteen years later and the MDGs may well be forgotten by 2015.

Promises are easy to make because they can be broken with impunity. Moreover, the notion of partnership which underpins them also impedes accountability: "In a world of partnerships, no one is to blame, failure is unfortunate, and we move on to planning more of the same for the next decade". The failure to reach the first global target on gender parity in 2005 was accompanied by the British Secretary of State for International development's statement: "there is no escaping the fact that we have collectively failed".

Global strategies addressed to the poor were created through consensus-building and this lowered political commitments to a minimum to which all could agree: only primary school, and only by 2015. Avoiding the language of human rights or public responsibilities, each child's birthright, instead of being affirmed, was converted into a long-term development goal. Education is seen as governmental expenditure, not investment, and is legitimized only if it is proved to be effective in reducing poverty. Primary school leavers are a mass of low skilled cheap labour (A survey of business in India, for example). Without the requirement of a minimum primary school duration, what hope is there for early school leavers, as cheap labour, to break out of their own poverty let alone contribute to the general welfare of their country?

In the example of Angola, children are able to leave school at the age of nine. If these children had three more years of quality education, the country might formally comply with stated MDGs, but this type of 'education' is not worthy of its name. Although it is well known that at least six years of education are necessary to sustain literacy, and that UNESCO and UNICEF assume primary school lasts six years (UNESCO/UNICEF 2005: 14), as yet there is no global 'quality control'.

Previously, free and compulsory education was linked to the elimination of child labour in 1921 by the International Labour Organization (ILO), setting the minimum school leaving age at 14, and raised to 18 in 1999 for children victimized by intolerable forms of child labour (Tomaševski 2004: 41-42). Eighty-year-old human rights correctives have been abandoned along with the understanding that the right to education unlocks other rights when guaranteed. Moreover, its denial precludes the enjoyment of all other human rights. Human rights safeguards for education encompass its quantity and quality and reach much further: all human rights apply in education and education should be designed so as to enhance all other human rights (Tomaševski 2006). "How we ever let a bank decide educational policy will be a puzzle for educational anthropologists of the future" astutely observes Davies (2004: 6).

WHY EDUCATION SHOULD NOT HAVE BEEN ENTRUSTED TO WORLD BANK'S ECONOMISTS

In the field of human rights, international cooperation is seen as support for governments to comply with their human rights obligations. Particularly within education, the pledge has been that any government willing but unable to ensure primary education will obtain the funds it needs. Despite governments attempting to hold creditors and donors accountable for their pledges, aid, if forthcoming at all, is less than what is asked for, comes later than is needed, and demands notorious conditionalities. This necessitates forcing governments to ignore other human rights guarantees and produce, instead, the required strategies that make them eligible for funding. As a leverage of control, the problem with economics (as singled out in

John Kenneth Galbraith's obituary), is the wilful denial of the presence of power and political interests.

One-size-fits-all straightjackets fitted through economies of scale and efficient delivery models appear to be useful in the reduction of poverty while generating an education not worthy of its name. Education as free and compulsory is absent from the World Bank's vocabulary as this would integrate international and domestic expressions of human rights law and necessitate obliging governments to provide sustained and adequate funding. Instead, education is analysed in terms of supply and demand, reducing learners to consumers of educational services, and eroding the notion of equitable access to education when consumption of this service is applied to children. Broadening access to education in World Bank terms is "delivering this service to those not currently consuming" (Winkler 2000: 120).

An efficient education, denying even teachers' human rights, cannot facilitate children's learning through the imposition of budgetary cuts. This impoverishment of education also triggers an exodus by those who can afford to purchase a free market education, and where public education is deemed to be of poorer quality (see also Mahal 2005: 596). This observation comes with thanks to the World Bank for "having financed some of the research" (ibid. : 552).

Perhaps more encouraging, there is a great deal of worldwide opposition to the World Bank's educational model, and this opposition is the focus of this report: All children, no matter how poor, must go to school, and that in terms of international human rights law is the *right to education*. Regardless of the Bank's derogatory terminology that resists education as a free public service or "handout," and the assertion that people do not like public services to be free, worldwide protests of the conversion of previously free to for-fee services belie their claim.

The resistance to education as a human right informs and underpins many global strategies. Notwithstanding, the World Bank avoids both the term *right* and its implications, following the USA model of denying that education is a right, or using the term *human rights* in the proliferation of recipes for *development*. Perhaps arguably, the UN Secretariat possesses the expertise on differences between human rights and commercial law in terms of establishing market conditions of supply and demand that strengthen a people's ability to meet their own needs. By "creating the conditions in which the market can supply the services they demand" (OHCHR 2006: 2), the two become conflated and it is necessary to ask *why*.

The simple answer is that intergovernmental actors place themselves on a collision course with their influential constituency if denial of the right to education is tackled. The biggest shareholder, the USA, would necessarily become a target for critique. Denying that compulsory education is a governmental responsibility through the rationale of channeling *excess demand* for education to private schools is a purposeful effort to reduce demand on public education (Chapman 2002: 26). *Excess demand* cannot exist in compulsory education since all children have the right to education because they need the processes of socialization and qualification which education entails. It's our own future that's jeopardized when our children are deprived.

HOW WOULD HUMAN RIGHTS LAW ALTER GLOBAL TARGETS?

International human rights law mandates the progressive realization of the right to education, and anticipates that international cooperation would facilitate this process beginning with the 1948 Declaration that aimed to broaden entitlements. Domestically, paying for the education of other people's children is ensured through taxation although there is no international equivalent to remedy the burden for the poorest states. Consequentially, the term *right to education* is frequently avoided because access to education doesn't implicate governmental responsibilities. *Access* incorporates education purchased on the free market or financed through charity. If there is no access to education, this can be defined as *excess demand* or lamented as inequitable but cannot trigger an accusation of human rights violation.

If the purpose of international human rights law is to provide safeguards against *abuses of power*, its exclusion from current global targets is *de facto* an inherent abuse. To assume commitment by individual governments and intergovernmental agencies where there is none impedes the agency necessary to expose and oppose its absence. This is precisely the work of human rights in exposing violation. For intergovernmental agencies, "partnership with Government is not an option but an obligation" (Cantwell 1997: 77). This partnership becomes uncomfortable when governmental abuses of power collide with their formal commitments to education or poverty reduction.

WHY ARE HUMAN RIGHTS VIOLATORS BAD EDUCATORS?

Comparing public investment on education with military expenditure, this report demonstrates the effect of governmental priorities. Laws mandating priority for human rights in resource allocation are turned on their head when priorities are bestowed on repression and warfare. An indirect toll is exacted on education by silencing opposition to such distorted priorities (Tomaševski 2005e). Two paradigmatic examples illustrate why this ongoing lack of educational commitment ought to be exposed and opposed:

(a) A government denying human rights as a matter of policy is likely to deprive people of education lest they learn that rebellion against oppression is their birthright. While rich governments of poor countries could easily finance education, the poverty of the country is used as an excuse not to do so. For intergovernmental agencies to step in to perform the job that the government will not do requires exposure of abuses, thus necessitating silence regarding human rights often resulting in these intergovernmental agencies themselves being retrospectively defined as facilitators of human rights violations.

(b) A government may transform education into institutional brainwashing, instructing people that theirs is the best, indeed the only way of life. The urge to enroll all children in school so as to attain global numerical targets avoids a question which should be asked: if education amounts to

> institutional brainwashing, would it not be better to defend the right of children and young people *not* to go to school?

International partners of such abusers are unlikely to hold them accountable for broken promises because they also have a track record of broken promises. This is why human rights and corresponding governmental obligations matter and this is precisely why they are avoided in global targets.

Free public education was instituted, among other reasons, to make new generations economically self-supporting, which was cheaper than suppressing their wrath triggered by the perpetual pauperism such as the Governor of Virginia in 1676 lamented. There is inherent difficulty to be found in ruling a people, "poore, endebted, discontented, and armed" (Tomaševski 2001: para. 11). The fact that public authorities should take charge of education because it is too dangerous not to do so continues to hold true. The question is whether governments have done all they should have done to enable new generations to learn what they need to know, particularly when macro-level exclusion has been globally institutionalized by legitimizing micro-level "strategies to ensure that certain populations do not develop" (Bradbury 2000: 4). Respect of freedom thus impedes governmental abuses in *compulsory education* wherein human rights law bestows upon parents the freedom to choose education for their children. While guarantees of collective freedoms–borne of the painful experiences of imposed education on indigenous and other minority populations–are meticulously and fiercely litigated in regions around the globe (see also Tomaševski 2005c), they are not mentioned in current global targets for education.

Using human rights as the lens for examining education necessitates challenging exclusion from education and also questioning the broad purpose of education. In this way it is clear that schooling, which is what the global targets prioritize, is not the end but merely a means for education. Whether used for good or ill (Waters & Leblanc 2005: 131), all-encompassing compulsory education without human rights safeguards institutionalizes indoctrination. Economists have found this a useful explanation for governmental insistence on providing, rather than only financing education, and this represents the difference between being uneducated and the wrong "type" of education (Lott 1990). Human rights safeguards have been designed, nationally and internationally, to slant education towards the good and away from the ill but they tend to be ignored.

Human rights violations, however, inevitably impose themselves as an issue which cannot be ignored: this is the proudest accomplishment of human rights activism of the past four decades. Whenever human rights are ignored in the design of development finance strategies, responses tend to be chaotic (see also Tomaševski 2000), but human rights law requires an analysis that asks the kind of questions 'bean counters' avoid. Anything else converts "education" into a technical exercise which might work on paper, but not in real life.

WHY SHOULD WE CARE?

Education should provide children with the qualification and socialization they need before venturing into adulthood. Often, they are forced to exit school into conditions of right-lessness, politically and economically. Children who grow up under repression are unable to confront it because they know of no alternative.

Organizing protest campaigns is most difficult where they are most needed (see also Conway; McLaren and Jaramillo this volume). A government responsive to popular demands prioritizes education whereas a dictatorship depletes it of funding. Considered in conjunction with the fact that there are 150 soldiers for every 100 teachers in the world, this is a litmus test of the global education priority and vindicates the right to education as intrinsic in the battle for human rights. That the language of the right to education is rarely used is a consequence of the Cold War ending elsewhere but not in the implementation of human rights law, policy and practice. Advocacy for education as an entitlement, a right against the state, often leads to a label of populism or worse. Nevertheless, some governments have pledged the abolition of charges in primary school in an effort to make education gradually free which could alter pessimistic forecasts relating to the future of education encapsulated within Millennium Development Goal #2. But thus far there has been far too little publicity for this process and not enough political or financial support from the large institutions and governments that can afford these choices.

This report argues that primary education should be freed from obstacles so that all children can go to school, but much more information is needed to facilitate the momentum for rolling back charges in primary education. Moreover, levying charges in primary education is illegal in many countries, but the law is unknown–or worse–it is ignored. Nothing can be more harmful for the rule of law than international support for national policies that are illegal. This will change only after such apparent abuses of power have been brought into the open and effectively opposed. The best argument for opposing this practice of ignoring domestic and international expressions of law is evidenced in the educational toll of betrayed global promises to universalize education.

SUB-SAHARAN AFRICA

Educational toll of World Bank recipes

Coming out of a decade of despair that did not begin that way with new independence, Sub-Saharan Africa is not expected to ensure primary education for all children by the year 2015. Having promised in 1961 that free, universal compulsory education would be a reality by 1980, it was designed as a free public service and provided by the governments of the region. However, the global blueprint at the time was subsidy-without-liberty, with no international attention for denials of freedom to education, and this ended with education as a free public service being replaced by the free market.

The de-privatization of the 1960s was supplanted with the privatization of the 1990s during which enrolments in African primary schools declined by 10 per cent (Colclough & Al-Samarrai 1998: 3). Where *nationalized* education in de-privatization was seen as the key to nation-building through state control of schools, curricula and teachers, free and compulsory education was expected to trigger indigenous development.

These hopes were short-lived as, on the advice of the World Bank (Tomaševski 2003: 73-73) mandated cost-sharing of education was transferred from governments to families and communities with the rationale of accountability. Critique was directed at the conversion of the previously 'free' into 'for-fee' primary school because it inevitably led to the economic exclusion of the poor. Noting that cost-sharing was more appropriate in post-primary education, the World Bank nevertheless hailed the significant sums raised by school fees in primary school (World Bank 1990: 44-45). They remained silent on governmental obligations to secure free primary education, never mentioning that education ought to be compulsory. Acquiescing that although many states recognize education as a right, it did not state this as an affirmation of governmental obligations to secure free primary and compulsory education that would entail support for corresponding budgetary allocations (see World Bank 1980; World Bank 1999). Because education is a right guaranteed in international human rights law as well as within many national constitutions, it forms part of domestic law in most of the World Bank's borrowers (Florestal & Cooper 1997: 15). This law, however, did not inform the World Bank's design of education although its policies are formally committed to promoting the rule of law. Educational policies violating country laws proliferated as "formally unconstitutional" and "technically illegal" (Kattan & Burnett 2004) fees were noted in World Bank surveys (UNESCO 2006a: 84).

In a 2001 report addressing user fees in health, water, and education, a World Bank statement opposing user fees in education acknowledged the inevitable economic exclusion of the poor but charges were to be opposed only where levied by the central government, and not by local authorities or schools (World Bank 2001). This policy was justified by the nomenclature of *community participation*. These are routinely triggered by insufficient funding for education by the centrally government, often due to debt servicing as the conflict of interest, and ensuring loan repayment *versus* freeing education from debt burden or debt servicing. This necessitated tackling *excessive demand* by tapping households for payment of quality education (Sosale 2000: v) so as not to cost the state anything (Chauveau 1998: 113)–thus triggering private education and a re-design of public education with an onus of absolving governments of responsibility altering for free to for-fee. Charges, so named by the World Bank, were introduced but not recorded (see also Conhye & Coulibaly 1999: 36), thereby maintaining education as legally free yet for-fee in practice.

Reports from many African governments under international human rights treaties often referred to structural adjustment programmes which made legally mandated free education fiscally impossible. As poverty reduction strategies became the key for international development finance–especially debt relief–

primary education, defined as a lever for poverty reduction and poverty reduction strategies was expected to accommodate two conflicting requirements: increasing public investment in primary education to reduce poverty and maintain affordable investment by WB standards.

FREEING EDUCATION FROM DEBT BONDAGE

Poverty Reduction Strategy Papers (PRSPs) are formal, country-owned strategies that require World Bank approval (Tomaševski 2005d), and which despite this review, had not detected where charges were levied in order to develop strategies to eliminate them. The necessary funds to replace charges were expected from debt relief. Although debt relief has facilitated the abolition of school fees in some countries, only primary education is eligible and although it is cheaper, it is not free. Because public funding for education was–and is–insufficient to cover direct, indirect, and opportunity costs of school, the definition *free* education was reduced to *fee-free* since not all financial obstacles keeping children out of school were eliminated in many states thereby ensuring international human rights law and national constitutions were often ignored.

CONSTITUTIONAL GUARANTEES *VERSUS* FISCAL POLICIES

Constitutional guarantees reflect the requirements of international human rights law mandating free and compulsory primary education, and obliging governments to ensure it. Making education free and compulsory requires public funding, but governmental and intergovernmental policies for financing frequently do not follow what the law mandates. The constitution may mandate primary education to be free but the government may levy or tolerate charges. Governments declining their own responsibility for violating constitutional guarantees point fingers at Washington, D.C. - headquarters of the World Bank and the International Monetary Fund (IMF) - and cite structural adjustment programs as the cause of the impoverishment of public education.

Where children are the majority of Africa's population, and poor children the majority within that majority, increasing numbers of governments promise to make education free to accommodate all children. The pledges, translated into government policy and often made when associated with changes of governance, are each new government's promise to undo the damage done by previous regimes regarding investment in education. This was a corollary of democratization: if given a voice, people will insist on free primary education.

EDUCATIONAL COST OF MILITARY EXPENDITURE

Distorted priorities in resource allocation are best exemplified by the gross imbalances between military expenditure and investment in education and, even more, in the paucity of reliable data. High military expenditures in many African countries were associated with warfare or repression, but neither has increasing public investment for education through reductions of military expenditure been successful. Alongside corruption, it is the biggest obstacle in channelling money to education (Tomaševski 2003: 9-14), and warranted monitoring by both the IMF and the WB in the 1990s.

Furthermore, despite the 2004 Security Council affirmation of the importance of school in halting and preventing recruitment and re-recruitment of child soldiers (United Nations Security Council 2004: para. 8-9), its main priorities have been security-and-survival, postponing education for a time when normalcy might be restored. Ironically, normalcy has proved impossible without an investment in education and that investment is estimated at 11.5 per cent of GDP (Kitaev 1999: 28-31).

TROUBLING GLOBAL TARGETOLOGY

The obstacle course which most African governments have to navigate to obtain global financial support for expanding and improving education is exemplified in the MDGs, which have set the bar too low by reducing the human right to education to 'primary schooling' alone. Defining its role as strengthening the private sector's role at non-compulsory levels of education, and aimed towards the release of public resources for the primary level, the WB's commitment to private financing of secondary and university education has discouraged families and communities because the cost is far beyond the reach of the vast majority. However, UNESCO Institute for Statistics finds that no country has ever universalized primary school without a minimum of 35 per cent secondary-school enrolments (UNESCO 2004: 8, 13).

Obviously, education cannot be *the* priority for an African government because an investment in primary school yields an economic rate of return only after children reach adulthood and start working. This means that economic benefits of today's public investment in primary education will materialize in a decade or two. The pressures of daily survival, for governments or families, take priority over investment in education. This reinforces the need for external support, which is evidenced in the fact that children aged 5-15 constitute 13 per cent of the population in OECD countries but more than 30 per cent across African states (World Education Indicators Programme [WEI] 1999). Lifelong learning is publicly financed in the OECD member states (UNESCO 1998: 29) while in most African regions meagre funds have to be stretched to school the large proportion of children in the population. As a consequence, today's child in the OECD will enjoy 18 years of education, and an African child will have *access* to a mere 3 years of schooling (UNESCO 2004: 4).

Because education has not been made free, it has not been universalized. This report applies the yardstick that stems from international human rights law whereby each government is obliged to make education compulsory and should be held accountable for failing to do so. This accountability extends to international organizations which have lowered the global benchmark to a mere completion of primary school by the end of 2015 thereby denying children's rights to education as well as undermining corresponding governmental obligations.

EASTERN EUROPE AND CENTRAL ASIA

Transition from the Second to the Third World

During the Cold War, global surveys by the UN used to single out then-so-called "socialist countries of Eastern Europe" for having achieved "universal, compulsory and free education at the primary level" (United Nations 1975: para. 494). They never-named this the 'Second World' although in-between the First and Third Worlds it had as one of its defining features free public services as the pillar of human rights (see also Tomaševski 2003: 36-66). This has now been abandoned along with the universalization of education which has disappeared with it.

The most visible consequence of the end of the Cold War was to make "Eastern Europe" invisible: Central European nations joining the European Union on their way to becoming First World; relegating the remainder ineligible for EU membership as Third World re-classifications. The end of the Cold War imposed upon its winners and losers a double transition, to market economy and democracy. The free market, education included, constituted an ideological given and basic public services were no longer free of charge.

Creating capitalism necessitates capital although safeguards against acquiring capital informally, clandestinely, and illegally were thought of late in the transition process. Corruption was attributed to excessive state intervention in the economy. Reducing the role of the state through privatization was supposed to reduce corruption while democratization would reinforce that process through increased transparency and accountability. The opposite often took place as corruption was "privatized" and "democratized" (White 1996: 150.). Free and all-encompassing public services were previously defined as human rights to health and education, but financial sustainability required governments to convert public services from free to for-fee (see also Tomaševski 1994: 98; Farkas 2004).

Today's educational profile of the region still reflects the heritage of decades of all-encompassing, free and compulsory education. The population is, perhaps, overeducated but formal accomplishments measured in years of schooling do not lead to employment, least of all to poverty reduction. On the contrary, the process of impoverishment took place despite all that education. This casts doubt on the assumption underpinning global anti-poverty strategies whereby education leads to poverty reduction. There is only a minuscule difference in unemployment rates in this region which can be attributed to education.

The transition from government-funded to market-based education has had a profound and negative effect as the previous *right to* became *access to education.* Educational enrolments decreased, especially during the "short, sharp shock" when the free market was introduced in the early 1990s. Budgetary allocations to education diminished and large parts of its cost were transferred to "the consumers." Education during the Cold War was free only in the sense that government was paying all direct and most indirect costs (see also Simons 1980). Freedom *of* and *in* education had been obliterated. Education was a top-down, command-and-control mechanism. All-encompassing enrolments were ensured because education was compulsory and free.

Educational governance was not based on the law but on the Communist Party's policy so as to conform to the official ideology and the constitutionally enshrined responsibility of a "communist upbringing" (see also Simons 1980: 18, 359).

This model of free, state-provided education laid down by the communist constitutions was transferred to numerous international instruments on economic, social and cultural rights generated during the Cold War. The inter-governmental nature of international human rights law-making made this inevitable because inter-governmental organizations reflect the views and priorities of their powerful constituents. After the Cold War, educational design was altered; the law defining education as a human right, ignored.

That short, sharp shock in education

The former region of Eastern Europe had consisted of 9 countries, but the first post-Cold War decade created 27 countries. Fragmentation prioritized education as an instrument of nation-building. The replacement of public by privately-financed education was *not* debated as a human rights question but institutionalized as part of the transition to the free market. As John Kenneth Galbraith put it, "there is the private sector and there is the public sector. Once there was capitalism and socialism" (Galbraith 2004: 47).

Educational statistics deteriorated after the changes, and coincided with the rapid impoverishment of the population. Although education remained compulsory, because it was no longer free, one in five children could no longer finish schooling in the 1990s. The ideological underpinning of re-designed education was 'choice'. Denied in the former socialist and/or communist model, ushering choice in education was hailed as an improvement and private schools, previously non-existent, supplanted inadequate government-funded institutions. People who could purchase education abroad were free to do so; those without purchasing power were denied choice and by abandoning financial responsibility for education, governments forced public schools to become self-financing.

Enter for-fee education

In its new 2001 model for education, the WB introduced charges formally in line with the privatization of financial responsibility for education. Additionally, informal charges that were not explicit and public were gleaned exacerbating the problem. Keeping education free, as mandated by the law, is promised on adequate budgetary allocations, but where budgets are small a seemingly generous allocation may be below the actual cost of education. Where public funds for education have proved insufficient, children's parents have had to provide the necessary but missing funds or children have had to abandon school. Despite all its faults, centrally planned, Soviet-styled education had been free.

Cost recovery versus constitutional guarantees of free education

The new model based on user charges permeated national policy-making through the World Bank's policy advice, conditions for loans and debt relief, and the associated research and increased impoverishment so as to re-classify countries from the Second to the Fourth World. Constitutional guarantees of free education became irrelevant and were replaced by the PRSPs which transferred policy-making on education from national capitals to Washington, D.C.

A requirement in the debt relief process and a blueprint for fee or for-fee primary education, the PRSPs of 4 countries of this region opting for-fee primary education contravene their own constitutions. Conflicts between constitutional guarantees and governmental policies remain to be reconciled. The World Bank's recipe has been to change the constitutions or to circumvent them (World Bank 2000: 45). Most countries opt for circumvention.

Often, a government will portray different realities of education. It will assert that education conforms to the human rights law in its human rights reports and argue the opposite while seeking funding from international creditors and donors.

Educational cost of militarization

The toll of high military expenditure has been expressed by an International Monetary Fund research team as rule of inverse correlation: the higher the military expenditure, the worse a country's governance (Tomaševski 1986). High military expenditures illustrate the opportunity cost for education. International financial support to education in such conditions is likely to fuel corruption (Transparency International 2003).

A lesson from decades of human rights work is another rule of inverse correlation: the absence of information of human rights violations points to the denial of human rights. In such conditions education amounts to little more than institutionalized indoctrination. Integrating human rights in education necessitates reaching beyond the "sector of education" to examine the state of human rights in each country as well as the interface between education and human rights.

ASIA AND THE PACIFIC

Divergent models of education

There is a variety of educational models in Asia and most of them are not rights-based. Educational guarantees in national constitutions follow one of two approaches: *pluralist*, affirming freedom of education, particularly in religious communities; and *uniformist*, imposing upon children compulsory attendance in public schools which are uniform throughout the country.

Besides different approaches to education, the extremes of impressive educational accomplishments and huge number of out-of-school children also reflect Asia's diversity. Successes of "the Asian tigers" (Singapore, Hong Kong,

Taiwan, and Korea) in international assessments of the learners' performances, especially in mathematics, are well known (Suter 2003: 20-21). Their price is less well known. Teaching to test and rote learning is disliked by both pupils and teachers while use of corporal punishment instills fear (Chapman & Adams 2002: 3).

Conversely, large numbers of Asian children do not get any schooling and the absence of compulsory education laws reflects tolerance of educational exclusion. The continued paucity of rights-based approaches to education derives from the reluctance of many Asian governments to commit themselves to universally recognized human rights and to bestow upon the people a right to challenge their violations.

Even when guarantees to free education exist, governmental policy may be to levy charges or to tolerate them as fees finance a larger portion of the costs of public education in Asian than in other developing nations (Tan & Mingat 1992: 40). A 2002 World Bank report survey revealed that charges in primary education were widespread owing to its low priority in budgets (Adams 2002: 10). When user charges are necessary to support schools even in the public sector, the word *necessary* indicates the gap between the law and policy.

It is necessary to ask why education as a public responsibility receives such a low budgetary priority when considering the educational policies of the past in terms of consistent public investment that have borne fruit.

Questionable economic returns to education

The financial crisis in Asia in 1997-1998 (Gill 1998) highlighted the importance of education as previous public investment in education facilitated weathering the crisis, and contributed to questioning many global recipes related to economic or educational development. The Asian Development Bank, for example, has argued that globalization has increased the economic value of higher education compared to the value of lower levels of education. This perpetuates a vicious circle where the wealthy take more education, and taking more education helps families create more wealth (Asian Development Bank 2003: abstract; 5)–precisely why education was made a public responsibility.

Primary education does *not* generate return on investment. Primary school leavers do not work nor should they: they are children. Return on investment necessitates secondary and higher education as economic returns on primary education are negligible (Todaro 1997: 396). Even where primary education is free in terms of not creating direct costs for families, it creates opportunity costs which are much higher for poor families than for wealthy ones.

The attractiveness of education as a parental investment depends on employment prospects of school-leavers and university graduates: where no prospects exist, the investment is a poor one. It is not only the interests of children which governments safeguard by investing in education, but the whole of society benefits when education serves as societal glue. Armed and political conflicts highlight the cost of neglecting education.

150 soldiers to 100 teachers

In the zero-sum game in which budgets are limited by conflicting priorities, the preference for military expenditure over educational investment is reflected in the region. There is an implicit global endorsement of low prioritization of education in fiscal allocations because it is rarely challenged. It is taken as a "fact" rather than an outcome for political decisions. Such political decisions create costs for education but also additional costs in coping with militarization.

MIDDLE EAST AND NORTH AFRICA

The post-9/11 concern for education

The global interest for education in the Middle East, particularly for religious education, was triggered by the US war-on-terror. Post-9/11 fears that religious schools might breed terrorism and the lack of knowledge in the global educational industry about religious education generated much more heat than light. *Education* has turned out to be much more widespread than formal government-provided *schooling*–considering the findings from a puzzling survey on literacy illustrates that a much greater number of people know how to read and write than the number of people that went to school (UNDP 2003: 8).

Formal schooling provides only one educational venue. Where education is designed in accordance with the global model which focuses on its poverty-reduction or wealth-generation dimensions, the abyss between what children learn in and out of school is huge. That model obliterates the primordial role of education to transmit cultural values and rules of conduct to the next generation–in the broadest meaning of culture–as the way of life. Sadly, this also includes the culture(s) of victimhood and varying explanations of the causes and the consequences of conflicts and warfare in the Middle East.

The design of education stemming from global strategies such as MDGs prioritizes quantitative targets, and consequently, they are presented as a technical exercise. Because the underpinning discipline here is economics, there is no mention of the politics of educational policy and no mention of religion. Considering MDGs and related educational strategies as forms of global central planning, the vocabulary itself is couched and squeezed in the administrative and spiritless language of the World Bank.

The instrumentalization of education for poverty reduction, and the World Bank as the key architect of the resulting global strategies, emphasize "efficient delivery" and "economies of scale"–strategies that clash with the reality of current models. Analyzing *how* education works and *why* it works that way provides the necessary basis for understanding what changes might be desirable and feasible and how they may be facilitated.

Parallel systems of education

An essential feature of the Middle East is that it is neither unified nor uniform. The 2005 Arab Development Report described three educational systems that run in parallel–government-provided, private, and religious, to conclude that these three "mutually exclusive sectors" (UNDP 2005: 147) weaken the social fabric. Government-provided education in the region has changed profoundly in the last two decades.

According to a 2002 Arab Development Report (UNDP/AFESD 2002: 53-54), education has begun to lose its significance as a means of achieving social achievement, turning instead to a means of perpetuating social stratification and poverty based upon the chasm between very expensive private education enjoyed by the better-off minority, and the poor-quality government education for the majority.

Because the Middle East has some of the wealthiest oil-exporters in the world, the yardstick for assessing public investment is inevitably raised. The meaning of *free* education is very broad in countries which are both wealthy and generous. While an upswing in oil prices in 2006 might increase public investment in education and undo some of the budgetary restrictions of the previous decades, the turmoil of warfare reflected in relentlessly high military expenditures has isolated education from official and popular political priorities (Kuwait National Commission for Education 1996: 13).

Increased budgetary allocation to education may have resulted in improved educational statistics but their impact may also be a negative one where high unemployment rates amongst graduates contradict assumptions that education leads directly to poverty-reduction or wealth-creation. What then are the youth to do with the schooling that the governments have provided?

International human rights law provides the framework for seeking answers because it forces the joining of separate sectors by the principle that human rights are interconnected and indivisible. The affirmation of basic human rights principles in the regional and national law is, however, quite fragmentary.

Commitments to the human right to education

The assumption behind international human rights law whereby national law is created and changed through democratic processes does not fully apply in the Middle East. In some countries, secular and religious laws exist in parallel while in others religious law takes precedence. In 1979, the new Islamic Republic of Iran challenged the legitimacy of secular law, including the Universal Declaration of Human Rights which is generally deemed to constitute the universal minimum accepted by governments (Tomaševski 2000: 158-164).

Although such uncertain status of internationally guaranteed human rights inhibits much human rights work, the right to education in the sense of individual entitlement to public services fares well. The Cairo Declaration on Human Rights in Islam, presented to the UN by Iran in 1992, and the Arab Charter on Human Rights, adopted by the League of Arab States in 1994, affirms the right to education for every citizen as "the quest for knowledge is an obligation and the provision of education is a duty for society and the State (Permanent representative of the Islamic Republic of Iran to the United Nations Office at Geneva 1992: 4, Article 9). Elementary education is compulsory and free (Arab Charter on Human Rights 1996: 57-64).

However, governmental policies consistent with this commitment to free and compulsory elementary education did not find favour with the World Bank– diagnosing that free and compulsory education that was publicly provided has been a central tenet of the social contract but objecting since this resulted in the crowding out of private delivery through lack of demand and some consequent ossification in educational development (World Bank 1998: 5, 7).

The heritage of education as a public responsibility is reflected in the constitution and laws of most Middle Eastern countries, however governmental policies vary in defining what free education means and in ensuring that such formal guarantees are translated into domestic practices. Where the government is both willing and able to eliminate all financial barriers that might keep children out of school, the definition of free is broad as international human rights law requires. Education can be called *free* where the government pays teachers' salaries and where families are supposed to bear all other costs. This "technically free" education leaves "indirect costs of uniforms, tutoring and books that parents often cannot afford or wish to pay" (Rihani 1993: 46). Transportation is an additional expense. Much as in other regions, there is a close correspondence between effective guarantees of free education and the universalization of primary schooling. Making education free is a necessary but insufficient condition for making formal schooling all-encompassing.

Educational toll of militarization

An implicit rule of statistics is that particularly large military expenditures are never fully reflected in the official statistics. It is the opposite in education and no official statistics are available where public investment in education is low. UNESCO recommends a minimum of 6 per cent of a country's GDP as necessary to be allocated to education. Two countries in the region meet this minimum, but for eight others, this statistic is unavailable.

LATIN AMERICA

Divergent human rights policies

Different ways in which governments in the region define human rights epitomize its diversity. Cuba and Costa Rica have attained impressive educational accomplishments pursuing profoundly different policies; Argentina has better statistics on primary education than the United States of America; Brazil and Mexico have shown the world what needs to be done to make primary education genuinely free. International cooperation should have supported these commitments but has proved to be an obstacle. The many human rights battles needed to transform military dictatorships into democracies have gone with much too little international support much too late. That fact that regional educational commitments have subsequently been raised to the universal completion of secondary education speaks volumes.

The region has a long heritage of free public education. This heritage has facilitated heightened expectations of what governments should do while indigenous movements have emphasized what they should *not* do, namely hispanicize rather than educate (Tomaševski 2006: 26-32).

Much as everywhere else, the cost of for-fee education is expressed in the numbers of children out of school. If charges are levied, the number of children and young people who go to school automatically diminishes (UIS 2001: 46). This finding shifts the Unfortunately, free *versus* for-fee models also revive Cold War debates about what human rights are and are not, and the language of human rights is subsequently not used in educational debates because of the automatic triggering. The human rights policy of the United States of America, whose federal government denies that there is such a thing as the *right to education* (Tomaševski 2001: para. 23-29), keeps the Cold War alive by pitting governments who priorize social and economic rights against the US which, in turn, labels that model as a remnant of a failed communist system (see also Tomaševski 2005b: 215-220).

The period which became known as *la década perdida* (the lost decade) amplified substantive disagreements about governmental obligations in education: Do governments provide or merely regulate education; were governments obliged to make primary education free or were they to levy charges so as to diminish fiscal deficits and facilitate debt servicing? The recipe came from the US capital, headquarters of the World Bank and the International Monetary Fund, and is thus known as the Washington Consensus (The key parts the Washington Consensus which have particularly affected education have been fiscal discipline [reduction of budget deficit, often entailing diminished budgetary allocations to education], altered priorities in public expenditure [routinely converting secondary and tertiary education from free to for-fee], tax reform [where cutting marginal tax rates regularly results in 'strategic deficits' and governmental revenue becomes insufficient to finance public services, including education], privatization [legal, regulatory and tax incentives for private educational institutions], liberalization of trade in education services, and protection of property rights, including intellectual property rights [which then transforms knowledge from a public good into a traded commodity]). This blueprint effectively denied the right to education by making corresponding governmental obligations impossible. Adequate and sustained funding for public education was then undermined by prioritizing debt servicing, and the shortfall in budgetary funds was made up by levying fees and other charges which victimised, in particular, children (CODEHUCA 1993). By weakening public education, the human rights impact of the Washington Consensus is profound. Whatever national guarantees of free education there may have been were made irrelevant. The symbolic gesture by Brazil and Argentina of paying debts to the International Monetary Fund so as to regain autonomy epitomizes the road travelled. Part of that journey was the privatization of the financial responsibility for education. A parallel system of public and private, free and for-fee schools exist everywhere except Cuba.

Free education provided by the state is routinely impoverished, while for-fee, private education offers consumers the best education that money can buy. The USA is used as the model and is also the magnet, being the largest exporter of educational services and "importer" of migrants from South America. A changed vocabulary followed and *access* to education replaced the *right* to education, thus educational statistics do not differentiate between education accessed through purchase and education which is available free of charge—blurred further by the levying of charges in public education. There is no controlled vocabulary as yet in Spanish because the phenomenon is new and policies introducing charges come from Washington, in English, hence the use of the World Bank's term *school fees*.

Constitutional guarantees of free education

The law in the region is uniform in guaranteeing free education with one exception. There are differences in the length of the educational cycle defined as free and compulsory. Education may be defined as both a right and a duty. If education is compulsory for children, it is also compulsory for their parents and for the state. The very notion of compulsory education denotes rejection of a parental right to deny education from their children. Having made education compulsory, the state has a heightened obligation to ensure that all children can comply with compulsory educational laws. This includes the elimination of all financial obstacles that prevent children from completing the compulsory education cycle.

The reason for transferring a part of the cost of education to families and communities is an inadequate investment in education. Human rights research always shows that formal guarantees can be a reflection of governmental policy but also a substitution for it. Clearly then, it is the priorities in budgetary allocations that reflect a commitment to education or its neglect.

Obviously, inadequate public investment in education impedes the attainment of the global minimum of primary schooling for all. The reason is not so obvious. It may be a particular government's unwillingness to invest in education of the poor, or its inability to do so. This inability has been an object of intense controversy because of the global policies for debt servicing over the past three decades.

The educational toll of the Washington Consensus

Regional commitments to ensuring free education for all children are reflected n the relatively high correspondence between constitutional guarantees and governmental policies in the region. The scope of freedom which a government has at a particular time is constrained by its debt burden and conditions for its servicing. Individual governments have often described the harm inflicted upon public education by debt servicing. Their reports under human rights treaties have referred to the Washington Consensus as *the* driver of their shift from free to for-fee education.

The two pillars of the Washington Consensus (see Williamson 1990) particularly relevant for education were to curtail excessive state intervention and to eliminate budget deficits. The first part translated into cutting down "oversized" public sectors, including education. The second part entailed decreased budgetary allocations to education, which made levying payments to make up for shortfalls inevitable. Increased social investments aim to remedy the damages wrought during this "the lost decade" by broadening democracy to include economic and fiscal decision-making. But another part of the Washington Consensus stands in the way, and is epitomized by the notion of *strategic deficit*. Such 'deficit' was created by reducing the size of governmental revenue so that there was no option but to cut public services. A key obstacle was the merger between inability and unwillingness to tax proprietary classes.

Fiscal commitments to education

Law is symmetrical with children's entitlement to free education, and thus, entails corresponding governmental obligations. Making constitutional guarantees of free education effective revolves around budgetary allocations to education. Discretionary allocations impede the realization of the right to education because they are unpredictable and routinely much below the cost of schooling. If the budget is small, the allocation to education is likely to be below its cost. Decreased military expenditures have been a "human rights dividend" secured in many states in this region through the replacement of military dictatorships by democracy.

Increased public investment in education has facilitated the universalization of primary education in many countries and the regional commitment is now to universalize secondary education. This process has revealed how broad the definition of free education should be so as to enable *all* children to go to school. Nevertheless, the financial barriers which children need to overcome to go to school are three-fold: direct, indirect, and opportunity costs (Tomaševski 2005c: 24-29). Eliminating charges is the first necessary step but this alone does not make education free.

THE CARIBBEAN

Varied constitutional models

Different from the prevalence of constitutionally guaranteed free and compulsory education in Latin America, in the Caribbean there is an emphasis on safeguards for freedom in education. Constitutionally guaranteed freedom of education also supports parallel systems of private and public, religious and secular education. This dividing line routinely coincides with for-fee and free schools. Private schools tend to be religious and to charge fees although they are often subsidized by government.

These differing models of education originate from legal traditions implanted during periods of colonization (see also Tomaševski 2003: 44-50), but constitutional guarantees prioritize freedom to provide education by both religious communities and private entrepreneurs. Education is still seen primarily as a parental responsibility with constitutional guarantees of religious and economic freedom offering choice, and because education is generally not free, choice is determined by the family's purchasing power. Because choice is exercised at one's own cost, the poor have no choice–children can only go to school if it's free.

Conflicts between constitutional guarantees of free education and governmental policies of levying charges demonstrate that the Caribbean has been affected by the trend to privatize financial responsibility for education much as the rest of the world. In countries where education was defined as a public responsibility and governments obliged to ensure free education, contrary governmental policies have impeded the universalization of education and undermined this rule of law.

THE WEALTHY WEST

Double standards

Globalized strategies such as the MDGs and 'Education for All' have formally divided the world into two parts. They speak to the poor and the wealthy parts of the world – the latter supposed to help the poor move towards the benchmarks it has so well defined that it is willing to finance. The MDGs were formally adopted by the United Nations but were designed by the OECD four years earlier (OECD/DAC 1996). A low threshold has been laid down for the poor while the rich continue performing to a much higher standard.

Grounded on the criterion of affordability, public investment in education is much higher in rich than poor countries, both in absolute and relative figures. The right to education should have globally institutionalized a minimal entitlement for all humans premised on two characteristics: (a) that it is a *human right* rather than an entitlement limited to citizens, and (b) that governmental *human rights obligations* are universal rather than circumscribed by national borders. Not having happened, the trend points in the opposite direction as found in OECD annual educational assessments: (a) the proportion of private funding of primary and secondary education tends to be higher in countries with low levels of GDP per capita (OECD 2001: 88.); (b) education reproduces existing patterns of privilege (OECD 2002: 99).

Within the OECD education is free and a variety of governmental subsidies reduce private costs of raising and educating children. The existing global pattern of privilege is reinforced with the OECD prolonging education from an average of 11 to 15 years of full-time education. Externally, these creditor and donor governments have committed themselves to support no more than primary school in the poorest states which is usually five years long or less.

Such denials of access to education on the grounds of poverty should not be tolerated, but is a corollary of the commitment rhetorically shared by all OECD governments to ensure that all children are well-educated—despite the variance in national policies defining this and operationalizing how this is best ensured. There is unanimity regarding this commitment (Kahn & Kamerman 2002) since education was made compulsory and free more than a century ago in most wealthy states and ample 'evidence' has accumulated on its advantages since those times

Governmental policies which need to be in place to keep education free and compulsory reach far beyond the sector of education because research has also documented the negative impact of poverty on children's school attendance and educational attainment. Universal entitlements (e.g. family or child allowances) are provided in some countries, means-tested policies in others, or a combination of the two–both having been proven to reduce child poverty as well as improve educational performance (Kamerman, et al. 2003). It should be noted here that children are defined as poor when they *live in households in which disposable incomes are less than half of the median income in a given country* (OECD 2005: 56).

Governmental policies to alleviate the cost of raising and educating children do not exist in poor developing countries. Education may be nominally free in poor countries but the cost of raising children may be exorbitant because most, if not all, public services are for-fee. The requirement that education be made compulsory for all has been abandoned in both the MDGs and the EFA strategies. This feature has made education a service provided "in the exercise of governmental authority" in the vocabulary of international trade law (Tomaševski 2005a: 10-15). This has made education as compulsory for the government as it is for the child and parents, and the government is obliged to make and keep compulsory education free.

The heritage of compulsory and free education

All-encompassing and compulsory education was introduced in this region beginning in the 19th century with the rationale summarized by Richard Hawker in 1877 that identified four key arguments behind universal, state-funded education in New Zealand.

- Social control
- Need for an educated electorate
- Investments in economic productivity
- Equal individual rights (Coxon, et al. 1994: 44).

Economic productivity is mentioned much more often than social control in government policies but that emphasis alone does not necessarily drive the educational practice. Experience has shown that education would never become compulsory unless it was also free, and the link between the elimination of child labour and free and compulsory education formed part of the oldest expressions of international human rights law. Noteworthy as well, the term *primary education* has fallen into oblivion because the educational cycle which is legally defined as compulsory is much longer.

Clearly, the definition of *free* means that no charges are levied for enrolment and tuition but the practice of states frequently varies beyond that minimum. In the majority of countries, the legal definition of *free* education is broad and governmental policy is to offset all costs related to education. In its comparative surveys of free and for-fee education, the OECD has noted that only in non-European countries, Japan and the United States, around 10 per cent of students attend schools "predominantly financed through unsubsidized household payments" (OECD 2001: 127). In the European Union, 89 per cent of the overall cost of education is borne by the public purse. Charges may be levied in pre-primary education and at the university but not in compulsory education. Moreover, family allowances exist in all European countries without exception. In general, they are awarded when children are born and paid up to the end of compulsory education (EURYDICE 2005).

When is education free?

Definitions of *free* education include a range of subsidies provided to offset the cost of enrolment, tuition, books, meals, computers, sports, to encompass transportation for children who live far from school, or extra-curricular activities (United Nations, 2002, para. 386). Finland, the country that has become known as *the* impressive performer in international ranks by virtue of its learning accomplishments, also serves as an example of the generous provision of everything that is needed for pupils to achieve impressive results.

> Municipalities are obliged to provide basic education, as well as materials and tools, free of charge to children of compulsory education age in their area. One healthy meal is served every day free of charge to those attending school. In cases where the journey to school is longer than five kilometres or, considering the age and circumstances of the pupil, too tiring, free transport to school must be arranged. Disabled children are entitled to have an attendant and such school aids as they need to be able to attend school, without any extra cost to themselves (United Nations 1999: para. 437).

Governmental responsibility towards subsidy and liberty

The European Union illustrates two facets of governmental human rights obligations, to ensure education for all children while respecting freedoms *of* and *in* education. Parental freedom to educate their children in non-state schools or at home has impeded the recognition of a state's right to impose public schooling by making it compulsory in the EU's key human rights documents. The European Union's Charter of Fundamental Rights has thus prioritized parental freedom of choice in defining the right to education, but has not repeated the formula from international human rights treaties [free and compulsory education] which assumes the state's power to impose education. Rather, it has referred to "the possibility to receive free compulsory education". That formulation reflects the limited competence of the European Union in education as well as in human rights and the requirement to respect national differences. Governmental obligations are to ensure that education is free by offering good quality education to all school age children while respecting parental freedom to opt out of public schooling.

In some European countries governments are obliged to provide even-handed financing to all formal compulsory schooling. In others, opting out of public school also means relinquishing the right to free education. Ireland's 1937 constitution provides an illustration of the complexity of a constitutional formula designed to impede the state from imposing education while obliging it to ensure that education is provided, and is worth quoting in full:

> The State acknowledges that the primary and natural educator of the child is the Family and guarantees to respect the inalienable right and duty of parents to provide, according to their means, for the religious and moral, intellectual, physical and social education of their children.
>
> Parents shall be free to provide education in their homes or in private schools or in schools recognized or established by the State.
>
> The State shall not oblige parents in violation of their conscience and lawful preference to send their children to schools established by the State or to any particular type of school designated by the State.
>
> The State shall, however, as guardian of the common good, require in view of actual conditions that the children receive a certain minimum education, moral, intellectual and social.
>
> The State shall provide for free primary education and shall endeavour to supplement and give reasonable aid to private and corporate educational initiative, and when the public good requires it, provide other educational facilities or institutions with due regard, however, for the rights of the parents, especially in the matter of religious and moral formation.
>
> In exceptional cases, where parents for physical or moral reasons fail in their duty towards their children, the State as guardian of the common good by appropriate means shall endeavour to supply the place of the parents, but always with due regard for the natural and imprescriptible rights of the child.

It must be emphasized that education financed and provided by the state is a fairly recent outcome in modern history, and that the inherited mosaic of the pre-state provision of education, especially by religious communities, has greatly influenced contemporary models. Constitutional guarantees for freedom of education have impeded state monopoly over education, which was a key feature of Soviet-modeled systems and triggered explicit safeguards against this model in the Western part of Europe during the Cold War. However generous the interpretations of the meaning of *free* might be for some, they are not shared amongst all Western countries many of whom have also formally introduced charges.

SUMMING UP: THE FINDINGS AND THEIR IMPLICATIONS

*Resolve and resources (*not *resources alone)*

The review of policy-based charges in primary school in wealthy, post-industrializing countries has again fully demonstrated the need to scrutinize the fate of the poor in rich countries. The tyranny of statistical averages portrays these countries as having universalized education but this is often not the case. As the United States has lower enrolments in primary school than Argentina, there is no automatic association between the wealth of a country and its educational performance. US school enrolments in 2001/2002 were reported at 94 per cent, meaning that 6 per cent of school-aged children (6-11) were out of school: some 1.3 million (UNESCO/ UNICEF 2005: 78).

Wealthy post-industrializing countries provide more and better education but differences between them demonstrate the impact of an effective recognition of the human right to education or its absence–differences much more apparent in poorer regions of the world. The word *compulsory* is missing from the global agenda as it would entail defining education as a public service and a public responsibility. Instead, the global vocabulary revolves around supply and demand.

The global pattern of economic exclusion

The purpose of this report is to make the global pattern of poverty-based exclusion from primary school visible so that the findings can illuminate and inform intertwined, interdependent global strategies for poverty reduction, debt relief, human rights and education. It uses the absence of poverty-based exclusion from education as the benchmark. It is paradoxical that this benchmark is absent from all global strategies, even when they claim to be designed to reduce poverty through education. If education is priced out of the reach of the poor, as is often the case, this paradox becomes glaringly obvious and it is necessary then to simply ask *why* this is so.

When is education not free?

Making (or keeping) education free has positive effects on children's enrolments. However, most of the available data refer to educational enrolments rather than attendance and completion, and in most countries primary education is much too short to genuinely benefit children.

Children are pushed out of school as the expenses of going to school start mounting. The experience accumulated in eighty years of governmental legal obligation to make education free and compulsory teaches us that education cannot be universalized (and then made compulsory) unless it is free.

One important reason for charges is that education routinely receives less funding that is necessary for schools to function and for teachers to be able to teach. This fact is cloaked under widespread unwillingness to determine the cost of education and thereupon to calculate necessary budgetary allocations. Another reason is that education is not affirmed as a human right in quite a few countries.

The cost of education varies between and within countries, depending on a range of factors including the percentage of school children in the population, its dispersion or geographical concentration as well as the diversity of the educational intake with regard to language or religion. The ability of families to contribute to the cost of education also varies. Those who are too poor to afford the cost may be exempt from charges but these exemption are routinely too cumbersome or too humiliating to comply with, or else too expensive to administer. More importantly, the cost of education cannot be transferred to a family which is too poor to bear it. In consequence, children have to work rather than to go to school. The result is a stunted childhood and a future denied.

What would it take to make education free?

The boundary between public and private education has been obliterated by conditioning access to public school payments. This conflicts with the very notion of free and compulsory education, where education is free at the point of use because getting educated is mandatory for all children. Education is an individual entitlement of each child. Access to school conditioned by the ability to pay, a defining feature of private education, has been imported into public education thereby privatizing it.

The confusing vocabulary relating to the payments imposed in public education demonstrates the novelty of this phenomenon. And the World Bank's term, *user fees*, is widespread because many of these charges originated in its design of education and it ahs become *the* source of official information on the incidence and prevalence of school fees.

The World Bank's contribution to the *2006 Education for All Global Monitoring Report* was entitled "Fees still exist in a large number of countries" with the small print indicating that the data was collected informally by World Bank task teams. The commissioned paper which should have clarified educational charges did no such thing. It merely lists five types of fees which the World Bank chose to ask about and what various task teams said about them (see also Bentaouett 2006). This has enabled the World Bank to publicly state that it did not promote school fees and define as *fees* only those charges that it did *not* promote.

This symptom of unwillingness to tackle he problem will not be addressed unless it is publicised, hence this report. It is inspired by the requirement of international human rights law that primary education should be free for all children.

It is meant to act as an incentive to reconsider the ends and means of global strategies for education. As long as they are based on the refusal to see clearly the breadth and depth of poverty-based exclusion form education, they cannot hope to remedy it.

Primary education is an investment with no immediate return and is therefore part of public law. Education is a public good because it represents the most widespread form of institutionalized socialization of children and not merely the transmission of knowledge and skills. Children can be deprived of schooling but they learn out of school, especially about their rights-lessness.

Children cannot wait to grow, hence their prioritized right to education. Education constitutes one of the few globally accepted duties for children because it is compulsory. Children are given the legal right to education because they lack a political voice that would enable them to secure their education through the political process.

After the turn of the millennium, there has been an increasing global consensus on the need to make primary education free. Paradoxically, this has not led to identifying charges which have converted previously free education into for-fee.

Governments battling to provide free primary education are exposed to counter-pressures. International human rights law demands ensuring free primary education. Debt relief strategies demand fiscal accountability. Debt servicing takes precedence over human rights obligations because sanctions for non-compliance are immediate and expensive. The World Bank has joined those who would advocate the elimination of fees (World Bank 2003: 5; 23.) but has not proceeded to apply this rhetoric where it could have made a difference, such as in debt relief.

Human rights law shares with global poverty reduction strategies the experience that poverty is a key barrier to universalizing education. In primary education, the key governmental obligation is that of result. Where direct, indirect and opportunity costs preclude access to education, the government has to ensure that they are gradually eliminated. The prerequisite is to identify these costs and, then, develop a strategy for their elimination.

Making education free necessitates acceptance of governmental powers to raise revenue through taxation and to prioritize the right to education in its budgetary allocations. In poor countries with young populations, domestically generated funds are often insufficient and international cooperation has been anticipated as a means to close the financing gap. Its basis is discretion of each creditor and donor. The bonds of solidarity that the universal right to education necessitates do not exist as yet. This report builds on the increasing global consensus that primary education should be free and argues that, at the very least, international cooperation should facilitate rather than hinder the universalization of education.

The key to a changed global design of education is an affirmation that education is a public responsibility. This report aims to facilitate such a change.

REFERENCES

Adams, D. (2002). *Education and national development: Priorities, policies and planning, Education in developing Asia* (Vol. 1). Manila & Hong Kong: Asian Development Bank & Comparative Education Research Centre of the University of Hong Kong.

Arab Charter on Human Rights. (1996). *The review of the international commission of jurists* (Geneva, No. 56/1996).

Asian Development Bank. (2003). *'Key Indicators 2003'(Special chapter): Education for global participation*. Retrieved from www.adb.org

A survey of business in India, *The Economist*, June 3, 2006.

Bentaouett, R. (2006). *School fees* (Commissioned paper for the 2006 Global Monitoring Report). Paris: UNESCO. Retrieved from http://portal.unesco.org/education

Bradbury, M. (2000, June 3). Normalising the crisis in Africa. *The Journal of Humanitarian Assistance*. Retrieved from www.jha.ac/articles/a043.htm

Cantwell, N. (1997). *Starting from zero: The promotion and protection of children's rights in post-genocide Rwanda july 1994 – december 1996*. Innocenti Insights, Florence: UNICEF International Child Development centre.

Chapman, D. (2002). *Management and efficiency in education: Goals and strategies. Education in developing Asia* (Vol. 2), Manila & Hong Kong: Asian Development Bank & Comparative Education Research Centre of the University of Hong Kong.

Chauveau, F. (1998). *Stratégies pour les jeunes défavorisés: Etat des lieux en Afrique francophone sub-saharienne*. Paris: Institut international de planification de l'éducation.

CODEHUCA. (1993). *Los niños de la década perdida*. San José (Costa Rica): Comisión para la defense de los derechos humanos en Centroamerica.

Colclough, C., & Al-Samarrai, S. (1998, November). *Achieving schooling for all: Budgetary expenditures on education in Sub-Saharan Africa and South Asia*, IDS (Institute for Development Studies Working Paper No. 77). Brighton: Home office.

Conhye, B., & Coulibaly, M. (1999). *Policies, procedures and strategies for the allocation of resources for education in Sub-Saharan Africa: A review of the literature*. Dakar: ADEA (Association for the Development of Education in Africa) and CODESRIA (Council for the Development of Social Science Research in Africa).

Coxon, I., et al. (Eds.). (1994). *The politics of learning and teaching in Aotearoa – New Zealand*. Palmerston North: Dunmore Press.

Davies, L. (2004). Comparative education in an increasingly globalised world. *Comparative Education Bulletin, 7*.

EURYDICE. (2005, July). *Key data on education in Europe 2005* (6th ed.). Office for Official Publications of the European Communities. Retrieved from www.eurydice.org

Farkas, L. (2004, February 6). Education, education, and more education. *EUMAP Feature*. Retrieved from www.eumap.org/articles

Florestal, K., & Cooper, R. (1997, June). *Decentralization of education. Legal issues*. Washington, DC: World Bank.

Galbraith, J. K. (2004). *The economics of innocent fraud: Truth for our time*. London: Penguin/Allen Lane.

Gill, R. (1998). *Asia under siege: How the Asian miracle went wrong*. Singapore: Epic Management Services.

Kahn, A. J., & Kamerman, S. B. (Eds.). (2002). *Beyond child poverty: The social exclusion of children*. New York: Institute for Child and Family Policy, Columbia University.

Kamerman, S. B., et al. (2003, May 20). *Social policies, family types and child outcomes in selected OECD countries* (OECD Social, Employment and Migration Working Papers No. 6, Doc. DELSA/ELSA/WD/SEM(2003)6, 20 May 2003).

Kattan, R. B., & Burnett, N. (2004, July). *User fees in primary education*. Washington, DC: World Bank. Retrieved from www.worldbank.org/education/pdf/EFAcase_userfees

Kitaev, I. (1999). *Private education in Sub-Saharan Africa: A re-examination of theories and concepts related to its development and finance*. Paris: International Institute for Educational Planning, UNESCO/IIEP.

Kuwait National Commission for Education, Science and Culture and the Department of Planning, Ministry of Education. (1996). *National report on the development of education: State of Kuwait*. Presented at the International Conference on Education, 45th Session, Geneva, 1996.

Lott, J. R. (1990, April). An explanation for public provision of education: The importance of indoctrination. *Journal of Law and Economics, 33*.

Mahal, A. (2005, November). Policy implications of the distribution of public subsidies on health and education: The case of Karnataka, India. *Comparative Education Review, 49*(4).

Obituary: John Kenneth Galbraith, *The Economist*, May 6, 2006.

OECD. (2005). *Society at a glance: OECD social indicators* (2005 ed.). Paris: OECD.

OECD. (2002). *Education at a glance: OECD indicators*. Paris: OECD.

OECD. (2001). *Education at a glance: OECD indicators* (2001 ed.). Paris: OECD.

OECD/DAC. (1996). *Shaping the 21st century: The contribution of development cooperation*. Paris: OECD.

OHCHR [Office of the High Commissioner for Human Rights]. (2006). *Frequently asked questions on a human rights-based approach to development cooperation* (Doc. HR/PUB/06/8). New York and Geneva: United Nations.

Permanent representative of the Islamic Republic of Iran to the United Nations Office at Geneva. (1992). *Letter dated 8 April 1992 for the preparatory committee of the world conference on human rights* (U.N. Doc. A/CONF.157/PC/35).

Rihani, M. (1993). *Strategies for female education in the Middle East and North Africa.* Amman (Jordan): UNICEF Middle East and North Africa Regional Office.

Simons, W. B. (1980). *The constitutions of the communist world.* Alphen aan den Rijn: Sijthoff & Noordhoff.

Smith, P. (2006, March). (Assistant Director-General for Education at UNESCO) *Building a world of learning for all.* Paris: UNESCO.

Sosale, S. (2000). *Trends in private sector development in world bank education projects* (Policy Research Working Paper No. 2452). Washington, DC: World Bank.

Suter, K. (2003, November). Pacific storms. *The World Today.*

Tan, J.-P., & Mingat, A. (1992). *Education in Asia: A comparative study of cost and financing.* Washington, DC: World Bank Regional and Sectoral Studies.

Todaro, M. P. (1997). *Economic development.* London: Longman.

Tomaševski, K. (2006). Removing obstacles in the way of the right to education. *Right to Education Primers, 1.* Retrieved from www.right-to-education.org

Tomaševski, K. (2005a, Winter). Globalizing what: Education as a right or as a traded service. *Indiana Journal of Global Legal Studies, 12*(1), 10–15.

Tomaševski, K. (2005b). Has the right to education a future within the United Nations? A behind-the-secenes account by the special rapporteur on the right to education 1998–2004. *Human Rights Law Review, 5*(2), 215–220. Retrieved from www.right-to-education.org

Tomaševski, K. (2005c). *Human rights obligations in education: The 4-A scheme.* Nijmegen: Wolf Legal Publishers.

Tomaševski, K. (2005d, October 5). Not education for all, only for those who can pay: The world bank's model for financing primary education. *Law, Social Justice & Global Development* (An electronic law journal). Retrieved from www.right-to-education.org

Tomaševski, K. (2005e, January). Strengthening pro-poor law: Legal enforcement of economic and social rights, ODI: www.odi.org.uk/rights

Tomaševski, K. (2004). *Manual on rights-based education: Global human rights requirements made simple.* Bangkok: UNESCO.

Tomaševski, K. (2003). *Education denied: Costs and remedies.* London: Zed Books.

Tomaševski, K. (2001). *Special rapporteur on the right to education: Mission to the United States of America, 24 September–10 October 2001* (Doc. E/CN.4/2002/60/Add.1). Paris: UN Commission on Human Rights.

Tomaševski, K. (2000). *Responding to human rights violations 1946–1999.* The Hague: Martinus Nijhoff Publishers.

Tomaševski, K. (1994). Human rights in Eastern Europe. In P. Baehr, et al. (Eds.), *Human rights in developing countries yearbook 1994.* Oslo: Kluwer Law and Taxation Publishers, Deventer & Nordic Human Rights Publications.

Tomaševski, K. (1986). Limits to diversity: Soviet and East European human rights policies and international standards. *Soviet Union/Union Sovietique, 13*(1), 45–110.

Transparency International. (2003). *Global corruption report 2003. Special focus: Access to information.* London: Profile Books.

UIS (UNESCO Institute of Statistics). (2001). *América latina y el Caribe: Informe regional.* Montréal: UNESCO Institute of Statistics.

United Nations. (1999). Doc. E/C.12/4/Add.1.

United Nations. (2002). Doc. CRC/C/8/Add.45.

United Nations. (1975). *The realization of economic, social and cultural rights: Problems, policies, progress.* New York: United Nations.

United Nations Security Council. (2004, April 22). Resolution 1539.

UNDP. (2005). *Arab human development report 2004: Towards freedom in the Arab world.* New York: United Nations Development Programme, Arab Fund for Economic and Social Development, and Arab Gulf Programme for United Nations Development Organizations, UNDP, Regional Bureau for Arab States (RBAS).

UNDP. (2003). *The millennium development goals in Arab countries.* New York: UNDP.

UNDP/AFESD. (2002). *Arab human development report 2002: Creating opportunities for future generations.* New York: United Nations Development Programme and Arab Fund for Economic and Social Development.

UNESCO. (1998). *Teachers and teaching in a changing world: 1998 World education report.* Paris: UNESCO.

UNESCO. (2002). *Education for all: Is the world on track?, EFA global monitoring report 2002.* Paris: UNESCO Publishing.

UNESCO. (2004). *Global education digest 2004: Comparing education statistics across the world.* Montréal: UNESCO Institute for Statistics, Montreal. Retrieved from www.uis.unesco.org

UNESCO. (2005, March). *Report by the Director-General on the follow-up to the EFA strategic review and UNESCO's strategy for the 2005–2015 period* (Doc. 171 EX/8). Paris: UNESCO.

UNESCO. (2006a). *Education for all global monitoring report 2006.* Paris: UNESCO. Retrieved from www.unesco.org

UNESCO. (2006b, March). *Report by the director-general on global action plan to achieve the education for all (EFA) goals* (Doc. 174 EX/9). Paris: UNESCO.

UNESCO/UNICEF. (2005). *Children out of school: Measuring exclusion from primary education.* Montréal: UNESCO Institute for Statistics.

Waters, T., & Leblanc, K. (2005). Refugees and education: Mass public schooling without a nation-state. *Comparative Education Review, 49*(2).

White, G. (1996). Corruption and the transition from socialism. In M. Levi & D. Nelken (Eds.), *The corruption of politics and the politics of corruption.* Oxford: Blackwell Publishers.

Williamson, J. (1990). What Washington means by policy reform. In J. Williamson (Ed.), *Latin American adjustment: How much has happened?* Washington, DC: Institute of International Economics.

World Bank. (2003). *Opening doors: Education and the world bank.* Washington, DC: World Bank.

World Bank. (2000, September). *Hidden challenges to education systems in transition economies.* Washington, DC: World Bank.

World Bank. (2001, September). *World bank issue brief.* Washington, DC: World Bank.

World Bank. (1999). *Education sector strategy.* Washington, DC: World Bank.

World Bank. (1998). *Education in the Middle East & North Africa: A strategy towards learning for development.* Washington, DC: World Bank.

World Bank. (1990). *Primary education.* Washington, DC: World Bank.

World Bank. (1980). *Education sector policy paper.* Washington, DC: World Bank.

World Education Indicators Programme (WEI). (1999). *Education at a glance 1999.* OECD Database.

HENRY A. GIROUX

DISABLING THE FUTURE

Youth and the Politics of Disposability

War and violence have become the most prominent organizing principles of American life, evident not only in the ongoing and ill-fated wars in Iraq and Afghanistan, but also in the increasing assault being waged at home on democratic values, social provisions, and increasingly all of those populations considered either unpatriotic because they do not conform to the dictates of an imperial presidency or disposable because they have been deemed the human waste of global neoliberalism The war at home has given rise not only to a crushing attack on civil liberties–most evident in the passing of the Military Commissions Act of 2006–which conveniently allows the Bush administration to detain indefinitely anyone deemed an enemy combatant without having recourse to the traditional right to challenge his or her detention through legal means–but also to an assault on those populations now considered disposable and redundant under the logic of a ruthless market fundamentalism. Disposable populations are less visible, relegated to the frontier zones of relative invisibility and removed from public view. Such populations are warehoused in schools that resemble prisons, dispersed to dank and dangerous work places far from the enclaves of the tourist industries, incarcerated in prisons that privilege punishment over rehabilitation, and consigned to the increasing army of the permanently unemployed. Rendered redundant as a result of the collapse of the social state, a spreading virulent racism, a growing disparity in wealth, and a take-no-prisoners market fundamentalism, a growing number of individuals and groups are increasingly demonized and criminalized by virtue of their status as immigrants, young people, being poor, unemployed, disabled, and confined to low paying jobs. Considered the human waste products of the new authoritarianism under the Bush administration such groups join the ranks of those who because of their misfortunes are viewed as having a personal weakness or who because of their racial and stateless presence are increasingly addressed as a threat to the social order (Bauman 2004). Unfortunately, the Bush administration seems dangerously incapable of questioning itself, even as it trivializes democratic values, redistributes wealth upward, aggressively attempts to destroy the welfare state, subordinates the needs of society to the dictates of corporate power, and views misfortune as a weakness.[1]

The definitive weakness is the inability to participate in the capitalist dream. Everybody is now a customer or client, and every relationship is judged against the bottom line. The ever-proliferating consumer and entrepreneurial subject replaces the concept of the responsible citizen, as the former complies with the neoliberal

S.A. Moore and R.C. Mitchell (eds.), Power, Pedagogy and Praxis: Social Justice in the Globalized Classroom, 55–71.

mantra, "privatize or perish." In this system of cost effectiveness, self-reliance is the ultimate virtue, which is another way of saying that people must face the increasingly difficult challenges of the social order alone. In short, private interests trump social needs, economic growth becomes more important than social justice, and the militarization and commercialization of public space now define what counts as the public sphere. The consequences for politics, democracy and public life are devastatingly obvious in the growing gap between the rich and the poor and in the downward spiral of millions of Americans into poverty and despair. The haunting images of New Orleans following Hurricane Katrina–of dead bodies floating in flooded streets, and of thousands of African – Americans marooned on rooftops, abandoned in the Louisiana Superdome, and waiting for days to be rescued from the roofs of flooded houses–serve as just one register of the racism, inequality, and poverty in America.

THE VILIFICATION OF YOUTH, AND THE IMPOVERISHMENT OF CHILDREN

This eroded democracy and emaciated social state comprises the environment in which America's youngest citizens form their concepts of power, democracy, security and citizenship. A great deal of criticism has been written about the passing, in the name of "homeland security," of new anti-terrorist laws that make it easier to undermine those basic civil liberties protecting individuals against invasive and potentially repressive government action, but there is a thunderous silence on the part of many parents, educators, and politicians regarding the ongoing insecurity and injustices suffered by young people in this country. Moreover, the state's increasing reliance on repressive and punitive policies is intensifying these injustices. In the security state, current concerns about terrorism and security almost completely ignore what these terms mean outside of a violent attack against property and persons. As a result, there is a sense of moral and political indifference, if not cynicism, about the forms of domestic terrorism suffered by children who are poor, hungry, homeless, neglected, lacking medical care, or suffering physical abuse by adults. Children have fewer rights than almost any other group and, consequently, their voices are almost completely absent from the debates, policies, and legislative practices that determine and ostensibly meet their needs.

All of these issues raise the fundamental question of what it might mean to take youth seriously as a political and moral referent in order to gauge not only the health of a democratic society, but also to define the obligations of adults to future generations of young people. Democracy increasingly appears damaged, if not fatally wounded, as those who are young, poor, immigrants, or economically marginalized people of color are excluded from the operations of power, the realm of politics, and crucial social provisions.[2] For over a century, Americans have embraced as a defining feature of politics the idea that all levels of government would assume a large measure of responsibility for providing the resources, social provisions, and modes of education that enabled young people to prepare in the present for a better future, while expanding the meaning and depth of an inclusive democracy. This was particularly true under the set of policies inaugurated under President Lyndon Johnson's Great Society programs of the 1960s, which were designed to eliminate both poverty and racial injustice. Not only did the Great Society initiative pass the Civil Rights Act of 1964, it also created the Neighborhood Youth Corps, and funded a number of job training agencies and community development programs. As part of a broader educational program, Johnson produced Project Head Start, and passed laws allowing federal aid to elementary and secondary schools. Since 1980s, however, all of the programs have either been cut back or eliminated and the cuts to funding show no signs of stopping. For example, President Bush budget proposals for 2008 contain cuts in funding to "elementary secondary education (including for special ed and drug-free programs), low-income housing, housing for poor people with disabilities, pollution control and abatement, health care research and training, and money for the prevention and prosecution of violence against women" (Rothschild 2007). The Bush plan would also cut hundreds of thousands of children nationwide from the State Children Health Insurance Program, "cut child care-assistance for 300,000 kids from poor families....and gouge Headstart by $100 million" (Rothschild 2007). Taking the social contract seriously, American society once exhibited at least a willingness to fight for the rights of children, enact reforms that invested in their future, and provide the educational conditions necessary for them to be critical citizens. Within such a modernist project, democracy was linked to the well-being of youth, while the status of how a society imagined democracy and its future was contingent on how it viewed its responsibility towards future generations. The end of that project can be seen in the new American reality under the second Bush administration. Instead of a federal budget that addresses the needs of children, the United States now enacts federal policies that provide tax cuts for millionaires and the weakening or elimination of basic social provisions for children at risk. As *New York Times* op-ed columnist, Paul Krugman, points out compassion and responsibility, under the Bush administration, has given way to "a relentless mean-spiritedness" and "President Bush as someone who takes food from the mouths of babes and gives the proceeds to his millionaire friends" (Krugman, 2005). For Krugman, Bush's budgets have come to resemble a form of" top-down class warfare" (Krugman, 2005).Bush's egregious funding decisions, however, are more than just class warfare; they attack the very concept of youth that was once widespread in America–that young people as a group of people deserve our protection and care.

But the category of youth and a valuing of the people it represents did more than affirm that modernity's social contract was rooted in a conception of the future in which adult commitment was articulated as a vital public service; it also affirmed that those vocabularies, values, and social relations were central to a politics capable of defending vital institutions as a public good and contributing to the quality of democratic public life. At stake here was the recognition that children constitute a powerful referent for addressing war, poverty, education, and a host of other important social issues. Moreover, as a symbol of the future, children provided an important moral compass to assess what Jacques Derrida calls the promises of a "democracy to come" (Derrida 2001: 253). A vocabulary that focuses on children's current and future social importance was particularly central to public and higher education, which often defined and addressed its highest ideals through the recognition that how it educated youth was connected to the democratic future it hoped for and its claim as an important public sphere.

But just as education has been separated from a viable model of democratic politics, youth have been separated both from the discourse of the social contract and from any ethical commitment to provide young people, through the public sphere, with the prospects of a decent and democratic future. Media, government policies, social institutions and popular culture increasingly construct youth as a problem rather than as a resource for the future, in which we need to invest. Instead, we frame youth largely as a generation of suspects and treat them as a disposable population, fodder for a barbaric war in Iraq, or we accuse them of causing most of society's problems. The young now constitute a crisis that has less to do with improving the future than with denying it. As Larry Grossberg points out,

> It has become common to think of kids as a threat to the existing social order and for kids to be blamed for the problems they experience. We slide from kids in trouble, kids have problems, and kids are threatened, to kids as trouble, kids as problems, and kids as threatening. (Grossberg 2005: 16)

Punishment and fear have replaced compassion and social responsibility as the most important modalities mediating the relationship of youth to the larger social order. No longer "viewed as a privileged sign and embodiment of the future" (Grossberg 2001: 133), youth are now increasingly demonized by the popular media and derided by politicians looking for quick-fix solutions to crime. As a result, youth are associated with a rising crime wave, but what is at stake in this discourse is really a punishment wave, one that reveals a society that does not know how to address the social problems that undercut any viable sense of agency, possibility, and future for many young people. For example, John J. Dilulio Jr., a former Bush advisor, argued in an influential article published in the conservative *Weekly Standard* that society faced a dire threat from the emerging generation of youth between the ages of 15 and 24, whom he called "super-predators" (Dilulio Jr. 1995). Former Secretary of Education William Bennett repeated the charge in a book co-authored with Dilulio, in spite of the fact that youth crime has dramatically and continuously declined since the mid 1990s (Bennett, Dilulio Jr., and Walters 1996).[4] Hollywood movies such as *Thirteen, Clueless, Brick, Hard Candy,* and *Alpha Dog* similarly represent youths as either dangerous, utterly brainless, or simply without merit. A recent episode about youth on *Sixty Minutes* is suggestive of this kind of demonization. Focusing on ways in which young people alleviate their alleged boredom, the show focused on the sport of "bum hunting," in which young people search out, attack and savagely beat homeless people while recording the event in an homage to the triumph of reality television. As reprehensible as this act is, it is also reprehensible to vilify young people by suggesting that such behavior is in some way characteristic of youth in general. Then again, in a society in which the marketplace's limited imagination sees youth only as either consumers or billboards to sell sexuality, beauty products, music, athletic gear, clothes, and a host of other products, it is not surprising that young people can be so easily misrepresented.

The popular demonization of the young now justifies responses to youth that were unthinkable 20 years ago, including criminalization and imprisonment, the prescription of psychotropic drugs, psychiatric confinement, and zero tolerance policies that model schools after prisons. In the latter case, the No Child Left Behind policy now provides financial incentives to schools that implement zero tolerance policies, in spite of their proven racial and class biases. Drug sniffing dogs, metal detectors, and cameras have become common features in schools, and administrators willingly comply with federal laws that give military recruiters the right to access the names, addresses, and telephone numbers of students in both public schools and higher education–even though there have been numerous cases of rape and sexual abuse by recruiters who used their power to commit criminal acts against children. For instance, a report by the Associated Press revealed that over 100 young women in 2005 were preyed upon sexually by military recruiters. The six-month investigation found that "Women were raped on recruiting office couches, assaulted in government cars and groped en route to entrance exams [and that at] least 35 Army recruiters, 18 marine Corps recruiters, 18 Navy recruiters and 12 Air Force recruiters were disciplined for sexual misconduct or other inappropriate behavior with potential enlistees in 2005" (*Sexual Abuse* 2006). [4] Trust and respect now give way to fear, disdain, and suspicion, creating an environment in which critical pedagogical practices wither, while pedagogies of surveillance flourish. Under such circumstances, children have fewer rights than almost any other group and also have fewer institutions protecting these rights. What are we to make of third graders being subjected to strip searches in Kansas City, Missouri (Dorfman 2002). What are we to make of the fact that, in Chicago alone, over 3 million students, mostly poor African--Americans, were suspended because of zero tolerance laws; or that the proportion of 15-17-year-olds in jail is expanding at twice the rate of the prison population as a whole; or that, while spending on education increased by 374 per cent, spending on prisons increased 823 per cent in the last decade? (Giroux 2003: 48-49).

Alongside the criminalization of youth, we see the criminal erosion of educational care for the young. Instead of providing a decent critical education to poor young people, President Bush and his cohorts serve them more standardized tests (Kornblut 2005: A26), enforce abstinence programs instead of scientifically informed sex education, and advocate creationism updated as Intelligent Design instead of scientific reason.[5] Youth who are poor and racially marginalized fare even worse and often find themselves in classes that are overcrowded and lacking in basic resources; they are also subject to policies designed to warehouse young people rather than educate them or provide even basic literacy skills. Rather than offering young people vibrant public spheres and the skills to make use of them, the Bush government gives them a commercialized culture in which consumerism is the only condition of citizenship.

The impoverishment of the American educational system reflects the literal penury of American children. The hard currency of human suffering that impacts children is evident in some astounding statistics that suggest a profound moral and political contradiction at the heart of one of the richest democracies in the world: the rate of child poverty rose in 2004 to 17.6 per cent, boosting the number of poor children to 12.9 million. Moreover, children make up a disproportionate share of the poor in the US, in that they are 26 per cent of the total population, but constitute 39 per cent of the poor (Chelala 2006). Just as alarmingly, 9.3 million children lack health insurance, and millions lack affordable child care and decent early childhood education. Most telling, however, of the priority the United States gives to the care of its youth is this: among the industrialized nations the United States ranks first in billionaires and in defense expenditures and yet it ranks an appalling 25th in infant mortality (Center for Family Policy & Research 2007).

As we might expect, behind these grave statistics lies a series of decisions to favor economically those already advantaged at the expense of youth. Programs that benefit young people are being slashed. At the same time, the Bush administration drains the public treasury of billions of dollars through tax cuts for the rich, a disastrous war in Iraq, and appropriations for a bloated military budget, which in 2007 is around $439 billion, not including an additional $120 billion funds requested by the Pentagon "to pay for the wars in Afghanistan and Iraq" (Goldstein 2006: A01). Savage cuts to education, nutritional assistance for impoverished mothers, veterans' medical care, and basic scientific research help fund tax cuts for the inordinately rich. Laura Flanders defines Bush's recent budget as a hit list targeting teens and kids because it calls for cuts in emergency medical services for children, cuts in K-12 education funding, cuts in vocational education and the highly successful Head Start Program. There are food-stamp cuts and a five-year freeze on child care. A $41 million college loan program is eliminated. The whole National Youth sports Program which has provided athletics for low income kids is cut, as in cut out. (Flanders 2005)

I think Paul Krugman once again gets it right in claiming that under the Bush administration, "The hijacking of public policy by private interests" parallels "the downward spiral in governance" (Krugman 2003: A39). This inversion of the government's responsibility to protect public goods from private threats further reveals itself in the privatization of social problems and the vilification of those who fail to thrive in the corporate state. Too many youth within the degraded economic, political, and cultural geography occupy a "dead zone" in which the spectacle of commodification exists alongside the imposing threat of massive debt, bankruptcy, the prison--industrial complex, and the elimination of basic civil liberties. Indeed, we have an entire generation of unskilled and displaced youth who have been expelled from shrinking markets, blue collar jobs, and the limited political power granted to the middle-class consumer. As ***New York Times*** **columnist** Bob Herbert points out, more than five million youth between the ages of 18 and 24 are out of school, work, and hope (Herbert 2003: A35). Rather than investing in the public good and solving social problems, the state now punishes those who are caught in the downward spiral of its economic policies. Punishment, incarceration, and surveillance represent the face of the new expanded state. Consequently, the implied contract between the state and citizens is broken, and social guarantees for youth, as well as civic obligations to the future, vanish from the agenda of public concern. As market values supplant civic values, it becomes increasingly difficult "to translate private worries into public issues and, conversely, to discern public issues in private troubles" (Bauman 1999: 2). The new collective agreement, then, is that alcoholism, homelessness, poverty, and illiteracy, among other issues, are not social, but rather individual problems–matters of character, individual fortitude, and personal responsibility. Those who fall prey to any social ill are doubly offensive to America's ethos of capitalism: in failing to "get ahead," they both threaten to reveal the flawed execution of an individualism that masquerades as meritocracy, and they question, even if not deliberately, America's ultimate measure of subjectivity: the ability to consume goods. Black youth are especially disadvantaged since they are jobless in an economy that does not need their labor and they hence occupy the status of flawed consumers, or as Zygmunt Bauman argues, they constitute "surplus populations"(2005: 39). *New York Times* columnist Bob Herbert points out that

> black American males inhabit a universe in which joblessness is frequently the norm [and that] over the past few years, the percentage of black male high school graduates in their 20s who were jobless has ranged from well over a third to roughly 50 percent....For dropouts, the rates of joblessness are staggering. For black males who left high school without a diploma, the real jobless rate at various times over the past few years has ranged from 59 percent to a breathtaking 72 percent.
>
> (Herbert 2007: A25)

As Herbert argues, "These are the kinds of statistics you get during a depression." (2007: A25). Yet, even while the spectacle of commodification appears as a standard against which disadvantaged youth are found lacking, consumerism's evils are becoming more apparent and more widely publicized, though certainly not widely rejected. Ardent consumers and disengaged citizens provide fodder for a growing cynicism and depoliticization of public life at a time when there is an increasing awareness not just of corporate corruption, financial mismanagement, and systemic greed, but also of the fact that a democracy of critical citizens is being replaced by a democracy of consumers. How we untangle this contradiction will determine the fate of democracy, and the civic health and future of a generation of children and young people.

At the current time, however, solutions involving the social problems have become difficult to imagine, let alone fund. For many young people and adults today, the private sphere has become the only space in which to imagine any sense of hope, pleasure, or possibility. Culture as an activity in which young people actually produce the conditions of their own agency through dialogue, community participation, public stories, and political struggle is being eroded. In its place, we are increasingly surrounded by a "climate of cultural and linguistic privatization" in which culture becomes something you consume, and the only kind of speech that is acceptable is that of the fast-paced shopper (Klein 1999: 177). In spite of neo-conservative and neoliberal claims that economic growth will cure social ills, the market has no way of dealing with poverty, social inequality, or civil rights issues. It has no vocabulary for recognizing and addressing respect, compassion, decency, ethics or, for that matter, its own anti-democratic forms of power. These are political issues, not merely economic concerns. A political system based on democratic principles of inclusiveness and nonrepression, in contrast, can and does provide citizens with the critical tools necessary for them to invest public life with vibrancy, while expanding the foundations of freedom and justice.

In order to strengthen the public sphere, we must use its most widespread institutions, undo their metamorphoses into means of surveillance, and reclaim them as democratic tools. Schools, colleges and universities come to mind–because of both their repressive use and their nonrepressive potential. The current state of youth bears heavily on both public and higher education; as childhood is constructed as a state of apolitical innocence, "the student" remains one of the few popular conceptions of youth whose political potential we are still capable of recognizing. Childhood as a core referent for a vibrant democracy and as a focal point of social justice is disappearing in a society that not only rejects the promise of youth, but also the future itself "as an affective investment" (Grossberg 2001: 133). Thus, the crisis of youth signals a dangerous state of affairs for the future; specifically, it portends a crisis in the very idea of the political and ethical constitution of the social and the possibility of articulating the relevance of democracy itself. In what follows, I argue that youth as a political and moral referent does not only refer to young children, but also to those youth who inhabit our institutions of higher learning, and who are posed to become adults by virtue of the knowledge, capacities, and skills they learn as critical citizens, workers, and intellectuals.

HIGHER EDUCATION AND THE CRISIS OF THE SOCIAL

In keeping with the progressive impoverishment of politics and public life over the past two decades, the university is increasingly being transformed into a training ground for the corporate workforce, rather than a public sphere in which youth can become the critical citizens and democratic agents necessary to nourish a socially responsible future. Anyone who spends time on a college campus in the United States these days cannot miss how higher education is changing. Strapped for money and increasingly defined in the language of corporate culture, many universities seem less interested in higher learning than in becoming licensed storefronts for brand name corporations–selling off space, buildings, and endowed chairs to rich corporate donors. College presidents are now called CEOs and are known less for their intellectual leadership than for their role as fund-raisers and their ability to bridge the worlds of academe and business. Venture capitalists scour colleges and universities in search of big profits to be made through licensing agreements, the control of intellectual property rights, and investments in university spinoff companies. In the age of money and profit, academic subjects gain stature almost exclusively through their exchange value on the market. This is all the more pronounced as the Bush administration attempts to wield more control over higher education, cut student aid, plunder public services and push states to the brink of financial disaster. As higher education increasingly becomes a privilege rather than a right, many working class youth either find it financially impossible to enter college or, because of increased costs, have to drop out. Those students who have the resources to stay in school are feeling the pressure of the job market and rush to take courses and receive professional credentials in business and the biosciences as the humanities lose majors and downsize. Not surprisingly, students are now referred to as "customers," while some university presidents even argue that professors should be labeled as "academic entrepreneurs."[6] As higher education is corporatized, young people find themselves on campuses that look more like malls (the humanities building at the University of Alberta is a mall) and they are increasingly taught by professors who are hired on a contractual basis, have obscene work loads, and barely make enough money to pay the loans for their cars. Tenured faculty are called upon to generate grants, establish close partnerships with corporations, and teach courses that have practical value in the marketplace (see also Fancy and Spearey; Connolly this volume). There is little in this vision of the university that imagines young people as anything other than fodder for the corporation or appendages of the national security state. What was once the hidden curriculum of many universities–the subordination of higher education to capital–has now become an open and much celebrated policy of both public and private higher education (Aronowitz 1998: 194).

Despite the corporatization of the university, higher education has still been attacked by right-wing ideologues such as David Horowitz and Lynne Cheney, who view it as the "weak link" in the war against terror.[7] Horowitz acts as the figurehead for various well-funded conservative student groups such as the Young Americans and College Republicans, which perform the ground work for his "Academic Bill of Rights" policy efforts to seek out juicy but rare instances of "political bias"–whatever that is and however it might be defined–in college classrooms. These efforts have resulted in considerable sums of public money being devoted to hearings in multiple state legislatures, most recently in Pennsylvania, in addition to helping impose, as the *Chronicle of Higher Education* puts it, a "chilly climate" of self-policing of academic freedom and pedagogy (*Forum* 2005: B7-13). In an even more blatantly McCarthyist effort, the Bruin Alumni Association of UCLA has posted on its website an article called, "The Dirty Thirty," in which it targets what it calls the university's "most radical professors" (*Bruin Alumni Association* n.d.). Radical, according to this group, appears to mean, among other things, opposing the war in Iraq, supporting affirmative action, and attacking "President Bush, the Republican Party, multinational corporations, and even our fighting men and women" (Jones n.d.). The Bruin Alumni Association does more than promote McCarthy-like smears, intolerance, and anti-intellectualism through a vapid appeal to "balance" it also offered, at least initially, $100 in "compensation" to any student willing to provide information on a "radical" professor's political views (Jones 2006). Of course, this type of classroom intervention has less to do with protesting genuine demagoguery than it does with attacking any professor who might raise critical questions about the status quo or hold the narratives of power accountable.[8] Illegal and unethical spying at the national level now seems to offer yet another strategy to harass professors, insult students by treating them as if they were mindless, and provide a model for student participation in the classroom that mimics tactics used by fascist and Nazi plants in the 1930s.

A more pervasive threat facing higher education comes from the ongoing militarization of public life. In its assumption that military power is the highest expression of social truth and national greatness, the Bush administration opens a dangerous new chapter in American military history that now gives unfettered support to what C. Wright Mills once called a "'military metaphysics'–a tendency to see international problems as military problems and to discount the likelihood of finding a solution except through military means" (Wright Mills 1956: 222). The influence of militaristic truths, values, social relations, and identities now permeates and defines American culture. As higher education is pressured by both the Bush administration and its jingoistic supporters to serve the needs of the military--industrial complex, universities increasingly deepen their connections to the national security state in ways that are boldly celebrated. Universities invest their resources, engage in research projects, and accept huge amounts of defense contract money in order to provide the personnel, expertise, and tools necessary to expand the security imperatives of the US government. The CIA and other intelligence agencies are developing diverse connections to higher education and, in the process, are not only shaping academic programs, but are also allocating vast sums of money for research projects (Giroux 2007). Public universities such as Penn State, Carnegie Mellon, the University of Pennsylvania, Johns Hopkins, and a host of others, expand the reach and influence of the national security state by entering into formal agreements with agencies such as the FBI (*Penn State's Spanier* 2005). Graham Spanier, the president of Penn State University, argues in a statement pregnant with irony that the establishment of the National Security Higher Education Advisory Board, which he heads, "sends a positive message that leaders in higher education are willing to assist our nation during these challenging times" (*Penn State's Spanier* 2005). Such commentary reads like a page out of George Orwell's *1984* and counters every decent and democratic value that defines higher education as a democratic public sphere.

EDUCATED HOPE IN DARK TIMES

The corporatization and militarization of higher education, the dumbing down of rigorous scholarship, and the devaluing of the critical capacities of young people mark a sharp break from a once strong educational tradition in the United States, extending from Thomas Jefferson to John Dewey, which held that freedom flourishes in the worldly space of the public realm only through the work of educated, socialized citizens. Within this democratic tradition, education was not confused with training; instead, its critical function was propelled by the need to educate students and thereby create citizens capable of defining and implementing universal goals such as freedom, equality, and justice. If we were to value schools and universities as social tools, we could continue this tradition and support its role in deepening the relationship between an expanded notion of the social and the democratic foundation that gives the social its vitality.

In order for higher education to become a meaningful site for educating youth for a democratic future, educators and others need to reclaim higher education as an ethical and political response to the demise of democratic public life. At stake here is the role of the university as a public sphere committed to increasing the possibilities of democratic identities, values, and relations. This approach suggests new models of leadership, organization, power, and vision dedicated to opening higher education up to all groups, creating a critical citizenry, providing specialized work skills for jobs that really require them, democratizing relations of governance among administrators, faculty, and students, and taking seriously the imperative to disseminate an intellectual and artistic culture. Higher education may be one of the few sites left in which students learn the knowledge and skills that enable them not only to mediate critically between democratic values and the demands of corporate power, but also to distinguish between identities founded on democratic principles and identities steeped in forms of competitive, unbridled individualism that celebrate self-interest, profit making, and greed.

Addressing education as a democratic endeavour begins with the recognition that higher education is more than an investment opportunity, citizenship is more than conspicuous consumption, learning is more than preparing for a job in the defense industries, and democracy is more than making choices at the local mall. Reclaiming higher education as a public sphere begins with the crucial project of challenging, among other things, corporate ideology and its attendant notion of corporate time. Corporate time, with its accelerated and fragmented pace, is increasingly replacing public time. In public time, time does not equal money; instead, time acts as one measure of the opportunity to debate, to imagine, and to have a positive impact on the social world. It allows consequential and cumulative change, and it recognizes that the present contributes to the shape of the future. In these ways, it differs greatly from corporate time, which imagines time as units of labour, production, sales, consumption, or increases and decreases in the value of currencies and stocks.[9] The primary difference between the two modes of time, then, is that only public time recognizes personhood.

By taking back higher education as a site for public time, we could foster dialogue, thoughtfulness, and critical exchange. This would, in turn, provide opportunities for knowledge that deepens democratic values, while encouraging pedagogical relations that question the future in terms that are political, ethical, and social. Higher education is a hard won democratic achievement, and it is time that parents, faculty, students, college alumni and concerned citizens reclaim higher education as a fundamental public good rather than merely a training ground for corporate interests, values, and profits. Higher education also needs to be defended against those religious and secular ideologues who harbor a deep disdain for critical thought and healthy scepticism, and who look with displeasure upon any form of education that teaches students to read the world critically and to hold power and authority accountable. Education is not only about issues of work and economics, but also about questions of justice, social freedom, and the capacity for democratic agency, action, and change, as well as the related issues of power, exclusion, and citizenship. These are educational and political issues, and they should be addressed as part of a broader effort to re-energize the struggle for social justice and democracy.

ACADEMICS AND PUBLIC LIFE

Professional academics have a strong role to play in the revitalization of education's ability to positively affect the social struggle, not only because they "belong" in the ivory tower, but also because they have a unique opportunity to throw open its doors. Institutions of higher education resonate with their democratic possibilities when viewed as deeply ethical and political spaces in which intellectuals assert themselves, both as professional academics and as citizens whose knowledge and actions presuppose specific visions of public life, community, and moral accountability. This view suggests that higher education be defended not as an adjunct of the corporation or the national security state, but as a vital public sphere in its own right, one whose ethical and educative dimensions directly impact on civic life. Academics must maintain this defense by redefining their role as public intellectuals who can move between academic institutions and other public spheres in which knowledge, values, and social identities are produced.

Further, if the university is to remain a site of critical thinking, collective work, and public service, educators will have to redefine the knowledge, skills, research, and intellectual practices currently favored in the university. Central to such a challenge is the need to position intellectual practice "as part of an intricate web of morality, rigor and responsibility" that enables academics to speak with conviction, use the public sphere to address important social problems, and demonstrate alternative models for bridging the gap between higher education and broader society (Roy 2001: 6). Connective practices are key: it is crucial to develop intellectual practices that are collegial rather than competitive, refuse the instrumentality and privileged isolation of the academy, link critical thought to a profound impatience with the status quo, and connect human agency to the idea of social responsibility (see also Connolly; Fancy and Spearey this volume).

Connection also means being openly and deliberately political in one's intellectual work. Increasingly, as universities are shaped by a culture of fear in which dissent is equated with treason, the call to be objective and impartial, whatever one's intentions, can easily echo what George Orwell called the official truth or the establishment point of view. Lacking a self-consciously democratic political focus, the university intellectual, under the corporate model of leadership, is often reduced to the role of a technician or functionary engaged in formalistic rituals, unconcerned with the disturbing and urgent problems that confront the larger society. In opposition to this model, with its claims to political neutrality, I argue that public intellectuals should combine the mutually interdependent roles of critical educator and active citizen. This requires finding ways to connect the practice of classroom teaching with the operation of power in the larger society. I think Edward Said is on target when he argues that the public intellectual must function within institutions, in part, as an exile, as someone whose "place it is publicly to raise embarrassing questions, to confront orthodoxy and dogma, to be someone who cannot easily be co-opted by governments or corporations" (Said 1994: 11). In Said's perspective, the educator as public intellectual becomes responsible for linking the diverse experiences that produce knowledge, identities, and social values in the university to the quality of moral and political life in wider society. Such an intellectual does not train students solely for jobs, but also educates them to question critically the institutions, policies, and popular values that limit the role of citizen to that of consumer; such a student is, in turn, capable of rethinking his or her role and identity within the public sphere.

In addition to their responsibility to prepare students to engage critically with the world, academics must also recognize the impact their students will have on a generation of young people twice removed from the university. The importance of such an educational challenge and project is evident in the findings of a survey conducted a few years ago by the John S. and James L. Knight Foundation. According to the survey, 36 per cent of US high school students believed that "newspapers should get government approval of stories before publishing" (Toppo 2005). This view, clearly much more at home with facism than with critical democracy, is legitimated by the students' lack of education about student rights, First Amendment freedoms, and the meaning of a substantive democracy. Education cannot be decoupled from political democracy; a deliberately politicized education should take place at all levels of schooling, but it must gain its momentum in colleges and universities among students who will go back to the schools, the churches, the synagogues, and the business world in order to produce new ideas, concepts, and critical ways of understanding the world in which young people live.

In order for pedagogy that encourages critical thought to have a real effect, it must include the message that all citizens, old and young, are equally entitled, if not equally empowered, to shape the society in which they live. If educators are to function as public intellectuals, they need to provide the opportunities for students to learn that the relationship between knowledge and power can be emancipatory, that their histories and experiences matter, and that what they say and do counts in their struggle to unlearn dominating privileges, productively reconstruct their relations with others, and transform, when necessary, the world around them. More specifically, educators need to argue for forms of pedagogy that close the gap between the university and everyday life. Their curricula need to be organized around knowledges of communities, cultures, and traditions that give students a sense of history, identity and place. Said illuminates the process when he urges academics and students to accept the demands of "worldliness," which include "lifting complex ideas into the public space," recognizing human injury outside of the academy, and using theory as a form of criticism to change things (Said 2000: 7). Worldliness requires that we not be afraid of controversy that we make connections that are otherwise hidden, deflate the claims of triumphalism, and bridge intellectual work and the operation of politics. It means combining rigor and clarity, on the one hand, and civic courage and political commitment, on the other.

It also necessitates that we incorporate the tools of popular culture into critical pedagogy. Educators need to construct pedagogical approaches that do more than make learning context-specific; in effect, they need to challenge the content of established canons, and, similarly, to expand the range of cultural texts that count as "really useful knowledge." As public intellectuals, university teachers must begin to use those electronically mediated knowledge forms that constitute the terrain of mass and popular culture. I am referring here to the world of media texts–videos, films, music, and other mechanisms of popular culture that operate through a combination of visual and print culture. What I am suggesting here is that educators challenge the traditional definition of schooling as the only site of pedagogy by widening the application and sites of pedagogy to a variety of cultural locations and, in doing so, alert students to how public pedagogy operates through the educational force of the culture at large.

Public pedagogy similarly ensures its relevance by demanding curricula that reflect students' lived experiences, and by using the classroom itself as a site of democratic participation. The content of curricula should affirm and enrich the meaning, language, and knowledge forms that students actually use to negotiate and inform their lives. Academics can, in part, exercise their role as public intellectuals via such curricula by giving students the opportunity to understand how power is organized through an enormous number of "popular" cultural spheres including libraries, movie theaters, schools, and high-tech media conglomerates that circulate signs and meanings through newspapers, magazines, advertisements, new information technologies, computers, films, and television programs. Needless to say, this position challenges neoconservative Roger Kimball's claim that "Popular culture is a tradition essential to uneducated Americans."[10] By laying claim to popular media, public pedagogy not only asks important questions about how knowledge is produced and taken up, but also provides the conditions for students to become competent and critically versed in a variety of literacies, while at the same time expanding the conditions and options for the roles they might play as cultural producers (as opposed to simply teaching them to be critical readers).

Finally, academics need to challenge their own status as experts. Although it is central for university teachers to enlarge curricula to reflect the richness and diversity of the students they teach, they also need to decenter the curriculum. That is, as Stanley Aronowitz points out, students should be actively involved in governance, "including setting learning goals, selecting courses, and having their own autonomous organizations, including a free press" (Aronowitz 2004: 207). Changing the distribution of power among teachers, students, and administrators further encourages students to become agents in their learning process; it also provides the basis for collective learning, civic action, and ethical responsibility. Student agency emerges from a pedagogy of lived experience and struggle, not from mere formalistic mastery of an academic subject. If academics willingly give students the opportunity to experience expanded agency first-hand within the classroom, they help students develop the skills to imagine and create new power structures in the greater community.

I have suggested that educators need to become provocateurs; they need to take a stand while refusing to be involved in either a cynical relativism or doctrinaire politics. This suggests that central to intellectual life is the pedagogical and political imperative that academics engage in rigorous social criticism, while becoming a stubborn force for challenging false prophets, fighting against the imposed silence of normalized power, "refusing to allow conscience to look away or fall asleep," and critically encountering all those social relations that promote material and symbolic violence. [11]

NOTES

1 I analyze neoliberalism in great detail in *The Terror of Neoliberalism* (2004b).

2 In terms of political marginalization, there are useful parallels to be drawn by comparing the degree to which children, immigrants, racialized populations and the poor are disallowed from participation in public and political spheres. I do not suggest that these groups have the same concerns or experiences in terms of political exclusion; however, they suffer from common factors that I explore throughout this essay, including the legal and extralegal silencing of their political voices, and popular imagery suggesting their inherent inability to participate socially as well as their "refusal" to be proper consumers. Interestingly, even while popular media depicts the younger generation as overly materialistic, it also repeatedly portrays as newsworthy the fact that young people are consumers at all. The news regularly reports that marketing now targets young people (or gay people, or specific racial groups) as if it were inconceivable or even alarming that these populations have economic, and therefore political, clout.

3 For an analysis of the drop in youth crime in the 1990s, see Levitt (2004).

4 Cited in CBS News, "Sexual Abuse by Military Recruiters," April 20, 2006. Online: http://www.cbsnews.com/stories/2006/08/19/national/printable1913849.shtml.

5 I have taken up this critique in great detail in *The Abandoned Generation* (2004a).

6 I discuss this phenomenon in "Academic Entrepreneurs: The Corporate Takeover of Higher Education" (2006).

7 This charge comes from a report issued by conservative group The American Council of Trustees and Alumni (ACTA), founded by Lynne Cheney (spouse of Vice President Dick Cheney) and Joseph Lieberman (Democratic Senator). ACTA also posted on its website a list of 115 statements made by allegedly "un-American Professors." See Jerry L. Martin and Anne D. Neal (2002).

8 For a much more detailed account of this type of attack on higher education, see Susan Searls Giroux and Henry A. Giroux (2006), *Take Back Higher Education.*

9 Public time similarly differs from the fragmented model of time implied by news media, in which catastrophes exist in the time pocket of the news clip; each day, new catastrophes appear, only to be forgotten and replaced the next day with a different set of catastrophes. News stories are seldom followed long enough to suggest that events spring from complex causes and have equally complex repercussions, and the very fact that stories are so quickly dropped implies that, no matter how catastrophic an event, its social importance is minimal.

10 Kimball is cited in Levine (1996: 19).

11 All of these ideas and the quote itself are taken from Said (2004: 142).

REFERENCES

Aronowitz, S. (1998). The New Corporate University: Higher education becomes higher training. *Dollars and Sense, 216*, 32–35.

Aronowitz, S. (2004). A different perspective on educational equality. *Review of Education, Pedagogy, and Cultural Studies*, 26.2, 193–210.

Bacevich, A. J. (2005). *The New American militarism*. New York: Oxford University Press.

Bauman, Z. (1999). *In search of politics*. Stanford: Stanford University Press.

Bauman, Z. (2004). *Wasted lives*. Cambridge, England: Polity Press.

Bennett, W. J., Delulio Jr., J., & Walters, J. P. (1996). *Body count: Moral poverty...and how to ain America's war against crime and drugs*. New York: Simon and Schuster.

Bruin Alumni Association. (n.d.). Dirty thirty: Ranking the worst of the worst. *UCLA Profs.com: Exposing UCLA's Radical Professors*. Retrieved January 23, 2006, from <http://www.uclaprofs.com/articles/dirtythirty.html>

Chelala, C. (2006, January 4). Rich man, poor man: Hungry children in America. *Seattle Times*. Retrieved January 11, 2007, from <http://www.commondreams.org/views06/0104-24.htm>

Derrida, J. (2001). The future of the profession or the unconditional university. In L. Simmons & H. Worth (Eds.), *Derrida down under*. Auckland, New Zealand: Dunmarra Press.

Dilulio, J. (1995, November 27). The coming of the super-predators. *The Weekly Standard*. Retrieved January 14, 2007, from <http://www.mcsm.org/predator.html>

Dorfman, D. L. (2002, March 29). Punishment for strip searches. *New York Times*. Retrieved December 1, 2006, from <http://query.nytimes.com/gst/fullpage.html?res=9C02E0DD1F3BF93AA15750C0A9649C8B63>

Flanders, L. (2005, February 13). Bush's hit list: Teens and kids. *Common Dreams New Center*. Retrieved January 17, 2006, from <http://www.commondreams.org/views05/0213-11.htm>

Forum: A chilly climate on the campuses. (2005, September 9) *Chronicle of Higher Education*, pp. B7–B13.

Fox Pivan, F. (2004). *The war at home: The domestic costs of Bush's militarism*. New York: New Press.

Giroux, H. A. (2003). *Public spaces/private lives: Democracy beyond 9/11*. Boulder, CO: Rowman and Littlefield.

Giroux, H. A. (2004a). *The abandoned generation: Democracy beyond the culture of fear*. New York: Palgrave Macmillan.

Giroux, H. A. (2004b). *The terror of neoliberalism*. Aurora, ON: Garamond Press.

Giroux, H. A. (2006). Academic entrepreneurs: The corporate takeover of higher education. In *America on the edge: Henry Giroux on politics, culture, and education*. New York: Palgrave Macmillan.

Giroux, H. A. (2007). *The university in chains: Confronting the military-industrial-academic complex*. Paradigm Publishers.

Goldstein, A. (2006, February 5). 2007 Budget favors defense. *Washington Post*, p. A01.

Grossberg, L. (2001). Why does neo-liberalism hate kids? The war on youth and the culture of politics. *The Review of Education, Pedagogy, and Cultural Studies*, 23.2, 111–136.

Grossberg, L. (2005). *Caught in the crossfire: Kids, politics and America's future*. Boulder, CO: Paradigm Publishers.

Herbert, B. (2003, January 6). Young, jobless, hopeless. *New York Times*, p. A35.

Herbert, B. (2007, 15 March). The danger zone. *New York Times*, p. A25.

Jones, A. (n.d.). *Open letter from the Bruin Alumni Association. About the BAA. Bruin Alumni Association*. Retrieved March 3, 2006, from <http://www.bruinalumni.com/aboutus.html>.

Jones, A. (2006). *The fight for academic freedom at UCLA. UCLA Profs.com: Exposing UCLA's radical professors*. Retrieved March 2, 2007, from <http://www.ucleprofs.com/articles/uclaprofsbooklet.html>

Klein, N. (1999). *No logo: Taking aim at the brand bullies*. New York: Picador.

Kornblut, A. E. (2005, 13 January). Bush urges rigorous high school testing. *New York Times*, p. A26.

Krugman, P. (2003, December 5). Looting the future. *New York Times*, p. A39.

Krugman, P. (2005, February 11). Bush's class-war budget. *New York Times*. Retrieved January 12, 2007, from <http://www.nytimes.com/2005/02/11/opinion/11krugman.html?ex=1265864400&en=c5baff37424e2a5d&ei=5088&>

Levine, L. W. (1996). *The opening of the American mind: Canons, culture, and history*. Boston: Beacon Press.

Levitt, S. D. (2004). Understanding why crime fell in the 1990s: Four factors that explain the decline and six that do not. *Journal of Economic Perspectives, 18*(1), 163–190.

Martin, J. L., & Neal, A. D. (2002). *Defending civilization: How our universities are failing American and what can be done about it*. The American Council of Trustees and Alumni. Retrieved March 3, 2006, from <http://www.goacta.org/publications/Reports/defciv.pdf>

Penn State's Spanier to Chair National Security Board. (2005, September 16). *Penn state live*. Retrieved May 27, 2006, from <http://live.psu.edu/story/13530>

Rothschield, M. (2007, February 7). Bush's budget priorities: Fund war, provide tax breaks for the rich, deprive the poor. *Common Dreams News Center*. Retrieved February 9, 2007, from <http://www.commondreams.org/views07/0207-25.htm>

Roy, A. (2001). *Power politics*. Cambridge, MA: South End Press.

Said, E. (1994). *Representations of the intellectual*. New York: Pantheon.

Said, E. (2000). Scholarship and commitment: an introduction. *Profession*, 6–45.

Said, E. (2004). *Humanism and democratic criticism*. New York: Columbia.

Searls Giroux, S., & Giroux, H.A. (2006). *Take back higher education*. New York: Palgrave.

Sexual abuse by military recruiters: More than 100 women raped or assaulted by recruiters in past year. (2006). *CBS News*. Retrieved January 17, 2007, from <http://www.cbsnews.com/stories/2006/08/19/national/printable1913849.shtml>

Toppo, G. (2005, 30 January). US students say press freedoms go too far. *USA Today*. Retrieved June 3, 2006, from <http://www.usatoday.com/news/education/2005-01-30-students-press_x.htm>

Thornburg, K., Ball, K., & Mumford, J. (2007, January) The state of children and families: 2007. *Center for Family Policy and Research*. Retrieved March 1, 2007, from <http://web.missouri.edu/~umchescfprwww/MOchildfam07.pdf>

Wright Mills, C. (1956). *The power elite*. (Reprinted 1993). New York: Oxford University.

JANET CONWAY

DIALOGUES ACROSS DIFFERENCE AT THE WORLD SOCIAL FORUM

Decolonizing 'Open Space' [1]

INTRODUCTION

Struggles over hegemonic knowledges and the production of critical, oppositional knowledges are central to both the field of critical pedagogy and the politics of emancipatory social movements. Despite such convergence, consideration of social movements as spaces and agents of knowledge production is largely absent from critical scholarship. A book such as this, addressed to social justice educators, which seeks to explore the relations among power, pedagogy and praxis in globalized contexts, provides an opportunity to examine the knowledge practices of contemporary global justice movements and explore their relevance to critical pedagogy.

Since its appearance in 2001, the World Social Forum has become an increasingly significant site for the agglomeration, encounter and transformation of movement knowledges arising from subaltern struggles rooted in specific social and geographical locations/identities. The World Social Forum (WSF) is itself an innovation, or a product of the knowledges of the anti-globalization movement (Leite, 2005). This chapter will examine the World Social Forum as a praxis that is remaking the manner in which social movements from around the world recognize and interact with each other and, in so doing, is transforming the political culture of anti/alter-globalization movements worldwide.

In the discussion that follows, I propose that the Social Forum is a pedagogical and political space that is enabling the emergence of communicative practices across previously unbridged, indeed largely unrecognized, differences. In particular, I will analyze the methodology of "open space" as central to the dynamics of recognition and dialogue across difference at the WSF. The WSF's practice and theory of open space is itself a significant movement-based political innovation, or a knowledge practice. However, this putatively horizontal and utopian space is also marked by unequal power relations and, in particular, legacies of colonialism. The praxis of open space is itself contested and conflictual, but also reflexive and giving rise to further knowledge and, in some time-places of the WSF, a deepened praxis of decolonization. In conclusion, I will consider the emergent knowledge claims embodied in and through the evolving praxis of the WSF and their relevance to emancipatory politics and pedagogy.

S.A. Moore and R.C. Mitchell (eds.), Power, Pedagogy and Praxis: Social Justice in the Globalized Classroom, 73–89.

JANET CONWAY

THE WORLD SOCIAL FORUM: CONCEPT AND HISTORY

Originally conceived as an alternative to the World Economic Forum held annually in Davos, Switzerland, the World Social Forum (WSF) was initiated at the height of the anti-globalization mobilizations to convene groups and movements of insurgent civil society from around the world. The idea was to create a forum for the free and horizontal exchange of ideas, experiences and strategies oriented to enacting and generating alternatives to neoliberalism. The gathering would be thoroughly international but anchored geographically and experientially in the global South. The first WSF, held in Porto Alegre, Brazil in January 2001, attracted 15,000 participants. Its astounding success led organizers to commit to the WSF as a permanent process. Each January since then, the event has taken place, growing exponentially in size, diversity, complexity, and importance so that it is now regularly attracting over 100,000 people annually.

After three years in Porto Alegre, Brazil, the WSF moved to Mumbai, India in 2004 and in 2007, to Nairobi, Kenya. Brazil remains the homeplace of the WSF but there is a widespread commitment to moving the world event geographically to other sites in the global South. This is a strategy for expanding and deepening the Forum's inter-continental and cross-cultural character. In a related move, at the second WSF in Porto Alegre in 2002, organizers called on participants to organize similar processes in their own places, defined by their own priorities, and at whatever scale made sense to them. Social forums have proliferated inspired by the world event and organized in accordance with the WSF's Charter of Principles, with regional scale processes emerging with particular vigour and importance.

Central to the functioning of the WSF to date has been the understanding that the WSF is not a deliberative process. The WSF *qua* WSF does not make decisions, issue statements, nor embark on common actions. Rather, the WSF is best understood as an open, autonomous, and civil society "space" in which participants are invited to self-organize, to advance their campaigns, and to mount activities for one another, aimed building broad political convergence across difference. The WSF is not a unitary entity. No one can therefore 'represent' the WSF. This understanding is becoming increasingly contentious in and beyond the WSF's International Council[1] but it has been definitive of the WSF thus far.

The civil society entities present at the World Social Forum vary considerably depending on the location of the event but are in every case amazingly diverse in their demographic make-up, organizational forms, cultural expressions, geographic roots and reach, strategies, tactics, and discourses.[1] In any analytical discussion about the WSF, it is critical to maintain a distinction between the World Social Forum and its constituent social movements and networks. The latter act in and beyond the WSF but also help constitute the WSF as event and space. The WSF is both more than and different from the sum of these movements; and the movements are more than and different from the sum of their practices vis-a-vis the WSF. The WSF and its constituent movements all have their own particular and evolving praxes.

The development of the World Social Forum, understood as an annual event, is central to most discussions, but it is critical to recognize that the WSF is more accurately represented as a world-wide, movement-based, multi-scale, and multi-sited cultural process. The world event/process is significantly re-created when it is taken up by groups in different parts of the world, and this changes what follows, locally and globally, although not in any mechanistic or predictable way. Likewise, when the Social Forum is enacted locally and regionally, it assumes specificities that flow from place and scale, the historical-geographic conjuncture in which the process/event occurs, and the discourses, practices, preoccupations and strategies of its constitutive social movements.

THE WSF: "A PEDAGOGICAL AND POLITICAL SPACE"

The World Social Forum is a new kind of public space, both pedagogical and political, that is creating new conditions of possibility for emancipatory movements. But what is the character of this "open space"? And what is the relevance of this praxis for movement-based pedagogy and politics?

The WSF is an in-gathering of the groups and movements of civil society at a new scale. Even though there are antecedents – in the UN conferences and parallel NGO fora, in the *encuentros* of the Zapatistas, in the mass anti-globalization demonstrations – the expanding array of forces now regularly convened in one space by the WSF is unprecedented. This is true in terms of the diversity of groups, movements, modes, issues, and constituencies represented, the expanding geographic and cross-cultural reach, the sheer numbers of participants, and in the accessibility of the Forum and the program to any group anywhere who can mobilize the resources to participate. It is a public space imbued with the ethos of the anti-globalization movements in their stunning diversity: simultaneously militant and oppositional, alternative and innovative, affirmative and festive. Its pluralist, multi-centric and non-deliberative character allows the movements and groups of globalizing civil society to make themselves visible to one another on their own terms, and to encounter and transform one another in new ways.

For already well-established transnational networks, the WSF allows activists to advance their work in focused and concrete ways while simultaneously communicating it to a broader audience and building broader alliances. For highly localized movements, who are just finding their ways into transnational civil society spaces, or those who have little cross-sectoral coalitional experience, the WSF is a place both to learn of new 'others' and to assert one's own right to be present in and to this worldwide convergence against neoliberalism.

From the beginning, there has been a *de facto* recognition and valorization of the emergence of resistance and alternatives to neoliberalism from the most local to the most global. The creation of conditions for contact, recognition and inter-change among movements and organizations working at a variety of scales, in a range of modes, and on a multiplicity of issues and fronts, and with a pluralism of strategic approaches has been one of the most significant innovations of the World Social Forum. Each instantiation of the WSF in whatever place at whatever scale is characterized by the participation and valorization of activisms operating at a variety of scales, and the (possibility of) horizontal exchange among them. This aspect is closely related to the presence, role and status of 'place-based' movements in the processes and events constituting the WSF, their own evolving multi-scale politics/practices, and the relation of these practices to their "subaltern strategies of localization" (Escobar, 2001).[1]

A dramatic claim by 'local' movements on the 'world' event took place in Nairobi in January 2007. A slum-dwellers' organization called the People's Parliament stormed the gates and disrupted a press conference to protest the cost of registration fees which they claimed made the World Social Forum inaccessible to poor people from the city. At an assembly of social movements on the last day of the Forum, their spokesperson, Wangui Mbatia, had this to say:

> For many of us this is the first WSF. What I like about the WSF is that it brings the world to me as a Kenyan poor person: not only the world but the best of the world. In this room, I have met people who believe in the same things as the Peoples Parliament and people who are courageous enough to believe that a better world is possible. I am concerned that there are many Kenyans have not been able to attend the WSF. We have had to come every single morning to get those doors open so that ordinary Kenyan citizens can attend the WSF. We believe the WSF is a conversation by, between, and amongst people. It is not fair that 90 per cent of the people in the rooms are not Kenyans. That is not just. We have fought day after day after day to get in. But we are not just fighting to get in: we are fighting to be recognized because we are people too (*Short report of the Social Movements Assembly, World Social Forum, Nairobi, 16h-18h, 24 January*, 2007).

This eruption by a poor people's organization politicized the question of who the 'open space' of the WSF is for, which constituencies should have privileged access to it, and whose presence should not simply be left to their own self-organizing capacities, especially in terms of resource mobilization. Furthermore, it intensified the questions of place and scale: which places and scales of activism should be privileged at any particular Forum? Should a *World* Social Forum in Nairobi privilege the participation of Nairobi slum-dwellers? Kenyan organizations? Or strive first and foremost to be a pan-African edition of a world process, as the leadership of the African Social Forum had in mind? The protests by the Peoples' Parliament, which attracted much support from WSF delegates and some organizers, signalled a boiling point for issues that have been simmering from the beginning of the Social Forum process with varying intensity in different places and with various responses by different organizing committees: how 'local' should the world event be? How cosmopolitan? What kind of international? How subaltern? How intellectual?

In the space of the World Social Forum, perhaps most notably in the 2004 edition in Mumbai, India, some of the poorest and most subjugated peoples in the world came to participate and make claims. Of the 80,000 official delegates, about 30,000 were dalits (untouchables) and a great number of these were adivasis (tribals). Of these, 40-45% were women. They came both demanding and offering recognition, solidarity, and dialogue vis-a-vis the thousands of other movements and groups gathered in the WSF. These movements of extremely poor and marginalized people had heretofore been largely invisible on the international stage despite impressive levels of self-organization and forays by individual leaders into UN-sponsored international fora. These groups recognized and helped construct the WSF in India as a transnational political space of a new kind.

Similarly in Nairobi, the Mau Mau Veterans' Association, survivors of the mid-20th century anti-colonial struggle against the British, enjoyed their first opportunity to speak of their experience to an international audience while, in their own words, they "are the unseen and the unheard of Kenyan society," their claims for land and recognition repeatedly rebuffed by successive post-colonial regimes. The Masaai, a tribal group of pastoralists being systematically displaced from their land by 'development', were in the 2007 WSF in the hundreds, visibly present in the space and organizing their own discussions primarily for their own constituency.

In Caracas, Venezuela in 2006, 400 activities or about one-third of the planned events were proposed by newly emergent local groups. In a society in the throes of the Chavez-led Bolivarian revolution with little experience of autonomous civil society formations, the social forum was an opportunity for these groups to encounter each other, to articulate for themselves their hopes and visions for Venezuela in the transnational space created in their city by the presence of the World Social Forum (Lander, 2006). These claims on the Social Forum by localized subaltern groups appear to be growing over time and as the WSF moves geographically, as place-based movements recognize the potential for their own struggles in the Social Forum's arrival in their city, country or region. The degree to which place-based subaltern groups can make these claims is also, of course, contingent both on their organizing capacity and on the particular politics of in/exclusion practiced by the local organizing committee. However, as the world process has unfolded and each major social forum event throws up new problematics and plural visions of both the Forum and the movement, organizers have demonstrated relentless reflexivity and constant innovation. The process is not perfectly linear, systematic, nor comprehensive, and certainly not conflict-free, but the culture of learning and the openness to experiment seems deeply entrenched and is creating conditions for great political creativity.

For instance, the claims of place-based subaltern groups for recognition targeted to the movements and groups of civil society from across the world gathered in the WSF regularly enacts a new kind of public space. To borrow a formulation from Nancy Fraser, the WSF embodies an emergent "alternative, postbourgeois conception of the public sphere." (Fraser, 1997, p. 72) It is 'placed' but transnational, localized but characterized by an expanding globality. Although Fraser is silent on the questions of place and scale, her rethinking the public sphere in response to Habermas is helpful in illuminating the significance of the WSF's praxis of open space. In contrast to Habermas's defense of a single public sphere of rational democratic deliberation, Fraser observes and argues for a plurality of competing publics (in permanent struggles for democracy). In particular, she notes the regular emergence of "subaltern counterpublics" who expose and contest the exclusions of the formal, official, putatively egalitarian and universally accessible liberal public spheres (Fraser, 1997, pp. 75, 81).

The WSF is a new kind of political space created by and helping to consolidate a transnational subaltern counter-public, or what Keck and Sikkink (1998) call emergent "transnational civil society." However, the WSF is not a single, overarching public sphere and, to date, its key architects have repudiated the notion that it can be or should be. It is a 'space of spaces,' a sphere of multiple public spheres.

Dalits, tribals, feminists, queers, indigenous peoples and others constitute subaltern counterpublics within the WSF. They participate in the WSF, intent on the need for their own spaces on their own terms, engaging in their own deliberative processes, or not. They are also simultaneously making a claim on the WSF as a whole and on its constitutive movements, agitating for recognition, inclusion and solidarity. Their voices are still muted in the deliberations about the WSF process in the International Council, but the WSF methodology allows space for "parallel discursive arenas where members of subordinated social groups invent and circulate counter-discourses, which in turn permit them to formulate oppositional interpretations of their identities, interests and needs." (Fraser, 1997, p. 81)

Fraser argues that multiple publics are preferable to single public in both stratified and (relatively) egalitarian societies because of the persistence of inequality and the cultural/rhetorical specificity of any one public sphere and the effects of both these conditions on the participation of marginalized groups (1997, pp. 82–83). She goes on to argue that this does not rule out the possibility of more comprehensive cross-cultural arenas. This becomes a question of practical politics and experimentation, not a conceptual impossibility. The WSF is that kind of more comprehensive, cross-cultural, political space that is allowing for the social learning and multicultural literacy that Fraser thinks are necessary pre-conditions for more inclusive processes and spheres of democratic deliberation.

The WSF as an autonomous, open, pluralistic and non-deliberative space is allowing for the communicability of struggles across different kinds of difference. While the WSF is not a space free of power struggles, its de-centred character allows for more rather than fewer perspectives and constituencies to get a hearing, and a broader rather than narrower range of social forces to claim the WSF as their own. The creation and preservation of such spaces is central for the development and transformation of political subjectivities in democratic dialogue.

In these ways, the WSF constitutes a new kind of public space and a new culture of politics in its foundational recognition of difference and irreducible multiplicity, coupled with a will to mutual intelligibility and concrete solidarity. However, this dynamic is very uneven and highly contingent on the particularities of place. With the move to India and the entry into the WSF of the tribals and the dalits, for example, the process seemed to enter a new phase. Before Mumbai, the impressive diversities in the WSF had been at least partially bridged through mutually-intelligible discourses of Western emancipatory political traditions. Those from outside the West who did attend the WSF in Brazil were likely to be Western-educated, or schooled in the transnational movement discourses of the NGO and UN networks. But historic silences and exclusions *within* the West were also reproduced in the WSF, rendering indigenous political discourses marginal, even unintelligible, to a majority of participants, for example. The cultural particularity of the putatively universal discourses of Western emancipatory traditions has become more apparent and is more broadly acknowledged by key European and Latin American voices in the WSF since Mumbai, although the effects on the WSF as a global phenomenon and particularly on its Latin American/Brazilian pole remain ambivalent. The mounting of the 2007 world event in Nairobi foregrounded African movements, histories, and discourses in ways very important for the WSF, but the barrage of criticism following the event emanating largely from European sources and with scant reference to the particularities of the African context highlighted the coloniality of knowledge/power in and over the WSF.

THE ASYMMETRIES OF 'OPEN SPACE'

The most contentious and enduring debate about the Social Forum, including among its proponents, has to do with the assertion that it is a "space" to serve, incubate, and advance progressive movements, but is not itself a movement. The Brazilian founders of the WSF vigourously defend the Forum as an open space for free association of non-party civil society entities that are united in their opposition to "rule of the world by money" but are otherwise stunningly diverse. They see the praxis of the Forum as fostering the emergence of a new political actor that of "planetary civil society," imbued with a new political culture. It is society that will change the world, not the Forum itself, but the WSF is singular in the functions it has assumed. In particular, the Forum is a space to unlearn the practices of the 20th century left, its hierarchies, violence and authoritarianism, and to learn how to resolve conflicts non-violently, to dialogue with difference, to learn how to live with diversity, and to recognize multiple paths for changing the world (Whitaker, 2007).

Whitaker and other Brazilian founders also insist that the Social Forum is not a space of power, but one of consensual association, self-management and horizontal exchange. The fact that the Forum is not an entity in itself, does not issue statements, take positions, or embark on actions, protects it and its participants from being consumed by internal struggles for hegemony. Its non-deliberative character frees its participating groups to encounter one another, to listen and to learn, and to be transformed in ways they could not be otherwise. In this view, the Forum's central function is one of cultural transformation of the movements and groups of civil society that respond to its summons.

The critics of 'open space' argue variously that the concept itself is wrong-headed and depoliticizing in its embrace of liberal pluralism; that the Forum is not really open in its exclusion of parties, governments and armed groups; that it excludes proponents of neoliberalism; that the open space is a free market, wherein those with more money and organizational muscle can dominate; that the open space has degenerated into a festival or, in the words of Hugo Chavez, a Woodstock of the left. Others observe that all social spaces are riven through with power and inequality, and that the Social Forum is no exception.

In my view, the Forum as a political form and organizing methodology has generated unprecedented creativity and collaboration among disparate actors in major world regions. The limits of this undertaking are not yet in sight and it is a grand experiment which needs to be respected, nurtured and safeguarded. In Whitaker's words, the WSF has issued a powerfully compelling "summons" to which hundreds of thousands of people and thousands of organizations have responded. The WSF's embrace of pluralism and diversity is, in my view, *post-liberal* in its clear condemnation of neoliberal capitalism and the inequalities and oppression it has entrenched. In placing a premium on practice, in opposing the hegemony of "any single way of thinking," in cultivating an ethic of solidarity among suffering and struggling people, their organizations and movements, and in asserting its critical positionality in the Global South, the WSF's praxis of pluralism is something new, both post-marxist and post-liberal, the broader implications of which have hardly been hinted at.

Affirming this however, is not to say that the praxis of open space is entirely straightforward, unproblematic, or without risks. It is surprizing, to say the least, that the WSF has not been targeted for infiltration or take-over by its enemies, or by the enemies of its enemies. There is no indication that right-wing forces or reactionary, fundamentalist anti-imperialist movements have exploited the openness of the Forum to enter, participate, or mount their own activities under more benign banners. In India, organizers decided to expand the criteria for participation to ensure that Hindu nationalist movements, which were anti-neoliberal and anti-imperialist but also anti-Muslim and anti-feminist, were not welcome in the Forum. In Kenya, in response to the heavy presence of churches in the 2007 WSF, some of them overtly homophobic and anti-feminist, there has been a call by some for stricter guidelines for activities in the WSF venue. While wanting to err on the side of openness, organizers are grappling with the call for greater oversight to *protect* the space as one hospitable to and respectful the full range of emancipatory movements, even as many recognize that understandings of "emancipatory" are plural, shifting and sometimes uncertain.

It is also critical to recognize that inequalities among movements get reproduced in the open space unless there is affirmative action to ensure that marginalized and minority populations are present and their voices and perspectives amplified. Feminist commentators on the WSF have been most insistent about this, noting that women regularly make up half the participants but only a tiny fraction of the speakers at the WSF, and protesting the historical marginality of feminism as a perspective despite the founding presence of feminist networks in the WSF (Conway, 2007; Vargas, 2003; Alvarez, Faria & Nobre, 2004). In some Social Forum processes, organizers have made explicit choices to reach out to marginalized constituencies to encourage and support their participation. Indian organizers sought out the *dalit* movements. In Nairobi, organizers subsidized the participation of 6,000 slum dwellers. Organizers of the Caracas edition of the 2006 polycentric World Social Forum actively supported and subsidized the participation of poor peoples' organizations from the US and of indigenous peoples from the Andean region. In the practical politics of organizing Social Forums, some groups of organizers have actively sought to compensate for historical marginalization and contemporary inequalities. However, thus far, these practices and other kinds of political decisions by organizers affecting the character of the space of any particular event have not informed the discourses about the praxis of 'open space,' including by the organizers! Here, as in many instances of movement-based knowledge production, practice is leading and theory is lagging.

Finally, on the question of difference, recognition, and the possibility of communicability, the challenges are far greater than the discourses of open space admit.

As a new kind of movement space, the WSF is enacting a new culture of politics among social movements that is both allowing for and requiring communicative practices across identities/differences that had not previously encountered one another, or if they had, had not been ready, able or open to negotiate their differences. However, mutual intelligibility among movements, including those who share opposition to neoliberal globalization, is not a given.

Ever-expanding diversity is arising from sheer multiplicity of forms of domination/resistance to which the movements of the Social Forum attest and the array of places and scales from which they arise. Some movements are more experienced with working across (some kinds of) difference than others. For all the movements, the sheer array of diversity in the WSF is confronting them with a historical challenge and invitation to unprecedented degrees of reflexivity, solidarity and transformation.

Furthermore, the movements are encountering each other on a historically unequal playing field. Some movements (and their discourses) have been hegemonic relative to others, historically and currently, in and beyond the Social Forum. Some voices and movements remain far more excluded and 'subaltern' than others, including in the WSF. This raises very profound questions about the character of the WSF's putatively 'open space,' its limitations, inequalities, and exclusions and, in particular, the need for a praxis of *decolonization*, in any place-based instantiation of the WSF and in its world-scale process.

TOWARDS A PRAXIS OF DECOLONIZATION

Recognizing the character of contemporary world order as one of "global coloniality" (Escobar, 2004) has put decolonization on the agenda of movements world-wide, not just in their frontal contestations with hegemonic powers, but in the relations between movement themselves, especially across North/South, indigenous/non-indigenous, and modern emancipatory/subaltern 'other' divides. In profound ways, this demands a decolonization of knowledge, including the emancipatory knowledges of modernity which have been so central to the politics of many progressive movements worldwide.

Movements have to recognize their own histories of colonialism and exclusion, male supremacy and racial hierarchy in order to engage with one another, in and beyond the Social Forum. Although this is a task for all, it is not equally so. It seems inescapable therefore, that subaltern perspectives must be privileged or, at least, met with thoughtful silence and practical solidarity while movements contemplate their historical and current positionality in creating "colonial difference."[1] This recognition is controversial but I believe foundational to advancing movement dialogues in and beyond the WSF

There are some very important initiatives within the Social Forum process that reflect this recognition. One of the most pre-figurative was the 1st Social Forum of the America held in 2004 in Quito, Ecuador. Ecuador is home to one of the strongest, most dynamic and politically potent indigenous movements in the world, where Aymara and Quechua peoples make up more than 40% of the national population.. The key national indigenous networks, CONAIE and ECUARNARI, were prominent members of the organizing committee of the ASF which declared gender and diversity as transversal axes.

In Latin America and beyond, this event issued a major challenge to prevailing Social Forum practices. In Brazil, the Social Forum has been the purview of more traditional constituencies of the Latin American left – in Brazil, notably the PT (Workers Party), the CUT (central labour federation) , and peasant (Via Campesina) and landless movements (Movimiento Sem Terra–MST). While a plethora of other movements and political orientations have been present, these entities with their predominantly socialist and statist discourses have cast long shadows. The choice of Porto Alegre as the site of the WSF has also been significant. While it is a city that has had a PT administration since the late 1980s and is the home of globally-acclaimed experimentations in participatory budgeting, it is also in the south of Brazil. With a population of predominantly German origin, many small and medium sized agricultural operations, and a healthy economic base, it is a light-skinned and relatively prosperous part of Brazil, far from the favelas of Recife, the Black Brazil of the North East, or the indigenous presence in the Amazon. The experiences and political discourses of the Afro descendants and indigenous peoples have been barely audible in the World Social Forum in Brazil.

The Americas Social Forum in Quito issued a strong challenge to Porto Alegre from within the Latin American orbit in the 1000 strong indigenous people present, in their prominent presence on panels not narrowly about indigenous issues, in the visibility of their art forms, music and dance throughout the event, in their distinct political discourses, visions, projects and processes, and in their twin insistence that they need the World Social Forum, and the world-wide movement against neoliberal globalization needs them.

The Americas Social Forum was organized by a coalition of indigenous, feminist and queer organizations. The Forum was also the occasion for the 1st Forum on Sexual Diversity. The tensions among the discourses of these movements were not resolved in Quito but they were on the table, being named and explored, even as these movements actively collaborated in conceiving and mounting the event. Their various constituencies co-occupied the space, shared platforms, organized their own discussions, facilitated cross-movement dialogues, ate, assembled and marched together.

This Social Forum is an example of how an ensemble of place-based movements seized a Social Forum in its entirety, in this case, at the regional scale, to enact and advance the possibility of dialogue across colonial difference. There are also numerous smaller-scale cross-sectoral initiatives underway within the open space of other Social Forum events that, as a whole, demonstrate less awareness of colonial difference. One such example is the feminist-sponsored "cross-movement dialogues" which are explicitly premised on a recognition of the inter-sectionality of oppressions and identities represented by the major emancipatory movements. Fostering cross-movement dialogue and breaking down sectoral silos emerged as key priorities in the feminist strategy sessions preceding the 2004 WSF. In Mumbai, feminists from across different networks and regions went on to host an inter-movement dialogue involving two speakers from each of four movements: women's, sexuality rights, labour and dalit rights/racial justice movements. Each was asked to speak to how their movement had incorporated class, gender, race and sexuality questions, the dilemmas and problems they had confronted and the strategies they had employed. Activists from the other movements were asked to respond. Then the second speaker from the original movement was asked to comment, refute or clarify. This proceeded through four rounds and was moderated. This format was repeated with great success the following year in Brazil (Gandhi and Shah 2006) (Shah, October 2005).

Gandhi and Shah, two organizers of the inter-movement dialogues see this initiative as contributing to the evolving methodology of the WSF which seeks to promote exchange among diverse visions and struggles. They are also aware of the inherent tensions and contradictions in the movements' attempts to simultaneously recognize difference while avoiding essentialism. They write:

> In our experience, social movement activists who have to strike a balance between pragmatism, theorization and strategy agree to a rejection of sweeping categorizations but usually retain the concept of categories itself. However, most have not sufficiently come to grips with the politics of differences and the notion of conflicting identities. As movement activists, we need to not only accept difference, diversity and plurality but try to incorporate these ideas within our movements and strategies. This was the underlying motivation behind the organizing of the 'Inter-Movement Dialogues' as a methodology for a collective reflection on inter category and intra category approaches to deepen our theory and bridges across movements (Gandhi & Shah, 2006, p. 73).

Santos calls the dialogical and political task of building articulation, aggregation and coalition among all the different movements the work of "translation," which allows for mutual intelligibility across difference. "The work of translation is to turn incommensurability into difference, a difference enabling mutual intelligibility among the different projects of social emancipation. The goal is to construct an ethical and political position without grounding it in any absolute principle." (Santos, Nunes & Meneses, 2007, p. l) Without prior consensus that there is not and can be no general theory of social transformation, translation is a colonial undertaking-no matter how postcolonial it claims to be. The task of translation is to generate new knowledges and practices capable of confronting neoliberal globalization and oriented to plural conceptions of social emancipation. Global social justice is not possible without global cognitive justice – the recognition of and engagement with the subaltern knowledges suppressed by modernity and rendered backward, primitive, or traditional by eurocentrism, on their own terms towards new and plural understandings of emancipation (Santos, 2005). The capacity for and fruit of translation appear to be cumulative as experience of the WSF accumulates. Santos argues that the extraordinary power of the WSF lies precisely in its refusal of the idea of a general theory. The alternative to a general theory, he suggests, is the work of translation. He and his colleagues further argue that "dialogues between knowledges may lead to regional or sectoral universalisms constructed from below, that is, to counter-hegemonic public spheres – or ... 'subaltern cosmopolitanism'" which start from recognition of the plurality of knowledges and of world views. While I am more reticent about using the language of universalism, the foundational claim that recognizing pluralism creates new possibilities for political convergence is clearly borne out in the Social Forum.

EPISTEMOLOGIES FOR SUBALTERN COSMOPOLITANISM

Through their everyday practices of survival, resistance, and solidarity, progressive social movements produce new and distinct knowledges about the world as it is and as it might be. Movement-based knowledge is largely tacit, practical and unsystematized. It is partial and situated, grounded in activist practice, arising from concrete engagement in social struggle, and embedded in specific times and places. However partial, these knowledges are crucial to imagining and enacting alternative and more emancipatory futures. Through their practices and discourses, which are permanently emergent, emancipatory movements are pre-figuring other possible and more just worlds. Movements are constantly inventing based on necessity, desire, and struggle. They are often informed by theory but they are not waiting for theory.

In my previous studies of knowledge production in social movements, I found that coalitions of social movements are a particularly fertile location for the production of new knowledges (Conway, 2006). They are pedagogical and political spaces in which the sustained encounter across constituencies and issues produces new cultural, political, and organizational practices. Coalitions are spaces of experimentation and this is especially important in a period of flux and uncertainty in both practice and theory. Because coalitions are constituted by a fundamental recognition of diversity and respect for pluralism, the knowledges that arise in and through coalition politics are particularly prescient for the building of a world with the space for many worlds, to use the Zapatista formulation. The knowledges produced in coalitions demonstrate the possibility of action premised on partial and provisional knowing – on politics that is simultaneously committed and open to what it does not yet know.

Epistemologies arising from the experience of coalition politics indicate that most contemporary oppositional movements do not claim absolute knowledge about the world and how it should be and much less how to manage it. This involves a break with older imaginaries of science, emancipation, revolution and utopia and are provoking new post-modern democratic imaginaries. Feminists have theorized the new epistemology most systematically as one of partial, positional and situated knowledges. Drawing on experiences in coalition politics, they have argued for the possibility of dialogue among partial knowledges, mutual learning, expanded solidarity and concrete collaboration that does not require either perfect knowledge or perfect agreement. In fact, this epistemology for "rainbow coalition politics" is premised on difference, on the recognition of diversity, on irreducible pluralism (Harding, 1998; Haraway, 1991; Yuval-Davis, 1993; Hill Collins, 2000).

Where pluralistic and open-ended attitudes to knowledge prevail in the movements, new politics are flowering, with implications far beyond the movements themselves. This dynamic has been central to the political convergence that produced the 'anti-globalization' movement. It is evident in movements like the Zapatistas and in spaces like the World Social Forum. Santos talks about this as a recognition of the "ecology of knowledges" and argues that it is not possible to imagine let alone advance alternatives for emancipatory social change without profound epistemological shifts associated with this recognition of the plurality of knowledges (Santos, et al., 2007, p. xlix).

The WSF is not a coalition but, as a space of sustained encounter across difference, is a site for similar dynamics in terms of movement-based knowledge production and for the emergence of knowledges premised on recognition of diversity and pluralism and on dialogue and solidarity across difference.

In my view, the power and potential of the Social Forum as a new political form and process rests on five features: (1) its character as a non-deliberative yet highly participatory and inclusive 'space of spaces' with multiple centres; (2) its global diffusion as a form and method through the proliferation of local and regional social fora; (3) the increasing internationalization, inter- and multi-culturalism of the global process, signaled by the WSF's move from Brazil to India in 2004 and to Kenya in 2007; (4) the incorporation of place-based and localized movements in a new kind of internationalism; and (5) a growing recognition of multiplicity, of diversity and pluralism as organizing principles in fostering a new politics for a new world with the space for many worlds within it. These features have emerged in practice and become definitive even as their significance can only as yet be dimly perceived. Their possible meanings depend on how future political practice, experimentation and debates over the future of the WSF unfold. Nevertheless, that the World Social Forum is a world-historic movement-based political innovation is indisputable. The practices that constitute it are knowledge practices which embody new ways of doing politics. They are harbingers that point beyond themselves.

The Social Forum as a particular political form and methodology can be characterized as itself a praxis of knowledge production that is generating new discourses and practices for an alternative world. The Social Forum is fostering new cultures of politics among social movements. One can discern the outlines of a new democratic imaginary taking shape in the global "convergence of difference."

Central to the new democratic imaginary is a new epistemological stance captured in the Zapatista slogan, "walk forward questioning" (quoted in Hardt and Negri 2003). This attitude toward knowledge undergirds all the new social movements even as it remains contentious on the left. It embodies the recognition of the limits of ones' own knowledge (and the knowledge of any particular movement, organization, politics, or program), alongside the necessity and possibility of acting while remaining open to what one does not yet know.

The primacy of diversity, pluralism and participation in the politics of the new social movements is in opposition to the neoliberal and neo-imperial project that is systematically suppressing difference, even the *possibility* of difference, through its monocultures.But this politics of recognition and difference is and needs to be premised also on an "epistemology of the South," on the acknowledgement of colonial difference and the need to break with eurocentrism. This is underway but highly uneven and contingent on the place and the place-based movements of particular iterations of the Forum.

In promoting the "convergence of difference," the World Social Forum recognizes diversity and pluralism, not as problems to be overcome but as conditions to be embraced, valued, promoted and protected. Recognition of diversity and the promotion of pluralism are fundamental to the WSF and to its deep-seated resistance to the hegemony of "any one way of thinking." Diversity will simply always be. New differences – new identities, ways of life, belief systems – will always be emerging. No one politics will ever adequately incorporate this irreducible reality. At the same time, the WSF is actively and successfully promoting the *convergence* of difference and increasingly, *dialogue* across difference.

In important ways, this is a 'post-liberal' politics in that it is situated within a shared, indeed non-negotiable, opposition to neoliberal globalization and grounded in acts of practical, cross-movement solidarity that transcend seemingly income-mensurable differences. Commitment to dialogue and a foundational recognition of pluralism does not imply the absence of firmly-held values or political commitment, but it does require an epistemology embracing partial, situated, positional knowing as the basis for open, provisional but 'reliable-enough' knowledge for politics. Movements' need to act and the diverse discourses and practices constantly emergent will always outstrip the best available theories.

The belief in and demonstrated capacity to act on provisional knowing, and to act together with others who think, live and dream differently, relies on a culture and politics of social learning and capacity building, and a shared willingness to confront the exclusions of one's own movement. It suggests notions of democracy, revolution, and utopia as open-ended projects-in-process, worked out in practice, open to question and to new 'others' and always needing renovation. The architects of the World Social Forum embody this in particularly powerful ways when they insist that the WSF is not a unitary entity or agent, but rather a "pedagogical and political space." (Fisher & Ponniah, 2003, p. 6)

The new democratic imaginary places a premium on practice. A new world is coming into being in and through the practices of progressive social movements. In this roiling politics of seemingly limitless diversity and pluralism, one recognizes one's allies through their concrete practices of solidarity. It is also through practice that the movements are producing the knowledges they need in the making of another world with the space for many worlds within it. Through countless concrete initiatives, experiments and projects, and reflection on their successes and limits, the movements learn, teach, change, try again.

The World Social Forum has been central to the convergence of both anti-globalization and anti-war movements. It has been the site for the emergence of the inter-movement dialogues and the growing claims of indigenous peoples on progressive movements world-wide. Its processes and methods are promoting extraordinary levels of self-organizing world-wide and sowing new trans-nationalisms. The Social Forum is successfully fostering *convergence* among movements world-wide through the promotion of *pluralism*. It is this extraordinary paradox, that embracing diversity is producing unprecedented co-ordinated action on global and other scales, that is key to the generative power of the Social Forum and suggestive of a new democratic, decolonized and decolonizing politics on a world scale.

(a) This article is one of a series on the World Social Forum and is the fruit of an ongoing research project funded by the Social Sciences and Humanities Research Council. For other related works, see Conway, 2002 2004b 2003b 2003a 2004a 2007 forthcoming.

(b) It is critical to maintain a distinction between the WSF and its governing and organizing bodies, the key ones being its International Council (IC) and International Secretariat. While IC deliberations are an important pole in shaping the world-scale WSF process, the proliferation, dynamism, geographic dispersion and multiculturalism of WSF processes continually overwhelm the IC and any occasional attempts to control and or represent the WSF.

(c) The WSF is open to any group anywhere in the world who professes opposition to neoliberalism, who is not a political party and who is not engaged in armed struggle. See the WSF charter of principles at http://www.forumsocialmundial.org.br.

(d) While all social movements have their own spatialities and territorialities, they are not all place-based in the same ways or to the same degrees.

(e) The term "colonial difference" highlights the divides and inequalities flowing from movements differently positioned along North/South, indigenous/non-indigenous, modern emancipatory/subaltern 'other' axes in the WSF.On colonial difference, see works by Mignolo, Dussel, and Quijano. For discussion, see Escobar 2004; Grosfoguel 2005.

REFERENCES

Alvarez, S., Faria, N., & Nobre, M. (2004). Another (also feminist) world is possible: Constructing transnational spaces and global alternatives from the movements. In J. Sen, A. Anand, A. Escobar,

& P. Waterman (Eds.), *World social forum: Challenging empires* (pp. 199–206). New Dehli: Viveka Foundation.

Conway, J. (2002). Power of social forum is its global diffusion. *Humanity and Society, 26*(3), 254–256.

Conway, J. (2003a, 2003 Spring). Engendering the world social forum. *McClung's*, 23–25.

Conway, J. (2003b). *Feminist views are necessary for global change*. Retrieved June 26, 2003, from www.rabble.ca

Conway, J. (2004a). Citizenship in a time of empire: The world social forum as a new public space. *Citizenship Studies, 8*(4), 367–381.

Conway, J. (2004b, June). Place matters: India's challenge to Brazil at the world social forum. *Antipode: A Radical Journal of Geography, 36*(3), 357–360.

Conway, J. (2006). *Praxis and politics: Knowledge production in social movements*. New York and London: Routledge.

Conway, J. (2007 forthcoming). The empire, the movement and the politics of scale. In R. Keil & R. Mahon (Eds.), *Leviathan undone? Towards a political economy of scale*. University of British Columbia Press.

Conway, J. (2007, April). Transnational feminisms and the world social forum: Encounters and transformations in anti-globalization spaces. *Journal of International Women's Studies, 8*(3), 49–70.

Escobar, A. (2001). Culture sits in places: Reflections on globalism and subaltern strategies of localization. *Political Geography, 20*, 139–174.

Escobar, A. (2004). Beyond the third world: Imperial globality, global coloniality and anti-globalisation social movements. *Third World Quarterly, 25*(1), 207–230.

Fisher, W. F., & Ponniah, T. (2003). Introduction: The world social forum and the re-invention of democracy. In W. F. Fisher & T. Ponniah (Eds.), *Another world is possible: Popular alternatives to globalization at the world social forum* (pp. 1–20). London & New York: Zed Books.

Fraser, N. (1997). Rethinking the public sphere: A contribution to the critique of actually existing democracy. In *Justice interruptus: Critical reflections on the postsocialist condition* (pp. 69–98). New York & London: Routledge.

Gandhi, N., & Shah, N. (2006). Inter movement dialogues: Breaking barriers, building bridges. *Development, 49*(1), 72–76.

Haraway, D. (1991). Situated knowledges: The science question in feminism and the privilege of partial perspective. In *Simians, cyborgs and women: The reinvention of nature* (pp. 183–201). London and New York: Routledge.

Harding, S. (1998). *Is science multicultural? Postcolonialisms, feminisms and epistemologies*. Bloomington and Indianapolis, IN: Indiana University Press.

Hardt, M., & Negri, A. (2003). Foreward. In W. F. Fisher & T. Ponniah (Eds.), *Another world is possible: Popular alternatives to globalization at the world social forum* (pp. xvi–xix). London & New York: Zed Books.

Hill Collins, P. (2000). *Black feminist thought: Knowledge, consciousness, and the politics of empowerment* (2nd ed.). New York and London: Routledge.

Keck, M. E., & Sikkink, K. (1998). *Activists beyond borders: Advocacy networks in international politics*. Ithaca, NY: Cornell University Press.

Lander, E. (2006, January 23). Presentation by leading member of the organizing committee of the Caracas edition of the 2006 polycentric World Social Forum to an orientation session for WSF delegates from Canada and Quebec, Caracas.

Leite, J. C. (2005). *World social forum: Strategies of resistance*. Chicago: Haymarket Books.

Santos, B. D. S., Nunes, J. A., & Meneses, M. P. (2007). Opening up the canon of knowledge and recognition of difference. In B. D. S. Santos (Ed.), *Another knowledge is possible: Beyond northern epistemologies* (pp. xix–lxii). London: Verso.

Santos, B. D. S. (2005). The future of the world social forum: The work of translation. *Development, 48*(2), 15–22.

Shah, S. (2005, October). *A dialogue between movements held at the World Social Forum (WSF) in Porto Alegre, Brazil on the 28th January 2005: A report*. Mumbai, India: Akshara–a Women's Resource Centre.

Short report of the Social Movements Assembly, World Social Forum, Nairobi, 16h–18h, 24 January. (2007).

Vargas, V. (2003). Feminism, globalization and the global justice and solidarity movement. *Cultural Studies, 17*(6), 905–920.

Whitaker, C. (2007). *A new way of changing the world*. Nairobi: World Council of Churches.

Yuval-Davis, N. (1993). Beyond difference: Women and coalition politics. In M. Kennedy, C. Lubelska, & V. Walsh (Eds.), *Making connections: Women's studies, women's movements, women's lives* (pp. 3–10). London and Washington: Taylor & Francis.

MARY KELLETT AND BEN WARD (AGED 10)

CHILDREN* AS ACTIVE RESEARCHERS

Participation and Power Sharing

*the term is used for brevity and encompasses all young people

Keywords: children as researchers; participation; children's rights; adult-child power relations; social justice

INTRODUCTION

If not quite a 'groundhog day' moment, the notion of children* as active researchers does have a certain sense of *deja vue* about it. We have been here before with other similarly disempowered groups. The emancipation of women, of black and minority ethnic groups and of disabled people all emanated from positions of exclusion and relative powerlessness before they were accepted as strong, distinct research voices in their own right (see Martusewicz and Reynolds, 1994; Oliver, 1997; Gordon, 1995; Usher, 1996; Aspis 2002). This has given rise to a new flank of 'critical approaches' to research (Cohen et al. 2000) and there is now widespread acknowledgement that methods pertinent to 'insider' perspectives are not only welcome but essential. It is from within this paradigm of critical research that the concept of children as researchers in their own right – or 'active' researchers, as is the preferred terminology of this author–is beginning to emerge (Sinclair, 2004; Alderson and Morrow, 2004; Kellett 2005).

This is fundamentally different from 'co-participation' in adult-led projects where children typically engage at the data collection level but frequently play no part in setting research questions, designing methodologies, analysing data or disseminating findings (Kellett, 2005a). A shift in our thinking is required to accommodate child-led research that is *supported* rather than *managed* by adults. Valuing children's perspective and participation in decisions that affect their lives is an essential pre-requisite to embracing them as active researchers.

CHILDREN'S STATUS AND PARTICIPATION IN RESEARCH

The emergence of children as active researchers comes in the wake of the UNCRC (1989) which directed that children should be informed, involved and consulted about all activities affecting their lives (articles 12 and 13). This has brought about changes in our thinking about child status and recognition that children are social actors in their own right (James, Jenks and Prout, 1998). Christensen and Prout

S.A. Moore and R.C. Mitchell (eds.), Power, Pedagogy and Praxis: Social Justice in the Globalized Classroom, 91–103.

(2002: 480) outline four ways that children and childhood have been identified in research: the child as object, the child as subject, the child as social actor and the child as participant/co-researcher. The first of these sees children as objects acted upon by others, dependent and in need of protection by adults who appropriate the role of interpreters of their lives and thus exclude them entirely from the research process.

The second viewpoint positions children as subjects putting them more into the foreground of the research process and orienting this towards a child-centred perspective. However, although the desirability of involving children is acknowledged it is tempered by judgements about their maturity and cognitive ability. Adult researchers still exert power in deciding whom to include and exclude. In the third perspective of children as social actors they 'act, take part in, change and become changed by the social and cultural world they live in' (Christensen and Prout, 2002: 481). This research approach does not necessarily make a distinction between adults and children and there is no automatic assumption that methodologies will need to be adapted for them. The fourth researcher perspective is concerned with children having an active participant role in the process of the research. Increasingly, this mode of active participation is developing into a quasi-partnership of children as co-researchers. *A crucial aspect here is the degree to which adults are willing to share knowledge.* At the most controlling end this can amount to a 'pretence of shared work' (Alderson, 2000) characterised by manipulation and tokenism. Power relations still predominate.

POWER RELATIONS

As Taylor (2000:21) noted, it is adults who write about the issues of rights for children and this is indicative of the power relations that confine children to subordinate roles in their societies. From a rights-based agenda, the perspective of children as social actors still places them as a socially excluded, minority group struggling to find a voice.

This suggests an imperative to engage with children at an active rather than a passive level. While we may have moved on from the white coat, laboratory-style child research, much adult-led research about children is still undertaken in power-laden settings. Contexts where there are ready-made research population samples, notably the 'captive audiences' available in school classrooms are popular. Here, the balance of power is heavily skewed towards adults. Arguably, school is a location where children are *least* able to exercise participation rights. In UK schools, adults control children's use of time, occupation of space, choice of clothing, times of eating–even their mode of social interaction.

Feminists challenged the validity of research based on a masculine way of looking at the world, on the basis that the ensuing knowledge generated was grounded in the male experience. In a similar vein, ideology critics argue that much child research is located in adult-dominated contexts and the knowledge generated is grounded in the adult experience. Generational issues feature prominently in adult-child power relations. Alanen (1992) maintains that there is a form of 'generational ordering' at work in the way children are contained in the 'private' world of the home and the family and excluded from the 'public' world of politics and economics.

Mayall (2000: 120) argues that the asymmetrical power relationship of childhood versus adulthood is a principal of social organisation:

> Adults have divided up the social order into two major groups – adults and children, with specific conditions surrounding the lives of each group: provisions, constraints and requirements, laws, rights, responsibilities and privileges. Thus, just as the concept of gender has been key to understanding women's relationships to the social order, so the concept of generation is key to understanding childhood.

Table 1 Support versus Management

adult support	**VERSUS**	**adult management**
enabling: training children in research process		**influencing:** allowing adult interests/agendas to influence what children research\
sustaining: training children in data collection skills		**limiting:** only teaching children certain skills thereby reducing their ability to make 'informed choices'
supporting: paving the way with gatekeepers		**judging:** suggesting that their ideas are not 'worthy' enough to research
helping: assisting children with transcription work, literacy and numeracy		**hijacking:** appropriating content and/or ownership of children's projects
empowering: seeking dissemination platforms for child researchers		**forbidding:** withholding consent for children to engage in research initiatives

EMPOWERING CHILDREN AS ACTIVE RESEARCHERS

This author suggests that we have now reached a point where we need to conceptualise a fifth dimension to Christensen and Prout's four-pronged perspective (2002) on children and childhood in research. Moving through children as objects, children as subjects, children as social actors and children as participant researchers, we have now arrived at a conceptualisation of children as active researchers in their own right.

This status enables children to set their own research agendas, explore issues about their lives which they, rather than adults, determine are important and to research them with their eyes and from their perspectives. Engagement in research has been shown to have a significant impact on their self-development and political agency (Kellett et al 2004). Moreover, research *by* children generates valuable new knowledge and understanding about childhood and children's lived experiences. A principal barrier to this happening is children's lack of research knowledge and skills. Many adults also lack these skills so any notions of the barriers being within-child deficits do not hold currency. A longitudinal research initiative (Kellett, 2003; 2004; 2005; 2005a) has been exploring the concept of children as active researchers since 2002. Various cycles of the project have focused on different barriers to children's empowerment, optimal ways to develop children's research knowledge and skills and effective ways to minimise adult filters by shifting the balance to *supporting* children's research rather than *managing* it.

A CENTRE DEDICATED TO RESEARCH BY CHILDREN

One of the outcomes of this ongoing project has been the establishment of *The Children's Research Centre* at the Open University (see http://childrens-research-centre.open.ac.uk) and the development of an extensively piloted programme of training that enables children to engage with research process without diluting the core principles of empirical enquiry (Kellett, 2005). The Children's Research Centre is dedicated solely to supporting and promoting research *by* children and evaluating its impact and is the first of its kind in the UK. It offers diverse groups of children a taught programme on aspects of research process followed by assistance to design and carry out their own research projects about aspects of their lives that concern or interest them. The centre supports a variety of outreach programmes with links to numerous schools and community organisations and has worked with more than 80 children on a wide range of research topics which children have self-identified.

Featured in this chapter is a small research study by a ten-year-old boy and some illustrated examples of other research by children which demonstrate the potential of children as active researchers to foster greater power sharing, more political agency and increased social justice for children.

Children's research contributions

The Children's Research Centre has supported children as young as nine to undertake their own research. While these studies are necessarily small scale, two outcomes are becoming increasingly apparent: firstly that children as young as nine can contribute valuable original knowledge from an insider perspective, knowledge that would otherwise remain closed to adult researchers; and secondly that engaging in research has an empowering effect on children's self-esteem, sense of self worth and political agency (Kellett, 2003).

INVESTIGATING WHAT CHILDREN THINK ABOUT THE WAY THEY TRAVEL TO SCHOOL

BEN WARD, AGED 10

Introduction

I have been attending a research club, called the OK club at school on a Monday lunchtime (O K stands for Original Knowledge!) We learn about research and the different ways of collecting information, and also the things you need to think about, like ethics, which means making sure no-one is hurt by the research, and how your research needs to be systematic and sceptical.
I am concerned about the environment and about pollution from vehicles. I have noticed that lots of my friends come to school in cars when they live really close by and I was interested to find out what the real picture is and also children's opinions about how they travel to school. I think I am in a better position than adults to find this out because I understand where children are coming from. I decided on my research question which is 'What do 9 and 10 year-olds think about how they get to school?'

Methodology

At first I was thinking about doing interviews, but I decided to do a questionnaire instead, because you can get information from lots more children that way. I didn't want it to be an adult questionnaire, I wanted it to be relevant to kids my age. These are some of the questions I decided to ask:

- How far children lived from school
- How they got to school
- Who decided how they travelled to school (adults or children or both)
- Whether this choice was influenced by concerns for the environment and health

Children's preferred way of getting to school (and how different this might be to their parents)

I made it quite simple so that children could easily understand it, and used tick boxes so they didn't have to write too much if they didn't want to, but left space for them to write more if they wanted. Then I tried it out on my brother and sister (who are 12 and 8) to see if the questions were clear. I gave out the questionnaire to a Year 6 class (aged 10) and a Year 5 class (aged 9) and got 57 completed questionnaires back (a few children were away).

Analysing the data

First of all I did tally counts on all the questions and then my adult supporter helped me turn these into percentages and then into graphs to make it easier to see where the patterns were. Here are the graphs of what I found out.

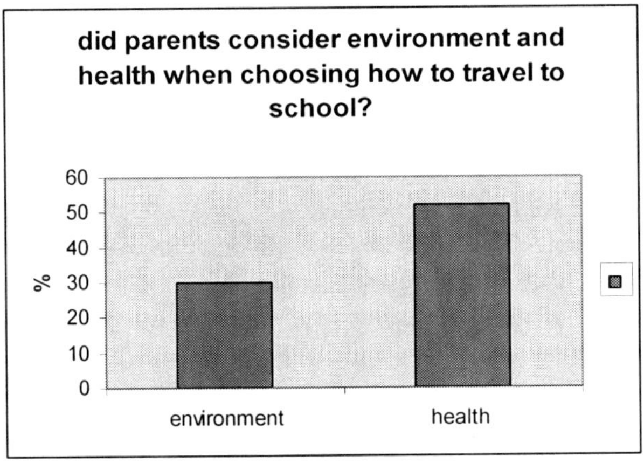

Figure 1: What do parents consider when they choose how to travel to school?

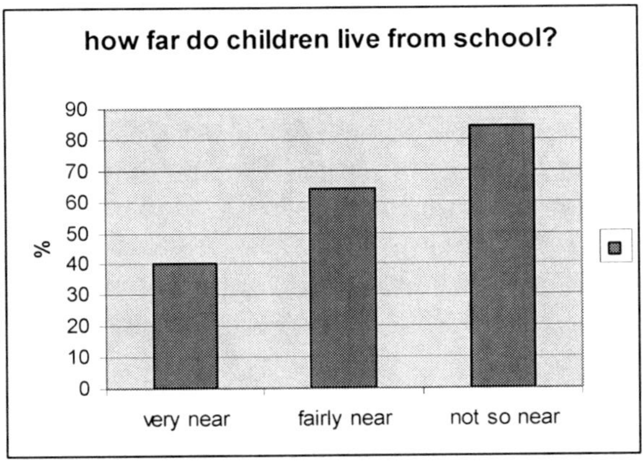

Figure 2: How far do children live from school

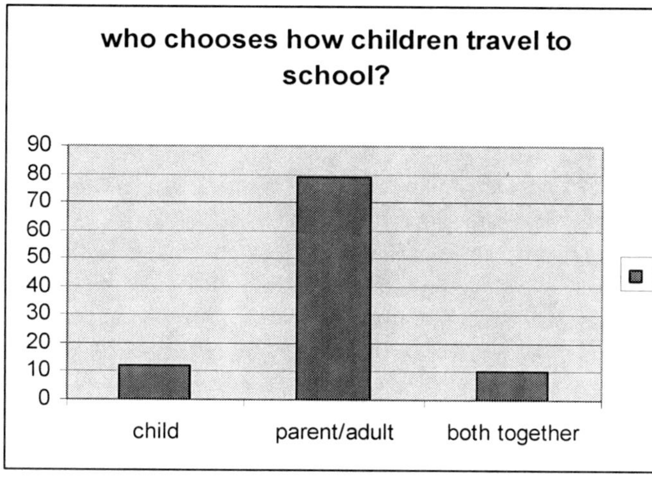

Figure 3: Who chooses how children travel to school?

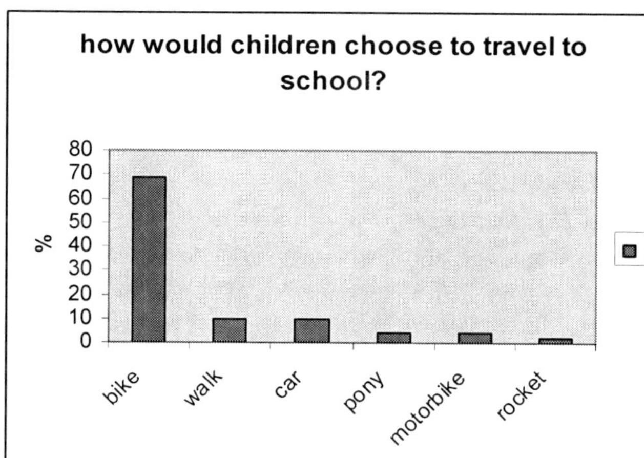

Figure 4: How would children choose how to travel to school?

From figure 1 you can see that children think that just under a third (30%) of their parents are concerned about looking after the environment when they choose their method of transport. This was less than I expected, but that may be because I think it's important and therefore assumed that others would agree with me but apparently not so many did. However, the questionnaires showed that just over half of the parents said that health was an important aspect in their decision about getting to school. I thought health would be quite high, because most people want to stay fit.

Figure 2 shows that 40% of the children who live very near their school travel by car every day. I find this very surprising because it is quite easy to walk, and would only take a short time, and might even be quicker than driving! The figure for children traveling to school by car who live fairly near is 64% which means that every day nearly two thirds of children living this close to school still travel by car. In the final category for those children living not so near the number is 84% but I would have expected this to be high because it is not easy to walk if you don't live near to school. (Although they could probably manage to cycle if they were allowed to). If you average out the findings from all of the children together (those who live very near, fairly near and not so near) then you can see that every day, nearly 60% are driving to school. For a primary school, where most children live fairly close, that seems a large percentage of people driving.

I think maybe it was this high because adults have other things to take into consideration, which children wouldn't have to worry about. For example they might have to drive on to work, straight after dropping the children off, so need the car for that - but it still might be quicker to walk the short distance to school and then go home for their car. Also, families may be in a rush in the morning, and not have time to walk or cycle. The other reason might be that adults are less energetic and active than children and so would rather use a less tiring way of travelling! But I was interested to find out if children agreed with their parents' decision to get to school by car.

From figure 3 you can see who chooses how children travel to school; in 12% of cases the children had the choice themselves, and in 10% of cases it was negotiated by both the children and the adults. I was amazed by the number of families where it was the adults who chose how the children travel to school; the figure was 79% which was much higher than I expected. And, as we saw from the last graph, often they decided to drive!

Figure 4 is the most important graph in my research because it shows what children themselves would choose to do if they were able to. I expected at least half of the children to want to go to school by car, and the other half choose to walk or perhaps cycle. In fact, as you can see, an amazing 69% of children want to cycle and only 10% of children want to drive. Also 10% of children want to walk. If we compare this graph with the results of how they really travel to school, it proves that the adults who usually choose, do not choose what the child would prefer and usually choose to drive even when cycling or walking would be quite easy (59% of adults choose to drive, 69% of children would choose to cycle.)

I thought it was funny that a few children put rocket or pony as their preferred method of transport, but it also shows that they weren't influenced by adults to put what they thought they should put, but had a completely free choice. This is one of the advantages of me doing the research because I am the same age as them and they might be more honest with me and put what they really think rather than what adults want! Most children did not put silly things and I think this proves that children are usually very sensible and responsible, perhaps more than adults think!

Conclusions

Even though this is only a small study I think it has shown up a big difference between how adults choose to travel when taking their children to school compared to what children themselves would choose. Most children end up coming to school by car, even when they live very close by. This is largely the adults' choice because only 10% of children would want this (about 80% would choose to walk or cycle). The children I have surveyed seem very concerned about transport and the environment but have little power or influence over what the adults choose for them. Perhaps if there could be more safe cycle paths more adults would let their children cycle to school then everyone would be happy and we would all be helping the environment.

REFLECTIONS ON BEN'S RESEARCH

Ben stated clearly that he did not want his questionnaire to be 'adult', he wanted it to be something that his peers could readily understand and identify with. Thus the value of child-led research is evident from the outset in that the research design and data collection tools are oriented from a child perspective and are likely to generate characteristically different data from adult-designed studies. This was shown by two nine-year-old researchers (see Carlini and Barry, 2005) who investigated what playground life was like for two girls who were nine but physically small for their age and easily mistaken for six-year-olds. Carlini and Barry claimed that adults' observation data would have been different because they are not party to the nuances of playground subculture which require an understanding of the kinds of games children construct and the unspoken rules that apply. Furthermore, in the child-child interviews they carried out they maintained that the two girls told them things they might not have told an adult researcher.

> We have been wondering whether adult researchers would have found out what we did if they investigated this topic…Rose and Kaz might not have told them as much as they were prepared to tell us because we are the same age as them – for instance Rose might not have told an adult about being bullied by someone younger. Also because we are used to the kinds of games that our age play at break times we can more easily see if something is different or unusual. (Carlini and Barry in Kellett, 2005:153).

Sceptics may criticise Ben for the somewhat naïve home-school distances he categorised in figure 2 as 'very near'; 'fairly near'; and 'not so near;' and attack the validity of the instrumentation. Ben would argue that when you are 9 and 10 being asked to choose between e.g. 'less than a kilometre'; '1-2 kilometres'; and 'over 2 kilometres' would generate far less accurate data because average 9-year-olds might not have the required estimation skills in their competence repertoire. However, 'very near'; 'fairly near'; and 'not so near;' are entirely meaningful to children of Ben's age and they know exactly what he means and respond with a consistency that can only be fully understood at child level. A similar argument can be made from the findings presented in figure 4 where the inclusion of rocket and pony as modes of transport underline the freedom offered by Ben in his open question for children to respond exactly as they felt rather than how they thought an adult would expect them to respond. Clearly a small minority of children in the study would like to come to school by pony or by rocket and these responses might have either been dismissed as 'silly' by adults or prevented from being expressed by restricting answers in closed-choice adult-designed categories. The inclusion of rocket and pony in the graph gives the reader confidence that the data has been generated from a genuine child perspective with no adult filters and no coercion or manipulation.

Furthermore, if one has this assurance that children had completely free choice (as evidenced by the rocket and pony data) it adds even greater potency to the dominance of the near 70% who cited bicycle as their preferred mode of travel, Despite the small scale of Ben's study and its child-like characteristics, it nevertheless delivers a giant-sized punch in terms of the message it conveys about where the power lies in decision-making and how differently children would approach this if they, rather than their parents, could exercise their right to choose how they travelled to school.

Ben presented his study to the Department of Transport, UK, where the strong trends in his data for cycling as the overwhelming child choice enabled him to lobby for more safe cycle paths. He was listened to attentively and promised that his findings would be taken seriously. When children's research, however small-scale, can have an impact and begin to influence policy in ways such as this, their agency as active researchers can play an important part in moving children's rights agendas forward.

Moving up the age range reveals more examples of research focused on participation and power-sharing in school environments. One forward-looking comprehensive school in a London borough ran a programme with a group of Year 8 (12 and 13 year-olds) students supported by the Children's Research Centre. The students first identified issues of concern among their peers and then went on to research these in some depth. Topics identified included students' perceptions of safety both in terms of school locations and times of the school day; students' perception of the extent to which their cultural identities were valued in school; and students' experiences of the lunch time break. The Year 8 students presented their research findings to the School Council who then took these forward to the School Governing Body. Providing evidence in the form of research data significantly enhanced the power of student voice in raising these issues and in subsequent transformative action. Similar student voice projects are well documented (e.g.

Fielding 2001; 2004) and point to a growing willingness to consult and involve students in school policy decisions. Though still relatively few in number, there are some examples of schools in the UK which invite students onto their governing bodies.

Other child researchers have undertaken studies concerning non school-based issues such as bereavement (O'Brien 2005), attitudes to parents' jobs (Kellett et al 2004), recycling and disability. In an initiative in five schools in Hertfordshire, supported by the Children's Research Centre, 10, 11 and 12 year-olds are researching topics as wide ranging as characteristics of sibling relationships, children's coping strategies to bullying, children's views about animal cruelty and attitudes to the curriculum. As the children as researchers initiative spreads, more children are being supported to undertake research in settings other than schools e.g. in youth groups, in community groups and as part of initiatives backed by children's organisations and charities. These have included studies by children on issues such as poverty in Africa (Bentley and Gambling, 2005), smoking, children's agency (Cole, 2004) young people staying safe, young carers, transport issues (Patil, 2005) youth danger and TV violence.

CONCLUDING THOUGHTS

Some sceptics maintain that children are not competent enough to engage in their own research and that adults can do it much better. The child competence debate was plagued by similarly sceptical views until robustly challenged (e.g. Hutchby and Moran-Ellis, 1998; Mortier, 1999; Woodhead and Faulkner 2000) as was the notion of children's inferior competence which was redrawn as 'different' from adults not 'lesser' (Waksler, 1991; Solberg, 1996). Therefore claims that children have insufficient knowledge, understanding and competence do not stand up to close scrutiny (Alderson, 2000; Kellett, 2005). With regard to childhood itself–in the sense of what it is like to be a child–it is children who have the expert knowledge (Mayall, 2000; Christensen and Prout, 2002). If the research areas that children undertake emanate directly from their own experiences then even the most skilled adult ethnographer cannot compete with children's own understanding of their worlds. Research *by* children is not going to replace adult research *with* children. There is room for both and each can, and should, inform the other. Children are not adults-in-waiting they have a status in the here and now with rights attached to that status. A growing and universal scholarly interest in childhood and children in society is already having an impact on children's rights agendas, moving these onto more secure platforms of legitimacy. Knowledge generated by children's own research has an important part to play in this legitimisation process. Progress is being made, although some would maintain that the pace of this progress is too slow, towards increased participation by children in democratic decision-making (Lansdown, 2002). There is an intellectual, political, legal and institutional momentum building in Europe (Franklin, 2002) in relation to child rights advocacy. It seems an appropriate time to consider children's own agency and research voice as part of that bigger picture.

REFERENCES

Alanen, L. (1992). Modern childhood? Exploring the child question in sociology. *Research Report, 50*. Jyvaskyla, Finland: University of Jyvaskyla.

Alderson, P. (2000). Children as researchers. In P. Christensen & A. James (Eds.), *Research with children'* (pp. 241–257). London: Falmer Press.

Alderson, P., & Morrow, V. (2004). *Ethics, social research and consulting with children and young people* (2nd ed.). Ilford: Barnado's.

Aspis, S. (2002). How valid is your research project? *Community Living, 15*(4), 17–18.

Bentley, D., & Gamble, L. (2005). *Young people's awareness of poverty in Africa*. Paper presented at Spotlight on Young Researchers conference, Open University.

Carlini, A., & Barry, E. (2005). Hey I'm nine not six!. In M. Kellett (Ed.), *Developing children as researchers*. London: Paul Chapman Publishers.

Children's Research Centre at The Open University, UK. Retrieved from http://childrens-research-centre.open.ac.uk

Christensen, P., & Prout, A. (2002). Working with ethical symmetry in social research with children. *Childhood, 9*(4), 477–497.

Cohen, L., Mannion, L., & Morrison, K. (2000). *Research methods in education*. London: RoutledgeFalmer.

Cole, D. (2004). *When can we have our say*. Retrieved from http://childrens-research-centre.open.ac.uk

Fielding, M. (2001). Students as radical agents of change. *Journal of Educational Change, 2*(2), 123–141.

Fielding, M. (2004). Transformative approaches to student voice. *British Educational Research Journal, 30*(2), 295–312.

Franklin, B. (2002). Children's rights and media wrongs: Changing representations of children and he developing rights agenda. In B. Franklin (Ed.), *The new handbook of children's rights: Comparative policy and practice*. London: Routledge.

Gordon, B. M. (1995). Knowledge construction, competing theories and education. In J. Banks & C. A. McGee-Banks (Eds.), *Handbook of research on multicultural education*. London: Macmillan.

Hutchby, I., & Moran-Ellis, J. (1998). Situating children's social competence. In I. Hutchby & J. Moran-Ellis (Eds.), *Children and social competence: Arenas of action*. London: Falmer Press.

James, A., Jenks, C., & Prout, A. (1998). *Theorizing childhood*. Cambridge: Polity Press.

Kellett, M. (2002). *Empowering able 10-year-olds as active researchers*. Paper presented at annual conference of the British Educational Research Association, Herriot Watt University, Edinburgh.

Kellett, M. (2003). *Enhancing pupils' learning skills through their engagement with research process*. Paper presented at Research in Practice Conference, Westminster Institute of Education, Oxford.

Kellett, M. (2004). Developing critical thinking skills in 10–12 year-olds through their active engagement in research. *Teaching Thinking Skills*, Issue 14, 32–40.

Kellett, M. (2005). *Developing children as researchers*. London: Paul Chapman Publishers.

Kellett, M. (2005a). *Adult free zones: Empowering children and young people as active researchers*. Paper presented at CHILDHOODS 2005 conference, Oslo.

Kellett, M., Forrest, R., Dent, N., & Ward, S. (2004). Just teach us the skills, we'll do the rest: Empowering ten-year-olds as active researchers. *Children and Society, 18*(5), 329–343.

Lansdown, G. (2002). *Promoting children's participation in democratic decision-making*. Innocenti Research Centre, Florence: UNICEF.

Martusewicz, R. A., & Reynolds, W. M. (1994). *Inside out: Contemporary critical perspectives in education*. New York: St Martin's.

Mayall, B. (2000). Conversations with children: Working with generational issues. In P. Christensen & A. James (Eds.), *Research with children: Perspectives and practices* (pp. 120–135). London: Routledge Falmer.

Mortier, F. (1999). Rationality and competence to decide in children. In E. Verhellen (Ed.), *Understanding children's rights*. Ghent: University of Ghent.

O'Brien, P. (2005). *How children are affected by bereavement.* Retrieved from http://childrens-research-centre.open.ac.uk

Oliver, M. (1997). Emancipatory research: Realistic goals or impossible dream. In C. Barnes & G. Mercer (Eds.), *Doing disability research* (pp. 15–31). Leeds: The Disability Press.

Patil, M. (2005). *Getting around as the child of a wheelchair user.* Paper presented at Spotlight on Young Researchers conference, Open University.

Sinclair, R. (2004). Participation in practice: Kaming it meaningful, effective and sustainable. *Children & Society, 18*(2), 106–118.

Solberg, A. (1996). The challenge in child research from "being" to "doing". In J. Brannen & M. O'Brien (Eds.), *Children in families: Research and policy* (pp. 53–65). London: Falmer Press.

Taylor, S. A. (2000). The UN convention on the rights of the child. In A. Lewis & G. Lindsay (Eds.), *Researching children's perspectives.* Buckingham: Open University Press.

United Nations. (1989). *Convention on the rights of the child.* Geneva: United Nations.

Usher, P. (1996). Feminist approaches to research. In D. Scott & R. Usher (Eds.), *Understanding educational research.* London: Routledge.

Waksler, F. C. (1991). *Studying the social worlds of children: Sociological readings.* London: Falmer.

Woodhead, M., & Faulkner, D. (2000). Subjects, objects or participants? Dilemmas of psychological research with children. In P. Christensen & A. James (Eds.), *Research with children: Perspectives and practice.* London: Routlege Falmer.

KAREN MUNDY

GLOBAL POLITICS AND LOCAL REALITIES IN THE REALIZATION OF THE UNIVERSAL RIGHT TO EDUCATION

In the 1990s, the international community saw a resurgence of interest in the achievement of "education for all." Beginning in the early 1990s with the Convention on the Rights of the Child and the Jomtien World Conference on Education for All, attention to the universal right to education steadily built momentum, culminating in the 1999 Dakar World Education Forum and the inclusion of education as two of the goals adopted at the United Nations Millennium Summit in 2000. Today it would be difficult to find any meeting of world leaders in which the universal right to education is not trumpeted as a common international goal. "Education for all" is a rallying call among heads of state and international financial institutions, and a focus for transnational advocacy by civil society actors. More recently it has emerged at the fore of meetings among the world's corporate leaders. Education for All is also an expanding arena for international development cooperation, characterized by widespread experimentation with new modes of aid delivery, new kinds of donor-recipient relationships and relatively high volumes of aid spending (Mundy 2006, 2007; Mundy and Murphy 2001).

Why has the global promise of EFA moved beyond international rhetoric to action now, and what kinds of limits and challenges still remain? To answer these questions, this paper provides a critical overview of the history of the Education for All (EFA) goal within the international community from 1945 to the present. It also highlights the EFA experience in two East African countries, Tanzania and Kenya. The paper concludes by considering what the current EFA experiment can tell us about the limits and possibilities for rights-based and redistributive form of global governance in our new century.

"EDUCATION FOR ALL" AND ITS IMPLEMENTATION IN THE POST-WORLD WAR II ERA

The idea that children have a right to attend school is so widely accepted today that it is hard to believe that schooling was not seen as an essential part of childhood in most parts of the world a mere 100 years ago. Yet in the 200-year period from the late 18th century to the late 20th century, "schooling"—formal, age-graded, classroom-based instruction—spread across Western societies and became the international standard for childhood socialization. Initially designed for the elite,

S.A. Moore and R.C. Mitchell (eds.), Power, Pedagogy and Praxis: Social Justice in the Globalized Classroom, 105–124.

by the early 20th century schooling (at least at the primary level) was increasingly being offered to all citizens, typically in systems run and funded by nation-states. So widespread had the institution of schooling become by the middle of the 20th century that the international community promised to uphold a "universal" right to education, first through the creation of the United Nations Education Science and Cultural Organization (UNESCO) in 1944; and secondly through Article 26 of the 1948 Universal Declaration of Human Rights, which states:

> Everyone has the right to education. Education shall be free, at least in the elementary and fundamental stages. Elementary education shall be compulsory. Technical and professional education shall be made generally available and higher education shall be equally accessible to all on the basis of merit (General Assembly of the United Nations 1948).

In the 1950s and the 1960s, newly independent countries around the world promised their citizens that they would expand access to schooling, replacing the highly restrictive systems inherited from colonialism with universal access. Universal primary education became a central part of the national development plans of post-colonial societies. Parents and children picked up the baton. Between 1960 and 1975, the number of children in school in developing countries increased by 122 per cent (Farrell 1999). Within years of independence, compulsory school laws were passed in virtually every country (Benevot and Resnik 2006).

The international community supported these post-colonial efforts to expand mass systems of public education. Aid to education, provided primarily through bilateral development aid (such as that given by the Canadian International Development Agency) was used to build the loyalty of postcolonial states during the Cold War; it also helped build economic ties to industrialized countries. But this was only part of the story. Educational aid also reflected the enormous commitment to education being made across Western welfare states after 1945, where expansion of access (at secondary and tertiary levels) and equality of opportunity had become central commitments. The idea that education could bridge social inequality was universally accepted, and countries with the most expansive domestic welfare states tended to offer international aid as an extension of their commitments to social equality at home (Mundy 1998). Large numbers of overseas volunteer teachers from the West reflected and reinforced mounting public support for the idea that rich countries should do their share to ensure that every child would get a chance to go to school.

A substantial research literature on the role of education in the development of the newly independent countries of the South also emerged in this period. Sociologists and political scientists carried out careful empirical work on the role played by education in constructing "modern" attitudes and behaviours (Inkeles and Holsinger 1974; McClelland 1961). Economists seeking to understand economic take-off discovered a residual role for a phenomenon that came to be labeled "human capital," and quickly embarked on rate of return studies to substantiate the claim that education enhances economic productivity (Becker 1962; Harbison and Meyers 1964; Schultz 1960). Both modernization theories and human capital theory promoted a functional view of schooling as an essential ingredient for national development. Education was linked to economic growth (greater national wealth); social development (more equitable distribution of wealth or opportunity); and political development (the creation of democratic systems) (Farrell 1999).

By the early 1970s, however, many scholars began to question the ambitions that lay behind the spread of modern schooling systems. Researchers challenged the earlier confidence in education's role in political modernization and economic growth, as well as its positive effects on social equality. Political scientist David Abernathy (1969) and sociologist Philip Foster (1965), for example, used their research in West Africa to question the wisdom of expanding education in contexts where economic growth was limited. Without the expansion of modern employment, Foster, Abernathy, and others warned that schooling might lead to widespread political dissatisfaction among the young, an unwillingness to work in agriculture, and to subsequent political destabilization (Huntington 1968). Other researchers began to show that while wealthier countries tend to have better educated populations, the expansion of schooling provides no guarantee of economic growth (Hannum and Buchman 2005). The effects of educational expansion are sensitive to context: for example, national political stability and position in the global trading system each structure the effects of schooling on individual, community, and national development (Ibid).

Questions about the role played by schools in the achievement of social equality were also raised. In the United States and the United Kingdom, educational sociologists like A.H. Halsey and James Coleman collected detailed data suggesting that schooling had minimal impact in altering the socio-economic status and life chances of children (Coleman and others 1966; Halsey, Heath and Ridge 1980). Family socio-economic background was indicated as playing a much larger role. Initial research from the developing world seemed to suggest that schooling did a better job of promoting intergenerational mobility in poor countries; but again, this outcome relied heavily upon the availability of new jobs, and in turn on high rates of economic growth (Farrell 1999). Subsequent research showed that even in contexts of economic growth, the equity-enhancing effects of each level of schooling seemed to weaken as it became universally available, passing pressure for access upwards to the next level in the educational system (Hannum and Buchman 2005). In most cases, elites manage to maintain their status by getting more education than the masses. Furthermore, although schooling could be shown to have positive effects on fertility (lowering the number of children) and on maternal ability to ensure children's health, it often also reinforces ethnic and gender inequality (Hannum and Buchmann 2005; Stromquist 1999).

A wave of theoretical and empirical work influenced by neo-Marxism explicated in detail the mechanisms through which schooling fed the reproduction of capitalist social relations on a global scale (Bowles and Gintis 1976; Carnoy and Levin 1985; Willis 1981). Led by Franz Fanon, Ivan Illich and Martin Carnoy, a countermovement of education and development theories emerged which blended neo-Marxist sociologies of education with dependency arguments to produce a hard-hitting critique of Western education as "cultural imperialism." These scholars posited that the expansion of education in the South was part of a larger process of "neo-colonialism," in which developing countries were integrated into a world economic system as supporting satellites of the West (Arnove 1980). Educational systems were thought to be playing several different roles in extending a new form of dependency. In the poorest and most marginal countries, schooling produced elite classes who identified with the values and culture of the West and were willing to exploit their own populations to emulate Western lifestyles. Schooling also acted as a legitimating mechanism that laid responsibility for failure in the world economy on the nation and the individual, rather than on the unequal and exploitative features of the world system itself (Fuller 1991; Illich 1971). Even in countries experiencing economic growth, schooling could still be viewed as producing a form of dependency—in this case habituating workers to competition in a global system of trade.

Alongside these criticisms from the left, the 1970s also saw the emergence of a variety of movements inside the developing world that focused on finding alternatives to dependent development. In Africa, for example, political leaders like Kwame Nkrumah and Julius Nyerere pioneered the idea of African socialism as an alternative to neo-imperialism (Nkrumah 1970; Nyerere 1969). Leading African thinkers, including novelists Chinua Achebe and Ngugi wa Thiong'o also began to expose the cultural dimensions of neo-colonialism, and explored African philosophy and indigenous forms of knowledge as alternatives to Western approaches to learning (Fanon 1963; Thiong'o 1986a, 1986b; Stromquist 1999). The spirit of these efforts is captured in the recent work of George Dei, who argues:

> ...for an approach to African development that is anchored in a retrieval, revitalization, and restoration of the indigenous African sense of shared, sustainable, and just social values. I contend that African peoples must re-appropriate their cultural resource knowledge if they are to benefit from the power of collective responsibility for social development. Indigenousness may be defined as knowledge consciousness arising locally and in association with the long-term occupancy of a place. Indigenousness refers to the traditional norms, social values, and mental constructs that guide, organize, and regulate African ways of living in and making sense of the world. Indigenous knowledges differ from conventional knowledges in their absence of imperial and colonial imposition. The notion of indigenousness highlights the power of dynamics embedded in the production, interrogation, validation, and dissemination of global knowledge about 'international development.' It also recognizes the multiple and collective origins and collaborative dimensions of knowledge, and underscores that the interpretation or analysis of social reality is subject to different and sometimes oppositional perspectives (Dei 2000).[1]

Such criticisms naturally led to proposals for alternative forms of education. Julius Nyerere, the longtime president of Tanzania (1961–1985), first captured this momentum in his well-known essay, "Education for Self-Reliance" (Nyerere 1967). Nyerere's interest in self-reliance shares a great deal with Mahatma

Gandhi's approach (described later in this book). He saw the inherited colonial education system in Tanzania as elitist in nature and oriented to "Western" interests and norms. Nyerere not only promised to make access to primary education free and to introduce universal adult literacy programs; he also envisioned schools as community institutions, supporting farms, workshops, and cultural activities that would help bridge the divide between school and rural society (Samoff 1999). In a move that attracted international attention, Nyerere expanded opportunities for adult education and initiated a national literacy campaign (Kassam 1994; Mundy 1993).

The 1970s saw the South–North diffusion of strong, alternative pedagogical models, emanating from socialist educational experiments in the developing world and from the writing and field-tested curriculum of Paulo Freire (1970). Freire built his approach to education around the concept of "conscientization," in which he integrated a commitment to education as the practice of freedom and the idea that a dialogue about the learner's own experience can be transformative. Freire criticized dominant elites for using a banking concept of education that encouraged the passivity of oppressed peoples. He argued instead that:

> ....the task of the humanists is to see that the oppressed become aware of the fact that as dual beings, 'housing' the oppressors within themselves, they cannot be truly human. This task implies that revolutionary leaders do not go to the people in order to bring them a message of 'salvation,' but in order to come to know through dialogue with them both their *objective situation* and their *awareness* of that situation — the various levels of perception of themselves and of the world in which and with which they exist (Freire 1970)

Such efforts at transformative pedagogy were picked up in a range of efforts to establish alternative forms of primary education for the poor. The development of alternative approaches to education also led organizations as different as UNICEF, USAID and the World Bank to more carefully target poor and marginalized populations in their development aid and at minimum to pay greater rhetorical attention to issues of equality, empowerment, and poverty (Mundy 1998).

GLOBALIZATION AND THE CRISIS OF EDUCATIONAL DEVELOPMENT IN AFRICA

Despite skepticism and debates about the role of education in development, the period from the 1960s to the mid-1970s was characterized by widespread expansion of public educational systems. In nearly all developing countries, whose prior colonially-inherited educational systems excluded the majority, changes were profound. Primary school enrolments, for example, increased more than six fold over a 30-year period in Sub-Saharan Africa. While fewer than half of all school aged children were in school in the early 1970s, by 1980, three-fourths attended schools (Samoff 1999). In some countries, enrolment ratios, particularly of girls, remained quite low (e.g., Francophone West Africa). But across the countries of East and Southern Africa, where governments promised universal and free access to schooling, it was not uncommon to find near to universal access to schooling. In Tanzania, for example, primary school enrolments expanded from 903,000 children in 1971 to 3,500,000 million in 1981—a rate of gross enrolments of close to 90 percent (Vavrus 2005).

However, this dramatic and rapid expansion of schooling in much of East and Southern Africa stalled after 1980. Some countries, like Tanzania and Kenya, experienced a severe reversal in the ratio of children enrolled in school. The central government and local communities in these countries re-introduced school fees. Educational infrastructure—school buildings, school materials, trained administrators and teachers—deteriorated dramatically, so that even when in school, children received an education of shockingly poor quality. A 1989 UNESCO report from Tanzania (where primary enrolment rates had plummeted to below 75 percent), describes the crisis:

> It is not uncommon to find a teacher standing in front of 80–100 pupils who are sitting on a dirt floor in a room without a roof, trying to convey orally the limited knowledge he has, and the pupils trying to take notes on a piece of wrinkled paper using as a writing board the back of the pupil in front of him. There is no teacher guide for the teacher and no textbooks for the children (Samoff 1999: 6).

Why did this deterioration in access to education occur? There are several answers to this question. First, African economies, already the most marginal in the global trading system, became even more peripheral during the great wave of economic globalization that began after 1975, in part because rich countries continued to raise barriers to agricultural and other primary commodities from the South. Many African governments also faced a sharp debt overhang, built up over years of borrowing from the West and its institutions for their development. As African government revenues declined, so too did available resources for schooling. Even governments that maintained a strong commitment to education saw per capita spending on education deteriorate by an average of five percent across the continent, to an average level of $85/per capita in 1995 (Ibid: 7).

Second, many governments in Africa were poor stewards of their nations. High levels of corruption and nepotism, weak administrative capacity, a tendency towards war, and relatively undemocratic political systems characterized many of the governments of the continent. In these contexts, intermittent promises of access to schooling were often used to broker patrimonial (father-child) relations between politicians and local communities. Used in this way schooling divided opposition and created "clients," rather than citizens with common perceptions and commitments to social and political rights. In contrast to rich country welfare states, where a strong national social settlement ensured access to education as a right of citizenship, in African countries education was often perceived as a tool of patronage. The hierarchical nature of many African school systems, as inherited from the colonial era, further entrenched inequalities. Administratively, African school systems tended to be organized in a top-down, centralized manner, with little room for participation or innovation (Ibid:13).

Finally, external political and institutional factors lay at the root of this crisis. From the late 1970s, African countries faced an increasingly harsh and punitive international community. The wealthier countries of the West were focused on domestic economic reforms to improve their own competitiveness in a globalized economic system, and were less willing to fund international development activities. Rich country governments refused to provide substantial debt relief or to drop trade barriers to the primary commodities produced by developing world countries. Instead they encouraged countries to adopt a standard set of "belt tightening" and liberalization reforms, often through their engagement with the International Monetary Fund (IMF) and the World Bank. "Structural Adjustment Programs" encouraged governments to place a cap on public spending—often with severe effects on educational provision. In cases such as Tanzania and Kenya, these caps on spending led to the reintroduction of user fees in health and education (Reimers 1994).

From the late 1980s, externally influenced educational reforms went much further, however, than the constraints and costs imposed by macro-economic adjustment. In addition, developing countries were hit by a set of educational reform proposals that had emerged across rich countries of the world, where policy makers had begun to question the sustainability of expansionary trends in public funding for education, and were seeking reforms that might guarantee greater efficiency as well as national competitiveness. The first generation of what we might think of as "globalization-driven" reforms in education began in the mid-to late 1970s when governments began to introduce "finance-driven" measures (e.g. cost cutting and the search for new, private sources of finance). A second generation of reforms focused on "competitiveness" —the efficient use of schooling to improve the productivity of the domestic labor force. Such reforms included standards based reform (principally the introduction of national testing regimes), and experiments in school choice and the privatization of educational service delivery (to increase inter-school competition and parental/student motivation) (Hanushek 1995). Finance and competitiveness driven reforms tended to "squeeze out" the expansive, equity-driven mandates of post-World War II educational systems (Ball 1998; Dale 2000). In turn, they eroded education's role in extending a social compact or settlement to the citizens of developing world countries.

In Africa, these reform measures were carried forward forcefully by the World Bank, which by the mid-1980s had emerged as the largest single financer of educational development as well as the largest education policy "think-tank" in the world (Carnoy 1995; Colclough 1991; Reimers 1994). The Bank's 1988 landmark publication *Education in Sub-Saharan Africa: Policies for Adjustment, Revitalization and Expansion* suggested that earlier goals of equality themselves could only be met through a substantial liberalization of educational systems. National systems of public education needed to be protected from elite capture, and returned to public accountability through the introduction of market-like mechanisms. Governments were told that they needed to encourage the private provision of education (directly funded by learners) not only because public finances could not afford universal systems, but also because private provision would enhance efficiency and quality. Governments were encouraged to step back from centralized systems of management and return schools to local control (albeit with new regulatory and accountability controls such as national testing regimes) (Colclough 1991; Hinchcliff 1993).

The impact of these reforms across Africa and the developing world has been mixed. Macroeconomic reforms have, despite their initially steep human costs, brought about a modest renewal of economic growth in countries like Tanzania, Kenya, and Malawi. At the same time, they have been decried for their negative impact on social equality, since the beneficiaries of economic growth are primarily in the modern sector of the economy, while producers in traditional sectors, like agriculture, continue to face trade barriers from the North. Further, without debt relief, governments are hard pressed to fund renewal of productive infrastructure: they simply cannot compete in a global market. These economic constraints create a steep barrier for educational change. Without an expanding labour market, it is unclear whether efforts to reform schooling will actually have a great impact on national productivity. Room for social mobility is also sharply constrained. The impact of structural adjustment reforms in Tanzania, for example, has been to shift pressure for access to the secondary level, where there is also a growth of private service delivery. Competition-driven educational reforms—including the decentralization of education, the encouragement of private service delivery and the devolution of financing to local communities—have had negative impacts on access and equality. Many reforms have floundered because they are introduced with no new resources for already fragile systems (Moulton and others 2002). Most observers agree that inequality of educational opportunity increased considerably in Tanzania between 1980 and 2000, "with a growing gap between those who can afford user fees and other school related expenses, and those who cannot." (Vavrus 2005: 183).

THE REVIVAL OF "EDUCATION FOR ALL" AFTER 2000

In recent years, the international context for educational development in Africa and other parts of the developing world has taken a somewhat more positive turn. Between 2000 and 2007, rich country governments substantially increased levels of foreign aid to Africa and made new commitments to debt relief. In addition, for the first time the international community has signaled that it will try to close the funding gap that prevents children in the poorest regions of the world from gaining access to schooling. Education emerged as a priority at the Millennium Summit of the United Nations and within the Millennium Development Goals set by the international community at this summit in 2000 (United Nations 2000)[2]. It also has gained renewed attention from the World Bank and the IMF, which now look for the achievement of universal access to basic education in their country lending programs (Mundy 2002, 2006).

These changes are particularly dramatic when placed alongside what has been widely assessed as the failure of the international community to achieve the goals established for education at the World Conference on Education for All in Jomtien,

Thailand in 1990 (Chabbott 2003; Torres 2000). The 1990s saw a precipitous decline in overall flows of aid, and an even steeper decline in aid for education. Instead of the "peace dividend" (expected by many at the end of the Cold War), issues of global poverty and inequality were sidelined as governments struggled to adjust to a rapidly integrating global economy.

The resurgence of interest in Education for All by the global community today is tightly linked to two new developments. First, the high-profile anti-globalization protests that surrounded the 1999 meeting of the World Trade Organization (WTO) in Seattle brought to the forefront the increasing public concern about the negative impacts of globalization. The growing strength, solidarity, and voice of such movements have placed pressure on rich country governments and major international organizations to recognize and respond to these concerns (Stiglitz 2003). Second, the rising importance of the European Union, with its more expansive approach to social welfare, has also contributed to new interest in global poverty within the international community. Thus, after more than a decade of declining aid and neo-liberal policy reforms, rich country governments and their multilateral institutions have begun to develop a consensus about international poverty and inequality that appears to offer a framework for a global "Third Way" (Alain 2005). This consensus links international development to democracy, good governance and human rights in a more extensive manner than ever before; while also strongly asserting the primacy of markets and capitalism.

Schooling appears to have re-emerged as a central part of this new international consensus or compact, in part because it fits with both the neo-liberal and pro-economic globalization approaches to development endorsed by the IMF and the World Bank, and the more equity conscious and globalization skeptic approaches adopted by the United Nations (Ruggie 2003; Therien 2005). Education straddles both equity and productivity conceptualizations of development, bridging the divide between the neo-liberal and social welfare orientations to global development. Thus, the World Bank argues:

> The expansion of educational opportunity, which can simultaneously promote income equality and growth, is a win-win strategy that in most societies is far easier to implement than the redistribution of other assets, such as land or capital. In short, education is one of the most powerful instruments known for reducing poverty and inequality and for laying the basis for sustained economic growth, sound governance, and effective institutions (World Bank 2002).

Others sum up the consensus about education somewhat more critically:

> A crude characterization of the current approach is to encourage internal and external trade liberalization, and simultaneously invest in health, education and good governance, so that people are able to take advantage of new economic opportunities (Maxwell 2005).

This growing international consensus about education is reflected in the seeming ease with which many development organizations and advocates are now calling increased global support for achieving the universal right to education (Birdsall and Vaishnav 2005; Sperling 2001). For example, the UN's Millennium Development Project Task Force on Education has argued for a "Global Compact on Education" to parallel the new consensus on global development. These calls demand significant reform of the aid business itself. Building on recommendations for donor harmonization and coordination advanced by the Organization for Economic Cooperation and Development [OECD], the UN Millennium Project urges donors to "commit new funds [7 billion/year] in a new way through a strong coordinated global effort that rewards and reinforces countries' measurable progress." (UN Millennium Project 2005). Rich nations are being asked to provide a long term, steady and reliable source of funding for the recurrent costs of schooling in the poorest countries of the world, as well as major improvements in terms of donor coordination, concentration of aid on the poorest countries, and the untying of aid to education. Indeed, since 2002, many donor governments have begun to pool their aid to provide funding for the recurrent costs of schools in the South—a first in the history of international development cooperation, which has generally shied away from directly paying for teachers' salaries and other recurrent costs of mass education. In some countries, such as Zambia and Uganda, upwards of 40 percent of the national education recurrent budget is now being funded by external donors (UNESCO 2005).

Education for All efforts have also been fed by the burgeoning of transnational social movements that have used education as a core venue for advocating for global redistributive justice. The right to education is supported by an increasingly active network of transnational advocacy organizations devoted to such issues as debt relief, Overseas Development Assistance (ODA) reform, human rights, and globalization. These actors have been particularly influential in forcing changes in international policies that reflect stronger commitment to social equality and poverty alleviation. Such advocacy work has included successful campaigns against World Bank and IMF policies on user fees in health and education (Mundy and Murphy 2001). In addition, the Global Campaign for Education (GCE), a powerful transnational advocacy network devoted to EFA, has also emerged in recent years. Initiated by OXFAM International, Actionaid, and the international association of teachers unions (Education International), the Global Campaign for Education now counts among its members a large number of national civil society EFA coalitions around the world, as well as some of the largest international nongovernmental organizations involved in education (e.g., CARE, Save the Children, Global March). The GCE has been instrumental in pushing bilateral donors, international organizations, and members of the Group of 8 industrialized countries to make concrete commitments of resources for EFA. It acts as policy watchdog at the international and national levels, raising issues of adequate financing and equitable distribution of opportunities in national educational planning exercises and in international fora; producing an annual "report card" on developing country and rich country contributions to EFA; and lobbying at the annual World Bank/IMF meetings to highlight the negative impact of IMF conditionalities (Mundy 2006).

These international initiatives have meshed with democracy reforms across many African countries to produce a return to ambitious plans for universal primary education in recent years (Stasavage 2005). Beginning with Malawi's first multi-party elections in 1994, a series of newly and democratically elected African governments have made "free primary education" an election promise. It appears that when free multi-party elections are held, governing parties see a strong incentive for introducing universal access to basic services. Such promises in Uganda, Kenya, Tanzania, and, most recently, Burundi have led to an enormous flood of students returning into the primary system after elections.

Political liberalization has also allowed for the development of an increasingly vocal network of civil society organizations across Africa. These organizations not only advocate for equity-driven approaches to national development; they also work with transnational advocacy groups to ensure that international organizations alter their social policy prescriptions. Thus two of the outcomes of political liberalization—universal free schooling and the expansion of local civil society organizations—have been mutually reinforcing. The concepts of "Education for All" and the "right to education" have now re-emerged as a central part of the social and political landscape in African countries. Political activism by domestic and transnational groups ensures that EFA is something in which both government elites and the local public share a strong stake.

EDUCATION FOR ALL: THE VIEW FROM TANZANIA AND KENYA

Current challenges and dilemmas of educational development can be illustrated by reference to two East African countries, Tanzania and Kenya. Both countries have recently announced national policies supporting universal, free access to primary education. They share a long history of governmental efforts to use education to support economic and social development. Yet, in both cases, the re-introduction of universal access to primary education has raised many new dilemmas.

As noted above, Tanzania was host to a unique experiment in education during the 1960s and 1970s. Under Nyerere's policy of "Education for Self-Reliance," Tanzania was among the first countries in Africa to achieve universal enrolment of children at the primary level; it also achieved relatively high levels of literacy among adults, and introduced a curriculum that focused on rural productivity. But because Tanzania was among the poorest countries in Africa, these gains came at a cost: to achieve universal free primary education and adult literacy, the government severely limited access to secondary education, to less than five percent of the school-leaving population. Nyerere's education initiatives, like many of his government's social policy initiatives, were linked to centralizing processes of 'village-ization' and forced resettlement. Ironically, an authoritarian, one-party approach to governance in Tanzania formed the backdrop for policies meant to support universal access and self-reliance.

Kenya and Tanzania are frequently contrasted in the literature because of the sharply divergent development paths their governments chose after independence. While Tanzania pioneered a form of "African socialism," Kenya eschewed efforts at centralized socialism and instead adopted a market-oriented approach to development. In addition, Kenya has been the more prosperous of the two countries, not only because it is endowed with significant natural resources, but also because it inherited a more developed market economy and physical infrastructure from the colonial period. As a result, early Education for All experiences in Kenya and Tanzania were quite different.

At independence, Kenya began with much higher levels of participation in school than Tanzania.[1] Unlike Tanzania, the Kenyan government did not constrain expansion at secondary level in order to focus on universal primary education. Instead, it encouraged communities to build their own secondary schools through a movement known as "harambee"– Swahili for "let us all pull together." As secondary schooling rapidly expanded in Kenya during the 1970s, the government did little to guide its expansion in terms of either quality or distribution. Kenya, again in contrast to Tanzania, paid little attention to reforming its school curriculum to build a distinct national identity or alternative approach to development (Cooksey, Court and Makau 2005; Sivasubramaniam and Mundy 2006). Nor did it enforce its promise of "free" primary education. Despite announcements ending formal fees in 1974 and 1979, individual schools were quietly allowed to re-institute fees for attendance. Thus, although the central government maintained control over the educational system through a national examination system and school inspections, many aspects of Kenya's approach to education mirrored the laissez-faire, open-market approach to development adopted by its government.

This approach to educational expansion in turn contributed to the development of clientalist politics in Kenya, fed by the harambee school movement. Under harambee, individual politicians were encouraged to make frequent contributions to local harambee schools in order to build political support and patronage. Wealthy communities and ethnic groups were able to build more and better schools than poorer communities, and large geographic disparities emerged in terms of opportunity and quality. At the same time, harambee schools helped to deflect attention from central government, offering an outlet for popular educational aspirations without creating binding expectations that government should ensure quality or equity across the school system. Disparities in educational opportunity were rarely blamed on the central government (Buchmann 1999).

In the early 1980s, both Tanzania and Kenya entered a period of severe economic constraint, accompanied by neo-liberal economic and educational reforms (Samoff 1990). In both countries, primary schooling began to deteriorate. Steep declines in educational quality were accompanied by the stagnation and later erosion of enrolments.

In this context, national policies towards education in both countries during the 1980s began to change. In Kenya, the government tried to reassert centralized control over the educational system and to reign in educational expectations. In 1983, the government introduced a new primary cycle of eight years with a new focus on pre-vocational training for self-employment. It introduced secondary and tertiary quotas, and announced that educational policies would be closed to public debate. However, the Kenyan government continued to respond to popular demands for access to higher education: in the late 1980s it expanded university enrollments, further depriving elementary education of finances. Meanwhile, in Tanzania, the government removed the cap on secondary school enrolments, encouraged communities to sponsor private secondary schools, and opened new university spaces. Tanzania's innovative literacy and adult education programs were neglected, and efforts to create a curriculum reflective of local issues and African socialism fell by the wayside.

By the late 1980s, both Tanzania and Kenya began to experience external pressures to introduce cost-sharing policies into their education systems as part of structural adjustment lending. Neither country received significant increases in external aid, despite their economic crises. Indeed, charges of corruption within the Kenyan government led several donors to cease their external aid programs altogether.

Today, Tanzania is still one of the poorest countries in the world, with a per capita GDP of US $330 in 2004. One of every three Tanzanians lives below the poverty line of 26 cents (US) per day; and more than one out of every 10 children under the age of 18 has been orphaned by AIDS. However, the achievement of multi-party democracy (in 1995) and the election of a reform-minded government have allowed the country to experience renewed economic growth and to receive increased development funding from the international community since the late 1990s.

In 2003, the Tanzanian government abolished user fees for primary education, after a successful campaign launched by both domestic and international advocacy organizations. The process through which this occurred demonstrates how new forms of global and transnational accountability are emerging around universal rights, such as the right to education. In the Tanzanian case, research on the negative impact of user fees in education was produced by the education NGO Maarifa ni Ufunguo in 2000. This research was then used by American NGOs to lobby members of the U.S. House and Senate, who eventually passed legislation prohibiting the U.S. government from funding the World Bank if it imposed any form of user fees as part of its loan conditionality. The World Bank subsequently removed user fees from its loan conditions, and the Government of Tanzania declared free primary education (Kuder 2004; Maarifa in Ufunguo 2000). The Tanzania experience in turn stimulated a number of other African governments to remove user fees in education and declare universal free primary education. Today, Tanzania continues to boast a vibrant network of civil society organizations working to monitor their government's educational commitments.

In Tanzania, the public response to the declaration of free education was overwhelming and immediate: overnight, approximately 1.6 million new students entered the primary system (Haggerty and Mundy 2006). Since free primary education was announced in 2003, gross enrolment ratios have risen from a low of 77 percent in the mid 1990s back to levels of over 90 percent. However, expansion of the country's primary education system is heavily dependent on foreign donors. These donors have encouraged the government to decentralize the administration of the education system, so that today school councils in Tanzania have responsibility for preparing budgets and school plans, managing funds and salaries, and preparing financial reports. At the national level a greater variety of stakeholders participate in education policy setting, including civil society and citizens' organizations.[2]

In Kenya, the announcement of free primary education came in late 2002, the year in which the longtime rule of Kenya's African National Union party ended with the election of the National Rainbow Coalition (NARC) —a party formed from a number of opposition groups. As in Tanzania, the popular response to this announcement was overwhelming: following the implementation of free primary education, 1.2 million out-of-school children were absorbed into formal primary schools and 200,000 into non-formal education centres. There had been little planning for such a large response, and only a very limited budget for it. As a result the first few years of free primary education have been somewhat chaotic. A significant number of civil society groups now monitor the Kenyan government's implementation of free primary education, although in Kenya there appears to be less formal coherence in the policies advocated by these nongovernmental groups.

Table 1 National Profiles of Tanzania and Kenya

	Tanzania	***Kenya***
Total population	38.3 million (2005)	34.3 million (2005)
GDP per capita	US$330 (2005)	US$442 (2005)
ODA as % GDP	16.1% (2004)	3.9% (2004)
Date of independence	1961	1963
First multi-party elections	1995 (Change of leadership but not of party)	1992 (No change of leadership or party until 2002)
Universal free primary education	-first achieved in 1973 -re-introduced in 2003	-first promised in 1963; again in 1969, 1973 and 1983. -removal of fees for first 4 years of school implemented in 1974 -re-introduced, 2002
Transition to secondary education	33.2% (2004)	95.4% (2003)

Sources:
1. World Bank, "EdStats", http://devdata.worldbank.org/edstats/query/default.htm
2. United Nations Development Programme (2007) Human Development Report 2006. *Table 18. http://hdr.undp.org/hdr2006/pdfs/report/HDR06-complete.pdf.*
2. Unesco (2007) EFA Global Monitoring Report: GMR Data,
http://gmr.uis.unesco.org/Accessed June 20, 2007 from http://gmr.uis.unesco.org/
[all accessed June 20, 2007].

The opening up of access to primary education in Tanzania and Kenya has been viewed positively by the international community. Yet, for both countries, free primary education raises a host of questions. In both instances, free primary education relies very heavily on international aid. Foreign donors finance more than half of Tanzania's education budget (Khainga 2005). Kenya, while much less dependent on foreign aid, still requires external funding to meet new levels of enrolment. Such dependency puts the future of free primary education in a very vulnerable position: a small change in donor funding would place the education of thousands of children at risk. These high levels of dependency also tend to lead to donor driven policies, rather than local control and ownership (Samoff 2004). There is little sign, in either country, of efforts to "indigenize" the curriculum or use African knowledge as a basis for educational reform. (See Chapter Nine in this volume for a more in-depth discussion of indigenous knowledge and Education for All). In both Tanzania and Kenya, the strength of external influence is amplified by a decision among donors to pool their resources and develop regular measures to jointly monitor government expenditures and implementation of policies.

At the local level, the rapid expansion of access to education in Tanzania and Kenya has had sharp implications for the quality of learning. Even with the increase in donor funding, class sizes of over 100 students are not unusual at the primary level in either country. Materials and classroom equipment are in short supply. While donor agencies have focused their funds on providing school level funds for materials and improved classrooms, there is still a strong belief in public sector constraint and smaller public sector staffing among donors, thus teacher shortages are likely to continue.

Perhaps most importantly, it is still not clear what going to school can do for national or individual welfare, at least in the short term. While parents continue to see education as a stepping-stone towards modern employment, the availability of formal sector employment in Kenya and Tanzania is limited. In both countries the public continues to demand the expansion of secondary level education, and many observers expect that motivation to complete primary schooling will slacken if access to secondary education and formal employment does not improve. Reform measures that encourage terminal primary education focused on self-reliant skills for production—the core of Nyerere's message in "Education for Self Reliance" — continue to be sidelined by parents and governmental elites whose focus is climbing what Robert Serpell describes as the "narrow educational staircase" (Serpell 1999) towards greater individual mobility. The achievement of broad-based equality through education is in tension with competitive self-interest.

The Kenyan and Tanzanian governments are under enormous pressure today—both from domestic groups and international actors—to maintain momentum towards EFA, even as they face limited national budgets, unreliable aid flows, low levels of formal employment, limited access to rich country markets, and increasing popular demand for access to secondary and tertiary education. The fragile democratic regimes at the centre of politics in these two countries have nonetheless staked their claims for political legitimacy on the promise of universal free education. It is not surprising, then, to find that governments in both countries are scrambling to find ways of harnessing private sector partnerships to expand education, and endorsing donor-advocated reforms such as the decentralization of school management and budgets. Such reforms deflect attention away from the central government and also offer mechanisms for doing "more with less." They add to the heightened complexity and interdependencies that now frame achievement of the universal right to education in these and other developing countries.

CONCLUSION: GLOBAL POLITICS, LOCAL REALITIES AND THE UNIVERSAL RIGHT TO EDUCATION

The resurgence of interest in EFA by the global community today is tightly linked to two new developments. The first is the emergence of fragile and deeply paradoxical consensus about international development among G8 governments. This consensus links development to democracy, good governance and human rights in a more extensive manner than ever before; while also strongly asserting the primacy of markets and capitalism. Education bridges these two sets of development ideals. In addition, EFA has been fed by the burgeoning of transnational social movements that have used education as a core venue for advocating for global redistributive justice.

If education is now embedded in a widening consensus about the core features of "good" global governance and development, it is important to keep in mind that this consensus bridges what had been a fundamental divide between those agents that have been more concerned with social equality and fundamental human rights, and those less concerned with equity, who are convinced that global economic growth through greater global integration is the way forward. The fact that the international community – both official and nongovernmental–has chosen to establish the universal right to education as an important part of its emergent vision of world order suggests that there has been a turn away from the laissez faire neo-liberalism of the 1980s and 1990s. But this turn is certainly not complete, and there is still far to go before the right to education is guaranteed by the international community. We still lack an overarching mechanism for coordinating and ensuring a global entitlement to education.

The limits of the current emphasis on Education for All as a focal point for global redistributive justice is also apparent in the choice of education over other forms of social protection by the international community. To borrow from Therien's critical reflections on the wider emergence of a global development compromise, the new focus on basic education as a strategy for poverty reduction may be seen as a victory for those who continue to frame the problem of development as one of individuals who are not well adapted to the demands of the market, and states that need to bear responsibility for development failures. As such, we might view the resurgence of interest in EFA as part of a global consensus that actively avoids an understanding of development focused on global structural inequalities and the need for permanent national and global measures of redistribution and social protection (Therien 2005; Maxwell 2005: 4).[5]

The Tanzanian and Kenyan examples highlight many of the dilemmas and challenges surrounding the international call for universal primary education. Domestically, an orientation towards greater equity, self-reliance, and public accountability across primary and later levels of schooling promises enormous returns. However, these returns can only be realized if, at the level of the world system, there are guarantees of long term funding for the poorest countries, cancellation of debt, and access to the agricultural and other product markets in rich countries. The emergence of a transnationally organized global public that is critical of globalization and global economic inequalities, and that views the right to education as an important venue for expressing a commitment to redistributive justice on a global scale, is a hopeful sign. Such transnational networks can help pressure rich country governments to provide reliable, long-term international funding. They can also help ensure that the voices of local civil society groups, closest to indigenous knowledge and the everyday experiences of schooling, are heard by national educational policy makers.

Overall, the democratization of opportunities for learning in the developing world remains a fragile and easily reversible process. For children in many of the world's poorest countries, access to schooling has thus far remained a hollow privilege. While schooling brings children into a global community of childhood rights and expectations, it often also sorts children into poverty and alienates them from their local cultures in ways that harm local self-reliance. The challenge of offering every child an equal opportunity to learn requires both greater global resources for the achievement of educational for all, and more attention to the transformation of education itself. But we must also think beyond the provision of schooling, towards fundamental changes in world politics and the creation of a globally redistributive social order. Constructing forms of educational organization and governance that engage children and citizens in the realization of Education for All may feed this larger goal, by helping to prepare them for more active roles in social transformation.

NOTES

1 See also Ali Abdi, "African Philosophies of Education: Counter-Colonial Criticism," in Issues in African Education: Sociological Perspectives, ed. Ali Abdi and Ailie Cleghorn (New York: Palgrave Macmillan, 2005).

2 The Millennium Development Declaration sets out eight Millennium Development Goals (MDGs) with time bound, measurable targets. These targets, set for 2015, include reducing world poverty, the spread of HIV/AIDS, and the number of people without safe drinking water by 50%; reducing infant mortality by 66%; combating malaria; and promoting gender equity and environmental sustainability. Universal primary education and gender equity in education are MDGs number two and three.)

3 In 1961, Kenya had roughly 10 primary and middle school students for every 6 in Tanzania. See Brian Cooksey, David Court, and Ben Makau, "Education for Self-Reliance and Harambee." in Beyond Capitalism and Socialism in Kenya and Tanzania, ed. Joel Barkan, 201–33 (London: Lynne Rienner, 1994).

4 While the government is broadly favourable to civil society, it also reacts aggressively to criticism. In 2005, the government banned the influential education advocacy NGO, Haki Elimu from publicizing its research in print or broadcast media because it was critical of the government's EFA efforts.

5 Thus in Maxwell's view "Poverty reduction is good, but social inclusion is better," and "there has been too much focus [on health and education] in PRSP's and public expenditure plans, at the

expense of productive sectors and social protection." He argues strongly for more attention to food insecurity and malnutrition (Maxwell 2005: 4).

REFERENCES

Abdi, A. (2005). African philosophies of education: Counter-colonial criticism. In A. Abdi & A. Cleghorn (Eds.), *Issues in African education: Sociological perspectives*. New York: Palgrave Macmillan.

Abernathy, D. (1969). *The political dilemma of popular education: An African case*. Stanford, CA: Stanford University Press.

Alain, N. (2005). *The new politics of global poverty* [unpublished manuscript]. Université de Montréal.

Arnove, R. (1980). Comparative education and world systems analysis. *Comparative Education Review, 24*, 48–62.

Ball, S. J. (1998). Big policies/small world: An introduction to international perspectives in education policy. *Comparative Education, 34*, 119–130.

Becker, G. (1962). Investment in human capital: A theoretical analysis. *Journal of Political Economy, 70*, 9–49.

Benavot, A., & Resnik, J. (2006). Towards a comparative socio-historical analysis of universal basic and secondary education. In J. Cohen, D. Bloom, & M. Malin (Eds.), *Education all the children: A global agenda*. Cambridge, MA: American Academy of Arts and Sciences and MIT Press.

Birdsall, N., & Vaishnav, M. (2005). Education and the MDGs: Realizing the millennium compact. *Columbia Journal of International Affairs, 58*, 257–264.

Bowles, S., & Gintis, H. (1976). *Schooling in capitalist America: Educational reform and the contradictions of economic life*. New York: Basic Books.

Buchmann, C. (1999). The state and schooling in Kenya: Historical developments and current challenges. *Africa Today, 46*, 95–115.

Carnoy, M. (1995). Structural adjustment and the changing face of education. *International Labour Review, 134*, 653–673.

Carnoy, M., & Levin, H. (1985). *Schooling and work in a democratic state*. Stanford, CA: Stanford University Press.

Chabbott, C. (2003). *Constructing education for development: International organizations and education for all*. New York: Routledge.

Colclough, C. (1991). Who should learn to pay? An assessment of the neo-liberal approaches to education policy. In C. Colclough & J. Manor (Eds.), *States for markets? Neo-liberalism and the development policy debate*. Oxford: Clarendon Press.

Coleman, J., et al. (1966). *Equality of educational opportunity*. Washington, DC: US Department of Health, Education and Welfare.

Cooksey, B., Court, D., & Makau, B. (1994). Education for self-reliance and Harambee. In J. Barkan (Ed.), *Beyond capitalism and socialism in Kenya and Tanzania*. London: Lynne Rienner.

Dale, R. (2000). Globalization and education: Demonstrating a "Common World Educational Culture" or locating a "Globally Structured Educational Agenda". *Educational Theory, 50*, 427–442.

Dei, G. J. S. (2000). African development: The relevance and implications of the 'indigenousness'. In G. J. S. Dei, B. L. Hall, & D. G. Rosenberg (Eds.), *Indigenous knowledges in global contexts: Multiple readings of our world*. Toronto: University of Toronto Press.

Fanon, F. (1963). *The wretched of the earth*. New York: Grove Press.

Farrell, J. (1999). Changing conceptions of equality of education: 40 years of comparative evidence. In R. F. Arnove & C. A. Torres (Eds.), *Comparative education: The dialectic of the global and the local*. New York: Rowan and Littlefield.

Foster, P. (1965). *Education and social change in Ghana*. London: Routledge.

Freire, P. (1970). *Pedagogy of the oppressed*. New York: Continuum.

General Assembly of the United Nations. (1948). Article 26, Universal Declaration of Human Rights. New York: United Nations.

Haggerty, M., & Mundy, K. (2006). Tanzania: Civil society participation and the governance of education systems in the context of sector-wide approaches to basic education [Working paper]. OISE/University of Toronto; Mimeo.

Halsey, A., Heath, A., & Ridge, J. (1980). *Origins and destinations: Family, class and education in modern Britain*. Oxford: Clarendon.

Hannum, E., & Buchmann, C. (2005). Global education expansion and socio-economic development: An assessment of findings from the social sciences. *World Development, 33*, 333–354.

Hanushek, E. (1995). Interpreting recent research on schooling in developing countries. *The World Bank Research Observer, 10*, 22–46.

Harbison, F., & Meyers, C. (1964). *Education, manpower and economic growth*. New York: McGraw-Hill.

Hinchcliff, K. (1993). Neo-liberal prescriptions for education finance: Unfortunately necessary or inherently desirable? *International Journal of Educational Development, 13*, 183–187.

Huntington, S. (1968). *Political order in changing societies*. New Haven, CT: Yale University Press.

Illich, I. (1971). *Deschooling society*. New York: Harper and Row.

Inkeles, A., & Holsinger, D. (1974). *Education and individual modernity in developing countries*. Leiden: Brill.

Kassam, Y. (1994). Julius Kambarage Nyerere. *Prospects: The Quarterly Review of Comparative Education, 24*, 247–259.

Khainga, D., et al. (2005). *United Republic of Tanzania: Education sector public expenditure review (PER), 2nd draft report*. Madrid, Spain: Altai Asesores, Neimacro Group.

Kuder, J. L. (2004). *The formulation of primary education in policy Tanzania within a global governance approach to aid and development*. Unpublished Ph.D. dissertation. Bristol: University of Bristol.

Maarifa ni unfunguo. (2000). *Cost sharing: A case study of education in Kilimanjaro*. Arusha, Tanzania: Maarifa ni Ufunguo.

Maxwell, S. (2005). The Washington consensus is dead! Long live the meta-narrative. *Working Paper WP/243*. London: Overseas Development Institute.

McClelland, D. (1961). *The achieving society*. Princeton, NJ: Van Nostrand.

Moulton, J., et al. (2002). *Education reforms in sub-Saharan Africa: Paradigm lost?* Westport, CT: Greewood Press.

Mundy, K. (1993). Towards a critical analysis of literacy in Southern Africa. *Comparative Education Review, 37*, 389–411.

Mundy, K. (1998). Educational multilateralism and world (dis)order. *Comparative Education Review, 42*, 448–478.

Mundy, K. (2002). Education in a reformed World Bank. *International Journal of Educational Development, 22*, 483–508.

Mundy, K. (2006). Education for all in the new development compact. *International Review of Education, 52*, 23–48.

Mundy, K. (2007). Education for all: Paradoxes and prospects. In D. P. Baker & A. W. Wiseman (Eds.), *Education for all: Global promises, national challenges*. Oxford, UK: Elsevier.

Mundy, K., & Murphy, L. (2001). Transnational advocacy, global civil society: Emerging evidence from the field of education. *Comparative Education Review, 45*, 85–126.

Nkrumah, K. (1970). *Consciencism; philosophy and ideology for de-colonization*. New York: Monthly Review Press.

Nyerere, J. (1967). Education for self reliance. *Ujamaa: Essays on socialism*. Dar es Salaam: Oxford University Press.

Nyerere, J. (1969). *Freedom and socialism. Uhuru na ujamaa; A selection from writings and speeches, 1965–1967*. Dar es Salaam: Oxford University Press.

Reimers, F. (1994). Education and structural adjustment in Latin America and sub-Saharan Africa. *International Journal of Educational Development, 14*, 119–129.

Ruggie, J. G. (2003). The United Nations and globalization: Patterns and limits of institutional adaptation. *Global Governance*, *9*, 301–322.

Samoff, J. (1990). 'Modernizing' a socialist vision: Education in Tanzania. In M. Carnoy & J. Samoff (Eds.), *Education and social transition in the Third World*. Princeton, NJ: Princeton University Press.

Samoff, J. (1999). No teacher guide, no textbooks, no chairs: Contending with crisis in African education. In C. A. Torres (Ed.), *Comparative education: The dialectic of the global and the local*. Lanham: Rowman and Littlefield.

Samoff, J. (2004). From funding projects to supporting sectors? Observations on the aid relationship in Burkina Faso. *International Journal of Educational Development*, *24*, 397–427.

Schultz, T. (1960). Capital formulation by education. *Journal of Political Economy*, *68*, 571–583.

Serpell, R. (1999). Local accountability to rural conditions: A challenge to educational planning in Africa. In F. Leach & A. Little (Eds.), *Education, cultures and economics: Dilemmas for development*. New York: Garland.

Sivasubramaniam, M., & Mundy, K. (2006). Kenya: Civil society participation and the governance of educational systems in the context of sector-wide approaches to basic education. Toronto, OISE/University of Toronto; Mimeo.

Sperling, G. (2001). Toward universal education: Making a promise and keeping it. *Foreign Affairs*, *80*, 7–13.

Stasavage, D. (2005). Democracy and educational spending in Africa. *American Journal of Political Science*, *49*, 343–358.

Stiglitz, J. (2003). *Globalization and its discontents*. New York: W. W. Norton.

Stromquist, N. (1999). Women's education in the twenty-first century. In R. F. Arnove & C. A. Torres (Eds.), *Comparative education: The dialectic of the global and the local*. New York: Rowan and Littlefield.

Therein, J. P. (2004). The politics of international development: Towards a new grand compromise? *Economic Policy and Law: Journal of Trade and Environmental Studies, Special Issue*.

Thiongo'o, N. W. (1986a). *Decolonising the mind: The politics of language in African literature*. Portsmouth, NH: Heinemann.

Thiongo'o, N. W. (1986b). *A grain of wheat*. Oxford: Heinemann.

Torres, R. M. (2000). *One decade of education for all: The challenge ahead*. Buenos Aires: International Institute of Educational Planning.

UN Millennium Project. (2005). Toward universal primary education: Investments, incentives and institutions [prepared by the Task Force on Education and Gender Equality]. London, Earthscan and the UN Millennium Project.

UNESCO. (2005). *Education for all global monitoring report 2005: The quality imperative*. Paris, UNESCO.

United Nations. (2001). United Nations millennium declaration. *United Nations UN Resolution A/RES/55/3*. New York: United Nations.

Vavrus, F. (2005). Adjusting inequality: Education and structural adjustment policies in Tanzania. *Harvard Educational*, *75*, 174–201.

Willis, P. (1981). *Learning to labour*. New York: Columbia University Press.

World Bank. (2002). *Achieving Education for All by 2015, Simulation results for 47 low income countries*. Washington, DC: World Bank.

PETER MCLAREN AND NATHALIA JARAMILLO

CRITICAL PEDAGOGY, LATINO/A EDUCATION, AND THE POLITICS OF CLASS STRUGGLE

Teaching in the Belly of the Beast

> Fox News host John Gibson: "Do your duty. Make more babies. That's a lesson drawn out of two interesting stories over the last couple of days. First, a story yesterday that half of the kids in this country under five years old are minorities. By far, the greatest number are Hispanic. You know what that means? Twenty-five years and the majority of the population is Hispanic. Why is that? Well, Hispanics are having more kids than others. Notably, the ones Hispanics call 'gabachos'—white people—are having fewer."
>
> Retrieved from AlterNet, December 28, 2006 at http://www.alternet.org/mediaculture/45983/.

Due to the fact that critical pedagogy constitutes a narrative of universal emancipation (at least those versions that have escaped attempts by post-modernists and neoliberals to domesticate them), critics on both the political left and the right not only have dismissed its politics as yet another example of the colonizing incarnations of the Western educational canon but also have rejected it as a valid means for social transformation. They have accused it of possessing, among other toxic attributes, an outdated and historically discredited working-class triumphalism premised on vulgar economic reductionism that should have been abandoned long before Fukuyama (1989) famously announced that the teething pains of capitalism were over and that liberal capitalist democracy had finally ascended to the zenith of humankind's ideological achievements through its ultimate victory over its conquered rival ideologies of hereditary monarchy, fascism, and more recently communism.1 Of course, the primary object of attack is Marxist theory itself, which has been making some significant inroads of late within the critical pedagogy literature (thanks to scholars such as Glenn Rikowski, Dave Hill, Ramin Farahmandpur, Noah Delissovoy, Mike Cole, Gregory Martin, Deb Kelsh, Juha Suoranta, and others), more specifically as the central theoretical armature of the critique of the globalization of capitalism and the pauperization of the working masses in the wake of recent 'free trade' agreements and the economic and military imperialism of the Bush Jr. administration. In this chapter, we attempt to discuss critical pedagogy in light of what we perceive to be the importance and efficacy of Marxist theory, particularly within the Marxist humanist tendency. We

S.A. Moore and R.C. Mitchell (eds.), Power, Pedagogy and Praxis: Social Justice in the Globalized Classroom, 125–148.

have chosen to accomplish this as part of a larger discussion of Latina/o education in the United States.

Our central position is that by grounding critical pedagogy in Marx's critique of political economy, educators are better able to challenge not only the exploitation of human labor that is endemic to capitalist society with its law of value, private property, and production for monetary return but also the assault on civil rights and human dignity that can be traced to the policy- making practices of the Anglosphere, not least of which has been directed at Latina/o populations through institutionalized forms of White supremacy and capitalist patriarchy.

Capitalist society requires that we routinely perform our labor in schools, in factories, in churches, at the voting booth, and on the picket line and that we educate ourselves to enhance our labor power (McLaren & Farahmandpur, 1999a, 1999b, 2000, 2001a, 2001b; McLaren & Jaramillo, 2002, 2004; McLaren & Martin, 2003; see also Rikowski, 2001a, 2001b). Consequently, we have borrowed the term used by Paula Allman (1999, 2001) *revolutionary critical pedagogy*—to emphasize critical pedagogy as a means for reclaiming public life that is under the relentless assault of the corporatization and privatization of the life world, including the corporate/academic complex. This is not a reclamation of the public sphere through an earnest reinvigoration of the social commons but its socialist transformation (McLaren, in press). The term *revolutionary critical pedagogy* seeks to identify the realm of unfreedom as that in which labor is determined by external utility and to make the division of labor coincide with the free vocation of each individual and the association of free producers, where the force of authority does not flow from the imposition of an external structure but from the character of the social activities in which individuals are freely and consciously engaged. Freedom as we are conceiving it, is freedom from necessity. Here, the emphasis is not only on denouncing the manifest injustices of neo-liberal capitalism, critiquing the current global crisis of overproduction, stagnation, and environmental ruin and on creating a counterforce to neo-liberal ideological hegemony but also on establishing the conditions for new social arrangements that transcend the false opposition between the market and the state.

Accompanied by what some have described as the "particular universalism" of Marxist analysis as opposed to the "universal particularism" of the postmodernists, critical educators collectively assert—all with their own unique focus and distinct disciplinary trajectory—that the term *social justice* all too frequently operates as a cover for legitimizing capitalism or for tacitly admitting to or resigning oneself to its brute intractability. Consequently, it is essential to develop a counterpoint to the way social justice is conceptualized and practiced in progressive education. This stipulates not only a critical examination of the epistemological and axiological dimensions of social democracy but also a contrapuntal critique of the political economy of capitalist schooling so that teachers and students may begin to reclaim public life from its location within the corporate-academic complex in particular and the military-industrial complex in general while acknowledging in both cases their violent insinuation into the social division of labor and capitalism's law of value. Amid the Bush regime's star-spangled war on hope, "full spectrum dominance" and freedom, post-Marxists and anti-Marxist educators have intensified their assault on anti-capitalist perspectives within the field of critical pedagogy. It is not surprising that this is the case, especially since Bush has declared the "war on terror" to be a war against regimes under the gnarled thumb of Old Scratch, regimes which the boy emperor has likened to totalitarian (i.e., Marxist) regimes of the Cold War. Consider his commentary during a West Point address in 2002:

> Because the war on terror will require resolve and patience, it will also require firm moral purpose. In this way our struggle is similar to the Cold War. Now, as then, our enemies are totalitarians, holding a creed of power with no place for human dignity. Now, as then, they seek to impose a joyless conformity to control every life and all of life. (cited in Domke, 2004, p. 112)

One wonders how the illegal and murderous deployment of cluster bombs, depleted uranium ordinances, white phosphorous shells, MK 77, SMAWNE thermobaric urban destruction bombs, and invasions of sovereign countries such as Iraq that kill, by some estimates, in excess of a hundred thousand civilians, contributes to what Bush Jr. refers to above as "human dignity". It has not escaped our notice that once the evil empires of the Cold War fell, new ones were created quickly to fill in the gap. They were created so that the actions of local despots of 'rogue regimes', such as Saddam Hussein and Manuel Noriega, could serve as justification for U.S. military intervention. The real despots are of a much larger scale—Bush, Blair and members of the transnational elite—but you won't find them sitting in the dock for war crimes. You will find them at their vacation villas sunbathing their buffed and thonged consciences in the glare of unreason and imperial arrogance.

J. Martin Rochester's (2003) "Critical Demogogues: The Writings of Henry Giroux and Peter McLaren," published in the Hoover Institute's flagship education journal, *Education Next*, constitutes a representative neoconservative assault on critical pedagogy. Demogoguery apparently is only acceptable when it is practiced by the leader of the world's sole superpower. A pedagogy designed to challenge the lies and deceptions of the U.S. ruling class and to counter the prevailing influence of neoliberal reform efforts (especially given the enfeebling efforts of the National Educational Association and the American Federation of Teachers to redress standards-based accountability measures) must be denounced in the name of democracy and objectivity by both liberals and neoconservatives. One of Rochester's (2003) charges against critical pedagogy is that it contributes to the development of a left-wing anti-intellectualism by means of emphasizing ideology over inquiry. For Rochester (2003), critical pedagogy is nothing less than a "chiliastic movement." Instead of participating in what are alleged to be critical pedagogy's pernicious forms of ideological indoctrination, Rochester sets the goal for teaching in terms redolent of a mawkish eulogy, maintaining that teachers must "reaffirm education as that which promotes," in the words of an 1830 Yale University report, "The Discipline and Furniture of the Mind." Rochester contends that it is impossible to teach a social justice agenda and at the same time foster a solid foundation of knowledge and understanding, a love of learning, and the tools for pursuing that learning. The latter, not the former, should be the first principle of education. The debates over values and truths should, Rochester argues, "be guided by a disposition toward objectivity, the spirit of free inquiry, and academic integrity rather than by chiliastic movements."

According to this assessment—what some critical theorists might refer to as a suprahistorical ethics of pure intentionality—not even history shaking movements such as a national literacy campaign can ever be guided by anything but craven self-interest, and therefore, revolution always makes for bad pedagogy. What fails to get explored by Rochester is exactly what is meant by the term *ideology*. As criticalists know, to employ ideologically free research practices is a Tantalusian illusion. The theoretical languages we use in our pursuit of knowledge about the social world become attributes of the actions of that world, they become part of our own self-comprehension. There is no laissez faire, universal-neutral methodology as theory and fact stand in a dialectical relationship to each other.

Seemingly objective facts are always already socially and historically produced or mediated (often as the reified thought of the bourgeoisie). Ideology achieves its purpose when it is able to erase evidence of its presence and often we are aware of its presence only retroactively, when it has exhausted its welcome and is replaced with another ideological effect. Here, we are not claiming that ideology is a purely passive social relation (i.e., determined by the economic base in a linear fashion), because ideological effects may react back on economic forces, reshaping the ideological field in general. What we are claiming is that Rochester lives in a perfumed world of unimpaired optimism where pedagogy is both taught and practiced from the fertile verdure of Mount Olympus, from the lazy sinecure of common sense, from an unsullied world of science where his categories of analysis are grounded in what seems to be the ontologically necessary dimensions of human existence—a perspective that itself is shrouded in a debilitating epistemological positivism. Rochester fails to understand how theory is a type of practice raised to consciousness. The 'theory' known as revolutionary critical pedagogy is both partisan and objective. It is partisan in that it prefigures the end of wage labor, property relations, and the social relations of capitalist exploitation. It is objective in that it addresses the materiality of life produced through human labor. Objectivity, grounded in class struggle, is the material condition of truth (Zavarzadeh, 2003). This insight would be useful for Rochester when attempting to understand critical pedagogy's methodological requirements for a unity of theory and practice. Rochester's own position of research as ideologically disinterested is a fraudulent and irresponsible claim as it assumes that research transcends its institutional technology and distinct historical configurations of power, knowledge, and social relations of production.

It represents the methodological practices of specific and historical subjects often in conflict among themselves. His normative epistemological pretensions and disposition towards heteronomy are inescapably illusory and enshrine in the language of objective science the interests of a particular social and political class disguised as general social interests. Inquiry that fails to address the social relations of production and totalizing epistemes that historically mediate the research question itself is not worthy of the name. Consequently, it is not surprising that the Hoover institute would support a critique of critical pedagogy under the banner of an ideologically purged pedagogy, given its own ideological allegiance to the imperialist imperatives of the current White House administration and other neoconservative organizations.

EMPIRE, THE CRUSH OF CIVILIZATION, AND POLITICS OF LATINO/A EDUCATION

> Right-wing pundit Ann Coulter on Rep. Maxine Waters, D-Calif., an African-American: "Congresswoman Maxine Waters had parachuted into Connecticut earlier in the week to campaign against [Sen. Joseph I.] Lieberman because he once expressed reservations about affirmative action, without which she would not have a job that didn't involve wearing a paper hat. Waters also considers Joe 'soft' on the issue of the CIA inventing crack cocaine and AIDS to kill all the black people in America." Retrieved from AlterNet, December 28, 2006 at: <http://www.alternet.org/mediaculture/45983/>

> Nationally syndicated radio host Neal Boortz on Rep. Cynthia McKinney's (D-Ga.) hairstyle: "She looks like a ghetto slut. ... It looks like an explosion in a Brillo pad factory. ... She looks like Tina Turner peeing on an electric fence. ... She looks like a shih tzu!" Boortz on McKinney's hairstyle (again): "I saw Cynthia McKinney's hairdo yesterday–saw it on TV. I don't blame that cop for stopping her. It looked like a welfare drag queen was trying to sneak into the Longworth House Office Building. That hairdo is ghetto trash. I don't blame them for stopping her." (Retrieved from AlterNet, February 29, 2008 at: http://www.alternet.org/mediaculture/45983/).

Since September 11, 2001, Bush has arrogated to himself the role of the Grand Panjandrum of the "civilized world" (i.e., the world with the most sophisticated military technology, the most powerful army, and a political administration that possesses the will and the determination to put those assets to use wherever and whenever it feels its national interests [i.e., profits] threatened). The Bush cabal's cunning political prestidigitations enabled it to govern the country with lies under the shibboleth of "exporting democracy" and those who were not hoodwinked and spoke out against such mass deception were labeled enemies of civilization (but why, we ask, did the U.S. not depose the regimes of Spain's Franco, Indonesia's Suharto, or Chile's Pinochet?). Imperialism's grand legacy of racism and White supremacy that has accompanied the virulent backlash against Marxist-driven instantiations of critical pedagogy is also affecting the agonistic terrain of Latina/o education in the United States. Are we not experiencing today the aftershocks of colonialism? And perhaps some new tremors? Ignoring the legacy of colonialism only worsens its effects. Pope Benedict XVI, who as Cardinal Joseph Ratzinger headed the Congregation for the Doctrine of the Faith (organized much the same way as when it was known as the Holy Inquisition), was a founding board member with "Neilsy" Bush of the Foundation for Interreligious and Intercultural Research and Dialogue that was created in Geneva Switzerland in 1999. Ratzinger, we might recall, made a famous intervention into George Bush's 2004 election, condemning any Catholic who voted for Kerry to having formally cooperated in evil because Kerry supports a woman's right to choose. Now this same Ratzinger, as Pope Benedict XVI, has condemned Marxism and unbridled capitalism for the problems facing Latin America. Recently in Aperecida, Brazil, he again attacked grassroots Catholic activists who were still influenced by liberation theology, a theology he tried to crush when he was a cardinal. While in Brazil, he made the outrageous claim that indigenous populations had welcomed the European priests who had arrived with the conquistadores, claiming that they had been "silently longing" for Christianity. He also said that colonial-era evangelization involving the proclaiming of Jesus and his Gospel "did not at any point involve an alienation of the pre-Colombus cultures, nor was it the imposition of a foreign culture." President Hugo Chavez of Venezuela has joined indigenous groups in condemning the Pope's remarks, claiming that Benedict XVI has ignored the enslavement and genocide of indigenous peoples in Latin America and the destruction of their native cultures, and has also ignored what in some cases amounts to the complicity of the Catholic Church in such violence and destruction. President Chavez proclaimed that "the bones of the indigenous martyrs of these lands are still burning." Clearly the legacy of colonial violence lives on, and not only in Latin America, but in North America as well. We see it's offspring today.

The defining principle underlying national policy initiatives (i.e., English- only propositions, anti-immigrant initiatives, and the No Child Left Behind Act of 2001) that both implicitly and explicitly target the education of Latina/o students is what we have termed *the politics of erasure*. Unilaterally designed to erase students' native language, national origin, and cultural formations, these initiatives arise out of an era marked by heightened nationalism and its attendant "fear factor" that views anyone outside of the xenophobic U.S. monoculture as a threat to U.S. citizenship. National policies reflect the larger capitalist ideology that dehumanizes those who do not conform, that disqualifies certain segments of the human race from full participation as citizens and instantiates a rhetoric of depersonalization. As a direct result of their demographic numbers, Latina/os have become both objects of inclusion (through assimilationist efforts) and exclusion (by restricting their access and opportunity to a quality education) in educational politics. On the surface, the politics of erasure seeks to incorporate a burgeoning Latina/o population into the economic, social, and cultural spheres of U.S. society. But the repressed underside of such initiatives is reminiscent of efforts designed to safeguard the cultural and linguistic homogeneity of what Gilbert Gonzalez (2001) has termed the "Ideology and Practice of Empire." Within this framework, education is perceived as the major apparatus of assimilating and acculturating a growing Latina/o population into the economic and social dimensions of an increasingly imperial and militaristic Pax Americana.

Unearthing and naming the ostensibly hidden narratives and ideological underpinnings of education policy is a necessary counterpoint to the reigning initiatives that evoke, at times, the popular support of Latina/os in pursuit of achieving the gross material benefits associated with American nationality. It is essential, therefore, that policy initiatives be understood in terms of their historical specificity, especially as this affects their functional imperatives for nation-states, which includes administering a commodity centered economy and its division of social labor (San Juan, 2002).

In education policy, the rhetoric of positive nationalism (i.e., equal opportunity for all) occludes both the racialized ideologies and class interests of the political elite who act either willingly or unknowingly—in the service of maintaining internal cultural homogeneity and an internal colonialism. One need only witness comments made recently by former House Speaker Newt Gingrich about bilingual education, in order to grasp the culture of the Anglosphere: "The American people believe English should be the official language of the government...We should replace bilingual education with immersion in English so people learn the common language of the country and then learn the language of prosperity, not the language of living in a ghetto" (Hunt, 2007, p. A20). When Gingrich said this to an audience of 100 members of the National Federation of Republican Women, the audience burst into wild cheering (Hunt, 2007, p. A20). Especially in light of today's war on terrorism, Latina/o entrepreneurs are needed to legitimize the economic objectives of the capitalist elite and provide ballast to the existing social division of labor, just as the rural and urban poor and middle class are needed as frontline troops in the country's imperialist wars. As an instructive example, consider the recent arguments set forth by the pugnacious and ideologically repulsive Harvard Professor Samuel Huntington. Huntington's (2004) commentary is predictably aligned to the ideological imperatives of U.S. citizenship. Addressing the issue of Mexican immigrants who have not assimilated into mainstream U.S. culture, forming instead their own political and linguistic enclaves, he writes the following: "There is no Americano dream. There is only the American dream created by an Anglo-Protestant society. Mexican-Americans will share in that dream and in that society only if they dream in English" (2004, p. 45). In linguistics, we would refer to the aforementioned coupling as cognates, but in Huntington's context, that speaks directly to the reactionary segments of the Anglo-Protestant population that he depicts, they represent two separate and incommensurable worlds divided by language, culture, and values. In his enfeebled defense of the Anglosphere as the sacerdotal eyrie of U.S citizenship, Huntington cites a number of scholars who characterize Latina/os, primarily those of Mexican decent, as a monolithic cultural group that possesses a "lack of initiative, self-reliance, and ambition" and has "little use for education; and acceptance of poverty as a virtue necessary for entrance into heaven" (2004, p. 44). Huntington's nativism is an unholy alliance of xenophobia and racism masquerading as a defense of the cultural identity of the U.S. (not to mention as scholarship). When seen in the context of critical pedagogy, Huntington's 'patriotism' is anything but a pleasant fiction of creating a vibrant democracy. Huntington's alarmist screed, premised on an unstated fear that

Mexican immigrants might one day engage in a reconquest of the U.S. Southwest, betrays at once a fear of the decline of an Anglo-Protestant majority and a defense of free-market capitalism. Such views are neither new nor limited to depicting the Latina/o population. The rise of industrialization, the emergence of world wars, the collapse of statist Communism and reformist Social Democracy and their replacement by "rogue regimes" as ideological counterpoints to "free market democracy", and the creation of the United States as the world's sole superpower has exacerbated an "us versus them" discourse that legitimizes cultural, political, military, and economic domination and mordantly attributes the 'dirt' that is 'out of place' in the living rooms of the ruling class to the immigrant Other. Huntington's work is but an academic gimcrack, the kind of crass racism you might find in a seaport bar only dressed up in the iron breastplate of the Angel of History—acrimonious ignorance disguised as moral profundity blown into our minds by a storm from paradise. It is the scholarly umbrage in which the most vile human sentiments take refuge from the light of reason. This is but a decaffeinated version of the eliminationist fantasy of conservative commentator, William Bennet, dressed up in language of serious scholarship. But we can clearly see the coxcomb pulled over Huntington's furrowed brow.

"LATINA/O": HISTORICAL AND MATERIAL DIMENSIONS

To understand the ways in which the education of Latina/o youth are being affected by what we term a *politics of erasure*, it is necessary to fully define *Latina/o*. We consider it important to highlight the arguments posited by Martha Gimenez (1997), who suggests that ethnic labels such as *Latino* or *Hispanic* work not only to solidify the negative stereotyping associated with that group but also to hide and deemphasize both the differences and similarities across ethnic enclaves. By differences, we are suggesting that Latina/os constitute a population of wide variation—across class and other social dimensions—and that they do not, by any measure, share or ascribe to an organic or pure cultural identity. By similarities, we are also suggesting that Latina/os, when viewed as individuals situated along an historical and material continuum differentiated by class status, share traits, experiences, and values with other "non-Latino" groups. The process of Americanization, acculturation, or assimilation is not a uniform process for Latina/os. Gimenez (1997) is particularly insightful on this point: "Dialectically... culture is not a thing one learns or unlearns (thus becoming acculturated): It is the lived experience of people shaped by their location in the class and socioeconomic stratification systems" (p. 231). In light of Gimenez's observation, it is necessary to view Latina/os as a social group in all of their iterations and to consider the material backdrop of their cultural formations (see Kincheloe & Steinberg, 1997). Here the alienation of Latina/o youth can best be understood by investing the ontological concept of alienation with social, historical, and economic content. Here, we take the position that although race, class, and gender invariably intersect and interact, they are not coprimary. We conceptualize class antagonism or struggle as one in a series of social antagonisms (race, class, gender, etc.) but argue that class most often sustains the conditions that produce and reproduce the other antagonisms. This is not, however, to argue that we can simply reduce racism or sexism to class. In other words, class struggle is the specific antagonism, the generative matrix that helps to structure and shape the particularities of the other antagonisms. It creates their conditions of possibility. The material basis of race and gender antagonisms can be traced to the means and relations of production within capitalist society—to the social division of labor that occurs when workers sell their labor power for a wage to the capitalist (i.e., to the ownership of the means of production). Regrettably, class exploitation is a topic that is very often ignored within schools of education. When it is discussed, it frequently deliquesces into a discussion of unequal resource distribution, and this ignores the fact that exploitation is a fundamental character of capitalism, that it is constituent of the labor-capital relation. Class struggle is a determining force that structures in advance the very agonistic terrain in which other political, racial, and gender antagonisms take place. However, we want to underscore that that in no way does this position ignore forms of nonclass domination. John Bellamy Foster (2005) makes an important observation when he writes the following:

> The various forms of non-class domination are so endemic to capitalist society, so much a part of its strategy of divide and conquer, that no progress can be made in overcoming class oppression without also fighting—sometimes even in advance of the class struggle—these other social divisions. (p. 17)

Among U.S. institutions, public schools bear the greatest burden to bring youth and their families into the neo-liberal regime. For educators such as Stanley Aronowitz (2004), schools serve as the primary mechanism to connect children and their families to the full spectrum of social life. Social life, in these terms, includes broad notions of citizenship, but it also, and perhaps most importantly, suggests the cultivation of a laboring citizen body. Aronowitz argues that

> the common school is charged with the task of preparing children and youth for their dual responsibilities to the social order: citizenship and, perhaps its primary task, learning to labor. On the one hand, in the older curriculum on the road to citizenship in a democratic secular society, schools are supposed to transmit the jewels of the enlightenment, especially literature and science. On the other hand, students are to be prepared for the work world by means of a loose but definite stress on the redemptive value of work, the importance of family, and of course the imperative of love and loyalty of one's country. (Introduction, 1.1)

We concur for the most part with Aronowitz's (2004) description of the public school, and we find it particularly relevant for Latina/os and other immigrant groups struggling assiduously on the margins for full incorporation into the dominant landscape of U.S. society. The notion that schools must ultimately shape and form future generations under the mantra of democracy-building or "loving one's country" becomes a necessary tool for policy makers and other members of the capitalist elite to justify pedagogical programs and initiatives designed to homogenize and unify a seemingly varied population. What is often overlooked is the role that schools play in serving as vehicles of profit maximization and in sustaining a commodity-centered economy predicated on the social division of labor. It is here that the linkages between the expansion of capital and schooling become more opaque—in terms of schools becoming transformed into commodities (through increased privatization) and in their role as commodity-producing (human labor power) institutions. Government-sponsored commissions clearly capture the interplay between schools, labor, capital, and citizenship. A report commissioned in 2003 on behalf of the G. W. Bush administration, *From Risk to Opportunity, Hispanics in the U.S.*, outlines these very relations. The report states that

> if the employment picture does not change, the economic consequences of an uneducated workforce will strain the economy of the United States. Hispanics are not maximizing their income potential or developing financial security. This leads to lost tax revenues, lower rates of consumer spending, reduced per capita savings and increased social costs. (p. 3)

This narrative antiseptically reduces the failed economic participation of Latina/os to an itemized list of discrete educational factors (see Miron & Inda, 2000). Against a backdrop of characteristics such as limited parent involvement, poor academic instruction and a lack of English or teacher accountability, an investment in school "improvement" is considered the only viable alternative toward eliminating the fiscal and social "crisis" associated with the Latinization of the United States. The Commission asserts that "school improvement may be an expensive short-term investment, but the ultimate profit resulting from an educated Hispanic workforce is much greater" (National Council of La Raza [NCLR], 2004, p. 3). When Latina/os' participation in the labor market is contrasted against indicators that measure their integration in education and other aspects of social life, the stage is set to "reform" or "rectify" those conditions associated with what is perceived as "failed assimilation." Across ethnic groups, Latina/os have the highest high school dropout rate, nearly 28%, and for newly arrived immigrants, the dropout rate stands at 40% (NCLR, 2004). Only 1 in 10 Latina/os ages 25 and older have received a bachelor's degree or higher, yet in the year 2002, nearly 1 in 5 of all those incarcerated in the United States were Latino (NCLR, 2004, p. 11). Close to 5 million English language learners reside in the United States, with the overwhelming majority being Spanish speakers. In the 2000-2001 period, Latina/os represented 10% of the school-aged population in the nation, a number that is expected to increase exponentially in the coming decades. When the "Latina/o experience" is viewed against these statistics, it provides the fuel and impetus for policy makers to create and implement educational initiatives to reverse the trend of so-called Latina/o failure. Such is the rationale behind increased standardization (as a way to equalize educational inputs and outcomes) of curriculum, testing mechanisms, and instructional techniques. For Latina/os and other segments of the population clinging to the rhetoric of positive nationalism, education policies conceived in this vein are configured and ideologically refitted ith irresistible appeal. But ultimately, such efforts come at the expense of an often cruel and violent pedagogy of dehumanization that places the burden on the young and "unacculturated" to adopt "ways of being" that are, indeed, foreign and alien.

The very system that incorporates Latina/os and other immigrant groups into the dominant "Whitestream" society is the same system that seeks to alienate them from their local histories, their culture, and the location where their knowledge is most readily inscribed, namely their language (Maldonado-Torres, 2004). Language, which serves to classify, categorize, and label human essence, relies on the process of internalization. Here, we are conceiving the process of internalization largely in relation to the function of language in identity formation. In other words, language represents a core construct of our subjectivity and the bulwark of our modes of self and-social-identification. In the words of Gloria Anzaldúa (1987), "ethnic identity is twin skin to linguistic identity—I am my language. Until I can take pride in my language, I cannot take pride in myself" (p. 81). With language valorized as the essentialized component of nationality and identity, English-only movements profoundly affect the Latina/o experience in public schools. Starting in California, with Proposition 227, an initiative that legally dismantled bilingual education instruction, and followed by similar propositions in Arizona and unsuccessful attempts in Colorado and Massachusetts, bilingual education is consistently thrust into politically pernicious and ideologically heated debates that negatively affect language minority students.

Although language policy has historically been sanctioned at the level of the state, the federal government's reauthorization of the Elementary and Secondary Education Act and the *No Child Left Behind Act* of 2001 marked a reversal of language policy by stressing the acquisition of English skills only (Crawford, 2002). By eliminating any reference to the term *bilingual*, by mandating achievement tests that measure the acquisition of English over subject-matter content (Abedi & Dietel, 2004), and by attaching a strict system of punishment and rewards to test results, the U.S. government has solidified a neocolonial model of education that legitimizes the sustained subordination of groups that fall short of gaining full membership into the dominant discourses of U.S. citizenship. Gutierrez, Asato, Santos, and Gotanda (2001) have referred to this phenomenon as "backlash pedagogy" rooted in "backlash politics, products of ideological and institutional structures that legitimize and thus maintain privilege, access and control of the sociopolitical terrain" (p. 337). In a similar vein, Donaldo Macedo (2000) writes that English-only initiatives are present-day forms of colonialism, designed to subordinate groups through the loss of their human citizenship. In conjunction with initiatives that support anti-immigrant hysteria (Proposition 209 in California, the elimination of the Immigrant Education Program in No Child Left Behind 2001) and measures to eradicate affirmative action programs, we are constantly reminded that becoming "American," from the standpoint of education policy, is an atrophic process that denies the full development of human subjectivity. This sentiment is clearly expressed in Gingrich's recent repugnant accusation that bilingualism poses "long-term dangers to the fabric of our nation" and that "allowing bilingualism to continue to grow is very dangerous" (Hunt, 2007, p. A20).

REVOLUTIONARY CRITICAL PEDAGOGY AS MARXIST HUMANISM

> Nationally syndicated radio host Rush Limbaugh, blaming America's "obesity crisis" on "the left," "liberal government," and "food stamps": "Because we are sympathetic, we are compassionate people, we have responded by letting our government literally feed these people to the point of obesity. At least here in America, didn't teach them how to fish, we gave them the fish. Didn't teach them how to butcher a – slaughter a cow to get the butter, we gave them the butter. The real bloat here, as we know, is in—is in government." (Retrieved from AlterNet, December 28, 2006 at: http://www.alternet.org/mediaculture/45983/)

As critical educators, we reject the notion that Latina/os and other marginalized student groups must selectively choose between the inflexible yet complementary tension of Americanism or un-Americanism, a binary construction that sets up a perfidious false opposition on which to base the concept of U.S. citizenship. We also reject the notion that schools must ultimately service the needs of capital rather than the humanizing needs of children and their families (De Lissovoy & McLaren, 2003). We denounce as well the reorganization of cultural hegemony and symbolic capital through the use of English as the only medium of classroom instruction—a nativist ploy to use monolingual "immersion" English classrooms to delegitimate or erase the daily lived experiences of linguistic minorities who are oppressed by a class-divided, racialized, and gendered social order, and to immure them inside a civic culture predicated upon property rights and the capitalist law of value production. At the same time, we are aware of the complex set of social relations that have compelled millions of working class and poor people from Latin America to leave their countries of origin in search of a viable alternative. The creation of composite national identities and the lived tensions and contradictions confronted in every aspect of social life in the United States by "immigrants" or "exiles" compels us to articulate a humanizing critical pedagogy that is rooted in the cultural, spiritual, and linguistic dimensions of everyday life. But a humanizing pedagogy is also grounded in a critique of the material social relations and practices associated with contemporary capitalist formations.

We have made an effort to note that the exploitation of our human capacity to labor (labor power) is not limited to regional or national geographical spaces alone. Rather, Latina/os in the United States and abroad are implicated in a web of transnational relations linked to the accumulation of capital and extraction of surplus value. Moving from the center to the periphery, it is instructive for us to engage critically social movements and popular education initiatives in Latin America as illustrative sites toward a humanizing critical pedagogy. Our own work in Venezuela in support of the Bolivarian revolution has taught us some of the promises and possibilities of a people who refuse to become peons within a transnational elite protectorate stage managed by Washington.

Determined to defeat US imperialism and the transnational capitalist class, Bolivarian educators are struggling to expand critical pedagogy throughout the country. President Chavez's own words to us at Miraflores palace—"be inspired by the Bolivarian revolution in your pedagogical work"—is advice we would offer teachers in the United States. Aleida Guevara March, daughter of Ernesto Che Guevara, offered us similar advice during a recent conversation in Havana, Cuba—to infuse our work with a profound respect for the creative capacity of humanity. In our ongoing work in Venezuela, we have been greatly impressed by the Bolivarian missions and their emphasis on human development and the creative capacity of all individuals to create democratic social formations able to address local needs in the context of a larger project of human emancipation by means of political transformation. These missions consist of anti-poverty and social welfare programs. We were fortunate to be able to visit some of them.

In one year, the Chavez government was able to graduate 1, 430,000 Venezuelans from Mission Robinson, a program launched in June 2003. Volunteers who work for Mission Robinson teach reading, writing, and arithmetic to illiterate adults using the "Yo Si Puedo" ("Yes I can") method developed in Cuba. This method uses a combination of video classes and texts which, in only 7 weeks, bring students to a basic literacy level. Indigenous peoples are taught to read and write in Spanish and in their own languages, in line with the indigenous rights outlined in the 1999 Bolivarian Constitution, Articles 199, 120 and 121. (Mission Robinson International has just been launched in Bolivia). Mission Robinson II provides basic education up to 6th grade, and Mission Robinson III teaches functional literacy and links these efforts to the creation of production units.) Mission Ribas, a two-year remedial secondary school program (that teaches Spanish, mathematics, world geography, Venezuelan economics, world history, Venezuelan history, English, physics, chemistry, biology, and computer science), targets five million Venezuelan dropouts. This program has a Community and Social-labor Component, where groups use their personal experience and their learning to develop practical proposals to solve community problems. We were fortunate enough to join in a group discussion of this component of the program in Barrio La Vega, and were especially impressed with the efforts of students there to design a day care center. Unemployed graduates of Mission Ribas (known as "lanceros") are encouraged to enroll in Mission Vuelvan Caras (About Face), where they receive training in endogenous development and are eventually incorporated into the formal economy. Mission Sucre provides a scholarship program in higher education to the most impoverished sectors of Venezuela, graduating university professionals in thee years as opposed to the traditional five years. Our work in an international think tank based in Caracas, Centro International Miranda, has six areas of focus in helping to further the Bolivarian Revolution. One of these areas is critical pedagogy. Whether Venezuela is marching in a truly socialist direction or will remain mired in a statist, topdown approach like the Lassalleans of the Gotha Program, remains to be seen. We remain optimistic.

A fundamental axiom of a critical humanizing pedagogy is a respect accorded to students' language and cultural identity. It begins, in the words of Antonia Darder (2002), "with the view that all human beings participate actively in producing meaning and thus reinforces a dialectical and contextual view of knowledge" (p. 135). Cultural workers in this tradition ask students to recollect the past; to situate the present socially, politically, and economically; and to strive toward a future built on a utopian universality. Such a utopia (we stress here a 'concrete' utopia built on a deep understanding of the present as distinct from an 'abstract' utopia premised on an idealist reading of the future) has the potential to create the conditions for groups to liberate themselves in their own contextually specific ways from all forms of oppression, exploitation, alienation, and degradation. A pedagogy built upon these perspectives and practices seeks to understand the underlying motives, interests, desires, and fears of draconian shifts in education policy, and it contests ascribed methods of producing knowledge. To challenge the erasure of students' cultural and subjective formations, a humanizing critical pedagogy refashions dialectically our self and social formation by challenging normative notions of citizenship and by underscoring what it means to be the subject rather than the object of history.

However, we clearly need more than a new normative foundation for a critical cultural cosmopolitanism; we also need a major shift in the mode of production. In addition to cultural solutions, workers need to seize political power on behalf of workers. Yet—in itself—this does little to eradicate the capitalist law of value. Moving beyond the capitalist law of value is a challenge that can be met by adopting a historical materialist critique and engaging in the struggle for socialism. Criticizing the model of "cultural schizophrenia" that informs the ideological ambivalence of "Chicana/o literature," Marcial Gonzalez (2004) advances a historical materialist critique that we believe is efficacious for the de-domestication of critical pedagogy. Historical materialism is important for Gonzalez, as it is for us, precisely because it "attempts to understand the dialectical relation between the particularities of existence and the larger social frameworks that give them meaning" (p. 180). It also helps us to grasp more fully and more deeply "the relation between universal processes and their local manifestations" (p. 180) in ways that the puerile prospects of postmodernism cannot. Furthermore, historical materialism provides the means for "understanding the complex categories of identity based on race, ethnicity, sexuality and gender, not as autonomous formations but as interconnected processes within the larger dynamics of social relations" (p. 180), so that we are able to recognize "the particularity and relative autonomy of race without jettisoning the causal character of class relations" (p. 181). From such a perspective, reality is perceived not as an absolute truth but as "a set of processes" (p. 181). The purpose of historical materialist critique is not to "correct faulty ideas" (p. 82) analytically but "to negate them" and demystify them as ideological correlates of real contradictions, and in so doing, "to transform them qualitatively" (p. 182).

REVOLUTIONARY CRITICAL PEDAGOGY AS A DIALECTICS OF PRAXIS

> Right-wing pundit Debbie Schlussel on Sen. Barack Obama, D-Ill.: So, even if he identifies strongly as a Christian ... is a man who Muslims think is a Muslim, who feels some sort of psychological need to prove himself to his absent Muslim father, and who is now moving in the direction of his father's heritage, a man we want as president when we are fighting the war of our lives against Islam? Where will his loyalties be?" (Retrieved from AlterNet, December 28, 2006 at: http://www.alternet.org/mediaculture/45983/).

In this section, we attempt to further situate revolutionary critical pedagogy in a Marxist-Hegelian optic, centered on a philosophy of praxis. To perform our revolutionary agency critically is to revisit the dialectical relation of theory and practice. What is important to us are the ideas of social change that are given birth in spontaneous movements and struggles and those developed in theory and made available to the "nonordinary" ordinary people. Raya Dunayevskaya (1973, 1978, 2000, 2002) has rethought Marx's relations to Hegelian dialectics in a profound way; in particular, Hegel's concept of the self movement of the idea from which Marx argued the need to transcend objective reality rather than thought. Dunayevskaya notes how Marx was able to put a living, breathing, and thinking subject of history at the center of the Hegelian dialectic. She also pointed out that what for Hegel is absolute knowledge, Marx referred to as the new society. Although Hegel's self-referential, all-embracing, totalizing absolute is greatly admired by Marx, it was, nevertheless, greatly modified by him. For Marx, absolute knowledge did not absorb objective reality or objects of thought but provided a ground from which objective reality could be transcended. By reinserting the human subject into the dialectic and by defining the subject as corporal being, Marx appropriates Hegel's self-movement of subjectivity as an act of transcendence and transforms it into a critical humanism.

In her rethinking of Marx's relationship to the Hegelian dialectic, Dunayevskaya parts company with Derrida, Adorno, Marcuse, Habermas, Negri, Deleuze, Mészáros, and others (Hudis, 2000, 2004a, 2004b, 2005a, 2005b). She has given absolute negativity a new urgency, linking it not only to the negation of today's economic and political realities but also to developing new human relations. She places a special emphasis on the negation of the negation or what she calls the "second negation." The second negation constitutes drawing out the positive within the negative and expressing the desire of the oppressed for freedom. Second negativity is intrinsic to the human subject as an agent; it is what gives direction and coherence to revolutionary action as praxis. A second negation permits abstract, alienated labor to be challenged by freely associated labor and concrete, human sensuousness. The answer is in envisioning a noncapitalist future that can be achieved, as Hudis (2000) notes, after Dunayevskaya, by means of subjective self-movement through absolute negativity so that a new relation between theory and practice can connect us to the realization of freedom.

Of course, Marx rejects Hegel's idealization and dehumanization of selfmovement through double negation because this leaves untouched alienation in the world of labor-capital relations. Marx sees this absolute negativity as objective movement and the creative force of history. Absolute negativity in this instance becomes a constitutive feature of a self-critical social revolution that, in turn, forms the basis of a permanent revolution. Peter Hudis (2000) raises a number of difficult questions with respect to developing a political project that moves beyond controlling the labor process. It is a project that is directed at abolishing capital itself through the creation of freely associated labor. The creation of a social universe not parallel to the social universe of capital is the challenge here. The form that this post-capitalist society will take is that which has been suppressed within the social universe of capital: socialism, a society based not on value but on the fulfillment of human need.

For Dunayevskaya (2002), absolute negativity entails more than economic struggle but the liberation of humanity from class society. This is necessarily a political and a revolutionary struggle and not only an economic one. This particular insight is what, for us, signals the fertile and protean power of Dunayevskaya's Marxist-humanism, the recognition that Marx isn't talking about class relations only but human relations. Domesticated currents of critical pedagogy are too preoccupied with making changes within civil society or the bourgeois "public sphere," where students are reduced to test scores and their behavior is codified in relation to civic norms. Marx urged us to push beyond this type of materialism that fails to comprehend humanity's sensuous nature and regards humans only as statistics or averaged-out modes of behavior. We need to move toward a new social humanity. This takes us well beyond civil society and the struggle for what has been called "radical democracy." We need to work toward the goal of becoming associated producers, working under conditions that will advance human nature, where the measure of wealth is not labor time but solidarity, creativity, and the full development of human capacities. This can only occur outside the social universe of capital.

Revolutionary critical pedagogy, built on the concept of absolute negativity, is needed to combat the ideological crisis that has occurred as a result of the defeat of communism, socialism, and national liberation movements and the radical wings of social democracy. Of course, one of the immediate goals of a revolutionary critical pedagogy is to work with social movements to disable the Bush administration from conflating leftist revolutionaries with terrorists. Guided by a cabal-like combination of Christian fundamentalists, global robber barons, far-right neo-conservatives, ultranationalists, arms dealers, oil tycoons, and militarists, the U.S. government's pursuit for the role of master and commander of the global capitalist system proceeds apace. Admittedly, it cannot be stopped by a revolutionary critical pedagogy, no matter how powerful its self-reflexive counter performances. But neither can it be effectively challenged without it. Today, it is urgent that we develop a coherent philosophy of praxis, but equally important must be our determination to live in our daily lives, our dialectical self reflexivity, as we navigate the perils of everyday existence and enact a politics of refusal and transformation.

A true renewal of thinking about educational and social reform must pass through a regeneration of Marxist theory if the great and fertile meaning of human rights and equality is to reverberate in the hopes of aggrieved populations throughout the world. A philosophically-driven revolutionary critical pedagogy, one that aspires toward a coherent philosophy of praxis, can help teachers and students grasp the specificity of the concrete within the totality of the universal—for instance, the laws of motion of capital as they operate out of sight of our everyday lives and thus escape our commonsense understanding. Revolutionary critical pedagogy can assist us in understanding history as a process in which human beings make their own society, although in conditions most often not of their own choosing and therefore influenced by the intentions of others. Furthermore, the practice of double negation can help us understand the movement of both thought and action by means of praxis, or what Dunayevskaya called the "philosophy of history."

The philosophy of history proceeds from the messy web of everyday social reality—from the arena of facticity and the tissues of empirical life—and not from lofty abstractions or idealistic concepts gasping for air in the lofty heights of some metaphysical crow's nest. Revolutionary critical educators engage students in a dialectical reading of social life in which "the labor of the negative" helps them to understand human development from the perspective of the wider social totality. By examining Marx's specific appropriation of the Hegelian dialectic, students are able to grasp how the positive is always contained in the negative. In this way, every new society can be grasped as the negation of the preceding one, conditioned by the forces of production, which gives us an opportunity for a new beginning. I think it is certainly a truism that ideas often correspond to the economic structure of society, but at the same time, we need to remember that history is in no way unconditional. The actions of human beings are what shape history. Both Freire and Dunayevskaya stress here that the educator must be educated. The idea that a future society comes into being as a negation of the existing one finds its strongest expression in class struggle. Here, we note that dialectical movement is a characteristic not only of thought but also of life and history itself. And here the outcomes are never guaranteed.

CLASS STRUGGLE IN A GLOBAL CONTEXT

CNN Headline News host Glenn Beck to Rep.-elect Keith Ellison, D-Minn.:

> "OK. No offense, and I know Muslims. I like Muslims. ... With that being said, you are a Democrat. You are saying, 'Let's cut and run.' And I have to tell you, I have been nervous about this interview with you, because what I feel like saying is, 'Sir, prove to me that you are not working with our enemies.'" (Retrieved from AlterNet, December 28, 2006 at: http://www.alternet.org/mediaculture/45983/).

If dialectical praxis within the larger project of class struggle is to serve as the centerpiece of critical revolutionary pedagogy, both in its fight against economic exploitation as well as racism and patriarchy, it is imperative that we chart out the lineaments of our anti-capitalist, pro-socialist struggle. Although it is important to acknowledge that the globalization of capital can be resisted, it is equally important to be aware of the strengths and limitations of our counter-hegemonic strategies and tactics. In short, we need a theory of counter-hegemony. William Robinson (2003) expands on this position:

> Globalization is the *resistible* renewal of capitalism. Globalization is always partial and incomplete, although the aspiration is one of universality and generalization. Any theory of historic change must address the question of how alternative projects arise, how resistance is articulated and how dominant structures are subverted. Theories of capitalist hegemony are incomplete without corresponding theories of counter-hegemony. (p. 319)

Here, Robinson (2003) rehearses Gramsci's distinction between a war of manoeuvre (frontal attack) and a war of position (a protracted struggle as in trench warfare, or in a war of attrition) as follows:

> A war of manoeuvre, associated with the traditional notions of revolution, can potentially succeed when the power that sustains the existing system is situated in a limited number of identifiable sites, like the police, military, etc. But the expansion of the state into new "private" and community realms under capitalism that Gramsci theorized, and the rise of a civil society in which the power of the dominant groups is anchored in ideological and cultural processes, implies that power is no longer limited to a number of sites and is more dispersed and multidimensional. The formal distinction between a war of position and a war of manoeuvre is clearly methodological, not real (organic), in the sense that social struggles involve both dimensions simultaneously. Which may be the most salient in strategies and practices of struggle is a matter of historical conjuncture and collective agency. (pp. 319-320)

Robinson (2003) convincingly argues that we must begin our anti-capitalist struggle with a strategic war of position, the exercise of resistance in the sphere of civil society by popular classes who are able to avoid co-optation and mediation by the nation-state—and this means resistance at the points of accumulation, capitalist production, and the process of social reproduction. Robinson revealingly elaborates this position:

> Social conflicts linked to the reorganization of the world economy will lie at the heart of world politics in the twenty-first century. The challenge is how to reconstruct the social power of the popular classes worldwide in a new era in which such power is not mediated and organized through the nation-state. The universal penetration of capitalism through globalization draws all peoples not only into webs of market relations but also into webs of resistance. (p. 320)

Drawing on the work of Kees van der Pijl, Robinson (2003) maintains that all three moments in the process of the subordination of society and nature to the reproduction of capital—original accumulation, the capitalist production process, and the process of social reproduction—generates its own form of "countermovement" of resistance and struggle. Consequently, it is to the social forces from below engaged in resistance at all three of these moments to which we should turn when developing our own counterhegemonic impulse.

> Robinson has established four fundamental requirements for an effective counter-hegemony that are worth repeating here. First, he argues that we urgently need to build a political force on a broader vision of social transformation that can link social movements and diverse oppositional forces. The resistance of popular classes needs to be unified through a broad and comprehensive "strategy of opposition to the broader structures that generate the particular conditions which each social movement and oppositional force is resisting (p. 321).

The challenge for popular social movements is how to fuse political with social struggles through the development of political instruments that can extend to political society (the state) the counter-hegemonic space currently being opened up in civil society through mass mobilization. Popular classes have nothing to gain by limiting their struggles to local and isolated "sites" of oppression and forsaking the development of a larger project of transformation, a project which includes a struggle against the state.

Here, it is important to "address how oppression and exploitation, and the immediate conditions around which popular sectors are struggling, are linked to and derive from a larger totality, that totality being global capitalism" (Robinson, 2003, p. 322). The organizational forms of a renovated left must include a commitment to supporting autonomous social movements, to social change from the bottom up rather than the top down, to democratic principles and practices within organizations themselves, and to an abandonment of the old verticalism in favor of non hierarchical practices. The second requirement for an effective counter-hegemony is building a viable socioeconomic alternative to global capitalism. To this end, Robinson (2003) asserts the following:

> Beyond calling for a mere change in the particular form of accumulation, a counter-hegemonic alternative needs to challenge the logic of the market in its program and ideology. If not, some new ideology and program designed from above by global elites, such as the so-called "Third Way" promulgated in the United States and the United Kingdom in the late 1990's, may well allow the global capitalist bloc to retain the initiative as crises extend and to forestall the possibilities of more fundamental change. An anti-neo-liberal agenda, however important, must develop into an anti-capitalist—that is, socialist—alternative. (p. 323)

The third requirement is that popular classes need to transnationalize their struggles. This means nothing less than expanding transnational civil society, which serves as an effective countermovement to global capitalism. Robinson (2003) further warns that

> the crisis and eventual collapse of neo-liberalism may create the conditions favorable to winning state power promoting an alternative. It is not clear, however, how effective national alternatives can be in transforming social structures, given the ability of transnational capital to utilize its structural power to impose its project even over states that are captured by forces adverse to that project. (p. 324)

The answer, for Robinson, is the challenging of the global elite "by accumulating counter-hegemonic forces beyond national and regional borders; to challenge that power from within an expanding transnational civil society" (p. 324). In the wake of this aim, his fourth requirement calls on organic intellectuals to henceforth subordinate their work to and in the service of popular majorities and their struggles.

In his latest book, *A Theory of Global Capitalism*, Robinson (2004) further elaborates on what a counter hegemonic movement should look like. He importantly notes that fundamental change in a social order becomes possible when an organic crisis occurs but that such an organic crisis of capitalism is no guarantee against social breakdown, authoritarianism, or fascism. What is necessary is a viable alternative that is in hegemonic ascendance— an appealing alternative to the existing capitalist social order that is perceived as preferable by a majority of society. Although the socialist alternative is unlikely to be considered a viable alternative by the majority of society any time soon, this should not dampen our efforts to bring us closer to that goal.

It is precisely an unyielding commitment to the Other that gives revolutionary critical pedagogy—nourished by Marxist roots—its ethical exigency and its affirmative starting point. Furthermore, it prevents critical educators from being caught in an endless vortex of negativity that previously trapped many critical theorists. In the language of dialectics, revolutionary critical educators negate the negation inflicted on the oppressed. They do so from the perspective of the affirmation of the oppressed. Not only does this negation of the negation have a roborant effect on critical praxis, it is the very bulwark of revolutionary activity.

As long as critical educators ignore the strategic centrality of class struggle (see Scatamburlo-D'Annibale & McLaren, 2003), the more difficult it will be for critical pedagogy to become a powerful catalyst in the ongoing struggle for a socialist democracy. Thus, we argue that a radically rearticulated revolutionary critical pedagogy needs to return to its Marxist roots; we do not use the concept of "returning" in the sense of going back to some prior or originary moment of a linear sequence in time. To return is not to regress but rather to move forward in awakening ourselves to our relationship with living history, which is both the source and destiny of the human subject: the self transcendence of our species being.

Our pedagogical project is directed toward a journey of self-discovery mediated by an infinite hope. Here, hope's infinite movement does not transcend human history but is embodied in finite, sensuous human beings struggling for freedom. As in the case of Hegel's true infinity, critical pedagogy's subject of history moves in and through otherness in the direction of a circle, a movement that returns into itself in its journey of selfawareness. Bad infinity, on the other hand, is a movement lost in the externality of the infinite, one of endless repetition and alienation. It is represented by a straight line in which experiences are never reconciled, in which the historical subject is endlessly lost and never reaches selfrecognition and the basis for a return to the self is, like in the case of Tantalus, forever out of reach (see McNally, 2004).

Critical pedagogy, as we envision it, avoids the bad infinity of mainstream pedagogy in which truth and justice are sought outside of living history in the precincts of a mystical otherness. In contrast, we underscore our conviction that the subjunctive world of the "ought to be" must be wrought within the imperfect, partial, defective, and finite world of the "what is" by the dialectical act of absolute negation. It is the search and struggle for a utopia in which the future is inherent in the material forces of the present. It is given birth out of the existing contradictions of the present moment. The critical pedagogy we are struggling to build works toward a transformation of the established mode of social metabolic reproduction through a form of concrete as opposed to metaphysical transcendence, through entering into the subjunctive mode of "what could be."

But in moving the struggle forward, we must not extend the concept of "what could be" to some ethereal hinterland beyond the reach of "what is" (Gulli, 2005). This is because we do not look to the externality of the infinite but rather to the infinite within ourselves, within our own pedagogical project, within our own acts of laboring, that we can describe our pedagogy as concrete utopian rather than abstract utopian.

To avoid falling into the pit of abstract utopianism, the realm of the "what is" must be inclusive of the "what could be" (Gulli, 2005)—which is, we maintain, the struggle for genuine universality (when history itself becomes a conscious and self-mediating process, that is, when history can unfold outside of the value form of labor under capitalism) rather than for an abstract universality (that exists outside of the historical time of real, sensuous human struggle in which concrete acts of labor are left behind)

Here, our self-activity and subjective self-awareness recognizes humankind's global interdependence and that only in our being for others can our own self-understanding be achieved. And even if the times are not propitious, we must nevertheless undertake an arduous and perhaps even harrowing journey in and through difference and return to a very different place from which we started out.

NOTES

This is a revised chapter that first appeared as McLaren, P., and Jaramillo, N. (2006). Critical pedagogy, Latino/a education and the politics of class struggle. *Cultural Studies Critical Methodologies, 6*(1), 73-93.

1 A defense of a Marxist-driven critical pedagogy against such attacks can be found in Peter McLaren's (in press) "Let Them Blister Paint: Response to Rebecca Martusewiczs'; Valerie

Scatamburlo-D'Annibale and Peter McLaren's (2004) "Class Dismissed? Historical Materialism and the Politics of 'Difference' "; Peter McLaren and Donna Houston's (2005) "The Nature of Political Amnesia: Response to C.A. Bowers"; Donna Houston and Peter McLaren's (2004) "Education and Environmental Crisis: Ecosocialist Critical Pedagogies in Theory and Praxis"; and in the opening chapter of Peter McLaren's *Capitalists and Conquerors: A Critical Pedagogy Against Empire*.

REFERENCES

Abedi, J., & Dietel, R. (2004). *Policy brief: Challenges in the No Child Left Behind Act for English language learners*. Los Angeles: National Center for Research on Evaluation, Standards, and Student Testing/UCLA (Winter).

Allman, P. (1999). *Revolutionary social transformation: Democratic hopes, radical possibilities and critical education*. Westport, CT: Bergin & Garvey.

Allman, P. (2001). *Critical education against global capitalism: Karl Marx and revolutionary critical education*. Westport, CT: Bergin & Garvey.

Anzaldua, G. (1987). *Borderlands/la frontera*. San Francisco: Aunt Lute Books.

Aronowitz, S. (2004). Against schooling: Education and social class. *Workplace: Online Journal for Academic Labor*. Retrieved October 30, 2005, from http://www.louisville.edu/journal/workplace/issue6p1/aronowitz04.html

Crawford, J. (2002). *The bilingual education act 1968–2002* (Spring). Retrieved October 30, 2005, from http://ourworld.compuserve.com/homepages/jwcrawford/T7obit.html

Darder, A. (2002). *Reinventing Paulo Freire*. Boulder, CO: Westview.

De Lissovoy, N., & McLaren, P. (2003). Educational "accountability" and the violence of capital: A Marxian reading. *Journal of Education Policy*, *18*(2), 131–143.

Domke, D. (2004). *God willing? Political fundamentalism in the White House, the 'war on terror,' and the echoing press*. London and Ann Arbor, MI: Pluto.

Dunayevskaya, R. (1973). *Philosophy and revolution*. New York: Columbia University Press.

Dunayevskaya, R. (1978). *Marx's 'capital' and today's global crisis*. Detroit, MI: News & Letters.

Dunayevskaya, R. (2000). *Marxism & freedom: From 1776 until today*. Amherst, NY: Humanity Books.

Dunayevskaya, R. (2002). *The power of negativity*. Landham, MD: Lexington Books.

Foster, J. B. (2005). The renewing of socialism. *Monthly Review*, *57*(3), 1–18.

Fukuyama, F. (1989). The end of history? *The National Interest*, *16*, 3–18.

Gimenez, M. (1997). Latino/"Hispanic"—Who needs a name? The case against standardized labeling. In A. Darder, R. Torres, & H. Gutierrez (Eds.), *Latinos and education, a critical reader* (pp. 225–238). New York: Routledge.

Gonzalez, G. (2001). The ideology and practice of empire: The U.S., Mexico, and the education of Mexican immigrants. *Cultural Logic*, *4*(1). Retrieved October 30, 2005, from http://eserver.org/clogic/4-1/gonzalez.html

Gonzalez, M. (2004). Postmodernism, historical materialism and Chicana/o cultural studies. *Science & Society*, *68*(2), 161–186.

Gulli, B. (2005). The folly of utopia. *Situations*, *1*(1), 161–191.

Gutierrez, K., Asato, J., Santos, M., & Gotanda, N. (2002). Backlash pedagogy: Language and culture and the politics of reform. *The Review of Education, Pedagogy and Cultural Studies*, *24*(4), 335–351.

Houston, D., & McLaren, P. (2004). Education and environmental crisis: Ecosocialist critical pedagogies in theory and praxis. *Educational Studies*, *36*(1), 27–45.

Hudis, P. (2000). The dialectical structure of Marx's concept of 'revolution in permanence.' *Capital & Class*, *70*, 127–142.

Hudis, P. (2004a). The death of the death of the subject. *Historical Materialism*, *12*(3), 147–168.

Hudis, P. (2004b, March). *Working out a philosophically grounded vision of the future*. Paper presented to the 2004 Convention of News and Letters Committees, Chicago.

Hudis, P. (2005a, March). *Directly and indirectly social labor: What kind of human relations can transcend capitalism?* Paper presented at a series on "Beyond Capitalism," Chicago.

Hudis, P. (2005b, September). *Organizational responsibility for developing a philosophically grounded alternative to capitalism.* Paper presented to the National Plenum of News and Letters Committees, Chicago.

Hunt, K. (2007). Gingrich lambastes bilingual education. *Boston Sunday Globe*, April 1, A20.

Huntington, S. (2004). This Hispanic challenge. [Electronic Version]. *Foreign Policy, 141*, 30–46.

Kincheloe, J. L., & Steinberg, S. R. (1997). *Changing multiculturalisms.* Milton Keynes, UK: Open University Press.

Macedo, D. (2000). The colonialism of the English only movement. *Educational Researcher, 29*(3), 15–24.

Maldonado-Torres, N. (2004). The topology of being and the geopolitics of knowledge: Modernity, empire, coloniality. *CITY Analysis of Urban Trends, Culture, Theory, Policy, Action, 8*(1), 29–56.

McLaren, P. (2005). *Capitalists and conquerors: A Critical pedagogy against empire.* Lanham, MD: Rowman and Littlefield.

McLaren, P. (in press). Let them blister paint: Response to Rebecca Martusewicz. *Educational Studies.*

McLaren, P., & Farahmandpur, R. (1999a). Critical multiculturalism and globalization. Some implications for a politics of resistance. *Journal of Curriculum Theorizing, 15*(3), 27–46.

McLaren, P., & Farahmandpur, R. (1999b). Critical pedagogy, postmodernism, and the retreat from class: Towards a contraband pedagogy. *Theoria, 93*, 83–115.

McLaren, P., & Farahmandpur, R. (2000). Reconsidering Marx in post-Marxist times: A requiem for postmodernism? *Educational Researcher, 29*(3), 25–33.

McLaren, P., & Farahmandpur, R. (2001a). Educational policy and the socialist imagination: Revolutionary citizenship as a pedagogy of resistance. *Educational Policy, 13*(3), 343–378.

McLaren, P., & Farahmandpur, R. (2001b). Teaching against globalization and the new imperialism: Toward a revolutionary pedagogy. *Journal of Teacher Education, 52*(2), 136–150.

McLaren, P., & Farahmandpur, R. (in press). *Teaching against globalization and the new imperialism: A critical pedagogy.* Landham, MD: Rowman and Littlefield.

McLaren, P., & Houston, D. (2005). The nature of political amnesia: Response to C. A. Bowers. *Educational Studies, 37*(2), 196–206.

McLaren, P., & Jaramillo, N. (2002). Critical pedagogy as organizational praxis: Challenging the demise of civil society in a time of permanent war. *Educational Foundations, 16*(4), 5–32.

McLaren, P., & Jaramillo, N. (2004). A moveable fascism: Fear and loathing in the empire of sand. *Cultural Studies: Critical Methodologies, 4*(2), 223–236.

McLaren, P., & Martin, G. (2003). The legend of the Bush gang: Imperialism, war and propaganda. *Cultural Studies: Critical Methodologies, 4*(3), 281–303.

McNally, D. (2004). The dual form of labor in capitalist society and the struggle over meaning: Comments on Postone. *Historical Materialism, 12*(3), 189–208.

Mirón, L. F., & Inda, J. X. (2000). Race as a kind of speech act. *Cultural Studies: A Research Volume, 5*, 85–107.

National Council of La Raza. (2004). *State of Hispanic America 2004.* Retrieved from http://www.nclr.org

Rikowski, G. (2001a, June). *After the manuscript broke off: Thoughts on Marx, social class and education.* Paper presented at the British Sociological Association Education Study Group, King's College London.

Rikowski, G. (2001b). *The battle in Seattle: Its significance for education.* London: Tufnell.

Robinson, W. I. (2003). *Transnational conflicts: Central America, social change, and globalization.* London: Verso.

Robinson, W. I. (2004). *A theory of global capitalism: Production, class, and state in a transnational world.* Baltimore: The Johns Hopkins University Press.

Rochester, M. J. (2003). *Critical demagogues: The writings of Henry Giroux and Peter McLaren. Education Next.* Retrieved October 30, 2005, from http://www.educationnext .org/20034/pdf/77.pdf

San, J. E. (2002). *Racism and cultural studies, critiques of multiculturalist ideology and the politics of difference*. Durham, NC: Duke University Press.
Scatamburlo-D'Annibale, V., & McLaren, P. (2003). The strategic centrality of class in the politics of race and 'difference.' *Cultural Studies: Critical Methodologies*, *3*(2), 148–175.
Scatamburlo-D'Annibale, V., & McLaren, P. (2004). Class dismissed? Historical materialism and the politics of 'difference'. *Educational Philosophy and Theory*, *36*(2), 183–199.

TERRY WOTHERSPOON

BALANCING GLOBAL CHALLENGES AND SOCIAL JUSTICE IN TEACHERS' WORK

The Case of Aboriginal Education

INTRODUCTION

Public systems of education are constructed around dual objectives to provide basic work and citizenship skills and to foster opportunities for social and economic participation for members of a society. These aims are typically understood as complementary to one another, but they frequently exist in a state of tension. The balance between them periodically shifts in the course of struggles to redefine and reshape education amidst challenges to accommodate changing social and economic conditions. Contemporary educational landscapes are especially volatile as social participants representing highly divergent interests attempt to redefine the role of schooling within transformations associated with the emergence of what is widely refereed to as a knowledge-based or information society.

Teachers frequently find themselves at the heart of educational contestation through their roles as front-line workers who must translate broad educational policies into concrete experiences and outcomes. Whether posed as agents or targets of reform, teachers are confronted with enhanced expectations regarding their professional roles and practices despite a proliferation of guidelines and duties which potentially restrict their capacity to achieve some of the objectives they are expected to fulfill.

The contradictory work relations experienced by teachers are the focus of this chapter. It begins with an overview of major priorities for educational reform driven by agendas to promote economic advancement for global competitiveness which coexist uneasily with a social justice orientation to facilitate social inclusion by diverse social groups. These policy directions are examined, in turn, as they come to be converted into educational practice. Attention is given to the ways in which educational reform can both alter and be shaped by teachers' work roles and workloads. Much of the discussion is conceptual, exploring the complex interactions among social, economic and political factors in conjunction with teachers' understanding of and responses to an explosion of educational reform initiatives. The chapter closes by exploring teachers' accounts of their work in specific community contexts in order to gain a fuller appreciation for how these dynamics come to be embodied through educational practice. In particular, the case of teachers who work in Aboriginal communities in two Canadian provinces,

S.A. Moore and R.C. Mitchell (eds.), Power, Pedagogy and Praxis: Social Justice in the Globalized Classroom, 149–164.

Manitoba and Saskatchewan, illustrates how policies to enhance education equity for Aboriginal people and broader strategies for economic participation and labour market development play out in the lives of teachers and the communities in which they work. The combination of pressures to rationalize teachers' work and the rationalizations that teachers employ to respond to these pressures contribute to high degrees of variance which ultimately pose risks that schools will fall far short of realizing formally stated objectives to advance either social justice or skills development in many communities.

GLOBALIZATION, COMPETITIVENESS AND SOCIAL INCLUSION

Teachers' work roles, along with educational relationships more generally, are being reshaped through the interplay among core policy directions and processes driving educational reform to promote economic competitiveness and broader social and economic participation across populations. Although broadly understood as consequences of economic globalization and framed in similar terms among major advanced capitalist economies represented by organizations such as the Organisation for Economic Co-operation and Development (OECD), these policies also have unique dimensions and implications as they come to be implemented within particular nation-states (Ozga, Seddon and Popkewitz, 2006: 7-8; Pierson, 2001; Brown, 2001: 236-241; OECD, 2001: 70).

At least five major dimensions represented in emerging policy environments pose substantial challenges for education systems, thereby heightening the tensions likely to confront teachers in their work relationships. First, intense competition exists among nations to produce more highly educated and skilled workers in order to foster technological innovation and productivity growth in knowledge-based economies. Second, these accelerated demands for education are accompanied by concerns to raise basic education and literacy levels throughout designated populations. Third, learning enhancement is promoted throughout the life course, thereby requiring modifications within educational institutions to ensure their relevance to changing societies and economic conditions while the range of effective learning alternatives is extended beyond formal education systems and institutional frameworks. Fourth, educational restructuring is occurring in a framework in which government services are subject to increasing public scrutiny, strategies to promote efficient delivery and cost containment, and demands for public accountability and transparency in decision-making. Fifth, as education's importance for social and economic participation and advancement increases, education systems are subject to claims from competing groups which seek educational services appropriate to their interests, needs and opportunities.

These policy considerations are manifestations of two more general, inter-related "agendas" of innovation and inclusion (Hale, 2002). Innovation agendas seek to foster competitive advantage and growth in the global economy through continuous advances in productivity driven by scientific discovery and application of knowledge in concert with innovative information and communications technologies. Inclusion agendas seek to address needs of diverse social groups, including those who have been historically marginalized and those displaced in the process of contemporary economic restructuring, in order to enhance their prospects for meaningful social and economic participation.

Educational enhancement, within agendas for innovation, is essential for expanding the pool of knowledge workers and contributing to the production and dissemination of new knowledge. In Canada, for instance, an innovation agenda formally introduced by the federal government in 2002 has targeted increased spending on research and development as a major priority, accompanied by measures to advance a skills and learning agenda and foster immigration of highly qualified labour. The skills and learning component of the strategy entails a combination of investment and improvement in early childcare and basic education along with enhanced accessibility and outcomes at the post-secondary level, bridged by greater co-ordination of transitions throughout the life course among education and work (Government of Canada, 2002: 12; see also OECD, 2001: 70). Education is valued, in this context, for its general ability to enable individuals to negotiate the demands associated with varied social sites, with special emphasis on the skills and capacities required for successful labour market integration. As innovation strategies gain prominence, labour market participation becomes the primary mechanism by which social integration and public participation are to be determined, although Canadian governments have not fully abandoned welfare state commitments to a broader array of social programs oriented to support the most vulnerable segments of the labour force and provide wider investment in children, families and lifelong learning (Jenson and Saint-Martin, 2003; Pierson, 2001: 438-440).

Agendas to promote inclusion or equity have emerged parallel to innovation agendas in order to facilitate widespread economic participation and manage political and social tensions induced by economic restructuring (Hale, 2002: 23). An inclusion agenda is motivated, in large part, by recognition that conventional labour market supplies are declining because of long-term patterns of population aging and low birth rates. Consequently, there is growing reliance to integrate segments of the population that have had lower than average levels of education, skill development and labour market participation. In Canada, these include the Aboriginal population (which is younger and has higher growth rates than the general population), single parents, persons with physical and mental disabilities, segments of immigrant populations, and other socially vulnerable or economically marginalized groups.

Policies to promote social inclusion are grounded in part upon human capital theories which emphasize that productivity can be accelerated when the population is equipped with knowledge, skills and capacities essential for economic development. Current conceptions of human capital refer not simply to specific forms of knowledge and learning outcomes, but encompass broader notions of core skills and capacities to learn and apply knowledge (as learning and learning how to learn are framed as lifelong enterprises). Social relationships and networks become increasingly important as people are expected to interact and work in a complex, changing array of institutional settings. Thus, given the centrality of economic considerations and sensitivity to labour market developments, there is a high degree of compatibility between the drive for innovation and the search for inclusion.

Inclusion agendas are also motivated by concerns about the potentially disruptive consequences of major social, political, and economic transitions. Widespread transformations in employment structures, workplaces, technologies, family and community relationships, health and social support systems, and broader social relations have far-reaching consequences, contributing to both temporary dislocation and longer-term uncertainty in people's lives. The impact of these changes is likely to be most severe for segments of the population which have fewest resources to protect themselves or are otherwise deemed to be at risk or vulnerable, but their reach also affects groups that experience erosion of previous entitlements or forms of security. Consequently, priorities to foster social inclusion can be understood as a form of "shock absorber" to manage potential political tensions created by social and economic dislocation. At the same time, they also leave open possibilities for various social groups or interests to raise demands for public services best suited to their particular needs or objectives.

Public schools and other educational institutions are key sites within which the politics and contradictions associated with innovation and inclusion agendas are being played out. The two sets of priorities appear in some respects to complement one another, extending and updating schools' historical purposes to foster work skills and social opportunities. In practice, these dimensions are not so easily reconciled. Schools represent a focal point for varied, often competing claims, ranging from criticisms that today's schools are better suited to meet requirements established in previous eras to responsibilities associated with the recognition that schools bring together people from heterogeneous backgrounds spending greater amounts of time engaged in learning activities. The next section addresses important questions related to the extent to which these tensions appear in and influence in public schools, especially as they are played out through teachers' work.

COMPETING EDUCATIONAL PRIORITIES AND TEACHERS' WORKLOADS

Demands to reshape teaching and reform schools are not new. Throughout the historical development of mass public schooling teachers have been portrayed, variously, as both impediments to reform and progressive agents of change (Lawn, 1996: 16; Ingersoll, 2003). Teachers and their organizations commonly represent themselves as advocates for social justice who are concerned, simultaneously (often in the face of extensive criticism and skepticism about their occupational contributions) to maintain a professional image and solid educational foundation for their work. This section examines some of the central dimensions of teachers' work, understood in the context of potentially competing policy priorities to foster economic competitiveness and social inclusion. Attention is drawn to the limitations contained in abstract notions about how teachers may contribute to enhanced social, economic and political participation by all students in a knowledge society when these conceptions fail to account for the more immediate challenges that enter into the lives of teachers and the students with whom they work.

Much ambivalence concerning teaching is rooted in the diverse purposes of public education as a system oriented to mould human personalities and provide an expanding array of knowledge and understandings in complex social milieux. Teachers, entrusted with core tasks to enable children to make the transition from private spheres of domestic life to diverse public roles and responsibilities, are both objects of intense public scrutiny and co-subjects of educational actions which are typically highly personalized and invisible to most observers. Consequently, educational reform discourse exhibits a recurrent refrain to implement mechanisms to ensure that teachers are doing what they are supposed to be doing which, as Smyth *et al.* (2000: 26-30) emphasize, is essentially about "teaching the curriculum." Teachers' tasks, understood in this way, appear to be deceptively straightforward, even when framed through a broad understanding of "curriculum" encompassing both formal learning objectives and informal or "hidden" dimensions of curricula. Closer scrutiny, however, reveals education to be a highly political, complex and shifting endeavour. Schools have symbolic and material significance that go beyond what is taught and how it is taught. They represent core values and ideas important to a given people or society and they bestow credentials that facilitate access to numerous desired places in the social and economic order. In a diverse society, both of these dimensions are highly contested, shaped by power relations through which dominant voices and interests are most likely to prevail. At the same time, as the previous section has suggested, schools are a focal point for the introduction of knowledge, practices, resources, and services that represent a variety of alternative interests including the needs of subordinate groups. The curriculum and dynamics around which teachers' work is organized, in other words, rarely exist in the form of a unified or coherent package, but represent instead a complex array of divergent and sometimes competing objectives and interests (Smyth *et al.*, 2000).

Teachers, in the confines of their own classrooms as well as in collaborative working arrangements with other educational staff, community members, and administrative personnel, convert curricular aims and objectives into ongoing and supposedly meaningful educational practice. This task involves recurrent efforts to manage, negotiate and carry out selected activities presented through what can often be an overwhelming range of priorities and possibilities. The following statements of purpose are typical of aims outlined in formal policy and curriculum documents, represented here from two Canadian provinces, Saskatchewan and Manitoba:

> The Goals of Education recognize the inherent worth and value of each individual. Education, then, should develop the potential of each person to the fullest extent. It should also enhance the ability of each individual to cope effectively in a changing physical, economic and social environment (Saskatchewan Learning, 2005: n.p.)

> The primary responsibilities of Manitoba Education, Citizenship and Youth are to facilitate the improvement of learning at the Kindergarten to Senior 4 (K-S4) levels, to enhance citizenship development, and to address transition (career development) issues for youth. Emphasis is placed upon enhancing learner performance, delineating roles and responsibilities across the education system, and facilitating the development and sharing of new knowledge (Manitoba Education, Citizenship and Youth, 2006: 2).

Framed in broad terms (and accompanied by more detailed statements of goals and practices to facilitate their realization), these curricular objectives appear relatively straightforward and benign. Nonetheless, even outlined in this abstract manner, they embrace several orientations or dimensions related to innovation and inclusion agendas, including specific knowledge and skills, citizenship roles, economic competitiveness, critical thinking, and social justice, which may not be entirely balanced or compatible with one another as they are given shape within particular social and community contexts.

Education policy and goals are implemented into practical actions in contexts in which boundaries and limits have already been established while new choices have to be made by key actors about such matters as which aspects will be given priority, what kinds and levels of resources are available, in what manner these resources will be distributed and employed, and how teachers will carry out these plans as they interact with other educators and students who possess distinct characteristics and orientations. Teaching, in these respects, involves an ongoing process of negotiation that unfolds as a dialectical relationship between institutional rules and organizational structures and more immediate contextual factors (Connell, 1985; Wotherspoon, 2006). There are powerful limitations that restrict the extent to which accomplishments and outcomes within any distinct school setting can alter social distributions of power and resources, but the dynamics that emerge in these contexts are nonetheless highly significant for the life courses and options encountered by any given individual and community.

RESTRICTING HORIZONS FOR SOCIAL JUSTICE THROUGH TEACHERS' WORK?

The adoption of inclusion orientations in educational policy has mixed implications for teachers and the students they work with, especially in communities which historically have experienced numerous barriers to educational advancement. Working in these circumstances can be conducive in many ways to the development of commitment to social justice among teachers. At the same time, differences within the teaching force and constraints in teachers' working conditions can serve to undermine prospects to fulfill these commitments. These relationships are being altered, often more indirectly than directly, by recent directions to reform schooling to enhance global competitiveness.

Teachers are positioned though their work roles to gain a strong appreciation for diverse strengths, challenges and desires brought forward by the students and community members with whom they work. Classrooms are not simply neutral sites in which students enter ready to learn. The immediacy of issues like poverty, hunger, Fetal Alcohol Syndrome, domestic problems, substance abuse, and students' uncertain futures is brought into the daily routines around which school activity occurs in many community contexts. The likelihood that teachers will see their roles not simply as educators but also as advocates for broader social reform is influenced, in part, by the composition of the teaching force and the character of teaching. Teaching, as a highly feminized occupation recruited predominantly from intermediate social class groups, tends to be idealized in terms of its ability to attract and foster individuals with a strong predisposition to serve in the public interest, work with children and youth, and engage in civic activities (Acker, 1999: 103-5; Lockhart, 1991: 36-7). Public school teachers are also state employees whose occupational interests are tied to the maintenance of a vital public sector. Teachers in many jurisdictions have seen their work conditions, along with life prospects for their students, eroded as a result of welfare state restructuring and the introduction of new forms of regulation (Robertson, 2000: 132-141; Smyth *et al.*, 2000: 3-9). The costs of reforms prompted by broad social and economic transformations, accompanied by political factors such as the advancement of neo-liberal agendas to promote market forces and limit the size and scope of state activity, and public demands for accountability, tax relief, spending constraint, efficiency, and responsiveness in government services, have frequently been downloaded into the classroom in various guises including reductions in teaching and support staff, wage restraint, limited school budgets and resources, and excessive workloads. These changes are occurring as teachers are also called upon to manage demands associated with the implementation of new curricula and administrative procedures, increased student loads, measures to integrate planning and consultation with other staff and community groups, and growing diversity within student populations.

Teachers have advanced various responses to this shifting education terrain, including vocal advocacy for a well-funded, broad-based public education system rooted in principles of social justice. The Canadian Teachers' Federation (CTF, 2004), representing most major provincial and territorial teachers' organizations across Canada, for instance, highlights its commitment to a public education system which is able to respond "to the complex goals and purposes of public education, and grounded in a vision that public schools work towards a common good that embraces democratic principles and social justice," in contrast with more narrowly-framed market driven conceptions of educational accountability.

Despite the potential appeal conveyed through this broad vision, the extent to which it is likely to be realized is limited by a combination of personal, situational and structural factors that characterize teaching. The absence of a unified professional orientation and approach to teaching even within the occupation is reinforced, in part, in circumstances where teaching remains a highly individualized and fragmented occupation leaving space for personal preferences and selective actions to guide what happens behind classroom doors. Although teacher individualism is not inherently a negative phenomenon (Hargreaves, 1993: 54-58), images relayed through personal recollections and media accounts of experiences with both "good" and "bad" teachers serve to construct and reinforce perceptions that teaching is a highly variable and unregulated enterprise. Such observations frequently enter into demands that teaching be more rigidly monitored, controlled and reformed, especially in the context of educational reforms to promote greater evidence-based practice and enhancement of a knowledge society (Smyth *et al.*, 2000: 37-46).

Contrasting sentiments are expressed in teachers' accounts, confirmed by findings of growing bodies of educational research, that teachers are being confronted with excessive workloads and rising demands on their time and energies which make it impossible for them to carry out effectively every aspect of their work (Easthope and Easthope, 2000). Teachers in many jurisdictions report a widespread litany of problems including rising class sizes, lack of preparation time, higher numbers and proportions of students with special needs in classrooms, excessive reporting requirements, disruptive students, and longer working hours (Schaefer, 2003; Smaller *et al.*, 2005). Workload pressures compel teachers to make choices, either deliberately or by default, about which aspects of work they will focus on, thereby short-changing or deviating from at least some elements contained within official curricula. This rationalization process often leads teachers to focus on duties regulated by strict time frames or administrative criteria, such as setting and marking assignments, reporting, meeting with parents and administrators, and other technical procedures. Increased concentration on a narrow range of pedagogical and administrative activities leave teachers with little time or opportunity to engage in the less visible but crucial social, interpersonal and caring dimensions of their work which are essential to the fulfillment of objectives to advance social justice.

These conflicting pressures are reinforced by tensions that accompany related strategies to reconfigure teaching, as evident in emerging discourses and concepts like reflective practice, data-driven or evidence-based decision-making, communities of practice, community engagement, and collaborative decision-making. The ongoing search for strategies to align education and teaching with broader social and economic transformations is focused around the reconstitution of teaching to provide for flexible learning, continual development and application of appropriate knowledge bases, enhanced student attainment, and commitment to lifelong learning (Bransford, Darling-Hammond and Lepage, 2005; Hargreaves, 2003; Troman, 1996). As with the more abstract innovation and inclusion discourses, these initiatives to redefine and reconstitute teacher professionalism give rise to particular problems as they come to be translated into distinct educational priorities, initiatives and practices in specific settings.

There are at least two inter-related levels through which the dynamics of educational practice are played out in this regard. At a symbolic level, broad statements of educational aims tend to be posed in neutral-sounding terms that are widely acceptable, stripped of the more concrete assumptions, struggles and intentions on which they are grounded. Educational reform is an expression of power relations and struggles over the distribution of privilege and resources which can therefore contain or deny access to valued opportunities and outcomes for some while advancing these for others. At the level of daily practice, teachers may be able to find "spaces" amidst the varied curricular frameworks and guidelines that can subvert the curriculum. Teachers' autonomy or resistance, understood this way, can be progressive when it is linked to strong ethical commitment to foster interests of students and communities who may otherwise be hurt by educational reforms. However, teachers' actions, not always inadvertently, can also be damaging to students' interests, fostering alienation, failure or disillusionment with education while reinforcing limits to their chances for social success.

The complex interplay involved in the application of educational reforms can be illustrated with reference to the implementation of various forms of information gathering procedures in schools and universities. Education, in common with many other workplaces and institutions, is subject to an increasing array of requests for data in the form of performance indicators, administrative reviews, reporting mechanisms, and feedback systems intended to guide reflective practice and facilitate rational decision-making. Employed in a conscientious manner in conjunction with professional discretion and serious deliberation among relevant actors, these data bases can be useful tools to set and achieve core educational objectives in an informed way. There are, however, serious risks posed by their application. Abstract commitments by agencies to rational or evidence-based decision-making can serve as influential ideologies or tropes which may be employed variously to justify particular kinds of institutional reform or to offer legitimacy to specific activities in response to demands for public accountability (which themselves may be constructed to achieve particular ends). Powerful lobby groups, media outlets, policy-makers and even educational institutions themselves have become part of the quest to create general or even universal standards by which educational performance can be assessed and ranked for such purposes as comparing or funding schools and universities, assessing students, or paying and promoting teachers.

The accumulation and interpretation of extensive data bases and reporting procedures can also become in themselves intensive self-reproducing organizational activities. In education and many other realms these exercises pose a dual threat to divert time and resources from core institutional mandates while they contribute to mechanisms by which individuals or agencies come to engage in impression management or "representational fabrications" that will enhance their performance ratings on key indicators (Ball, 2004). As designated data categories enter into policy processes in which crucial decisions are made about educational resources, growing concern has mounted in the United States and other nations that reliance on data and research that are too narrowly defined is reducing relatively complex and varied educational relationships to those activities that can be most readily measured and codified (Eisenhart and Towne, 2003). While sometimes seen as a "game" among participants seeking to present themselves in the best possible light or justify their actions through scientific evidence, the new relations of data collection and knowledge use can also be understood as part of a more significant transformation in social and economic relationships in the direction of a particular form of state-regulated market society. Ball (2004: 152) warns that, in education and other public services, these altered relationships reveal prospects for a profound shift in the nature of the relationship between workers and their work. Service commitments no longer have value or meaning and professional judgement is subordinated to the requirements of performativity and marketing; though obviously there is an important element of cynical compliance at work in the processes of individual and institutional fabrication. This is part of a larger process of ethical retooling in the public sector which is replacing concern for client need and professional judgement with commercial decision-making.

The new discourses regarding teachers' work and professionalism are emerging as educational policies are being reframed to accommodate major social and economic transformations. Though framed to suggest that market-based global economic competitiveness will both enhance and be enhanced by socially inclusive institutional orientations which create new opportunities throughout the population, these policies and discourses represent unequal structural relations which, in turn, are activated in specific school and social contexts in a selective manner, thereby potentially imposing significant barriers to progressive social change. In the next section, these relationships are explored by drawing upon teachers' observations about their work in settings where educational equity for designated student groups has been identified as a policy priority.

EDUCATION IN ABORIGINAL COMMUNITIES

Educational policy objectives to foster social inclusion and economic participation among diverse social groups appear in numerous specific manifestations. One of the major priority areas within Canadian jurisdictions is the need to improve educational participation and success and improve the quality of education for Aboriginal people. Commitment to principles of social justice as well as pragmatic human resource development considerations underlies efforts to address serious education gaps. Large segments of the Aboriginal population experience educational attainment levels and outcomes well below national averages, while severe barriers to full educational participation in many communities are compounded by a relatively young and growing demographic profile. These circumstances have prompted provincial, territorial, federal, and First Nation governments, along with local education authorities, to implement an extensive range of action plans, equity targets, programming and curriculum initiatives, and consultative processes, with mixed success to date (Assembly of First Nations, 2006: 16-17; Castellano, Davis, and Lahache, 2000; Schissel and Wotherspoon, 2003).

Aboriginal education guidelines and initiatives convey both explicit objectives and indirect role expectations for teachers. There is widespread, though not unanimous or unqualified, support within the teaching force for commitments and initiatives intended to improve educational success for Aboriginal people, with teachers expressing several reservations about the likely effectiveness of general policy objectives and their own contributions in the act of implementing change (Wotherspoon, 2006). This section draws from statements made by teachers surveyed in twenty-seven school districts (seventeen provincial districts and ten First Nations jurisdictions) in Manitoba and Saskatchewan, the two Canadian provinces with the highest proportions of persons of Aboriginal ancestry in their school-age populations. The research project combines qualitative and quantitative data from 344 respondents. Representative statements are presented here, drawn from open-ended parts of the survey and selected to illustrate the major themes which characterize how teachers understand their roles in educational environments driven by shifting policy agendas.

Teachers' responses reinforce the previous portrait of diverse and often uncertain educational directions, delivering mixed messages about their educational contributions and relationships in Aboriginal communities. There are indications that teachers feel they are making some progress in connecting with students and their communities in significant ways but the profile that emerges is clearly not one of either unconditional commitment to social justice or unambiguous development of core foundational skills associated with advancement in a knowledge-based society.

The broad policy frameworks and directions outlined in previous sections of this chapter serve as reference points that have tangible consequences for how teachers are managed and assessed as well as for the ways in which teachers approach and conduct their work. Manitoba and Saskatchewan school teachers identify an impressive litany of modifications in their schools and districts in response to priorities to enhance Aboriginal education. These range from specific curricular changes, such as the introduction of Aboriginal course content, native studies courses, incorporation of Elders' programs, or visits to sites of cultural significance to First Nations, to broader program supports and modifications to pedagogy and school organization.

The introduction of Aboriginal programming initiatives tends, overall, to be well received, conveying direct and indirect benefits for teachers and students. In a recurrent theme highlighted in a sizeable minority of cases, teachers suggest their schools have made progress in cultivating an inclusive, holistic orientation to encompass Aboriginal students and educational values. Two teachers working, respectively, in a large city high school and an elementary school in a smaller community, observe, for instance, that, "I am not aware of any institutions anywhere that foster more positive attitudes and communication among different racial and cultural groups [than my school]," and "Everyone has a voice – staff and student work together towards greater levels of respect and responsibility." Similarly, an urban elementary school teacher sees many of the new initiatives to be valuable since "most effective teaching takes place when learning in one area is facilitated in other areas." A rural counterpart reveals, more explicitly, how the "introduction of an Elder program has complemented and enhanced the Aboriginal content in my programs. It is also helpful in dealing with behaviour problems." Program innovations can also play an affirmative role by integrating cultural identity with more general educational growth, reflected in the observation by a teacher of Aboriginal ancestry working in a rural high school that such programs have "allowed me the use of my Cree language and values in my classroom on a daily basis." The circumstances depicted here suggest there is some hope to realize prospects for broad-based notions of education idealized by teachers' organizations and policy frameworks, in which schools are posed as caring communities that link orientations to inclusion, social justice and strong educational foundations.

Unfortunately, most school settings appear to fall well short of this ideal. Sometimes, teachers consider this failure to be the fault of policy-makers and other authorities whose visions do not take into account the full spectrum of classroom life. Formal policy guidelines and the way in which they are implemented suffer, in the words of one rural high school teacher, from a "lack of common sense by bean counters." Teachers frequently point to an absence in their schools or districts of compliance with formal guidelines or directives, emphasized by an urban teacher who cites the detrimental consequences of "the lack of programming ...for students of Aboriginal ancestry [for whom] the school is not a welcome place." In other cases, initiatives and programs that have been introduced are not effective because teachers do not have crucial information, resources, confidence or support to take advantage of them. A city high school teacher acknowledges that in her experience programs and services for Aboriginal students have "had very little impact as I was not aware of their availability," while a colleague in another community who states, "I'm sure there are excellent supports available in the community but the information isn't readily accessible."

These problems are exacerbated by a much more prevalent theme in teachers' accounts as they convey the tremendous effort and strains associated with their efforts to manage workload burdens and daily demands on their time. Teachers' concerns about workload management highlight the increasing complexity of their jobs, encompassing multifaceted responsibilities in the classroom and curriculum planning, administrative and reporting functions, engagement in extracurricular and community activities, and shifting interpersonal and interprofessional relationships occurring in conjunction with both curricular and organizational reforms. The ground on which schools have traditionally operated is being transformed, creating substantial uncertainty and dislocation not only for many teachers, but also for the diverse groups with whom teachers work. Teachers in the Manitoba and Saskatchewan schools, consistent with teachers surveyed in other Canadian research contexts (e.g., Smaller *et al.*, 2005: 19), express high levels of overall job satisfaction, but even many of those who feel that they are performing well reveal strong reservations about their ability to address adequately many core elements of their work roles. One part-time urban high school teacher expresses a widely-shared concern in her lament in that, "Personally I try very hard to read and reach all my students but I know that I can't. It doesn't help that even at 66% [of full-time] I may see 100 plus students a day and each for only an hour. How do I address all the possible issues and concerns and still cover curriculum?"

The interface between home and school is a major source of tension in these work roles. Teachers are highly conscious of circumstances which affect students' lives in and out of the classroom, although there is substantial divergence in their understandings of how these relationships affect and should be responded to in their work, ranging from high degrees of empathy with students and parents to disdain or even hostility. The following list illustrates teachers' characterizations of some of the factors they consider to be detrimental to Aboriginal children's education: "community poverty," "Aboriginal parents in our area are irresponsible," "lazy parents," "gangs" and dealings with the criminal justice system, "chronic unemployment," children "coming to school tired/hungry," "substance abuse, lack of involvement, students living on the street with no parental support or guidance," "transient families," "racism," and "Drinking in the community among many members. Neglect and abuse are also factors that hurt children." A rural teacher encapsulates many of these concerns in the observation that, "most of my Aboriginal students are living in despair. They are victims of poverty, abuse, and neglect. Parents are so involved in their own addictions that the children are left to their own devices. School is the only 'safe' place for them."

It is important to stress that these conditions and descriptions do not apply to all Aboriginal students and communities, nor do they represent the teaching circumstances and views expressed by all teachers. Nonetheless, teachers highlight, in their attention to circumstances that are not always part of the formal curriculum, the difficult task presented to them to negotiate the challenge to make their workplaces into inclusive, nurturing places that also offer solid educational foundations constructed through knowledge, skills and aptitudes for lifelong learning in a globalized context.

This is the point at which the relationship between formal school system directions and teachers' capacities to act as effective educational agents (in terms of the extent to which they are able to exercise or feel that they possess flexibility and selectivity in their work relative to rigid curricular expectations and system requirements) becomes most significant. There is a high degree of variability in these regards. Some teachers consider their teaching effectiveness, expressed broadly in terms of the service that they can provide to students, to be impeded by lack of flexibility in the system or by the standards and efficiencies which they and the school system in general are required to meet. Teachers must devote extraordinary effort and commitment to foster student success, in excess or in spite of formal curricular procedures, with long hours in and out of the classroom dedicated to community engagement and efforts to work with and reach their students. Others, by contrast, approach educational challenges by appearing to make no concessions to new mandates and priorities, such as the rural high school teacher who claims that, "I have been teaching the same way since I started teaching."

These conditions foster prospects for a powerful disconnection among schools, communities, and policy objectives. Many teachers blame community conditions, reinforced by actions and attitudes of parents, as serious impediments to their pedagogical efforts. Although rarely articulated in overtly racialized terms, a prominent discourse within teachers' accounts represents Aboriginal communities as the "other" counter posed against the school and teachers' own valiant educational efforts to maintain competitive standards.

The notion of disjuncture between the teacher and those outside the school may be understood in part as a product of individual values or cultures of teaching, but it is also connected to institutional and structural relationships. Teachers face a dilemma insofar as they are becoming increasingly subject to external judgement and assessment by parents, media and system representatives seeking measurable indicators of educational success or results while their daily work roles require them to invest considerable energy and resources, typically in less tangible forms that do not figure prominently within formal teacher appraisal, if they are adequately to attend to students' fundamental personal, emotional and physical needs. These conditions force teachers to make choices about how they will approach important aspects of their daily work routines, particularly if they perceive that their schools or state services systems are not supporting and reinforcing their efforts with sufficient resources and recognition.

Globalization, competitiveness and innovation agendas rarely appear in teachers' accounts of their work in Aboriginal communities, except when depicted as abstract educational principles. Nonetheless, these phenomena and what they represent – the need to maintain standards, the curriculum that must be taught against all odds, the administrative prerogatives that govern school-based activities, the ideologies of individual responsibility and entrepreneurship, and the forms and allocation of educational resources – stand as reference points that enable teachers at times to justify actions which may be detrimental to the students and community interests they are supposed to be serving. Posed in simple terms, teachers increasingly opt, or feel constrained, to choose between approaches that consider social problems to be getting in the way of their jobs and those that integrate responsiveness to social issues as part of their jobs.

CONCLUSION

Public school teachers are confronted with and called upon to mediate among an extensive array of curricular goals and educational priorities. These aims, which are commonly framed in policy documents and professional discourses as part of a seamless package in which education seeks to integrate enhanced prospects for social participation and opportunity among all social groups as it fosters economically-appropriate attributes and skills, are not as balanced as they appear. As the stakes associated with education rise in the context of globally competitive knowledge-driven societies, fierce contestation over valued social and economic resources expose deep inequalities embedded in the politics of educational reform and played out in particular ways within specific educational settings.

Even in contexts such as Manitoba and Saskatchewan, in which social justice orientations take formal precedence over neoliberal agendas devoted to retrench state services and expand private alternatives, new forms of marketization, fragmentation and division are appearing both within and as a result of public schooling. Teachers, often unwillingly, are complicit in these processes as they act selectivity to manage existing workloads and obligations to accommodate further curricular and organizational changes. Teachers and students alike are affected differentially as educational participants negotiate the limitations and freedoms that frame and are part of the "spaces" of everyday school activity. In conjunction with deep-rooted inequalities in social conditions, uneven resource distributions, and variations among school contexts, the collective weight of major social and economic transformations makes it difficult for local matters to count. Nonetheless, teachers' perceptions and orientations to their work reinforce the simple consideration that educational success or failure is also influenced by what happens in any given school and classroom. The pathway leading from effective responsiveness to immediate personal and community needs to meaningful participation in a globally competitive world and, more critically, to prospects to convert "moments" of possibility into a society reconfigured by effective commitment to social justice, is long and arduous. Teachers, along with members of the communities in which they work, require options to foster viable opportunities to work together as active participants in, and be supported by, nurturing educational environments if they are to avoid alienating those communities from education and the opportunities which depend upon school success.

REFERENCES

Acker, S. (1999). *The realities of teachers' work: Never a dull moment.* London: Cassell.

Assembly of First Nations. (2006). *Royal commission on aboriginal people at 10 years: A report card.* Ottawa: Assembly of First Nations.

Ball, S. J. (2004). Performativities and fabrications in the education economy: Towards the performative society. In S. J. Ball (Ed.), *The RoutledgeFalmer reader in sociology of education* (pp. 143–155). New York: RoutledgeFalmer.

Bransford, J., Darling-Hammond, L., & LePage, P. (2005). Introduction. In L. Darling-Hammond & J. Bransford (Eds.), *Preparing teachers for a changing world: What teachers should learn and be able to do* (pp. 1–39). San Francisco: Jossey-Bass.

Brown, P. (2001). Globalization and the political economy of high skills. In P. Brown, A. Green, & H. Lauder (Eds.), *High skills: Globalization, competitiveness, and skill formation* (pp. 235–262). Oxford, UK: Oxford University Press.

Canadian Teachers' Federation. (2004). Moving from the Cult of Testing to a Culture of Professional Accountability, Ottawa: Canadian Teachers' Federation Issues Paper. Retrieved December 6, 2006, from http://www.ctf-fce.ca/en/default.htm?main.htm

Castellano, M. B., Davis, L., & Lahache, L. (2000). Conclusion: Fulfilling the promise. In Castellano, Davis & Lahache (Eds.), *Aboriginal education: Fulfilling the promise* (pp. 251–255). Vancouver: UBC Press.

Connell, R. W. (1985). *Teachers' work.* Sydney: George Allen & Unwin.

Easthope, C., & Easthope, G. (2000). Intensification, extension and complexity of teachers' workload. *British Journal of Sociology of Education, 21*(1), 43–59.

Eisenhart, M., & Towne, L. (2003). Contestation and change in national policy on 'Scientifically Based' educational research. *Educational Researcher 32, 7*(October), 31–38.

Government of Canada. (2002). *Knowledge matters: Skills and learning for Canadians.* Canada's Innovation Strategy, Ottawa: Human Resources Development Canada.

Hale, G. E. (2002). Innovation and inclusion: Budgetary policy, the skills agenda, and the politics of the new economy. In G. B. Doern (Ed.), *How Ottawa spends 2002–2003: The security aftermath and national policies* (pp. 20–47). Don Mills, ON: Oxford University Press.

Hargreaves, A. (1993). Individualism and individuality: Reinterpreting the teacher culture. In J. Warren Little & M. W. McLaughlin (Eds.), *Teachers' work: Individuals, colleagues, and contexts* (pp. 51–76). New York: Teachers College Press.

Hargreaves, A. (2003). *Teaching in the knowledge society: Education in the age of insecurity.* New York: Teachers College Press.

Ingersoll, R. M. (2003). *Who controls teachers' work? Power and accountability in America's schools.* Cambridge, MA: Harvard University Press.

Jenson, J., & Saint-Martin, D. (2003). New routes to social cohesion? Citizenship and the social investment state. *Canadian Journal of Sociology, 28*, 1 (Winter), 77–99.

Lawn, M. (1996). *Modern times? Work, professionalism and citizenship in teaching*. London: The Falmer Press.

Lockhart, A. (1991). *Schoolteaching in Canada*. Ottawa and Toronto: Minister of Supply and Services Canada and University of Toronto Press.

Manitoba Education, Citizenship and Youth. (2006). *Annual report, 2005–06*. Winnipeg, MB: Government of Manitoba.

Organisation for Economic Co-operation and Development (OECD). (2001). *The new economy: Beyond the hype*. The OECD Growth Project, Paris: OECD.

Ozga, J., Seddon, T., & Popkewitz, T. S. (Eds.) (2006). Introduction: Education research and policy–steering the knowledge-based economy. In *Education research and policy: Steering the knowledge-based economy* (pp. 1–14). London: Routledge.

Pierson, P. (Ed.) (2001). Coping with permanent austerity: Welfare state restructuring in affluent democracies. In *The new politics of the welfare state* (pp. 410–456). Oxford, UK: Oxford University Press.

Robertson, S. L. (2000). *A class act: Changing teachers' work, the state, and globalisation*. New York: Falmer Press.

Saskatchewan Learning. (2005). *Saskatchewan education indicators kindergarten to grade 12: Fall 2005 update*. Regina: Saskatchewan Learning.

Schaefer, A. C. (2003). *The good, the bad and the indifferent: A comparison of elementary and secondary teachers' workload and stress issues*. Vancouver: British Columbia Teachers' Federation Research Report, June.

Schissel, B., & Wotherspoon, T. (2003). *The legacy of school for aboriginal people: Education, oppression, and emancipation*. Don Mills, ON: Oxford University Press.

Smaller, H., Tarc, P., Antonelli, F., Clark, R., Hart, D., & Livingstone, D. (2005). *Canadian teachers' learning practices and workload issues: Results from a national teacher survey and follow-up focus groups*. Toronto: The Work and Lifelong Learning Research Network Working Paper. Online. Retrieved December 6, 2006, from http://www.wallnetwork.ca/resources/Smaller_Clark_Teachers_Survey_Jun2005.pdf

Smyth, J., Dow, A., Hattam, R., Reid, A., & Shacklock, G. (2000). *Teachers' work in a globalizing economy*. London: Falmer Press.

Troman, G. (1996). The rise of the new professionals? The restructuring of primary teachers' work and professionalism. *British Journal of Sociology of Education, 17*(4), 473–487.

Wotherspoon, T. (2006). Teachers' work in Canadian aboriginal communities. *Comparative Education Review, 50, 4*(November), 672–694.

MAUREEN CONNOLLY

FREIRE IN THE (POST-MODERN) CLASSROOM

A Post-Colonial Tale

INTRODUCTION

My story begins in the final weeks of the 2006/07 academic year. As is my habit, I am reflecting on how the course I have just finished has measured up to the standards of transformative liberatory pedagogy, a praxis I have been living since 1987. It is also my habit to be unsparing in my critical reflection, and I am my own harshest critic. This is the thirteenth year I have taught the introductory course in Women's Studies. The numbers have increased steadily, going from a modest 100 to an impressive 300 students. "Doing" transformative, liberatory pedagogy can be tricky with classes this big, but I have persevered in my commitment.

If I am honest, I have to say my gut level reflection is one of "existential fatigue", and I am still grappling with the bone deep shock I experienced halfway through the fall term when I realized that we had spent the first four weeks coming to a shared understanding of the word "agency". My gut response then was that something was seriously wrong, that this resistance, reluctance, resentment and downright fear were about more than agency, the word or concept, and, indeed, were about agency, the lived experience. Interactions with my students and assessment of their work since then have only confirmed my suspicions.

My story really begins in 1987, when I read Ira Shor's edited collection Freire for the Classroom – A Sourcebook for Liberatory Pedagogy. Several essays spoke to me immediately, most notably Finlay and Faith's essay on Illiteracy and Alienation in American Colleges, Zimmet's essay on More Than Basics, and Freire's Letter to the North American Teacher. Already awakened by Freire's written works and revolutionary activism, I was absolutely ready for the promise and practicality of Shor's sourcebook. I embraced it unreservedly; it has animated my life as a teacher for the past two decades, and it remains a river – I never dip my hands into the same water twice.

Sometime over these past two decades, I have also crossed the line into mentoring, academic development and educational leadership. I have begun to facilitate curriculum reform in my own and other institutions; I work within/against the academic culture that is also the site of much of my scholarly inquiry, a culture I must continue to examine and write about. I have been relatively successful in using transformative liberatory pedagogy in the post-secondary context. In my paper, I will describe examples of the good, the bad and the ugly in educational

S.A. Moore and R.C. Mitchell (eds.), Power, Pedagogy and Praxis: Social Justice in the Globalized Classroom, 165–178.

leadership, instructional strategies, assessment and evaluation and content. I will also describe the increasingly textured challenges that the post-modern classroom brings. Finally I will suggest praxiological options.

The post-modern classroom is not a "what", but rather a "who": who is/are the post-modern classroom? They are the "millenials", a generation of learners who have come to (some form of) consciousness in a media-soaked, technology-normed culture; they are the microwave generation – they want it hot and they want it now; they are the generation who self-select as overachievers while they are struggling to achieve passing grades; they are the generation who believe they are immune from the influence of culture; they are my students.

The post-modern classroom is also the professoriate, a melange of inter-generational nomads spanning the silent generation, through the boomers, to the Gen Xers, as agitated, urgent and driven as the students they teach. They are the next generation of academics re-discovering funding and frontier research; they are the mid-career explorers hanging onto the remnants of a meritocratic code no longer relevant, more than slightly embarrassed for believing it ever was; they are the early crusaders, hoping that their legacy will have made some impact; they are my colleagues.

For my students, I wonder: How do I engage them in Freire's project of problematizing the existential situation, so elegantly demonstrated in the Zimmet article? How do I create an environment where agency is their desired outcome? How do I do this without becoming the hegemonic overlord, dragging them, kicking and screaming to their liberatory transformation? How do I maintain my standards of learning, pedagogy, and integrity without invoking a colonialist agenda in an ostensibly critical reflective classroom?

For my colleagues I wonder how do I mentor without pretentiousness and pride? How do I facilitate a mindfulness that fosters not only survival but authenticity? How do I function in educational leadership without being impositional?

These are the post-colonial tales of my paper. Through examples drawn from my earlier and more recent years in higher education contexts, I will examine, interrogate and puzzle over the tensions, paradoxes, risks and choices which characterize working from a Freirian orientation. I will refer to the works in Shor's 1987 collection and comment on their ongoing relevance. I will also employ post-colonial and semiotic phenomenological modes of analyses in my attempt to work through issues of power, pedagogy and praxis in the increasingly urgent and intolerant politics of contemporary academic culture.

1987 – FREIRE IN THE CLASSROOM: PEDAGOGY

In "Illiteracy and Alienation in American Colleges: Is Paulo Freire's Pedagogy Relevant?", Linda Shaw Finlay and Valerie Faith (1987) describe their efforts to improve the language skills of upper-middle-class American college students, based on the philosophy and methodology of Paulo Freire (p. 63). Much like my students in 2007, their students demonstrated weaknesses in and (on the surface, at least) apathy about reading, writing and intellectual curiosity. Finlay and Faith created a series of learning activities which moved students through Freire's "forms of consciousness"; they also drew on the work of the Russian cognitive psychologist Lev Vygotsky, whose work in the early half of the 20th century has an almost eerie cogency – much like Freire's – for early 21st century post secondary education, the context for my inquiry and my paper.

Both Freire and Vygotsky emphasize the importance of the interaction between persons and cultural elements in moving from inner speech to shared expression (i.e., from maximally compact inner speech to maximally elaborated written speech). Freire also developed an archeology of consciousness wherein he explored the spontaneous, pre-reflective attitude that most accurately characterizes a person's consciousness of the world. He proposed these as naive, superstitious and critical forms of consciousness and further proposed – echoing Vygotsky – that language (and expressive) habits held clues to these forms of consciousness and hence could be viable sites for dignified and transformative pedagogic interventions.

In determining the form of consciousness, the question to be asked is: Do people recognize how human action and language create their world? or, in Freire's terms, do they distinguish between what is natural and what is cultural? (Finlay and Faith, 1987, p. 65). Culture, being historically, materially and politically constructed or at the very least, conditioned, can, theoretically, be changed or acted upon by the humans inhabiting it. A failure to distinguish culture (the product of human action) from nature often impairs the ability to use language and other forms of expression critically, as well as the ability to act, and often contributes to feelings and lived experiences of alienation from culture, language and communication. In the archeology of consciousness, students and teachers focus on language use as the most accessible mirror of naïve, superstitious or critical consciousness (Finlay and Faith, 1987, p. 65).

The chief characteristic of naïve consciousness is an unreflecting acceptance of the absolute validity and unquestionability of the world as is and one's own views. Naïve thinkers cannot conceive of a basic perspective different from their own. Their thoughts and behaviours are connected insofar as those same thoughts (and values) are held unreflectively – i.e., there are no other alternatives to action but the ones governed by one's unreflectively examined thoughts and values. Superstitious consciousness is characterized by a recognition of cultural options but a concomitant sense of powerlessness to do anything about those options. Social institutions and practices are mysterious, endowed with almost magical status and are seen as monolithic entities outside of causes and control (e.g., "the media").Critical consciousness recognizes that cultural institutions are created and sustained by human purpose and action and language both shapes and reflects people's perceptions of cultural institutions (Finlay and Faith, 1987, p. 66). There is no innocent, separate "I" outside of or uninfluenced by culture; people shape and are shaped within culture; culture can be analyzed, deconstructed and, in principle, transformed by human action, language use being one of those actions.

It is important to realize that these forms of consciousness are not necessarily hierarchical – although in particular pedagogic contexts they can be seen as such.

Certainly "critical thinking" has become ubiquitous to the point of tokenism in the academic planning discourse of most post-secondary institutions. I will suggest, however, that it is the superstitious consciousness that is most prevalent in these same institutions, regardless of the purported embrace of critical thinking as a valued learning outcome.

Finlay and Faith discovered – with and through their students – that "Freire's philosophy is not simply specialized to teaching Third World people how to read and write, but is also helpful for examining particular cultures" (p. 83). Their early concerns with mechanical and technical skills lead them to re-imagine curriculum so that the study of language use was embedded in a consideration of the "nature of cultural institutions, the epistemological dimensions of language and the ethical dimensions of vocabulary, grammar, syntax and rhetoric" (p. 83). Once their students achieved a "meta-awareness" of their own lived contradictions within a consumer culture, the skills of writing and reading unfolded in a relevant, meaningful and timely fashion. Finlay and Faith go on to propose that since the issues they encountered with their students are not isolated, that is, that students at many levels of intellectual and skills development have these same problems, that the roots are attitudinal and cultural rather than solely mechanical and individual (p. 83).

A brief digression is called for, here, in order to support a more robust post-colonial and semiotic phenomenological analysis later. The work of an earlier contemporary of Freire and Vygotsky, Ernst Cassirer, provides a helpful juxta-positioning of the concept of "mythic consciousness" and its strategic implementation in the technique of modern political myths. Like Freire and Vygotsky, Cassirer did his theorizing in the context of an oppressive totalitarian state (pre WWII Germany) and, while not exiled from his homeland, Cassirer was forced to take refuge in America at the height of his writing productivity. In his Myth of the State, Cassirer (1946) describes mythic consciousness as a necessary, but not sufficient developmental/liminal phase of emerging conscious awareness of the world of others and one's relations and responsibilities in that shared world. Mythic consciousness is that which unbinds humans from those features, themselves inherent in humanity, which are sources of constraint or fear.

> In mythical thought and imagination we do not meet with individual confessions. Myth is an objectification of man's [sic] social experience, not his individual experience... in myth man [sic] begins to learn a new and strange art; the art of expressing, and that means of organizing, his most deeply rooted instincts, his hopes and fears (pp. 47-48).

Simply put, and at its most insufficient, mythic consciousness is the construction of a world governed by fulfillment or avoidance of deeply rooted instincts (sex), hopes (I do what I want) and fears (death and lesser constraints).

Cassirer relates a return to or dependence on mythic consciousness as a premise for particular developments of totalitarian or colonial agendas, an undergirding for what bell hooks (2000) proposes as the paradox and premise of western political thought: the right of the superior to dominate the inferior.Cassirer's proposition is that myth does not disappear – it goes underground until people have to face unusual and dangerous situations; it appears if people are confronted with a task that seems to be far beyond their natural powers – when rationality and skill fail, there remains always the power of the miraculous and mysterious (1946, p. 279). Invariably accompanying this turn to the mythic and magical is the willingness – and necessity – to consolidate and personify this power in a hero-leader. The "technique" of the modern political myth is the active manipulation of this process. Cassirer lays out the process: 1) change in the function of language (i.e., new words; charged words; semantic and magical uses of words; old words used in a new sense); 2) supplement the magic word by the introduction of new rites and the flattening of personality and individual responsibility through repetition; (the "group" is the moral subject whose purpose is acquiescence: people no longer question their environment – they accept it as a matter of course); 3) remove the "burden" (dilemma) of freedom and with it relieve people from all personal responsibility; 4) use the hero-leader to re-affirm that what is unfolding is the "will of the gods" and the rightful enactment of manifest destiny (pp. 282-288). Cassirer's mythic consciousness and its role in creating hegemonic structures is related to Freire's superstitious consciousness, and its role in reproducing internalized oppression. Interrupting mythic and superstitious consciousness is the post-colonial challenge of this paper.

In "More Than the Basics: Teaching Critical Reading in High School" Nancy Zimmet (1987) states that "because my students' alienation and insecurities about school were at the heart of their learning difficulties, I decided to make schooling itself the object of study, to problematize in Freire's words the existential situation" (p. 123). Like Finlay and Faith, Zimmet enacted Freire's approaches in her classroom with impressive results not only in improved language skills but in a marked improvement in critical thinking and application. She facilitated her students through a unit of readings about others' experiences in schools in an attempt, as Freire urges, to start objectifying situations in students' lives so they might be discussed. Zimmet also utilized Herber's (1978) three levels of reading in her application of Freire, these being

> ... literal, in which students simply determine what information is presented; interpretive, in which they look for relationships between statements and derived meanings; and applied, in which they question an author's premises, judge material in light of their own experience and formulate new ideas. (p. 124).

In guiding her students through Herbr's levels of reading, Zimmet also allowed her students to experience Freire's forms of consciousness, moving to a place of agency within and about their own experiences in school.

In his letter to the North American Teacher, Paulo Freire (1987) responds to editor Ira Shor's request to Freire for a reflective, epistolary commentary on the application of his pedagogic and political philosophy. Paulo Freire's work in literacy education formed the template for educational work in the development of critical consciousness. Freire's work is remarkable for many reasons, not the least of which is its insistence on affirming the role of *oppressed* or *othered* groups in the construction of the discourse which shapes and describes their reality. Freire is adamant about the necessity for silenced and marginalized groups to refuse the definition of their identity and possibility by those assuming to be more powerful. In keeping with his commitment to education for social transformation, Freire (1987) also articulated some *rules of engagement* for teachers.

> Since education is by nature social, historical and political, there is no way we can talk about some universal, unchanging role for the teacher... a teacher must be fully cognizant of the political nature of his/her practice and assume responsibility for this rather than denying it. When the teacher is seen as a political person, then the political nature of education requires that the teacher either serve whoever is in power, or present options to those in power... Professional competence, command of a subject or discipline, is never understood by the progressive teacher as something neutral. There is no such thing as a category called "professional competence" all by itself. We must always ask ourselves: In favour of whom and of what do we use our technical competence? (pp. 211-214)

Linking education to a consciousness of the relationship between expressive bodies and the culture which shapes and is shaped by the, Freire engaged illiterate adults in dialogical situated pedagogy which allowed the learners to move from a näive to a critical consciousness of the culture and the dominant forces within it. In Freire's archeology of consciousness, students who see themselves as makers of culture (i.e., as cultural agents) experience their relation to reality and their powers to change reality. This challenges their alienation. Their powers to change themselves and their reality are in their hands; this is not seen as an extraordinary act of human courage but rather as a basic act of human agency. Critical consciousness allows and enables this shift in responsibility. Superstitious consciousness, however, provides students with the desperation necessary to resort to the power of the magical and mysterious. A highly developed magic and connected with it a mythology always occurs if a pursuit is dangerous and its issues uncertain (Cassirer, 1946, p. 279).

For Freire, people become "enconscientized" by oppression – that is, they internalize the doctrine of a superstitious consciousness to the extent that they can oppress themselves, whether a hero-leader is present or not. Cassirer also presents this acquiescence as a fundamental ingredient in the technique of the modern political myth. His description is unnerving:

> ... They have ceased to be free and personal agents. Performing the same prescribed rites they begin to feel, to think, and to speak in the same way. Their gestures are lively and violent; yet this is but an artificial, a sham life. In fact they are moved by an external force. They act like marionettes in a puppet show – and they do not even know that the strings of this show and of man's whole individual and social life are henceforth pulled by the political leaders (1946; p. 286).

In Freire's model, alienation from forms of expression (especially language) leads to alienation from culture; for Cassirer, this alienation is also enacted in the disengagement from the burdensome trappings of freedom. For both, the results are a retreat from responsible, reflective engagement with the world of lived relation; and while this is achieved under the mantle of centralized power, it is the decentred "disciplinary practice" based power (á la Foucault) which makes its continuance possible. This active manipulation of instincts, hopes and fears which culminates in the pursuit of the metaphysical shelter of myth and magic is not accidental or coincidental. It is alive and well in contemporary academic culture.

ACADEMIC CULTURE 2008: PARADOX

Students learn about relations of dominance and subordination through the subtleties of the hidden curriculum (Bain, 1990) performed daily within the habitus of departmental and institutional politics (Bourdieu, 1977). *Hidden curriculum* refers to what is taught to students through institutionalized rituals, routines and habits. Typically, hidden curriculum has as much to do with the how, where, and who of the content as it does with the what of the curriculum, the agenda-ed character of the what notwithstanding (Brustad, 1997). Freire's (1987) insistence that the act of teaching and the teaching of subject matter are inseparable underscores Bain and Brustad. The teacher cannot present subject matter as if it were disconnected from an interpretive framework, yet the act of teaching also teaches learners about knowledge, values, and power distribution. How subject matter is taught affects not only what is learned, but also what is meaningful, i.e., what is worth knowing and doing.

Students at all levels encounter hierarchically organized subject matter and faculty members. Positivistic approaches to knowledge production tend to carry over into positivistic approaches to constructing teaching, learning, and supervisory contexts. Rigidity around contingency and diversity is usually performed and interpreted as rigorous standards. The mind-body dualism is so obvious as to be absurd. Similar dichotomies are visible between the status awarded research and teaching. Subject matter receives status according to its specialized parochialism – the more exclusive, the more significant. Literal reproduction and/or persistent penetration of the content density through successive and sustained application of (usually ambiguously articulated) hard work illustrates the barely concealed phallic character of knowledge production and transmission euphemistically termed teaching and learning in the majority of degree programs.

The fragmentation of the curriculum, the lack of infused concepts across disciplinary areas, the core-elective designations, the numbers of courses in specific disciplines deemed necessary, who is assigned to teach what course, what content is evaluated and how, and how faculty members achieve progress through the ranks and institutional status are all signs of the norms and inscriptions of a productive academic institution. Ideology critique, if presented as a legitimate theoretical framework for undergraduates, is usually housed in elective courses, and is interpreted as tangential.

Here, Spivak's (1988) chilling conclusion that the subaltern cannot speak without risking their own eradication should serve as a reminder that privileged subject positions often exist without such risk and often at the expense of those who cannot, or dare not speak. Academic privilege without personal and political reflection will allow these conditions of unequal power distribution to continue and will model this as appropriate behaviours for students to emulate.

Wendell's (1996) paradigm citizen is valorized in contemporary university culture. Norms and inscriptions of machine-like pace, efficiency and productivity characteristic of this paradigm citizen are the regulatory standards. Students learn to abuse their bodies through lack of sleep, poor nutrition, and the use of various stimulants; they learn impression management, ingratiation, and the judicious exploitation of friends and peers who can supply what they need; they learn crisis management techniques; sadly, they also learn to redistribute their priorities – relational, spiritual, political, well-being – according to these mechanistic, technocentric norms and inscriptions. Fortunately, they have excellent role models: faculty in increasingly economically driven universities operate under the same norms and inscriptions in order to progress as expeditiously as possible through the institutional ranks and toward international scholarly renown.

Lived bodies are a transgressive sign to these norms and inscriptions – i.e., bodies which need sleep, balanced nutrition, nurture; bodies which get sick, get hurt, get behind the pace; bodies which are unconventional or which bring contingency; bodies which are recalcitrant in their embodiedness. While I in no way wish to minimize the lived reality of persons with disabilities within ablist culture, I must also emphasize that any lived body is transgressive to non-human standards of pace efficiency, and productivity. Persons living with disabilities and chronic illness are most certainly displaced from participation, knowledge, and discourse production in many disciplinary cultures and in ablist culture in general. Persons pursuing the holy grail of Craig's (1998) severely able body perpetuate this displacement through their unreflective reproduction of a disembodied academic culture; however, as Craig also notes, regardless of the lengths and depths that people will go to avoid the encounter with their own lived body, sooner or later it calls to us all.

PARADOX EXAMPLE 1: PROMOTION AND TENURE

The tension between agency and structure is certainly experienced in institutional rituals associated with promotion and tenure. Faculty members at various stages of career wrestle with paradoxes of creativity, innovation, authenticity and orthodoxy. If we examine the technique of the modern political myth as proposed by Cassirer, we can see the strategic deployment of each step in the "progress through the ranks journey" of university professors. At my institution, the promotion and tenure process is governed by several articles in our Collective Agreement between our bargaining unit (the Faculty Association) and our administration.

In the Promotion and Tenure process, changes in language function are prevalent. Charged words such as "clear promise" and "achievement" are located within the rites of the disciplinary home world; candidates deemed insiders are socialized into the rites and rituals until the behaviour and belief are seamless and the acquiescence is then performed as excellence. This connection of language and ritual also serves to normalize harassing behaviours as "standards". Since cultural participants neither owned nor created these standards, they cannot be held responsible for the price exacted by their deployment. These standards of disciplinary purity are then championed by an exemplar who confirms and reinforces the unquestioned appropriateness of the whole process.

PARADOX EXAMPLE 2: ACADEMIC FREEDOM

Again, drawing from my home institution, academic freedom has evolved from being a safeguard against censorship to being a tyranny of unregulated excess. Early efforts in academic freedom supported a professoriate's right to teach and research in knowledge areas that might be considered "outside the norm" or outside the paradigmatic constraints. Recently, professors have claimed that their academic freedom has been compromised because they do not have chalkboards in their classrooms or because they will be expected to demonstrate accountability for student learning, two sites of engagement previously less fraught with protest and hostility. A siege mentality established, ordinary means of negotiation and problem solving are abandoned as insufficient; when rationality and skill fail, there remains always the power of the miraculous and mysterious (Cassirer; 1946, p. 279).

I have witnessed increasing incidence and intensity of academic freedom outrage (uber freedom, if you will) in the name of maintaining a ritual practice and avoiding accountability. Underlying manipulation of actual academic freedom quite possibly contributes to the overkill response in the teaching context. "Strategic grants" (language) are supported by application protocols and competition (rituals) accepted as not only legitimate practice but evidence of scholarship (acquiescence) and formally endorsed by recognition from key senior administrators. The sad reality that the context of choice (i.e., what I may research and how I may package it) is controlled by external agencies may be the fuel that is feeding the fires of academic freedom as "doing what I want" because I am the expert. The loss of agency in the choice of research contexts compels the urgency which has uber freedom as its (discharge) expression in the teaching context.

PARADOX EXAMPLE 3: MILLENNIAL ANGST

As mentioned previously, millennial learners bring distinct characteristics to academic culture. The children of the baby boomers, assured from birth that they are amazing regardless of the mundane nature of the achievement, believe that they are. Highly skilled in the deployment of technology and "plugged in" to all the information they want, they are also extremely loyal to friends and family and place affiliation as an equal priority with task completion. Having witnessed the failure of meritocracy in their parents (ironic, since it is the parent's work ethic which makes their children's consumer ethic possible), they are suspicious of its promises. They will learn from peers before consulting with a hierarchically appointed expert; they are creative, innovative and confident. At the same time, they expect that the parental structures that have been their invisible support (car, money, buffer, smoother) will continue, paradoxically while they perform as independent agents.

Of course, the paradox cannot be sustained under the weight of academic culture – deadlines, disciplinary conventions, expectations of evidence based argumentation – and the professoriate have neither the training nor the inclination to be cast in the role of parents. When the meltdowns occur, usually midway or near the end of the term, the tension between agency and structure in both professors and students mounts to unbearable levels. Within the students, their adulthood is both required and challenged; their peers, in the same boat, cannot help with the task requirements and affiliation is the only means of support. These are the ideal conditions under which students will resort to mythic or superstitious "solutions" – plagiarism, medical emergencies, terminal uniqueness (their situation is unlike or more desperate than any other), escape (trips, vacations), or distant disasters which nevertheless affect them deeply. Usually, around the same time, the students' professors are undergoing similar institutionally based dilemmas.

The tension between the structures associated with progress through the ranks and the agency associated with academic freedom is a lived reality for most faculty members. As a presumed unresolvable and inevitable feature of academic culture, it continues to reproduce relations of dominance and subordination and romantic notions of homogeneity and meritocracy; however, if accepted as an ongoing tension and not upheld as a master narrative, this lived experience can be a site of interruption and resistance and an opportunity to re-configure constraints.

POST-COLONIAL TALES: PRAXIS

What characteristics of a post-colonial orientation lend themselves to pedagogic and leadership applications in the post-modern, intergenerational contexts of millennial students and their paradigm citizen professors? At the risk of putting forth a tokenistic checklist, I offer the following for consideration:

- problematizing romantic notions of unity, homogeneity and meritocracy
- resisting facile rationalizations based in monolithic and essentialist representations
- interrogating the "naturalization of progress" (Briskin, 2004, p. 344), the common sense belief in a linear movement towards equality and that things will naturally get better, and of naturalism (Briskin, 2004, p. 345) which implies an inevitability about social organization
- recognizing the importance of local, fluid and contextualized sets of meanings and practices; of negotiated and renegotiated historical circumstances
- acknowledging a self in production ... a subject in process/on trial (Kristeva, 1984)

- building links cognizant of difference, "with local differences kept in focus and the gaze on difference refusing to construct exotic subject positions" (Briskin, 2004, p. 352)
- accepting the ongoing tension between agency and structure (reminiscent of Marx: humans make history but not in circumstances of their choosing); realizing that some degree of agency is always possible and resistance reconfigures constraints

This next section will propose options for "reconfiguring constraints" based in Freire's philosophy of transformative pedagogy and applying a post-colonial orientation to contexts of power and paradox in academic culture. I will provide analysis of several contexts of academic culture in order to explore alternatives based in the aforementioned characteristics of a post-colonial orientation. I will incorporate concepts described earlier in the paper (forms of consciousness, mythic consciousness, levels of reading) in both the analyses and exploration.

Again, at the risk of supplying a tokenistic – or worse – simplistic checklist, I offer the following as interruptions into business as usual, "natural" processes:

- forced dissonance
- paradoxical juxtapositioning
- adult, parent, child distinctions
- contextualized and historical details
- local relevance

Forced dissonance is actually anticipating and creating a crisis, of sorts. Habit strategies (in students and professors) will not be abandoned or questioned or changed unless they do not work in ways that are undeniable. In my classroom I achieve this with in-class, open book, immediate feedback, pre-practiced assessments that nevertheless result in grade spreads from less than perfect to failing. This demonstrates how preparation is a skill as important as literal information retrieval. For many of my students it is a helpful encounter with failure or being less than perfect. The key is then unpacking the experience so the students see the constituent elements and do not resort to "mythic" or superstitious rationalizations; rather they see links between action and consequences. These insights can also be nurtured with group-based in-class assessment followed by analysis. Open ended questions guiding the analysis are a significant component in the overall learning of both students and professors.

Paradoxical juxtapositioning is a somewhat perverse form of giving people what they say they want. Placing two (usually contradictory) elements side by side as if they could co-exist or be mutually supportive is one way of allowing a process to unfold which cannot reach a fulfilling resolution. The student or professor must then find ways to manage this tension (and, in the case of the student in my classes at least, analyze and report on it), or find an alternative. This allows for a self-located disruption of the belief that things will always work out for the best under forces outside of the student's or professor's control. It also encourages a more grounded consideration of what is theirs to control. I emphasize here that this exercise does not suggest control as a solution, but rather a consideration of the features where agency is possible, a recognition of the fluid and contextualized aspects of meaning and practices, and a commitment to negotiated and re-negotiated historical and actual circumstances.

Adult, parent, child distinctions are a pedagogical application of transactional analysis therapeutic constructs. I invite my students to enter into adult to adult relationships with me, where there is reciprocity around process and expertise. Because they readily agree, I am then able to use this agreement in a paradoxical juxtapositioning exercise halfway through the term when a percentage of them want me to be their parent (in a parent-child relationship). We cannot be adult to adult in one context, and parent-child around conventions in an academic paper. This forced dichotomy also forces dissonance, which is especially helpful for moving through or coming to terms with tension between agency and structure. Ironically, it also clarifies for the students what roles their parents do play in their lives. When undertaken as an explicit and transparent feature of pedagogy, this strategy allows faculty to set appropriate time, space and behaviour boundaries – boundaries which the new generation of faculty (the Gen Xers) seem to have significant difficulties establishing and maintaining. Adult, parent, child distinctions contribute to the recognition of local, fluid and contextualized sets of meanings and practices, and support Kristeva's (1984) powerful proposition of self as a subject in process/on trial, with the proviso that this work in progress is dependent on being "on trial".

Contextualized and historical details have been the touchstone of my work with faculty in the preparation of promotion and tenure dossiers and teaching award dossiers, and in my advocacy role in appeal of promotion and tenure decisions. An academic career trajectory is not self-evident; each element must be contextualized (e.g., choice of research dissemination form; disciplinary conventions and standards of practice; whether a course taught is core or elective, first year or fourth year) and placed against historical practices and developments. This can be accomplished with categorizing and summarizing techniques and with cues for the reader so that the document is not left to a "natural process" of collegial telepathy and presumed homogeneity. Historical and contextual descriptions have proven to be more effective than grandiose claims of achievement. In the classroom setting, providing context and background for students not only models this behaviour for them but also allows for current research on learning in the discipline to be included in the content. I have also found it helpful in teaching students to be more discerning regarding information and sources. Once they realize that context and history are the existential ground of agency and structure, they also realize that what counts as evidence is not as straightforward as they had previously assumed.

Local relevance is a strategy whereby particular subject positions can be expressed in ways that engender regard and respect rather than "othering" or "exoticizing". For example, millennial students have preferences for working in groups and having a high degree of autonomy. These are not necessarily contradictory if an assignment can be designed which includes the students' cultural interests, existing skill sets and a peer-based accountability structure. In my relatively large (300) first year class I have an assignment I call "Not a Paper"; students work in groups of no more than five and produce something that can be displayed in some form accompanied by a report on the group's process. Early confusion and anxiety (frequent questions on what do I want are answered with "I am open to anything as long as it is not a paper") are reduced with the tasks of meeting, keeping minutes, and signing off on decisions. Process is assessed as well as product – and while the products are usually amazing, the process descriptions are equally rich in context and history – i.e., local relevance.

Local relevance is also gaining ground in the promising use of a broader discourse to account for forms of scholarship. A faculty member's research can have significant and sustainable impact on local policy and practice; this form of scholarship is no less valuable – and certainly no less scholarly – than a paper in an international journal. The language of presentation of my scholarship to academic peers outside my research interests is my responsibility; I am the one to translate my maximally compact inner speech to (intelligible) maximally elaborated written speech. My peers must be prepared to listen with open minds. Our willingness to describe and appreciate each other's local differences is an exercise of agency within structure, a realization that some degree of agency is always possible, an enactment of resistance reconfiguring constraints.

TEMPORARY CLOSURE

I have attempted to show similarities between the academic contexts described in 1987 and those I inhabit in 2008; I have proposed that superstitious and mythic consciousness have power in academic contexts, are productive and effective forms of control and internalized oppression, and are active in contemporary academic culture; I have embedded Freire's philosophy in a post-colonial orientation to offering options to the dilemmas experienced by students and faculty in complex and contested lived relation. I remain convinced that Freire's pedagogic and political theorizing have relevance for intergenerational, neo-colonial academic contexts and more committed than ever to taking seriously his question: In favour of whom and of what do we use our technical competence?

REFERENCES

Bain, L. (1990). A critical analysis of the hidden curriculum in physical education. In D. Kirk & R. Tinning (Eds.), *Physical education, curriculum and culture: Critical issues in the contemporary crisis* (pp. 23–42). Bristol, UK: The Falmer Press.

Bain, L. (1997). Transformation in the postmodern era: A new game plan. In J. M. Fernandez-Balboa (Ed.), *Critical postmodernism in human movement, physical education, and sport* (pp. 183–196). Albany: SUNY Press.

Bourdieu, P. (1977). *Outline of a theory of practice*. Cambridge, UK: Cambridge University Press.

Briskin, L. (2004). Privileging agency and organizing: A new approach for women's studies. In A. Prince & S. Silva-Wayne (Eds.), *Feminisms and womanisms – a women's studies reader* (pp. 343–358). Toronto: Women's Press.

Brustad, R. (1997). A critical postmodern perspective on knowledge development in human movement. In J. M. Fernandez-Balboa (Ed.), *Critical postmodernism in human movement, physical education, and sport* (pp. 87–98). Albany: SUNY Press.

Cassirer, E. (1946). *The myth of the state*. New Haven, CT: Yale University Press.

Craig, T. (1998). Liminal bodies, medical codes. *Semiotics, 1997*. New York: Verso.
Finlay, L. S., & Faith, V. (1987). *Illiteracy and alienation in American colleges: Is Paulo Freire's pedagogy relevant?* In I. Shor (Ed.), *Freire for the classroom – A source book for liberatory pedagogy* (pp. 63–85). Portsmouth, NH: Boynton/Cook Publishers.
Freire, P. (1987). Letter to North American teachers. In I. Shor (Ed.), *Freire for the classroom* (pp. 211–214). Portsmouth, N.H.: Boynton-Cook.
Freire, P. (1973). *Education for critical consciousness*. New York: Seabury.
Freire, P. (1968). *Pedagogy of the oppressed*. New York: Continuum.
Herber, J. (1978). *Teaching reading in the context areas*. Englewood Cliffs, NJ: Prentice Hall.
Hooks, B. (2000). *Feminist theory from margin to center* (2nd ed.). Cambridge, MA: South End Press.
Kristeva, J. (1984). *Revolution in poetic language*. (Leon S. Roudiez, Trans.). New York: Columbia.
Said, E. W. (1978). *Orientalism*. New York: Vintage Books (Random House).
Shor, I. (Ed.). (1987). *Friere for the classroom – A source book for liberatory pedagogy*. Portsmouth, NH: Boynton-Cook.
Spivak, G. (1988). Can the subaltern speak? In C. Nelson & L. Grossberg (Eds.), *Marxism and the interpretation of culture* (pp. 271–313). Chicago: University of Illinois Press.
Vygotsky, L. S. (1962). *Language and thought*. Cambridge, MA: MIT Press. (Original work published 1934).
Vygotsky, L. S. (1978). *Mind in society: The development of higher psychological processes*. (M. Cole, V. John-Steinor, S. Scribner, & E. Souberman, Eds.) Cambridge, MA: Harvard University Press.
Wendell, S. (1996). *The rejected body – Feminist philosophical reflections on disability*. New York: Routledge.
Zimmet, N. (1987). *More than basics: Teaching critical reading in high school*. In I. Shor (Ed.), *Freire for the classroom – A source book for liberatory pedagogy* (pp. 122–128). Portsmouth, NH: Boynton-Cook.

DAVID FANCY AND SUSAN SPEAREY

MINDFULNESS AND THE EROSION OF THE HUMANITIES

> People think of meditation as some kind of special activity, but this is not exactly correct. Meditation is simply itself [...]. It is about stopping and being present, that is all. Mostly we run around doing. Are you able to come to a stop in your life, even for one moment? Could it be *this* moment? What would happen if you did?
>
> A good way to stop all the doing is to shift into the "being mode" for a moment. Think of yourself as an eternal witness, as timeless. Just watch this moment, without trying to change it at all. What is happening? What do you feel? What do you see? What do you hear?
>
> [...] By taking a few moments to "die on purpose" to the rush of time while you are still living, you free yourself to have time for the present. By "dying" now in this way, you actually become more alive now. This is what stopping can do. There is nothing passive about it. And when you decide to go, it's a different kind of going because you stopped. The stopping actually makes the going more vivid, richer, more textured. (Kabat-Zinn, 2005)

This chapter examines the potential that mindfulness meditation and related embodied awareness practices can bring to bear on pedagogy in the Humanities. Synchronous with the overall theme of this volume, we will begin to articulate the possibilities of how the integration of mindfulness-oriented awareness practices in the Humanities classroom can further enhance the ability of students and professors to more profoundly experience and explore the intensities, subtleties, and multifarious realities emanating from of the types of crises that litter the terrain of the current late-capitalist, neo-imperial geopolitical climate. Furthermore, we will argue that the quality and efficacy of these involvements are heightened in the context of the kind of intersubjective pedagogical relationships marked by ever-increasing qualities of transversal sharing of power that mindfulness awareness practices often encourage.

Even at first glance, the potential for mutual generativity between traditional Humanities pedagogy and mindfulness practices is pronounced given the emphasis that both modes place on capacities for observation, "open-mindedness," and a sophisticated affective reception by individuals of critical analysis, the world, as well as forms of artistic expression to which they give their attention. With regard

S.A. Moore and R.C. Mitchell (eds.), Power, Pedagogy and Praxis: Social Justice in the Globalized Classroom, 179–198.

to the nature of this beholding, Kabat-Zinn suggests that mindfulness and awareness practices, contrary to certain reigning assumptions about meditation, are not predicated on notions of disengagement, solipsism, passivity or the pursuit of transcendent states; rather, they invite practitioners to begin to address the plenitude and complexity of their present circumstances by engaging in acts of witnessing.[1] In a similar fashion, students and teachers are witnesses to the world, the texts, and fields with which they engage and study. Significantly, however, in mindfulness practice such acts of witnessing do not necessarily privilege the discursive or even the ocular, with its imperialist associations and reductively empiricist understanding of observation that positions learners at a distance from events, and as potential "masters" of their significance. Instead, witnessing from a mindfulness perspective can be understood to be a more dialogic and dynamic process that broadly invokes and mobilizes all the senses and faculties. The point of mindfulness practices is not to attempt a totalizing understanding of our experience in any given moment, but to register in increasingly subtle ways the vicissitudes and potentialities of what we already understand, and to acknowledge the inevitability of what remains beyond our grasp. It follows, then, that such an approach is not simply an affirmation or naturalization of so-called undifferentiated "authentic" experience rightfully challenged by the contemporary anti-essentialist poststructural theory of Derrida or Butler. As we will suggest, one way of conceiving of this more expansive mode of engagement with experience is to stress that mindfulness addresses *affect* in its subtlest manifestations.

For their part, we see the Humanities as "affecting," not in the sense of principally addressing the emotions (or more cynically, tugging at the heartstrings in potentially manipulative ways), but in the sense of tapping into, as Kabat-Zinn[2] suggests in the epigraph above, multiple dimensions of experience, while also alerting us to the ways that habits of intellect, of psyche, of body, of expression, and of processing sensory input are deeply ingrained and unconsciously reproduced and replicated. Optimally then, Humanities subjects engage not only the intellect, but also all the other senses and sensibilities; and they do so not by advancing arguments that present themselves as seamless,[3] nor by encouraging "blind faith" in a particular cosmological or ideological paradigm, but rather, by staging crises, making them evident, and leaving it to audiences to engage mindfully and ethically with what they witness. Eliciting this awareness and evoking multiple qualities of affective response (which perhaps begins by frustrating the ones on which we are customarily most heavily reliant) gives us the opportunity to shift or depart from ingrained patterns of reaction, thereby potentially opening connections between subjects that have previously not been considered or explored in a sustained way, reopening discussion around terms, definitions, concepts and ethical stances that may potentially have become sclerotized, as well as leading to the creation of entirely new concepts and expressions.

We propose that at its best, Humanities teaching and scholarship resists, on the one hand, the teleological and positivist imperatives that index learning towards eventual moments of revelation, discovery or mastery; and challenges, on the other hand, the assumption that the world can never be known, a position that frequently collapses into a nihilist stance, or into the kind of disengaged relativism that is often (falsely) attributed to postmodernist thinking. Humanities education encourages a more expansive and intensive engagement with the world even as it celebrates flux, open-endedness and multivalence; it attends just as scrupulously to the vast range and diversity of what has been expressed as it does to all that cannot be represented or articulated in language or fixed as objects of knowledge; it grapples with indeterminacy and contingency, with what Stephen Batchelor[4] has described as states of "perplexity" that suffuse the entire organism. Batchelor writes,

> Experience cannot be accounted for by simply confining it to a conceptual category. Its ultimate ambiguity is that it is simultaneously knowable *and* unknowable. No matter how well we may know something, to witness its intrinsic freedom impels the humble admission: "*I don't really know it.*" [...]
>
> The sheer presence of things is startling. They provoke awe, wonder, incomprehension, shock. Not just the mind but the entire organism feels perplexed. (Batchelor 1997: 97)

Our argument is that Humanities subjects must constantly work to hold in tension—or hold together— knowing and unknowing rather than trying to resolve the unknowing into a seamless or definitive argument of knowing. Furthermore, they must develop renewed ways of emphasizing that the states of perplexity that inevitably issue from increasingly subtle and probing engagements with the present moment operate at levels that extend far beyond the cognitive. It is precisely this gesture of "holding together and (or) in tension" of both what we know and what we do not—a gesture facilitated by mindfulness awareness practices—that can significantly re-orient temporality, agency, authority, and even subjectivity away from capture into teleological and instrumentalist paradigms and projects.

There is a strong tendency, even in the most sophisticated of scholarly analyses, to speak to only one or two dimensions of the experiences or issues under consideration, a tendency that has implications for the position accorded to the reader and the terms in which she or he is addressed. Such analyses frequently engage readers by appealing to their intellectual and perhaps moral[5] sympathies, and address them only to the extent that their consensus or affirmation of the arguments and positions presented is tacitly invoked. Viewed through the lens of mindfulness practices, such trends reinforce existing hierarchies of authority and discourage readerly response. Successful Humanities pedagogy insists that texts, histories, performances, and paintings remain open to multivalent, proliferating and contingent meanings: what is known and what is not known are not constants, but rather will vary from reader to reader as well as varying from context to context. Indeed, readers, auditors and viewers can always be understood to approach texts, arguments, images and performances from what Brian Massumi has termed the "boundary condition" of the present, (Massumi 2003: 212). Even if the text is ostensibly "known," the unknown or "not-yet-known" of the present-time necessarily enters the equation, a factor that contributes to why readers, viewers and auditors have agency and are participants in meaning-making. If we invoke only cognitive dimensions of experience and fixed systems of morality, then it is much easier to make authoritative pronoucements, to project solutions into a future time and space, and to render readers passive recipients of received truths. If, however, cognitive and moral certainties are constantly "shadowed by" other dimensions of experience—a quality of affective excess posited by Massumi that we go on to discuss below—then cognitive authority cannot be absolute, and affective dimensions must be engaged with.

Crucially, if knowing and not knowing are separated, and stability comes to be assumed as normative, if instability or not knowing is ignored, disavowed, displaced, isolated, or treated as a problem to be solved every time it surfaces and claims our attention, the experience of destabilization then becomes a source of what mindfulness practitioners, influenced by Buddhist psychology, describe as anguish. Mindfulness traditions teach practitioners to be "comfortable with uncertainty"[6] rather than responding to anguish with attempts to eradicate it or to restore stability. Batchelor argues that "as mindful awareness becomes stiller and clearer, experience becomes not only more vivid, but simultaneously more baffling;" that is, a fuller, more attentive and mindful engagement with the present moment actually *gives rise to* more subtle and profound forms of questioning (Batchelor 1997: 97). It is only by treating such questions as specific problems to be ultimately and definitively solved that we reactivate states of anguish and step up the pursuit of stability.[7] Repeated occlusion of the unstable and its capture into the stable normative — be it for individuals, disciplines, institutions or states — leads to what Batchelor describes as a process of "compulsive becoming" that demands ever increasing occlusion and capture in turn:

> Each time I think I have found a situation that solves my problems, it suddenly turns out to be a reconfiguration of the very situation I thought I was escaping from. My sense of having found a new lease on life turns out to be merely a repetition of the past. I realize I am running on the spot, frantically going nowhere. (Batchelor 1997: 74)

Significantly, Batchelor figures this process of compulsive becoming as one that instantiates increasingly "frantic" levels of activity while paradoxically also severely curtailing possibilities for mobility. The acceleration of velocity, in combination with the apparent variation of circumstances (which turn out instead to be repetitions of past in new guises) creates the illusion of fullness, activity and diversity; however, "running on the spot" does not open up new pathways or directions; it simply exhausts the runner. When this process of capture of affective flows becomes increasingly central to economic activity, as is currently the case in the "knowledge economies" of the economic North, the regulation of individuals' affective lives at the subtlest of levels, including inducements to confront any kind of anguish with increased stabilization and "security," become a central means of social control.

We feel that the possibilities for fuller affective involvement with Humanities pedagogy have been eroded for a variety of historically contingent reasons, including a number of the foci of our study here. The first of these is the corporatization of time in the academy as a means of containing and capitalizing on flows of affect in the form of intellectual labour, and the translation of such labour into marketable goods. Once at the heart of university curricula, Humanities subjects have become more and more marginalized, rationalized and instrumentalized as Humanities departments are closed down, amalgamated or turned principally to service delivery centres for students of more highly prioritized disciplines. Contemporary Humanities researchers are encouraged to conduct "interdisciplinary" projects that, more often than not, are funded by agencies that invoke models and standards of performance derived from other disciplinary traditions, often emphasizing a more positivist emphasis on the generation of knowledge, the genesis of knowing. Such a state of affairs informs our contention that we are writing at an historical juncture at which pedagogy in the Humanities, particularly in an institutional climate in the economic North, seems increasingly to emphasize a certain utilitarianism, a distance from, or mastery over the object of study. In this climate, the traditional foci of Humanities studies (the arts, languages, religion, philosophy) are either dismissed as overly fanciful, insufficiently practical or largely redundant concerns, or, alternatively, are earmarked as potential channels for understanding, accessing and appealing to the interests of larger markets for the production and consumption of goods and services.[8] The Humanities are being taken up in a variety of ways into the apparatus of capture of affective capitalization, and concomitant stabilizations, semiotizations, and literalizations are the necessary result.

We propose that the articulation and ongoing elaboration of a dialogue between mindfulness and bodymind practices and Humanities pedagogy will serve to foreground and to recuperate valuable dimensions of Humanities education currently being eroded by systematized forms of compulsive becoming tied to emergent formations of the affectivization of capital and the capitalization of affect. Rather than pursuing projects that can be understood to promote the containment or stabilization of a targeted problem, and by doing so, reasserting the primacy of hegemonic paradigms and forms of power, we are interested in how to bring the resonances of the many occluded crises of economic globalism to the fore in a fashion that is at once assimilable and enabling to students. We argue that exploring the convergences between mindfulness practices and Humanities pedagogy potentially opens a space for students and instructors to cultivate thinking and experiencing that mobilizes the personal sensitivities of the subject in a given context and that addresses itself attentively and ethically to questions of power, social justice and transformative potential, thus allowing the possibility of repeated rupture to the cycle of compulsive becoming. As part of this project, we will explore how the objectification of the body in the cultural theorizations of the last two decades has contributed to the corrosion of theorized possibility for agency and resistance to hegemony. The resonance between mindfulness practices and the Humanities allows pathways to increased agency as well as affective and/or discursive resistance to be pursued without either student or instructor necessarily succumbing to the increasingly prevalent positivist imperatives of advancing arguments and analyses that make claims of certainty, those of definitive or prescriptive judgment, or of the nihilist responses that frequently pose as the only viable alternative.

THE PROBLEM OF TIME, REFLECTION, AND CONTEMPORARY INSTITUTIONAL CULTURE

We argue that the stridently corporate culture of contemporary educational institutions in most Western democracies has had far-reaching effects on pedagogical practice and on the very terms according to which education is conceived, experienced and approached by students and educators alike. Henry Giroux, in "Public Time and Educated Hope: Educated Leadership and the War Against Youth" contends that the integration of corporate values, practices and institutional structures in academic contexts enforces a reorientation towards time as a commodity in ever scarcer supply, and that such commodification of time has had profound and proliferating repercussions. Giroux notes, for instance, that it is hardly accidental that protest culture has all but disappeared as a defining feature of post-secondary student life since the Reagan/Thatcher years, contending that the ability to speak to power is predicated upon the possibility that learners will have ample time to reflect, a possibility that has been virtually eradicated as corporate time has become more firmly entrenched in academic life. He argues that time to reflect is necessary in the first place so that learners can assimilate a certain level of understanding, and in the second, so that they might respond to that understanding, either by critically engaging with the processes of knowledge production through which it has been generated, or by exploring ways of working creatively with it. In an institutional culture oriented towards "productivity" and "efficiency," according to Giroux, "time to reflect" is encoded as "wasteful," insufficiently rationalized. This situation has been exacerbated for learners in contexts in which tuition hikes have been steep, and expenses such as books and the electronic equipment and attendant communications services necessary to conduct research and write papers are costly. In response to these circumstances, many students have taken on larger and larger part-time workloads in addition to their study commitments, further reducing their access to time to reflect.

Moreover, Giroux signals the crucial issue of how time "is mediated differently by institutions, administrators, faculty and students but also how it shapes and allocates power, identities, and space through a particular set of codes and interests" (Giroux 2003). To take as a case in point the issue of research time, we can see that time to reflect is allocated in direct correlation to status within the institutional hierarchy. The more prestigious research awards offer teaching release time, demonstrating that academic institutions, rather than endorsing the complementarity of teaching and research,[9] accord to the latter a much higher status, thus making sustained time to reflect relatively inaccessible to all but an elite minority. The result is that the teaching and administrative responsibilities of "research faculty" are offloaded on those further down the institutional hierarchy, whose uptake of these responsibilities reduces the proportion of their own research time. Research awards and fellowships also allocate budgets for the disposal of research assistants' time on more menial tasks. At Brock University, where we both teach, direct contact time between faculty and undergraduate students has for decades consisted of two lectures and one seminar per course each week in most subject areas. The seminars (generally 50 minutes per week for groups capped, at least theoretically, at 20 students) were once the cornerstone of the institution's claims to excellence. Brock is currently in the process of shifting from the status of a university dedicated principally to undergraduate teaching to that of a "comprehensive university" (a university that offers a variety of graduate programs in both interdisciplinary fields and discipline-specific areas), with the result that the seminar system is constantly under threat as insufficiently cost-effective. In other words, the undergraduate students' time to discuss and question ideas and concepts (rather than being the passive recipients of "top-down" "knowledge" as disseminated most often in increasingly large-group lectures) is increasingly becoming signaled as being unimportant, a luxury. A frustrating consequence of this rationalization of time is the frequency with which students come to ask for precise instructions as to how to achieve the grades necessary for admission into a particular graduate or professional program, and when asked to consider focusing their work on questions that matter most to *them*, dismiss this pursuit as not "worth" the time to investigate. In other words, the perceived scarcity of time to reflect, time to work and contact time with anyone not positioned in close proximity to them within institutional hierarchies serves to alienate students from themselves, from the exploration and expression of their most deeply-held values and interests, from dimensions of their own experience that do not have direct bearing on their potential "success" in a world of global capitalism. In effect, the commodification of time encourages their participation in the cycle of compulsive becoming. As Giroux observes, who and what one has time for is a good index of power relations.

It follows, then, that the commodification of time can disable widespread critical thinking within the academy, or reduce critical projects to largely reactive iterations of counter-hegemonic positions that serve to reinforce understandings hegemonic forms of power and knowledge as inevitable and normative. If, as Edward Said argued, the role of the public intellectual is to speak truth to power, it is, ironically, those who wield the most institutional power who will be best positioned to do so; the idea of democratization is expressed precisely through the entrenchment of structural inequity that passes itself off as meritocracy. The commodification of time also induces a climate of escalating competition which serves to atomize learners—and researchers—and to forestall collective endeavour; it instills a sense that the only possibility for success resides in mastering (rather than recognizing or critiquing) the terms of hegemonic discourse and in attempting to meet the continuously accelerating demands for "efficiency" and "productivity;" it reduces students and educators to the role of functionaries within the inherited system, thereby both diminishing their potential for agency and perpetually deferring any sense of achievement or emancipation; it erodes the education system's public role of fostering responsibility, critical citizenship and ethical action; and it imposes and justifies a regime of policing and regulation by blaming increasingly demoralized and alienated subjects for any hindrances to efficiency, and by diverting attention from the systemic nature of any problems that arise. Corporate time can be understood to advance and further stabilize in the academy the structures of an emergent form of working practice that Hardt and Negri have named "affective labour" (Hardt and Negri 2004: 108), one in which "education", understood as a training in the replication of hegemonic norms, as well as a complementary "attitude, character, and 'prosocial' behaviour [are recognized] as the primary skills employers need" (ibid).

Giroux (2003) advocates for a recuperation of what he terms 'public time' as a way of redressing the proliferating effects of its more privatized variant: Rejecting an instrumentality that evacuates questions of history, ethics, and justice, public time fosters dialogue, thoughtfulness, and critical exchange. Public time offers room for knowledge that contributes to society's self-understanding, that enables it to question itself, and seeks to legitimate intellectual practices that are not only collective and non-instrumental but deepen democratic values while encouraging pedagogical relations that question the future in terms that are political, ethical, and social.

While clear distinctions between public and private time are difficult to demarcate, Giroux signals certain characteristics that corporate time devalues and fails to cultivate. We argue that these qualities have profound ethical importance, and affirm Giroux's argument that knowledges which are not simply instrumentalized in the service of re-entrenching the dominant culture and its hierarchies of value, and which are not simply political in terms of advancing a prescribed agenda, are vitally important dimensions of experience for students to access and explore.

MINDFULNESS, ARREST, PAUSE

Pivotal to the understanding of the mode of witnessing that mindfulness practice encourages and privileges in the interruption of cycles of compulsive becoming is the point of complete arrest, the "full stop" that Kabat-Zinn invokes in the epigraph at the beginning of the chapter. Stopping enables us to interrupt the momentum of activity that is driven by, and serves to re-entrench, unconsciously reproduced patterns of affective, social, ideological, psychic, cognitive, embodied or emotional conditioning. Such interruptions open up possibilities for mindfulness practitioners to re-engage—and to move more fully, intensively and skillfully into—the present moment, thereby amplifying their capacities to exercise agency. Batchelor has argued that such interruptions are every bit as necessary in the context of mindfulness traditions themselves. He contends that the most emancipatory possibilities of *dharma practice*—"the teachings of the [historical] Buddha as well as [...] those aspects of reality and experience with which his teachings are concerned"— have been eroded as "Buddhism" has, over the course of the centuries and in its evolving forms and traditions, taken on the institutional trappings and cosmological concerns of a religion (Batchelor 1997: xi). Observing that "The four *ennobling* truths are not propositions to believe; they are challenges to act," (our emphasis) he makes the case that taking up such challenges offers practitioners a potential means of transforming understandings and experiences of agency, authority, subjectivity, ethics, causality and temporality, and of rendering the interconnections and interdependencies between these far more evident (Batchelor 1997: 7). Batchelor returns to the first principles of the historical Buddha's teachings, not in order to retrieve an "authentic" or "originary" or "pure" set of precepts, but to illuminate the ways in which these teachings, when approached through a probing and engaged agnosticism that was in many ways anticipated and modeled by the teachings themselves, offer a particularly valuable method for confronting the complexities of our own historical moment:

> The contemporary social engagement of dharma practice is rooted in awareness of how self-centered confusion and craving can no longer be adequately understood only as psychological drives that manifest themselves in subjective states of anguish. We find these drives embodied in the very economic, military, and political structures that influence the lives of the majority of people on the earth. Harnessed to industrial technologies, the impact of these drives affects the quality of the environment; the availability of natural resources and employment; the kinds of political, social and financial institutions that govern peoples' lives. Such a socially engaged vision of dharma practice recognizes that each practitioner is obliged by an ethics of empathy to respond to the anguish of a globalized, interdependent world. (Batchelor 1997: 112)

By foregrounding the proliferating and mutually-reinforcing forms of "self-centered confusion and craving," Batchelor suggests why the rush of contemporary life potentially escalates processes that alienate subjects from themselves, from each other and from the environments they inhabit, processes that, as we have argued, are all too often replicated in the very institutional structures and methodologies of contemporary post-secondary education. The emphasis placed in *dharma* practice on "clinging" and "craving" as the root causes and propelling imperatives of anguish has particular pertinence in the context of global capitalism. In such a system, "clinging" manifests in the shoring up and protection of individual and collective resources (often by force, and almost invariably at the expense of equitable distribution, conservation or renewal), while the production of "craving" in multifarious forms (always accompanied by the promise of its fulfillment in a future place and time) can be seen to animate and sustain the entire system. The examples cited by Batchelor of military, industrial, political and economic modes of compulsive becoming are suggestive of the antagonistic forms of authority engendered by this unreflective process, as well as its proliferating destructive consequences in terms of individual, social and environmental potentiality. Batchelor's observations also suggest why projects that address the impacts of these processes by attending to certain manifestations of confusion or alienation to the exclusion of others are unlikely to produce enduring forms of transformation.

Crucially, Batchelor's call to arrest the impetus of these drives is underpinned by an ethical imperative, which, along with its ensuing ethical inferences, has far-reaching pedagogical implications. In the most practical terms, as we have suggested, mindfulness opens the learning process to multiple dimensions of experience that extend beyond the cognitive or conceptual mastery of specific skills and discourses, and it does so by fundamentally reconfiguring understandings and practices of subjectivity and authority. In meditation, Batchelor contends, we have the opportunity to experience selfhood in a fashion different than that to which we are accustomed:

> And instead of a coherent personality that stretches back in an unbroken line to a first memory and looks forward to an indefinite future, we discover a self ridden with gaps and ambiguities. Who 'I am' appears coherent only because of the monologue we keep repeating, editing, censoring, and embellishing in our heads. (Batchelor 1997: 24)

And it is precisely the desire for and insistence upon this assumed "coherency" that impels us to repeat habitual patterns, to feel overdetermined by particular histories and limited in our choices, to experience ourselves as separate, and to work at consolidating the realm of "me" and "mine." In relinquishing these compulsions, Batchelor suggests, we open ourselves to possibilities of both self-creation and world-creation: "The self-creation of individuation and the world-creation of social engagement cannot exist apart from each other" (Batchelor 1997: 112). By breaking habituated patterns and accessing virtual potentials, new pathways open both for and between individual subjects. Furthermore, Batchelor suggests that an "unawakened existence, in which we drift unaware on a surge of habitual impulses" engenders forms of authority that necessitate the imposition "of our will on others either through manipulation and intimidation or by appealing to the opinions of others more powerful than ourselves" (Batchelor 1997: 6). He concludes, "Authority becomes a question of force rather than of integrity" (ibid). The latter, he suggests, is not founded on force, nor on accession to certainty or totalizing understanding, but in more subtle and dynamic ways: "While rooted in empathy, integrity requires courage and intelligence as well, because every significant ethical choice entails risk," and that the cultivation of integrity is necessary because "We are obliged to assume responsibility for choices whose potentially considerable consequences for others we cannot possibly foresee" (Batchelor 1997: 46–7; 113). That is, as Massumi succinctly puts it, "ethics is about how we inhabit uncertainty, together" (Massumi 2003: 218). We propose, then, that incorporating lessons and practices derived from secular mindfulness traditions does not necessarily encourage a student's induction into a particular religious or philosophical tradition, reinforce the primacy of goals of self-realization, or assert notions individualism and free-will that serve to sustain liberal and capitalist ideologies in their contemporary manifestations. Instead, the process of affective and intellectual re-appraisal that can arise from the "stopping" can serve as a critique of the compulsive nature of craving and as a critical intervention in capitalist processes of fuelling increasingly insatiable desires. As a necessary complement, such practices also offer students a valuable means of assuming greater degrees and qualitatively different forms of mutually-constituted authority in the process of their learning, and of cultivating modes of interaction that are not overwhelmingly or even significantly conflictual or willful, and therefore do not lead to deeper and deeper entrenchments of contesting imperatives. Instead, these modes of interaction give rise to "non-coercive" and necessarily empathetic practices of experientially-acquired ethics.

Affect and cultural theory

We might pause for a moment and ask, how does the materialist tradition informing Giroux's assertions conceive of the mindful bodymind that we are proposing provides means of answering the restrictions of corporate time? If mindfulness can be understood to be a pathway by which the rhythms of stabilization and crisis of affective economies shaping the academy can be effectively brought into view, if mindfulness can provide the student with approaches that can contribute significantly to ethically grounded agency, how does the materialist tradition from which Giroux writes envisage the bodymind, that interpenetrating fusion of thought and bodily experience, as a site of resistance to hegemony? In other words, what is it that is coming to a full stop, what is it that is witnessing, how has this been and how might it be conceived?

In addressing cultural theory's discussion of the body over the past two decades, Massumi explores how theorists have generally emphasized notions of the body's constructedness by exterior forces and semiotized positionality in the broader material forces of the social matrix. In addition, despite the challenge that feminist criticism has mounted to Cartesian bifurcation, the body and mind are generally viewed as entirely distinct from one another, and most discourses imply their mutual exclusivity. Certainly, post-secondary education addresses itself principally to the mind of the student. Even in disciplines such as physical education, kinesiology, the performing arts, which involve the cultivation of physical skills and abilities— and even in theoretical explorations of questions of embodiment— the body tends to be treated as an object of study to be "mastered" conceptually. Massumi argues that such theoretical imperatives overly simplify the reality of the body's relation to change and were pursued in a bid to avoid "a reductive empiricism that would dissolve the specificity of the cultural domain in the plain, seemingly unproblematic, 'presence' of dumb matter" (Massumi 2002: 1). In these models, the body can be understood to be resistant to hegemony only if it is challenging the regimes of representation and restrictive economies of signs that cultural materialist theory posits as being the networked sites of social control. This mediated body can only be understood to be resistant if it performs a disturbance unsettling to dominant semiotic codes. For its part, in this way of theorizing, the mind is responsible for discursive intervention into governmental and juridical formations.

But what of the body's capacity to sense, Massumi wonders? He is informed by the thinking of Gilles Deleuze, who argues that we are not fixed selves or subjects, but rather that our underlying identities are best understood as those of mobile individuals set in motion by unidentifiable intensities. Massumi emphasizes, following Bergson and Whitehead, that when discussing the body and the body's relationship to thought, process comes before coding: "Passage precedes construction" (Massumi 2002: 8). A way of describing the flow of sensation and change that occurs in the body and the thought that interacts with it is the notion of affect, a concept that can be understood to be part of the broader Deleuzian project of "trying-to-understand, and comprehend, and express all of the incredible, wondrous, tragic, painful and destructive configurations of things and bodies as temporally mediated, continuous events" (Colman in Parr 2006: 11).

It would be a mistake to assume that affect is simply an experiential and subjective force; rather it is an independent thing "sometimes described in terms of the expression of an emotion or physiological effect, but all the while trans-historical, trans-temporal, trans-spatial and autonomous" (Ibid.). Massumi elaborates, "[Affects] are our angle of participation in processes larger than ourselves. With intensified affect comes a stronger sense of embeddedness in a larger field of life—a heightened sense of belonging, with other people and to other places" (Massumi 2003: 214). He goes on to suggest that the most radically transformative actions are instantiated by tapping in to the intensities of embodied and intersubjective experience in any given present moment; and by working beyond inherited conceptual and moral paradigms, beyond the familiar and habit-dulled practices of cognition and judgment which simply prescribe and re-entrench existing patterns of movement and interrelation, often unwittingly. Significantly, rather than being understood as a private or deeply interior experience, affect can be conceived as the advent of potentially new *intersubjective* and *embodied* relations. Drawing on Spinoza, Massumi proposes an understanding of "the body in terms of its capacity for *affecting* or being *affected,*" and sees these capacities as fundamentally interconnected (Massumi 2003: 212). He elaborates:

> When you affect something, you are at the same time opening yourself up to being affected in turn, and in a slightly different way than you might have been the moment before. You have made a transition, however slight. You have stepped over a threshold. (Massumi 2003: 212)

It is in this place of transition that new configurations of authority can begin to emerge.

Nevertheless, the experience of affect is direct. Massumi explains when he states that:

> the directness I'm talking about isn't a self-presence or self-possession which is how we normally tend to think of our freedom. If it's direct, it's in the sense that it's directly in transition — in the body passing out of the present moment and the situation it's in, towards the next one. (Massumi 2003: 215)

Pivotal to this conception is the doubleness of bodies, the notion that "a body doesn't coincide with itself," that it is never entirely present to itself on account of the remains of affective potential following whatever a body says or does:

> Looked at from a different angle, this perpetual remainder is an excess. It's like a reserve of potential or creativity that is experienced alongside every actual production of meaning in language, or in any performance of a useful function—vaguely but directly experienced, as *something more*, a more to come, a life overspilling as it gathers to move on. (Massumi 2003: 215)

This excess, this surfeit of affect is what continues to resonate and proliferate, which implies that our experience is always more than can be theorized. Our affective experience is also always more than can be captured by a hegemonic system, regardless of what that system's ability to redirect flows of affect towards its own ends, such as those of capital, might be.

If not attended to, affect, as a result of its properties of resonance, transformation, and transmission, can readily become material and compel systems of knowing, of history; affect can become crystallized into restrictive circuits of habituation and power on an individual level and societal level, including the dynamic of affective capitalization referred to above. In that affect provides a potentially sophisticated way of discussing the types of flows of experience that mindfulness (and a traditional Humanities education) addresses, it provides us with pathways of understanding how the way that affect precipitates into thought, sensation and emotion in processes of teaching and learning can be understood to be so much more than the passive notion of "reflection" by which such activities are often described. Mindfulness offers an active engagement with the world that is uniquely positioned to allow us to thoroughly challenge patterns of compulsive becoming while also assuring the possibility of both captures and releases of flows of affect and its excesses into awareness, and ultimately, agency.

THE HUMANITIES IN/AND CRISIS

> The tradition of the oppressed teaches us that the 'state of emergency' in which we live is not the exception but the rule. (Walter Benjamin, Thesis VIII, "Theses on the philosophy of history")

One of our purposes in highlighting the conditions that frame pedagogical encounters in the Humanities classroom in our present place and time is to examine the operation of a very particular set of parameters and constraints[10] to which we are attempting to respond. As we have suggested, these constraints, insofar as they engender and entrench systematic forms of compulsive becoming, serve to accelerate processes that alienate learners from themselves and one another, to reduce their awareness of and access to significant dimensions of affective potential, and therefore to curtail possibilities for agency. As we gesture towards the potential consequences of leaving these constraints intact and unchallenged, of failing to rupture processes of compulsive becoming that narrow our range of experience and capacity for re-subjectification, and that play into hegemonic strategies of social control currently fueled by the capitalization of affect, and as we argue for the urgency of attending to processes that might restore to learners "a margin of manoeverability," we do not wish to suggest that the state of crisis in which post-secondary education currently finds itself is in any way aberrant, exceptional or unprecedented (Massumi 2003: 211). Such perennial crisis is not simply a temporary deviation from normative or desirable conditions that, once addressed, would facilitate a restoration of order. Rather, we hope to put this crisis in a broader context, to suggest that the purpose of Humanities education is precisely to take us to the heart of crisis, and to propose that mindfulness practices provide a generative way of negotiating the difficulties that such a project inevitably entails.

If we take seriously Walter Benjamin's often-cited argument that "the tradition of the oppressed" is one of almost continuous emergency, we must also acknowledge what this "teaches *us*." This is especially the case if we are among those whose privilege has shielded us from *necessarily* experiencing crisis as a constant condition—and most of us who teach and study in post-secondary institutions in the economic North would fall into that category, irrespective of the challenges we face. We must acknowledge that our various forms of conditioned behaviour—including our intellectual conditioning—have encouraged us to think of stability as normative—perhaps as our right—and to seek its restitution with ever increasing levels of tenacity when it eludes us. By the same token, we must recognize that this conditioning often prevents us from registering that whatever sense of stability we may have experienced is inextricably bound up with the states of instability to which the majority of the people in the world are almost constantly subject. And we must understand that when our feeling of stability is shaken, any attempt to regain "equilibrium" in the face of this type of crisis that fails to address patterns of implication, interconnection and interdependence is bound to escalate, rather than alleviating, the states of emergency that we—and others—experience (6). It is precisely by ignoring, isolating or displacing crisis in order to sustain our fictions of autonomy, stability and mastery—whether individual or collective; by attributing the root causes of instability to people and events in distant places and times; and perhaps most crucially, by indexing our responses to crisis—our encounters with the "unknowable"— towards a teleological quest for restoration of order and "knowing," that states of emergency spill over into catastrophe and mass violence.

Shoshana Felman, who situates our current historical moment at the end of a "post-traumatic century, a century that has survived unthinkable historical catastrophes" (Felman and Laub 1992: 1), has argued that the direct experience of crisis has enormous value, particularly in pedagogical terms, and that what distinguishes truly transformative learning from the transmission of knowledges and skills that serve to re-entrench hegemonic power and the ontological and epistemological foundations upon which it rests is the enactment of change through a bringing-to-crisis. In "Education and crisis, or the Vicissitudes of Teaching," a chapter that opens with the question, ""Is there a relation between crisis and the very enterprise of education?" (ibid.), she writes,

> I would venture to propose, today, that teaching in itself, as such, takes place precisely only through a crisis: if teaching does not hit upon some source of crisis, if it does not encounter either the vulnerability or the explosiveness of a (explicit or implicit) critical dimension, it has perhaps *not truly taught*: it has perhaps passed on some facts, passed on some information and some documents… (Felman 1992: 53)

Felman understands crisis as a shift in conditions that we register, perhaps traumatically, when we discover that our inherited frameworks (of language, epistemology, morality, semantics) fail to serve us, fail to provide us with meaningful or adequate forms of response to events. Like Batchelor, she suggests that we can never resolve or even understand the full import and implications of a crisis, but that it is in the act of confronting its emergence, encountering its complexity, and experiencing its affects that what she terms "precocious testimony"—not-yet-known and still-to-be realized understandings—can begin to be articulated. She contends that it is in literature and the arts that the fractures in old systems are first registered as crises not fully grasped or understood, and that witnessing these crises is part of what we do as writers and readers. Specifically, she, along with co-author Dori Laub,[11] explores how "art inscribes (artistically bears witness to) *what we do not yet know of our lived historical relation to events of our times*" (Felman and Laub 1992: xx). "Education in crisis" is presented as Felman's own "life testimony," a compelling account of teaching a graduate course on Literature and Testimony that focused on literary and cinematic acts of bearing witness to historical trauma. Near the end of the course, she explains, many of the students themselves began to experience symptoms of trauma in the immediate aftermath of viewing selected testimonies from the Video Archive for Holocaust Testimonies at Yale. As she addresses the eruption of trauma *in the classroom*, and not merely in the content of the course materials, she observes:

> Looking back at the experience of that class, I therefore think that my job as a teacher, paradoxical as it may sound, was that of creating in the class the highest state of crisis that it could withstand, without "driving the students crazy," without compromising the students' bounds.
>
> In the era of the Holocaust, of Hiroshima, of Vietnam—in the age of testimony—teaching, I would venture to suggest, must in turn *testify*, make something happen, and not just transmit a passive knowledge, pass on information that is preconceived, substantiated, believed to be known in advance, misguidedly believed, that is, to be (exclusively) a *given*. (Felman 1992: 53)

Felman's argument uncompromisingly celebrates what we see as the core values of the affective dimensions of a Humanities education, an encounter with the limits of the known that precipitates an ongoing exploration of states of perplexity. Moreover, her account of the experience of this course highlights precisely the value of introducing mindfulness practices as a means for students and instructors alike to cultivate skills that enable them to address moments of profound crisis. To push classes to the "highest state of crisis [they] can withstand [...] without compromising the students' bounds" is potentially to interrupt the reproduction of hegemonic knowledges and interests, and to create spaces for new ways of connecting to begin to be negotiated. Batchelor's account of entering into states of perplexity that suffuse the entire organism, like Felman's account of her students' symptoms and responses, suggest that such crises are registered and must be addressed not only in intellectual terms, but also psychically, emotionally, and somatically.

We contend that the cultivation of awareness practices provides a means of beginning to address crisis, while containing its most overwhelming impacts. Batchelor puts it thus:

> All of life is ceaseless mutation: emerging, modifying, disappearing. The relative constancy of still, centered attention is simply a steady adjustment to the flux of what is observed. Nothing can be relied upon for security. As soon as you grasp something, it's gone. (Batchelor 1997: 25)

That is to say, we are not suggesting that the crises with which students will inevitably be confronted in the classroom and in their lives will be somehow eradicated, resolved, remedied or stabilized by various forms of mindfulness or bodymind work. Rather, mindfulness practices enable students to tap into the potentiality for "emergence" that always inheres in states of "emergency," to the virtual dimension of acts and utterances that Massumi terms "the *excess,*" [...] vaguely but directly experienced, as *something more*, a more to come, a life overspilling as it gathers to move on" (Massumi 2003: 215). If indexed towards the realization of a particular goal or predetermined outcome—and revelation and resolution would be two obvious goals in an academic context— mindfulness practices, like Humanities scholarship and pedagogy, sacrifice their most radical emancipatory potential and simply entrench a new set of imperatives and their attendant constraints that will eventually manifest as yet another pattern of conditioning. When left open-ended, the full potentiality of affective connection remains available.

HOLDING TOGETHER AND (OR) IN TENSION

> ...if hope is separated from concepts of optimism and pessimism, from a wishful projection of success or even some kind of a rational calculation of outcomes, when I think it starts to be interesting — because it places it in the *present*. [...]
>
> The question of which next step to take is a lot less intimidating than how to reach a far-off goal in a distant future where all our problems will finally be solved. It's utopian thinking, for me, that's 'hopeless'. (Brian Massumi, "Navigating Movements")

And now, a return to a now: a specific, discernable moment in time; one that despite its having passed can draw us—by means of traces of affect precipitated into thought, language, and text—through the stormy moment of an unsettling anticipation of personal crisis and towards a threshold of destabilization threatening to harden into anguish. We will finish this chapter by sitting with and alongside the thoughts of a theatre studies student, an undergraduate wrestling with the fresh awareness of complexities inherent in his relationship with labour, critical analysis, and creative practice. Feeling trapped by a troubling state of perplexity as he attempts to write of his experience for an undergraduate thesis project, he sends the following email to his instructor:

> I'm having a bit of an ideological crisis with the paper theory work at the moment, I don't know if you have any suggestions but it's causing me a bit of distress. I go to work [at the scenography building shop] and assimilate into the culture and begin to think (and believe) that my thesis is bullshit, that it is impractical, that the existent structure [of society and the workplace] is necessary; in fact why am I even at school? In fact, I really hate actors, and all those silly creative impractical people. In fact, I should just find a good place to work, and ... well work. Then I see something like [a compelling theatre production] or read an article that blows my mind and I flip into another naturalized position of realizing I'm working in a factory that has nothing to do with the theatre. Which I think is something that I think I like sometimes, maybe. Do I like it? In opposition to this through my encounters with [cultural materialist] theory, I begin to question my values, my enjoyment of work. The respect I earn at work is directly related to my ability as a worker, therefore my place in production and my own oppression, right? If values of hard work, and quality work serve my employer and not me, if a large part of what I identify as self is a construction that places me at the bottom of a power structure why do I hold [these values]? Why is working hard good? Why is laziness bad? Which of these thoughts are authentic? Are any? If both thought processes are impressed upon me how do I navigate between them? I'm getting really confused. Because I agree with these theorists: Eagleton, Althusser, Barthes, etc., but I'm having a hard time with all the questions this brings up. And specifically this paper [about the materiality of theatre practices] and what I find interesting about it, and what is at the same time difficult, is that I'm not an astronaut or a deep sea diver bringing his/her world with him/her in exploration of another. I'm part of it, and fish don't write papers. Plus poststructuralism is making me second-guess, it's really hard not to be paralyzed by the stuff.

Struggling with being objective and distanced from the life that he is living even as he becomes even more involved with it through the increased sociopolitical awareness that an engagement with certain texts has brought him—grappling with being "in or out of the water" as it were—the student oscillates between letting himself follow further lines of questioning and then gesturing towards the stabilizing act of separating the unknown from the known ("the existent structure [of society and the workplace] is necessary"). The testimony that ensues from his witnessing over time is an affirmation of shifts from one ingrained framework of patterns of reaction to the another, with the juxtaposition of both sets of assumptions serving to defamiliarize and denaturalize the authenticating underpinnings of each of the two foundational codes ("Which of these thoughts are authentic? Are any?"). As he writes through this painful awareness of implication, interconnection and interdependence, as he experiences the vertigo—most likely experienced affectively throughout his entire being—of the heightened realization of a seemingly fractured coherence of self, a practice of mindfulness emerges as a potential pathway forward ("how do I navigate between them?"). A moment of arrest and pause that does not attempt an immediate reconciliation of apparent opposites nor promotes the suppression of the most anxiety provoking of the terms is a moment in which the full potential of affective connection can remain available. The rich affective excess of the testimony can this way become less of a threat, a threat that may risk traumatizing the beholder ("I'm having a hard time with all the questions this brings up"), when the student sits—literally and metaphorically—with the discomfort rather than fleeing to one secure yet potentially reductive position or another. In such a moment, the tentative asking of further questions can follow, which can in turn give rise to subtler and more profound lines of questioning. By continuing to break the cycle of compulsive becoming, a rupture initiated by the texts he has read and the discussion he has entertained in and out of class, the student can further recognize and critique the terms of the hegemonic mode that attempts, discursively and affectively, to entrain him into mastering and repeating it. This encounter with the limits of the known can precipitate into an ongoing exploration of uncomfortable states of perplexity all while mobilizing rather than shutting down the affective excess that clearly overflows in such moments of cumulative realization ("it's really hard not to be paralyzed by the stuff"). By engaging in this exploration and exchange in the public/private space between the student and professor in a moment of simultaneous containment, release, and pause, all parties reconfigure understandings and practices of subjectivity and authority in a dialogically and dynamically enacted moment of public time. This temporality of generosity—in which bound affective flows are released rather than captured/commodified—is the ethical mode in which the deferral of teleologies, in which the affirmation of irresolution, of working principles, and of temporary theses, all have increased potential for actualization. It is in such a time and place, this now, every now, that small but confident steps can be taken in the interstices between stultifying authoritative stances and the denial of any solid ground whatsoever, small but confident steps towards…

NOTES

1 As we will go on to elaborate, we understand "witnessing" in the sense in which it has been theorized by Shoshana Felman and Dori Laub in *Testimony: Crises of Witnessing in Literature, Psychoanalysis and History* and by Kelly Oliver in *Witnessing: Beyond Recognition*, that is, not simply as analogous with observation, but as an advent of understanding that emerges in the context of intersubjective encounters.

2 Kabat-Zinn has written a number of books on the application of awareness practice to stress management, and serves as the director for the Center for Mindfulness in Medicine, Health Care and Society at the University of Massachusetts Medical School.

3 In *Buddhism without Beliefs*, Stephen Batchelor uses as the epigraph for his chapter on imagination Richard Rorty's observation that "[A] talent for speaking differently, rather than for arguing well, is the chief instrument of cultural change." [from *Contingency, Irony and Solidarity*. Cambridge: Cambridge University Press, 1989, 7].

4 Born in Scotland, Batchelor trained as a Buddhist monk first in the Tibetan, and later in the Korean Zen tradition, before disrobing in 1985. He has since worked in a secular context teaching, writing,

translating and serving as a contributing editor of *Tricycle: A Buddhist Review*. In 1992 he became the co-ordinator of the Sharpham Trust, and later, co-founded the Sharpham College for Buddhist Studies and Contemporary Enquiry (1996). His research, which explores the role of dharma practice in the contemporary world, draws on a range of ancient Pali texts, and he has also translated into English several Tibetan texts by ancient and modern Buddhist teachers.

5 We use "moral" in Brian Massumi's sense, based on the distinction he draws between *moral codes* on the one hand, which he sees as inherited imperatives that posit stable and universal criteria for "right" and "wrong" (or "good" and "evil" in a more theological idiom), and *ethical actions*, on the other, which he understands as situational responses to intersubjective crises. Where moral codes demand conformity to established rules and protocols, ethical action involves risk, empathy, intensification of affect and creativity. Where a moral action might be understood in teleological terms to contribute to the production of a desired outcome, an ethical action is open-ended, and can be judged only in terms of the range of possibilities it opens up and sets in play in the present.

6 This phrase, coined by the American Buddhist teacher Pema Chödrön, serves as the title of her 2003 book, subtitled "108 teachings on cultivating fearlessness and compassion" (Shambala Press).

7 At a retreat led by Stephen and Martine Batchelor in Ixopo, South Africa from 30 December, 2006 to 8 January, 2007, participants were encouraged, as is typical during meditation, to attend carefully to bodily sensations, emotional and physical states, and to sounds, smells, and other sensory input as they sat in the meditation hall. Gradually the instruction not simply to label what was observed, but to question "what is this?" was introduced and elaborated. In question and answer sessions, many participants, including long-time practitioners, expressed how difficult they found it not simply to label and categorize what they had attended to, particularly the aural sensations such as bird calls, gusts of wind, the sound of rain, or of various activities in progress at the retreat centre. The habit of indexing attentiveness towards "knowing" was recognized as very powerful, and most often treated as an end in itself. One participant, however, told the story of labeling the call of a bulbul, and then asking "what is this?" and realizing how little, beyond invoking criteria for identification, he knew about the bird, how ridiculous it was to assume he knew it. He expressed the recognition as one that that induced a state of near hilarity, and that was enormously freeing.

8 It is interesting to note, on the one hand, the similar terms in which Humanities subjects have come to be viewed within the academy and those in which mindfulness traditions are often discussed (as frivolous, self-indulgent, superfluous, irrelevant; even "flaky"); and on the other hand, the similar ways in which both have been taken up by corporate interests as channels for the personal growth of employees or for the diversification of potential markets.

9 Ironically, the application form for the award under the auspices of which this current research is being conducted, Brock University's Chancellor's Chair for Excellence in Teaching, explicitly cites as one possible use for the funds awarded a buy-out of some of the recipients' teaching duties; we both felt, however, that our respective commitments to and interests in pedagogy would *not* best be served by reducing our contact time in the classroom.

10 Following Massumi, we do not equate the experience of freedom with the eradication of constraint, which would be neither possible nor desirable; rather, we recognize the accession to "degrees of freedom" in the capacity to work creatively *with* constraint. Massumi writes, "freedom, or the ability to move forward and to transit through life, isn't necessarily about escaping from constraints. There are always constraints. When we walk, we're dealing with the constraint of gravity. There's also the constraint of balance, and a need for equilibrium. But, at the same time, to walk you need to throw off the equilibrium, you have to let yourself go into a fall, then you cut it off and regain the balance. You move forward by playing with the constraints, not avoiding them. There's an openness of movement, even though there's no escaping constraint. (218-9).

11 *Testimony: Crises of Witnessing in Literature, Psychoanalysis and History* is a co-authored volume, but consists of chapters individually authored by either Felman or Laub. "Education in Crisis," with which the volume opens, is authored by Felman.

REFERENCES

Batchelor, S. (1997). *Buddhism without beliefs: A contemporary guide to awakening*. New York: Riverhead Books.

Benjamin, W. (1969). Theses on the philosophy of history. In *Illuminations*. Edited with an introduction by Hannah Arendt. Translated by Harry Zohn. New York: Schocken Books. 253–264.

Colman, F. (2005). Affect. In Adrian Parr (Ed.), *The Deleuze dictionary* (pp. 11–13). New York: Columbia University Press.

Felman, S., & Dori Laub, M. D. (1992). *Testimony: Crises of witnessing in literature, psychoanalysis and history*. New York and London: Routledge.

Giroux, Henry A. (2003). *Public time and educated hope: Educational leadership and the war against youth*. [Online]. Retrieved January 25, 2005, from http://www.units.muohio.edu/eduleadership/anthology/OA/OA03001.html

Hardt, M., & Antonio, N. (2004). *Multitude: War and democracy in the age of empire*. New York: Penguin USA.

Kabat-Zinn, J. (2005). *Wherever you go, there you are: Mindfulness meditation in everyday life*. New York: Hyperion Books.

Massumi, B. (2002). *Parables for the virtual: Movement, affect, sensation*. Durham, NC: Duke University Press.

Navigating Movements (2003). In M. Zournazi (Ed.), *Hope: New philosophies for change* (pp. 210–242). New York: Routledge.

WARREN LINDS AND LINDA GOULET

PERFORMING PRAXIS

Exploring Anti-racism through Drama

> Our relationship with the learners is one of the roads that we can do to intervene in reality over both the short and long term ... our relationship with the learner demands that we respect them and demands equally that we be aware of the concrete conditions of their world, the conditions that shape them (Freire 1998: 102).

This chapter will critically examine praxis in a program dealing with racism and discrimination in schools. We will explore how the theatrical process we use not only de-normalizes acts of discrimination, but also provides a space to develop an "as if" world, where an anti-oppression praxis (Adams, Bell and Griffin 1997; Kumashiro 2000) is modeled and enacted. Such a praxis involves looking at the relationship of identity, power and social change questioning structures of power in the world, communities and, most importantly, schools. We will look at how working against racism is possible to address in student-student relationships and problematize the program's difficulty in extending this work to identify, and change, institutional and societal beliefs and practices.

PRAXIS

Paulo Freire (1970) writes that praxis involves action and reflection where each element builds upon the other as "the act of knowing involves a dialectical movement which goes from action to reflection and from reflection upon action into new action" (31). These actions take place in the real, not some imaginary or hypothetical, world and this world is the world of people interacting with each other. As interaction around important issues, praxis is always risky, requiring that a person "makes a wise and prudent judgment about how to act in this situation" (Carr and Kemmis 1986: 190).

Word and action, action and reflection, theory and practice are all facets of the same idea. Actions as praxis is not merely doing something (what Freire describes as activism) or acting upon, or doing something for the sake of doing. Praxis is a creative act, and dialogic in that both our actions and the world are emergent in the action.

In praxis, the facilitator draws participants into a process of critical reflection by first discovering the generative themes that are the common experiences in one's social milieu, developed by people to make sense of the world around them. Once

S.A. Moore and R.C. Mitchell (eds.), Power, Pedagogy and Praxis: Social Justice in the Globalized Classroom, 199–217.

discovered, the facilitator or educator and participants work together to initiate new understandings of what is going on and one's place within it. The goal is to determine appropriate action and change.

In this chapter, we use Fregeau and Leier's (2002) division of the process of praxis to structure the discussion of our school based anti-racism program as follows:

- Understanding one's social reality
- Reflecting on that reality and experience
- Realizing that it can be changed and imagining how
- Deciding one has the power to make changes, and
- Taking action to make changes in that reality

1. UNDERSTANDING THE CONTEXT

The anti-racism program

A Canada-wide survey commissioned by the Dominion Institute (Ipsos-Reid 2005) in March 2005 found that one in six Canadians (17%) report that they have been the victims of racism. More specifically, the residents of the prairie provinces of Saskatchewan/Manitoba (27%) report they have been the victims of racism. Residents of the same provinces (76%) say that Aboriginal[1] people are the most likely to be the victims of racism.

In releasing the survey results, Rudyard Griffiths, Executive Director of the Dominion Institute commented that "these poll results unfortunately indicate that racism and discrimination are a fact of everyday life for millions of Canadians. Despite the advances we have made as a country to eliminate intolerance, we cannot become complacent about the need to challenge racism and discrimination at their every occurrence" (2).

The Ipsos-Reid poll showed approximately 30% of Canadians feel that schools and families would be most effective in promoting racial tolerance. At the same time, other studies have documented that schools are sites of racist incidents and practices (Huff 1997, Schissel and Wotherspoon 2003, Silver and Mallett 2002, Wilson 1991). In our program, we view the incidents of racism to have potential in anti-racism education. We include these incidents as part of the learning process as we examine, through experiential activities, racism as it occurs in the lives of students at school.

In 1994, a public school board in Canada created a program to develop the capacity of youth between the ages of 12-18 years for leadership in anti-racism and cross-cultural education in their schools. The school division has ten high schools and close to fifty elementary schools. Compared to other jurisdictions, the student body would seem to be dominated by Eurocanadians, although there is a cultural and racial mix. The largest group of racialized students in the school is Aboriginal and that is where the greatest amount of racial tension in the community exists. The students and teachers who participate in this program are from different cultural and racial backgrounds. The program motto – Together We Will Make a Difference! – reflects a belief that it is everyone's responsibility to work toward building communities where individuals are safe from discrimination, prejudice, stereotyping and racism. In this chapter we analyze the program in terms of praxis, focusing primarily on one aspect of the program, a retreat, although implementation in the schools is also included. The retreat is an intensive three day training that brings together school staff, students and facilitators in a setting away from their schools and the city. At the retreat, we use Power Plays (Diamond 1991), a Canadian adaptation of Brazilian theatre director Augusto Boal's (1979, 1992, 1995, 1998) Theatre of the Oppressed techniques along with community and trust building activities that explore issues of identity and power in order to facilitate the development of youth leadership to address acts and attitudes of school-based discrimination.

BUILDING A SPACE FOR COMMUNITY

Risks are inherent in discussing what we want to de-normalize. Racism and discrimination are risky subjects, partly because they are not talked about in school, and partly because the issues are a complex interweaving of power, identity, attitudes, behaviours, and institutional and cultural structures. Trust amongst participants is important to enable them to share their lived experiences of discrimination. We use many experiential activities that involve themes of exclusion and inclusion, and link them through debriefing to life in school. The goals of the retreat are to familiarize the participants (including adults) with the language of discrimination and racism, to enable trust to be developed, and for stories to begin to emerge that help both facilitators and participants understand the reality of students.

Experiential activities include warmup games and trust exercises that inform different levels of the creative process, provide experiences of issues of power (exercises that embody leaders and followers) and, at the same time, enable a safe space to emerge. We begin with "Who is Here?", an activity that introduces concepts of multiple identity and group membership. "Responding to Difference" explores how difference is constructed and dealt with both individually and in society. "Power Flower" (Burke et al 1991: 87-88) helps student identify who they are (and aren't) as individuals, and as a group, in relation to those who have power in society.

We engage in activities and debriefing on important aspects of racism. One game, "Discriminadot" (Selby 1988), introduces the notion of exclusion through the random placement of dots on participants' foreheads and asking participants to group themselves. Another, "Sticky Labels' explores how we are "labeled" by others in terms of negative and positive qualities that affect social interaction and status.

Theatre games are used to contribute to a sense of community through Boal's (1992) *Knowing the body*: feeling what we touch, listen to what we hear, and seeing what we look at. We work in small groups to develop our sensory consciousness of the world and share the storied lives of the participants.

The games, small group work and theatre activities build trusting relationships among participants that allow a deep level of sharing. A powerful sense of community is developed that extends beyond the retreat setting.

2. REFLECTING ON REALITY AND EXPERIENCE

Seeing our own and others' stories

> To try to know the reality that our students live is a task that the educational practice imposes on us: Without this, we have no access to the way they think, so only with great difficulty can we presume what then they know (Freire 1970: 102).

Stories are central to the learning process, as they mediate between self and others. As students develop different sets of images, they come to see their experiences reflected in those of others as they share common experiences. This forges bonds that grow out of, and expand, the program. Therefore, an integral part of the process is to enable participants to express themselves individually and collectively. Boal (1979) calls this "making the body expressive" (130). Turner (1982) suggests that "narrate" traces its lineage from the Latin narrare, "to tell," and Latin gnarus, "knowing," both deriving from the Indo-European gna, "to know" (86-87). Thus, narrative is a way of knowing, a search for meaning that privileges experience, process, action and risk. The shared roots of both storytelling and knowledge indicate the way knowing is shared through action. Knowing is achieved in representation through word, image or sound.

At the retreat, students begin to represent their world by sharing stories non-verbally through Image[2]. Based on the idea that a "picture paints a thousand words" (Jackson in Boal 1992: xx), students recall an incident or experience they have had and create a body shape or image to represent that experience. Imaging enables the participant to fill the body shapes with feelings and thoughts that come from the interplay between the physical shape and experience. Thoughts and words initially emerge from the individual's awareness of the static body in the Image and the world around the Image. Images can be activated into further motion, movements that arise out of the interplaying of the physical shapes of bodies and their interpretation in words and action.

Image as narrative is introduced through "Complete the Image" (Diamond 1990) which is first done by two people shaking hands in a frozen image in front of the whole group. Anyone who has an idea can jump up, tap one of a pair shaking hands and replace them in a new body shape in relation to the other, adding a new element, creating a different Image, a new story. After a few Images in pairs, more characters are added to one of the Images until there are six or seven people who are making a story out of the original paired Image. We then decode the image by asking the group what they see as the story, emphasizing that one image can be interpreted in many ways, from many perspectives[3]. When it seems the group has understood the method, we begin again. This time we ask the group to think of a particular theme like life in school, or racism in school while completing the image. We then ask the group to identify who has power in the Image story, who doesn't and why.

Such an Image is a tool of Bertolt Brecht's (quoted in Roman 1993) "complex seeing of analysis" (158) – a set of visuals which emerge from generative "themes which contain the possibility of unfolding into again as many themes, which in their turn call for new tasks to be fulfilled" (Freire 1970: 92) with rich ramifications in the lives of learners.

Just as there is a transformation from that of the story teller into the story shower, playing with Image leads to a transformation of meaning. "The image work never remains static....the frozen image is simply the starting point for or prelude to the action, which is revealed in the dynamisation process, the bringing to life of the images and the discovery of whatever direction or intention is innate in them" (Jackson in Boal 1992: xix–xx).

As text, Images are a form of communication between storyteller and audience. They access events, places and personalities that exist, not as isolated facts, but as inter-related representations that emerge as we remember (Simon 1994). The issues become clearer as we work through image. When we see another's images or hear his/her story, we as members of the group may invest that story and those characters with the colours of our own experience. We grasp the story and make it our own.

In this way, Images are tools to reflect upon action in the world outside the retreat. At the same time, constructing the Image is an act of creation so becomes something more than mere reflection. Through this process, Image brings to light what is otherwise hidden and withdrawn. In the case of Image, this language of "double seeing, where the image of the real is real as image" (Boal 1995: 43-44), the Image forms a kind of mirror with us being both inside and outside it. Imaging through performance invites participation through performance – embodied explorations of the interplay through body, mind, and imagination; we perform possibility and absence into being and becoming.

3. REALIZING THAT REALITY CAN BE CHANGED AND IMAGINING HOW

The "Wildest Dream"

Image work enables a listening to stories, overcoming the act of hearing, "since it entails not only hearing, but also feeling what is listened to, getting involved with what is being listened to, and being actually engaged with the speaker – and then, reflecting on all this, systematizing what has been listened to first" (Freire 2002: 13).

In our work at the retreat, students create images that tell the story of their experiences of power, oppression and racism in their lives. The image work produces a creative space for students to develop the capacity to represent and give expression to their view of experience and reality. The Images created by the students most often deal with stories of oppression in their lives at school, but sometimes includes experiences in families, with peers or in the community. As we examine each individual Image to identify commonalities and differences, students come to see their experiences reflected in those of others and recognize that they are not alone in their experiences of exclusion and powerlessness. This recognition of self in the experience of others illustrates the commonalities shared by students, forging bonds among them. A composite image is then created that incorporates the most powerful aspects of each of the individual images. We call the composite image the Image of Oppression. Students reflect on the Image of Oppression to identify the characters and their role in the Image. We discuss with the participants who has power over, who is under power, and how that power is expressed. We identify the central conflict in the Image. This exploration helps students deconstruct the power relationships inherent in racism and oppression and leads to an examination of how that power is developed and maintained.

The Image of Oppression is followed by an adaptation of an exercise called Your Wildest Dream which was developed by David Diamond (2000). Your Wildest Dream takes the Image of Oppression and asks the participants to make an Image that is not an opposite of the Image of Oppression, but one that takes us into our imaginations to explore what our dreams might be for an ideal that would represent, for example, 'A world without racism'. Then Images are made to represent the intermediary steps that could transform the Image of oppression (which is of a concrete situation) into the Image of the Your Wildest Dream, which is much more imaginative and abstract. As students come up with the intermediary steps between the Images, they discuss the possibilities for change and examine the consequences of the attempts to change. We begin to see the little changes that are necessary. Who is able to change first? How might other characters respond? What changes does this cause? What is blocking the desired changes? What will enable the change to occur? In the interplay between the Image and the discussion of transformation, students start to see where hope lies and what are the significant moments of change, creating an 'as if' world or, more accurately, a 'what if' world that is about 'what if we could change things' or "what if we acted to change things'.

Doing so gives student voice so that their issues lead the program within the structure set by the leaders. Sharing helps students overcome isolation and breaks the silence of oppression. Discrimination starts to be denormalized. On numerous occasions we have heard students comment that they thought bullying and discrimination were just the way things were but that hearing others' stories enabled them to understand that these acts were wrong and they should do something about it. Students come to see that they are not alone in their experiences of feeling oppressed. In the representation of a common incident of oppression they discover the features of domination and how it is enacted. Students come to understand how power is achieved through numerical strength, different forms of power, and coercion and fear. They can see how power is exercised in speech and in their body. In working through the stages from the incident of oppression to the wildest dream, students identify who the players are, the roles they play and gain some insight into the possibilities for change, for personal or societal intervention.

4. DECIDING ONE HAS THE POWER TO MAKE CHANGES

Forum Theatre

In engaging one's audience in this process of consciousness raising, the educator is required to help draw the audience into a process of critical reflection by first discovering the group's "generative themes" as the baseline for the dialogic encounter. These themes are the common elemental orienting concepts of one's social milieu, developed by people to understand the world around them; and once discovered, the educator and audience work together to initiate a self-generated new understanding of historical reality and one's place within it (Freire 2002: 81)

In the program retreat we have a student leadership team, composed of more senior students and past participants of the program who have experience in representing their reality through drama. We work with this group to develop a Forum play that incorporates their common experiences of exclusion, discrimination, prejudice, and racism. Each play includes various characters like oppressors, victims and bystanders, or potential allies of the antagonist and protagonist. The first time we perform the play for the participants in the retreat setting, we use it for discussion of the issues the characters in it are facing. We ask each audience member to think about which character's struggle they identify with the most. After the play, we ask the audience to help us create a Status Lineup, so that we can physically place the characters in the play according to the power they have in the scene. This leads to interesting discussions about who can potentially use their power; who will refuse; who will never have power; and what is the potential for certain characters to take action.

Later we perform the play using Forum Theatre (Boal 1979) with the retreat participants as audience members. Drawing on Boal's critique of the usual role of the audience in theatre, he developed the term spect-actor to change the role of audience to participant, where the audience is invited to suggest and enact solutions to dramatized problems. A situation is shown in an unsolved form (the Forum play), to which the audience (spect-actors) is invited to suggest and enact solutions. Many alternative solutions or interventions are enacted in the course of a single forum. The result is a pooling of knowledge, tactics and experience similar to what Freire calls praxis as "untested feasibility [inedito viavel]" (Freire 2002: 8). Thus, praxis is not merely behaviour; it is the possibility of doing something that has not been tried before and that can only be understood in terms of the commitments that informed it. Thus, interventions are rich concrete instances of 'what might be possible'.

After watching the play to its problematic ending, the play performance is repeated several times with students invited to become spect-actors. Students can and do intervene on behalf of a character they identify with, whom they see having a struggle to overcome power. "The keener the desire to take action, the more the spect-actors hurry on to the stage. They enact thoughts, rather than just speaking them"(Dwyer 2004: 199). We encourage students to try out their ideas for action as spect-actors, and that we can learn from each intervention, not just those that produce a more "satisfactory" result in the play. We find that as students see their peers go on the stage, everyone is likely to be more engaged and critically conscious. "There is a kind of knowledge – or perhaps, better a will to knowledge and power – which is apprehended in similar circumstances and which is qualitatively different from knowledge sitting in your seat as silent witness" (200).

We debrief each intervention asking both the actors as characters and the spect-actors who intervened what has happened and how the intervention affected their character. We also explore the barriers to action, because usually, each new action carries with it some kind of risk.

A recent play was about a teenage girl and her new 'brother'. The girl resents that her mother has begun living with an Aboriginal man. The mother hasn't got much time for her daughter and the man has also brought a son into the household. The girl has a lot of power in her school peer group and there are others wanting to become like her. There are also students with learning disabilities and several other characters who are caught between what they want and how they have to act because of peer pressure.

Jim, a student with a learning disability, was playing himself in the play. A spect-actor came on the stage and replaced a character who wanted to befriend Jim, but couldn't because of peer pressure. In the original play, Jim wanted to disappear whenever conflict occurred. As he put it in rehearsals, "that is the only way I can survive high school". Thinking that it was important to support Jim as the character isolated from the rest of the school population, the student spect-actor intervened on behalf of another character and went out of his way to befriend Jim. But Jim still ran away and did not respond to the overtures of friendship from the character.

In the debriefing after the intervention the facilitator asked Jim why he acted this way...wasn't it good that he had a potential new friend?

"Yes," Jim replied, "But he wasn't helpful before. He changed on a dime this time – he could always change again – so why should I trust him now"?

"Then", the facilitator asked Jim, "how does trust get built'?

Jim responded, "Trust has to be built one situation at a time".

As we see in this example, Forum Theatre provokes understanding by enacting possible strategies to assist a group or individual investigate possible solutions to particular challenges. To activate and dynamise audience and actors to explore other personas and other ways which give more power to a character in a situation is to learn another kind of behaviour that might help overcome oppression. It doesn't say do or don't this, but it does say, 'maybe you could try this or that, but it's up to you to decide in the end'.

> "We express the dreams we are able to fight for in view of the human possibility to project whatever s/he wants and thinks ....that carries the embryo of possible changes steered at a more humane future" (Freire 2002: 9).

If the play's structure is not only about life in schools but about larger issues of power, then the reverse is also true – the play can become a place to develop a *what-if world* where we play in the reality of the play to rehearse for the play of reality outside the stage. In bridging the gap between social justice theory, individual agency and social transformation, forum theatre is an aesthetic learning space where the actors and spect-actors are directing and involved in their own story. This event enables us not only to clarify where and what the central issues are, but also to experience and practice possible ways of dealing with those issues. Students come to see how individual actions impact the social situation and also how the social affects the individual. Often students recognize that in order to confront, diffuse or counteract the power of the oppressor, alliances or partnerships with others are needed. The social situation needs to be reconfigured before a shift in power relationships is possible. They come to recognize where interventions are possible in their lives and begin to explore ineffective actions and what effective interventions might look like. Rather than learning specific responses to a problem, forum encourages actors and spect-actors to explore and enact conceptions of effective actions.

This exploration of the student's reality is made possible when the space is created where students can take leadership in describing, naming, and acting upon their world.

5. TAKING ACTION TO MAKE CHANGES IN THAT REALITY

> You need one person to break the pattern (Student interview).

In the spring and summer of 2006, the authors were asked by the sponsoring school board to document the impact of the program and make recommendations for possible changes. Focus groups, student interviews, teacher interviews and a student drama workshop were used to ask students and teachers reflect on the program impact, both at the retreat and back in their schools.

PERSONAL CHANGE AND TRANSFORMATION

> The retreat was a life changing experience. I remember every single minute. I will always remember all of it (Focus group).

Students reported that the retreat was a powerful experience. Through the trust building exercises and sharing personal stories with others, students formed emotionally close relationships. They were not afraid to share their fears, frustrations, disappointments and negative emotions. A lot of the students appreciated what they felt was a safe environment. Students felt like they could open up and be themselves – some for the first time in their lives. Possibilities for action emerged as students exposed their thoughts, feelings and fears. Students thought this happened when they saw others 'step out of the box' – "then more people are brave" (Drama workshop) and people start shedding their facades. As one student leader put it, "we did not have to be somebody we were not. We did not have to keep up a façade" (Drama workshop) or continue how they acted in school with their guard up. "When we realized that people did not care who we were on the outside, we opened up" (Drama workshop). The experience of being able to show who they truly were was an emotional experience for the students. "I was crying after the retreat, cause you feel so secure about your feelings – that no one would judge you" (Focus group). The bonds of friendship developed at the retreat built an important support system for many students. They created a network of close friends that they stayed in touch with.

Students embraced drama as a method to learn about racism. Sharing stories of discrimination was an important part of the drama process. "I talk to people and they share stories about what happens to them and I can see they are affected by [racism]. [The stories] make you realize I have been through something like that too. You really realize that I am not the only one going through these things" (Focus group). The students reported that the Forum Theatre plays were "real" and presented them with a representation of the reality of discrimination and racism that occurs in school. Students said that it is a part of their reality that is not usually talked about anywhere else. The reality of the plays, the interventions, and discussions of the forum theatre process help to denormalize the acts of prejudice and racism that are part of students' daily lives. Dramas are "hard hitting, during these dramas you can see how it might feel to be discriminated against" (Focus group).

At these retreats participants identified issues in their personal lives and at the school with the goal of developing their own solutions to racism. They felt they gained insight into how they could respond to racism differently. "A friend of mine used to get really mad when someone called him a racist name. [After the retreat] he deals with the situation by giving them a long lecture. Even me, I know how to talk to people now if they are being racist" (Student interview). For others, it opens their eyes to the effect their actions have had on others. "[The anti-racism program] has changed my perspective of people and how I treat them. I used to be mean to people because of the color of their skin" (Focus group). The consciousness of and action against racism continued through the student involvement in their in-school anti-racism, anti-discrimination group.

CHANGES IN SCHOOL CLIMATE

> Ever since we did the play, I have seen slight changes. Before, in the cafeteria from one end to the other, you could hear people cracking the [discriminatory] jokes. Now, you hear it less (Focus group).

The experiences at the retreat served as a catalyst for developing solutions and taking action toward change through their school's anti-racism/anti-discrimination group and activities such as forum plays. Back at school, some of the students developed and performed forum plays for their fellow students and some were able to perform forum plays for elementary schools. More than one teacher stated that the plays got a good response in the school. "Our group received a lot of positive feedback about their play from both students and teachers" (Teacher interview). Participants stated they had noticed changes in their school from students who had stopped labeling, to people who were more inclusive of those who are different, to those who had more self respect for themselves.

Students also reported that activities in their school allowed students to be more different – to be themselves, to be open and to express themselves as individuals (Focus group). The students' cohesive anti- discrimination voice seemed to have had an impact on the other students at their school.

CHANGES IN THE COMMUNITY

The courage to act went beyond the school environment, it spilled over into the community. Many students told of the program giving them the awareness and confidence to challenge racist beliefs, expressions or actions, even of their family members including parents. One boy told of an incident where his brother used a racial slur when walking by an Aboriginal woman on the street. "I got mad and told him off. I told him it was wrong and that he shouldn't do that" (Focus group).

The program's school projects have gone beyond the walls of the schools as well. The plays developed by students have been performed for many community and educational groups. Thus we see that the use of drama in the program developed student voice, confidence in action, and skills in dialogical learning, while keeping the focus on the issue that brought us together – racism and discrimination. Drama enabled students to become connected to the issue, and through shared leadership with adults, come to recognize the use of drama to represent reality, and not just be seen as "play".

INSTITUTIONAL CHANGE

The anti-racism program had a profound effect on the students involved. However, institutional change was harder to achieve. The degree of impact on other students in the school and on the racism and discrimination in the schools varied from school to school. A couple of schools didn't have active anti-racism groups even though their students and staff had attended the retreat. At one school, the group wasn't sure how to address issues of racism beyond the level of awareness. At another, students believed that one activity, a play on labeling and stereotypes that they performed, had an impact on student interactions, by reducing the derogatory comments made by students in their interactions with others, but they believed they needed to do more to have a broader impact. At yet another, both students and teachers described the school wide impact that program had had on the climate of the school, especially the integration of the 'Alternative education' students (those with special learning needs) into the 'mainstream' student body. "The program has changed our school. Now students are more open to talking to other people. Now students see Alternative education students as human, as someone they will talk to. There is more courage to stick up for one another, to say when a joke is offensive" (Focus group).

Institutional change of schools around the issue of racism and student leadership in addressing racism is a slow process. In the case of this program, although the administration of the school division is very supportive of the program, in many cases, at the school level it is not perceived to be a priority. The lack of the program's status is evident in teacher involvement and in scheduling in the school. It is often difficult to recruit teachers as leaders for the program. Although the retreat can be a life changing experience for the students, it is can be difficult to get teachers to commit to attendance for the three days of the retreat. Often para-professionals (teacher's aides, school-community coordinators) from the school attend the retreat with students to "supervise" students. The paraprofessionals may not have the primary responsibility for the program back at the school. Despite the support of senior administration, at the school level the anti-racism program is seen as an extra-curricular activity, but lacks the status of the sports teams, choir or drama clubs. Many school anti-racism teams report difficulty finding time to meet due to scheduling conflicts with other school activities or because the anti-racism team is not the only extra-curricular responsibility of the teacher. Issues such as these prevent the program from becoming institutionalized and more fully integrated into school programming.

CHANGES IN POWER DYNAMICS

Although the impact of the anti-racism program varied from school to school, one systemic change was the leadership shown by students in the program. Students in the program were critically analyzing their school environment. They identified actions to address racism and discrimination in their schools. Students felt empowered to initiate ideas and make decisions for change in their own lives and in their schools so to some extent, decision making and problem solving around issues facing students in the school was shifting to the students, out of the hands of the administration, so to a limited extent, changed the power dynamics in the school. At the same time, we recognize that schools are hierarchical institutions where teachers are seen as the authority. Some of the teachers in the program find it hard to accept that students have the creativity and capability to come up with solutions to complex problems in their lives.

For example, one of the authors was jokering[4], facilitating a forum play where the Grade 6 boys kept intervening in the play with physical violence or shouts, swearing and insulting the person exerting power. One of the teachers we were working with came over to the joker and said, "Can't we just begin the performance by listing possible actions that the students could try out and then the students would see how these transformations work?"

This is to control, to provide a recipe of what to do and what not to do. We operate out of the assumption that what is not expressly forbidden is permissible.

The joker replied, "We don't say no, we say yes, and through the characters we explore students'-interventions. We challenge them to think of other ways to deal with the situation, keeping an opening for creativity. We let the spect-actors choose the interventions and see what transpires." But this isn't a passive form of leadership. We asked the audience, "What kind of suggestions have been made through these interventions? Is violence or swearing the only way to deal with bullies? Where do we get these ideas from? Are there any other suggestions?"

The role of the actors and the Joker is to help the spect-actors discover these alternatives.

PRAXIS ENABLING AN INTERROGATION OF THE PROGRAM

> Social theory is seen as a means by which people can achieve a much clearer picture of who they are, and to examine the real meaning of their social practices as a first step in becoming different sorts of people with different sorts of social arrangements. It is intended to free people from causal relationships by getting them to have different ends...it is not the ability to work with a system efficiently, but the power to alter this system fundamentally (Fay 1987: 89).

Praxis is the action and reflection of people upon their world in order to transform it. This requires both active reflection and reflective action. In this section we will use this process to interrogate the program in terms of knowledge (of racism), power, and changes in relationships in schools. In effect, we will explore how engaging in this program has enabled us to come full circle so that we engage in praxis as we interrogate our own approach as facilitators and as adults.

INTERROGATING RACISM IN SCHOOL

In drawing from their own experience, white people will often look at times in their lives when they have been oppressed and gain empathy through this experience with those who experience racism. In our anti-racism program students create the Forum theatre play but, because it is based on their experiences, students most often present the racism expressed in the personal and social relationships amongst different student groups. This student focus is understandable because most student bodies in high school are highly stratified. Students as audience members immediately recognize and identify with the racism and discrimination amongst different student groups. This is the overt racism that is denormalized in our program. What is not presented and what students and teachers do not address is the systemic racism of school as an institution where personalized racism amongst the students is the norm and those with power in the institution turn a blind eye to this issue or, worse yet, have beliefs about white students and racialized students that result in the unequal treatment of white and racialized students. These racialized beliefs of teachers are manifested in the lack of success of racialized students, lack of support for racialized student learning, disciplinary action imposed on racialized students, and push out of racialized students (Schissel & Wotherspoon, 2003; Silver & Mallett, 2002; Wilson, 1991).

The anti-racism program problematizes student-student relationships and power differentials in peer interaction, but ignores one of the key relationships in schooling and learning–the teacher-student relationship. The teacher-student relationship is where institutional and societal power and authority are enacted.

In our program, we don't explore the power and authority teachers and administrators have to determine what counts as knowledge, how that knowledge will be gained by students, and who has the right to participate in their school through disciplinary action and grading. This form of racism in schools remains unproblematized.

Although our three-day workshop has not yet done problematized institutional racism, there is a space to bring this aspect of racism into the program in the forum play. One way is to add the character of a teacher who uses her authority to perpetuate racial inequity. For example a teacher could be added to a play to intervene in a racial conflict in a way that favours the white students and reinforces the existing racialized peer power structure in the school. In this way, we could begin to interrogate the power structures of the institution of schooling.

INTERROGATING POWER STRUCTURES IN SCHOOLING

Transformative education or education as the practice of freedom (Freire 1973; Hooks 1994) that counters traditional education is based on acts of knowing fused from two interrelated experiences – "the creation of an authentic Dialogue between the learners and the educators as equally knowing subjects" (Taylor 1993: 54); and "the awareness of the real concrete context of facts, that is of the social reality in which we are living" (Taylor: 54).

Freire's approach is a transitive praxis where learner is both subject and object. Through an analysis of *Banking Education,* where the teacher's relationship to the student is to pour knowledge into the 'empty' student – "knowledge is a gift bestowed by those who consider themselves knowledgeable upon those whom they consider to know nothing" (Freire 1970: 58*)*. "In banking education an educator replaces self-expression with a 'deposit' that a student is expected to 'capitalize.' The more efficiently he does this, the better educated he is considered. To change the world through work, to 'proclaim' the world, to express it and to express onself are the unique qualities of human beings. Education at any level will be more rewarding if it stimulates the development of this radical, human need for expression" (Freire 1985: 21).

Freire's solution to the teacher-student relationship challenges the one-way relationship, creating a *critical pedagogy*. This involves posing problems that enable us to continuously inquire into our relationships in the world which impacts on our notions of self in relation to others and to the social structures in which we are embedded.

The idea of "equally knowing subjects" is integral to our analysis of the program and the relationship of students to teachers. The work with students in this program has brought into focus the contradiction where the drama process, with its emphasis on stories and interactivity, puts relationships of power into question. Globally, schools are sites of power (Fay 1982) and the process of education conforms to this power. Situating the program within the schools but outside the curricular structures has enabled us to work the cracks, where the work "is a challenge to authority, unpredictable disruption of norms, a kind of playing with fire" (Kershaw 1998: 68), but, in doing so, it has also limited the ability of the program to engage in long term change.

Herein lies the weakness of the continuation of our work: we engage students but not the teachers. In failing to reach the teachers, many may not have the view of themselves and their students as equally knowing subjects. Because teachers don't engage in an authentic exploration of racism in their lives and schools, they do not have the same awareness as the students of the context of the facts as do the students.

> True dialogue cannot exist unless the dialoguers engage in critical thinking–...thinking which perceives reality as process, as transformation, rather than as a static entity – thinking which does not separate itself from action, but constantly immerses itself in temporality without fear of risks involved (Freire 1970: 80-81).

Students identify the need for courage in confronting racism, but we fail to challenge the teachers to do the same. Working in a system of institutionalized racism, how might we explore with teachers their fears around change? In what ways can they be reflexive to examine their practices and identify possibilities for teacher actions that would confront the reproduction of racism and discrimination in their schools? How can they become collaborators with student in the creation of more equitable schools?

Freire (1998) sees the enactment of this process of a collaborative approach in education through democratic leadership. He sees the development of democracy as embracing diversity, where different truths need to be respected. He views the practice of respect for diversity (tolerance) as a virtue and as the balance between the abuse of authority and wonton permissiveness.

> The act of tolerating requires a climate in which limits may be established, in which there are principles to be respected...Under an authoritarian regime, in which authority is abused, or a permissive one, in which freedom is not limited, one can hardly learn tolerance. Tolerance requires respect, discipline, and ethics. The authoritarian, filled with sexual, racial, and class prejudices, can never become tolerant without first overcoming his or her prejudices (42).

In the light of the past intolerance in schools for minority ways of being and cultural knowledge, Freire's analysis of the need for teachers to embrace tolerance becomes clear. It contextualizes the importance of respect in education for diversity as respect becomes tied to tolerance and the development of democracy. The social system established in the classrooms is where the students learn, at the micro level, the practice of freedom and responsibility needed in a diverse and democratic society and world.

STUDENTS INTERROGATING THEIR REALITY

One of the critiques we have of the program is that we haven't yet found a way to prepare students for the awareness that emerges when they return to their schools from the retreat. This is illustrated by a story that one of the Student Leaders told to a workshop with pre-service teachers following one particular retreat.

The retreat ended on a Thursday afternoon. Participants went back to their schools on the Friday. Mark, the student leader, reported that during the following weekend students were calling him, telling him how they felt in their schools after the program. Suddenly, they kept seeing instances of exclusion and were having trouble coping with their new consciousness. Mark said that it was as if they started seeing their school communities and the interactions within it with new eyes, that they were 'becoming conscious' and found it overwhelming and hard to deal with. And they were asking him what they could do with these new feelings and thoughts.

This story illustrates how during the retreat, many students experience profound personal transformation that impacts how they now see and interpret their world back at home and school. Students are prepared to act differently. But when they go back into the school, others around them may not share their views or know how to respond to the student's new perspective or how to support the student.

FUTURE DIRECTIONS

The interrogation of the program has clarified that more work needs to be done with teachers if the program is to become an ongoing part of the school division's programming and if we hope to challenge the institutionalized racism in schools. However, as we continue the struggle to integrate the program into the institution of schooling, we need to be careful not to ignore the power of the retreat setting or to minimize the importance of personal transformation in the lives of individual student's.

> [The program] has impacted everything I am, it's the only reason I go to school, its one of the reasons I quit doing drugs and drinking and a lot of the bad things I got myself into. Its changed the way I look at things. It's one of the more positive things I have had in my life. I am actually really grateful I have had that experience (Aboriginal student interview).

> Now I am not so anxious to say that I am from Afghanistan, that I am from the ESL class or I am Muslim. I used to get anxious, like oh, what would the other person be thinking? Now I know that everyone has their own rights to what they believe. Some people would say you are Muslim, you are like a terrorist. But now I am proud of who I am. There are always someone that doesn't like you or who you don't like, you just need to ignore them (Afghani student interview).

It is important in this context of thinking about the relationship of individual and global or structural change to consider what Boal (1995) says:

> The smallest cells of social organization (the couple, the family, the neighbourhood, the school, the office, the factory, etc.) and equally the smallest incidents of our social life contain all the moral and political values of society, all its structures of domination and power, all its mechanisms of oppression. The great general themes are inscribed in the small personal themes and incidents...When we talk about a strictly individual case, we are also talking about the generality of similar cases......The propagation of ideas, values, of tastes is osmosis: interpenetration (40).

Osmosis means there is an interweaving of societal values in the body, values, ideas, tastes. The role of the team building process in the program is to make the dialogue between the world outside the retreat transitive and transparent, helping these values emerge for investigation. Because the retreat is in the world, it has the values of the world within it. So we must transform ourselves to transform the world.

> No one lives democracy fully, nor do they help it to grow, if, first of all, they are interrupted in their right to speak, to have a voice, to say their critical discourse, or, second, if they are not engaged, in one form or another, in the fight to defend this right, which, after all, is also the right to act (Freire 1998: 65).

A few years ago one of the authors led a Theatre of the Oppressed workshop with a group of high school students. Several months later, one of the student participants in the workshop attended a meeting of adult educators and described her experience. An audience member asked her what the effect of the theatre workshop had been on her high school experience. She replied that having gone through the workshop she realized that every time she saw a racist incident at her school she knew that even though only she saw it, there were many people at other schools 'standing behind her' and supporting any actions of intervention she might take.

Leadership in confronting oppression and racism requires the development of notions of collaborative and inter-generational leadership because systemic change most often requires the development of collective action. We can begin by having adult leaders and teachers reflect on the reality of institutional and systemic racism in their own lives and to enact democratic leadership that recognizes students as "knowers" (Gourd 2005), modeling the practice of shared and collaborative leadership.

Freire (1998) writes, "it is truly difficult to make a democracy...It is not what I say that says I am a democrat, that I am not racist or machista, but what I do" (67). To Freire, it is in the contradiction between saying and doing that we learn that we are in a challenging and ambiguous state which asks us to find a way out. Becoming consistent between saying and doing is a challenge that we feel drama helps us to overcome as it identifies contradictions and, at the same time, enables us to address them. It is this challenge that continues to inform our work in drama, youth leadership and anti-racism education.

> I've had quite a few racial encounters that were unpleasant. I want a world where no one has to go through that. If joining [the program] meant I could make a contribution to a world without racism, I was willing to do it (Focus group).

NOTES

1. In different parts of Canada and the United States, different terms are preferred to denote the original peoples of North America. In this chapter, as designated in the Canadian constitution, the term Aboriginal is used to be inclusive of First Nations, Métis and Inuit peoples, who are each recognized as distinct groups.
2. We use the capitalized Image to refer to the particular theatricalized use of bodies in frozen motion in a drama workshop. When uncapitalized, image refers to the visual concept.
3. Almost every time we do Image work the first response by participants to an image is – what is the person in the Image trying to say? and then the inevitably "guessing" begins. This happens even when I begin a sequence with a shaking hands exercise as I emphasize that there is no right or wrong answer. We add that the Image we show at the beginning allows everyone to "read into it" their own story. Despite these assurances, we feel the inertia and habit of "playing charades," of "guessing" what someone is trying to say remains so ingrained that participants cannot trust to let the image be, to come into its own meaning.
4. The Joker is the director/master of ceremonies of a workshop or performance. At a forum theatre performance s/he is the link between the play, the actors, and the audience. S/he explains the rules and discusses the interventions with both the characters in the play and the spect-actors from the audience who intervene in the action.

REFERENCES

Adams, M., Bell, L., & Griffin, P. (Eds.). (1997). *Teaching for diversity and social justice: A sourcebook*. New York: Routledge.

Arnold, R., Burke, B., James, C., Martin, D., & Thomas, B. (1991). *Educating for a change*. Toronto: Between the Lines.

Boal, A. (1979). *Theatre of the oppressed* (A. Charles & M.- O. McBride, Trans.). London: Pluto Press.

Boal, A. (1992). *Games for actors and non-actors* (A. Jackson, Trans.). New York: Routledge.

Boal, A. (1995). *The rainbow of desire: The Boal method of theatre and therapy*. (A. Jackson, Trans.). New York: Routledge.

Boal, A. (1998). *Legislative theatre: Using performance to make politics* (A. Jackson, Trans.). New York: Routledge.

Boal, A. (2001). *Hamlet and the baker's son. My life in theatre and politics* (A. Jackson, Trans.). New York: Routledge.

Carr, W., & Kemmis, S. (1986). *Becoming critical: Education, knowledge and action research*. London: Falmer.

Diamond, D. (1991). *Power plays: A joker's manual*. Vancouver: Headlines Theatre.

Diamond, D. (2000). Email to author, 12 April.

Dwyer, P. (2004). Making bodies talk in forum theatre. *Research in Drama Education, 9*(2), 199–210.

Fay, B. (1987). *Critical social science: Liberation and its limits*. Ithaca: Cornell University Press.

Fregeau, & Leier. (2002). Praxis and teacher visions of socially just school reform. In J. Slater, S. Fain, & C. Rossatto (Eds.), *The Freirian legacy: Educating for social justice* (pp. 172–183). New York: Peter Lang.

Freire, A.- M. (2002). Paulo Freire and the untested feasibility. In J. Slater, S. Fain, & C. Rossatto (Eds.), *The Freirian legacy: Educating for social justice* (pp. 7–14). New York: Peter Lang.

Freire, P. (1970). *Pedagogy of the oppressed* (M. Ramos, Trans.). New York: Seabury Press.

Freire, P. (1973). *Education for critical consciousness*. New York: Continuum.

Freire, P. (1985). *The politics of education: Culture, power, and liberation* (D. Macedo, Trans.). South Hadley: Bergin and Garvey.

Freire, P. (1998). *Teachers as cultural workers: Letters to those who dare teach* (D. Macedo, D. Koike, & A. Olivira, Trans.). Boulder, CO: Westview Press.

Hooks, B. (1994). *Teaching to transgress: Education as the practice of freedom*. NewYork: Routledge.

Huff, D. J. (1997). *To live historically: Institutional racism and American Indian education*. New York: SUNY Press.

IPSOS-REID and The Dominion Institute. (2005). *March 21st international day for the elimination of racial discrimination – Survey highlights.* [online]. Retrieved May 13, 2006, from http://www.dominion.ca/Downloads/IRracismSurvey.pdf

Kershaw, B. (1998). Pathologies of hope in drama and theatre. *Research in Drama Education*, *3*(1), 67–83.

Kumashiro, K. (2000). Toward a theory of anti-oppressive education. *Review of Educational Research*, *70*(1), 25–53.

Roman, L. (1993). On the ground with anti-racist pedagogy and Raymond William's unfinished project to articulate a socially transformative critical realism. In D. Dworkin & L. G. Roman (Eds.), *Views beyond the border country: Raymond Williams and cultural politics* (pp. 158–214). New York: Routledge.

Schissel, B., & Wotherspoon, T. (2003). *The legacy of school for aboriginal people: Education, oppression, and emancipation*. Toronto: Oxford University Press.

Selby, D., & Pike, G. (1988). *Human rights. An activity file*. London: Stanley Thornes.

Silver, J., & Mallett, K. (with Greene, J. & Freeman, S.) (2002). *Aboriginal education in Winnipeg inner city high schools*, Winnipeg Inner-City Research Alliance. Winnipeg: Canadian Centre for Policy Alternatives – Manitoba.

Simon, R. I. (1994). *Teaching against the grain: Texts for a pedagogy of possibility*. Westport, CT: Bergin and Garvey.

Taylor, P. V. (1993). *The texts of Paulo Freire*. Philadelphia: Open University Press.

Turner, V. (1982). *From ritual to theatre: The human seriousness of play*. New York: PAJ Publications.

Wilson, P. (1991). Trauma of Sioux Indian high school students. *Anthropology and Education Quarterly*, *22*(3), 267–383.

MARK SMITH

EDUCATIONAL OUTCOMES AND SOCIAL JUSTICE IN SCOTTISH RESIDENTIAL CARE

INTRODUCTION

This chapter considers, from a Scottish perspective, the position of children and youth in state care, specifically those placed in residential homes and schools. Scottish traditions of welfare in some respects bridge Anglo-American approaches with their roots in the poor law doctrine of less eligibility and European models of social education or social pedagogy. I begin by outlining Anglo-American traditions of social welfare, identifying within these the persistent specter of the poor laws, which are resurgent within current neo-liberal discourse with its emphasis on individual deficit and responsibility for actions. I identify some manifestations and problems of services based around neo-liberal ideologies. I go on to consider alternative perspectives on how we might care for children and youth based around more universal principles of 'upbringing' and social education, as embodied in European models of social pedagogy, but also with strong Scottish resonances as exemplified in the thinking behind the Kilbrandon Report (1964), which led to the establishment of the children's hearings system. I argue that aspirations towards social justice for children in state care are best served within broadly educational approaches to practice rather than those rooted in pathology or punishment, which seem to be embedded within dominant Anglo-American paradigms of social welfare. In seeking to draw such broad comparisons between systems, I am aware of the risk of stereotyping these systems and of papering over differences and nuances within them. The work of Jane Addams for instance offers testimony to attempts to establish a social model in the US. However, there do seem to be discernible ideological and practice distinctions between Anglo-American and European models (Smith and Whyte 2008) and it is these that are developed here.

THE POOR LAWS AND THE DOCTRINE OF LESS ELIGIBILITY

Anglo-American discourses of social welfare derive in large part from the 16th Century English Poor Laws, which sedimented what Jones and Novak term 'punitive and negative images of the poor' (1999: 5). In providing a rudimentary level of social welfare the Poor Laws differentiated between the deserving and the undeserving poor. The former, such as dependent children and the disabled, were acknowledged to be poor on account of circumstances beyond their control, whilst the latter, the able bodied poor, were adjudged to be responsible for their own

S.A. Moore and R.C. Mitchell (eds.), Power, Pedagogy and Praxis: Social Justice in the Globalized Classroom, 219–232.

predicament; the root of their poverty lay in a predisposition to laziness or fecklessness. Thus poverty was individualized, a product of moral deficit, shorn of any political or social context.

The Poor Law Amendment Act (1834) introduced to English welfare provision the doctrine of 'less eligibility,' the idea that support offered by the state should be less desirable than that which a person might experience without such recourse to such services. Workhouses, the institutional response to pauperism, housing both adults and children, were deliberately austere and unwelcoming places in order to prevent people wanting access to them and thereby becoming a financial burden on the authorities. Attitudes betraying roots in Elizabethan England have been instrumental in influencing welfare ideology across the Anglo-American world ever since, having been…

> … transplanted and adapted to the New World of North America where they continue to shape attitudes and policies towards 'the poor .... They reinforce a belief in self-help and the American Dream, which constitutes poverty as a failure (Lister 2004: 104).

The transplantation of a poor law ideology across the Atlantic was influential in shaping the development of social work in the US. Myers (2000) notes that American discourses about poverty evolved from a belief that it was a symptom of poor character to one portraying it is a result of psychological or familial dysfunction. As a consequence responses to social problems assume the form of individual or family therapies and fail to address wider structural determinants of social problems. This way of thinking made its way back across the Atlantic where the developing social work profession in the UK was heavily influenced by American psycho-social traditions (Higham 2001) and practice developed along casework models.

MORALITY AND MORALISM

Foremost among the individual deficits considered to cause poverty was moral impropriety. Ferguson (2007) identifies a persistent emphasis on dirt and virtue or a lack thereof in the motivations of welfare reformers. The London Foundling Hospital, established by Thomas Coram in the 18th century based its admission criteria around the marital status of a baby's mother (Oliver 2003). Throughout the 19th century reformers were driven by a moral purpose to eradicate vice. Their concern with poverty was secondary, borne out of a fear that this might lead to vice and immorality. Charities such as the National Society for the Prevention of Cruelty to Children (NSPCC), which developed in the late 1880s were underpinned by a puritanical zeal. Sex, especially where it might involve children, became a consuming force in the provision of welfare. The moral panic engendered by children and sex was also apparent in the work of organisations such as the National Vigilance Organisation (Webster 2005). Child protection, the predominant social work mode of intervention with children and families today, echoes a similar puritanical urge albeit a largely secularized one; it is a revivalist movement with roots in the same moralistic impulse that motivated 19th century reformers, an essentially conservative doctrine, which fails to accord children any agency over their lives, locating this with adults cast in a protective role. It also does nothing to challenge the causes of children's maltreatment and exploitation, which lie primarily in structural inequality.

THE USE OF RESIDENTIAL CHILD CARE OVER TIME

Residential child care can be considered in professional discourse, especially within those traditions critical of institutions (Jones and Fowles 1984) to exist separate from more mainstream welfare provision for children and youth. In fact its history merely reflects dominant ideas and ideologies about children and childhood. The concern of the early Victorian period focused on the threat caused by street urchins to public order, shifting from the 1860s, to a predominant concern with care and protection (from their own families), a phase that existed for most of the 20th century. Trends, emanating from the rise of psychiatry and psychology in the 1920s began to shift interventions towards a focus on particular behaviours or areas of concern, reflecting the growing prominence of treatment ideologies. More recently children's rights have become a powerful force in the delivery of residential care services (Fulcher and Ainsworth 2006). According to Grant and Gabor (2006) these eras are not discrete but 'overlap and interact and, as such, the evolution of new philosophies have not always meant the disappearance of old ones. The philosophies of days gone by still affect programmes today' (2006: 17). The persistence of doctrines of less eligibility and of rescuing children provides examples.

Approaches to residential care practice are not neutral but incorporate particular ideological preferences. Grant and Gabor (2006) argue that a treatment ideology merely supplants a focus on children's psyches for one on their souls, which was the concern of previous generations of practice. In both cases residential care is something imposed on children. The children's rights and consumer involvement agendas that have come to the fore in recent years bring with them their own problems as discussed later in the chapter. Neither of these underpinning ideologies identifies a structural dimension to the provision of care, either in respect of what brings children and youth into care settings or what they might experience while there.

RESIDENTIAL CHILD CARE: PROCESSING THE CHILDREN OF THE POOR

Whatever the dominant purpose of residential child care at any point of time, a role in processing the children of the poor has been constant throughout its history. As already noted its purpose in the Victorian period was to address problems of vagrancy and single parenthood. More recently, Bebbington and Miles (1989) compared the backgrounds of children admitted to care in the 1980s with a previous study from the 1960s. They found that levels of deprivation in the population had actually increased over this period, identifying a litany of disadvantage: low income, poor housing and marital discord. Berridge and Brodie (1998) considered children in residential child care to be among the most disadvantaged in society.

The effects of poverty are not only apparent in an inability to access the good things in life. Of more significance is the level of inequality existing in a society This impacts on variables such as life expectancy, homicide rates, levels of violence, educational attainment and also importantly on levels of trust and social cohesion (Wilkinson and Pickett 2007). Thus, widening gaps between the rich and the poor are likely to compound the impact of structural disadvantage. Widening inequality has been apparent across OECD countries in the past decade with the highest levels to be found in the USA, Ireland and the UK (Moss and Petrie 2002). UNICEF (2007) notes a stark divide between North-European countries where child well-being is at its highest in the Netherlands, Sweden, Denmark and Finland. The United Kingdom and the United States, those countries that have embraced neo-liberalism most enthusiastically, find themselves in the bottom of the ranking on measures of child wellbeing. This is manifest in more fractious inter-generational relationships and in children's subjective accounts of their sense of wellbeing.

Residential child care is charged to manage the casualties of neo-liberal political and economic systems. Perhaps inevitably the concern of staff in care establishments (often themselves poorly educated and valued, a point I will return to) is on control. At its most extreme the overwhelming urge to neutralize any perceived threat from children in residential child care and to assimilate them to dominant societal values is apparent in the experiences of 'the stolen generation' of aboriginal children, removed from their homelands and placed in residential schools in Canada and Australia in order that they might assimilate the dominant culture and be 'civilised'. Coldrey (2001) attributes the kind of abuses in residential child care, which have come to the surface in recent decades to a clash of the conservative working class culture of those who worked there with the counter-culture of those placed there.

RESIDENTIAL CHILD CARE AND SOCIAL WORK

The UK, unlike just about every other jurisdiction in the world, locates residential child care provision within the social work profession. This has implication for the way in which the service is conceptualized. Essentially, the history of social work is predicated on individualism. In the UK the profession traces its roots to the Victorian Charity Organisation Society (COS). The COS steadfastly upheld the 1834 Poor Law Amendment Act, which reaffirmed principles of deterrence and less eligibility. It blamed the poor for their plight, operating from a casework model, which it quite explicitly championed as promoting individualism and as a bulwark against socialist ideas (Ferguson and Lavalette 2007).

The professionalisation of social work in the 1970s saw the emergence of some more radical manifestations of social work practice which according to its proponents sought to respond to the poor in the context of the social and economic structure in which they lived (Bailey and Brake 1975). It also drew on ideas of community development as opposed to casework models of practice. However, in respect of residential child care, social work was influenced by the sociological literature of dysfunction (Jones and Fowles1984) which contributed to defining a professional identity for social work around the avoidance of institutional care. In so doing it failed to give cognizance to potentially more liberatory perspectives on residential care deriving from a European educational tradition. It also located the social work task in respect of children with the family and in that respect aligned itself with the family based conservative ideologies of the political Right. In many respects the influence of radical social work was more imagined that real. Nevertheless, the stereotype of the radical social worker created the conditions for a political backlash. The chosen field of conflict was child protection. Parton (1985) highlights how the death of one particular child, Maria Colwell in 1973 was used by Keith Joseph, the Conservative Minister of State for Social Services, to shift the focus of welfare services away from universal provision and family support towards more explicit targeting of problem families. Harnessing child protection for political purposes has been a feature of debate ever since.

THE RETREAT FROM WELFARE

The identification of social work with child protection effectively extinguished any radical flame within the profession, aligning it with neo-liberal doctrines valorizing the sanctity of the family. This was part and parcel of a wider retreat from welfare taking place across the US and the UK in particular from the 1970s. Professional antipathy to residential care coalesced with New Right concerns to cut the costs in public services. In respect of child care, fostering was considered to be cheaper and it had the added bonus of locating care within the private domain of the family.

MANAGERIALISM

The neo-liberal project sought to bring the public services to heel through an injection of what it considered to be private sector rigor. This was driven forward by the dogma of managerialism, 'a set of beliefs and practices at the core of which burns the seldom tested assumption that better management will prove an effective solvent for a wide range of economic and social ills' (Pollitt 1990:1).

Managerialism has been a device to control and regulate the public services workforce. Although it has its roots in 1980s Thatcherite ideology, there has been a massive growth in regulation across social care in particular since the election of the New Labour government in the UK in 1997 (Humphrey 2003). This is manifest in the establishment of various inspection and regulatory bodies. In Scotland, the Regulation of Care (Scotland) Act (2001) established a Care Commission, which inspects residential care homes against sets of care standards and has powers to demand improvements in services and to impose sanctions on organisations which fail to meet minimum standards. There have also been developments to regulate the workforce, involving the imposition of codes of practice, which McLaughlin (2007) argues are symptomatic of a lack of trust in professionals.

The Regulation of Care legislation also established minimum qualification levels for staff in residential child care. These were set at vocational qualification

(VQ) as opposed to the professional level qualification previously aspired to. Vocational qualifications can be argued to be pedagogically unsuited to the dynamic and relational nature of residential child care (Heron and Chakrabarti, 2002, Smith, 2003). They reflect a 'dumbing down' of the level of intellectual capacity and critical thinking required of workers, replacing professional judgment with bureaucratic regulatory mechanisms. The consequences of managerial approaches to the delivery of residential care are identified by Magnuson et al. who claim that "the bureaucratic organization of … care services has cost us ethically and pedagogically by constraining and demoralizing staff and clients and in the creation and recreation of a direct care practice in disarray" (Magnuson et al.1996).

In respect of social work Jones (2007) identifies the current role as comprising rationing and surveillance. He goes on to say…

> [t]alk to any frontline practitioners today and you will be regaled by tales of the mountain of paperwork which they recognize as being an attempt to regulate their work with clients. Agencies simply do not want thinking and creative social workers especially as inequalities deepen under neo-liberalism (2007:192).

CONTROLLING RESIDENTIAL CHILD CARE: CHILD PROTECTION AS A TOOL OF MANAGERIALISM

Child protection has acted as a particularly pernicious but clever tool in the managerial armoury. It can sound banal to challenge the notion of protecting children. However, the child protection industry that has developed in recent decades is more concerned with regulating the actions and indeed the thoughts of those who interact with children than it is about truly protecting children; were that its primary interest, its energies would of needs be directed at a structural level. Writing from an educational perspective Sachs and Mellor claim:

> [c]hild Protection policies, both in their form and content, act as regulatory frameworks which constrain and proscribe teachers' practices and … emphasize a 'safe' and 'risk averse' form of practice. They can also be seen as technologies of performance because they presuppose a culture of mistrust in professions (2005: 149).

FROM POVERTY TO SOCIAL INCLUSION; BLAMING THE VICTIM

Under the New Labour government elected in 1997 poverty in the UK has been rebranded social inclusion. Like child protection, social inclusion is one of those buzz words that we are all meant to celebrate–of course we are all in favour of social inclusion. However, Levitas (1998) identifies social inclusion, as promulgated by New Labour, as enforcing social cohesion around market forces while regarding deprivation and inequality as consequences of individual pathology. Thus the focus of social policy shifts towards raising individual opportunities and emphasising individual responsibilities. Those who do not appreciate attempts to include them in the resultant moral centre ground are subject to a range of authoritarian responses (Butler and Drakeford 2002). Those who fail to measure up to the requirements of the neo-liberal state are positioned as part of an underclass, of drug users, anti-social youth and young offenders.

In relation to youth the murder of two-year-old Jamie Bulger by two 10 year olds in Liverpool in 1993 was used to shift the focus of social policy from welfare to an increasing correctionalism. Recent years have seen a raft of legislation around anti-social behaviour, and a massive increase in numbers of children locked up. Since the inception of secure accommodation, initially as a welfare response to children's needs, there has been a relentless increase in its use. In Scotland the number of secure beds doubled over the course of the 1970s, trebled in the 1980s and quadrupled in the 1990s (Smith et al. 2005). Numbers of children locked up in England and Wales rose by almost 90% between 1992 and 2002 (Pitts 2005). By 2003, 'the level of child and youth incarceration in England and Wales vis-à-vis the under 18 population as a whole was four times that of France, ten times that of Spain, and one hundred times that of Finland' (Pitts 2005:186). Again the comparison between neo-liberal regimes and social democratic ones is instructive.

Despite the structural origins of the problems that bring children into care, the response of care systems is to individualise these; problems are conceptualised and addressed as though they were a product of personal or family pathology. Legislation identifying children in need fails conspicuously to identify poverty in its definition (Jackson 2006). Once placed in residential care children are subject to a range of technologies of intervention, such as anger management, cognitive skills or family therapy programmes, in order to smooth cognitive distortions so that they might return to a normative fold. Little consideration is given to the fact that children's behaviours may be perfectly understandable and adaptive responses to their social circumstances.

EDUCATION AS A TOOL OF SOCIAL INCLUSION

One example of the social inclusion agenda in respect of children in care is around education, where there is a marked divergence in the educational attainments for children in care compared to those in the wider community. Within a social inclusion frame the political drive is for children in care to have the same opportunities for education, including further and higher education as their peers and to provide them with additional support to compensate for previous deprivation or disadvantage. Children and those who care for them are blamed for the fact that educational attainments compare unfavourably with those of the general population. Targets have been set to boost their qualification levels and a range of initiatives has been introduced to bring this about. Thus, children's homes have been provided with computers and fitted out to provide homework space, to little avail, as qualification levels have not improved.

Attempts to bring children in care up to speed educationally through improving examination results betray a particular view of education as a commodity, which can be expressed and measured according to examination results and linked with employability. Yet, in the scheme of things children achieving one or two basic level qualifications are unlikely to see their life chances substantially improve. It might just build in a level of discontent among those who get them but are still consigned to menial work or who can't get a job even with their qualifications. Such instrumental views of education also deny any liberatory or transformational potential of the educational experience (Freire 1974). A similar point can be made of the residential care workforce. Tied to a VQ model themselves they are unlikely to encourage aspirations towards an educational experience which might raise awareness among those they work with.

CO-OPTING CHILDREN'S RIGHTS

Langan (2002) notes that, 'One of the most significant trends of the past decade has been the deployment of formerly radical themes in a new framework of regulation' (cited in Lavelette and Ferguson 2007: 26). The way in which children's rights agendas have been co-opted is a case in point. While a focus on children's rights has been argued by some commentators to provide a blueprint for the development of residential child care (Frost Stein and Mills, 1999) the reality is somewhat different. Any emancipatory possibilities of a rights-based agenda have been hijacked by what Butler and Drakeford (2003) identify as "the far less emancipatory paradigm of child protection" in which children's rights are subsumed beneath their supposed need to be protected by adults. Parton (1991) argues that political interest in children's rights has to be understood within the new politics of welfare which speaks a language of consumer choice rather than political or civil rights (cited in Butler and Drakeford 2003). The rights agenda has thus become part and parcel of the neo-liberal state apparatus. Dahlberg and Moss (2005) note further that...

> ...(it is no coincidence that the prominence given to rights coincides with the dominance of advanced liberalism and increasing recourse to law as a means of mediating relationships) and premised on particular values and a particular understanding of the subject as a rational, autonomous individual (30).

Agencies that provide residential child care have appointed or contract to employ children's rights officers. They also fund children's advocacy projects, which purport to be a voice for children in care. Children are increasingly presented with "statements of rights (and entitlements) and ...told of a complaints procedure should they feel they are being mistreated by programme staff" (Fulcher and Ainsworth 2006: 291). In such a climate, statements of rights are about protecting agencies from liability more than they are meaningful affirmations of their hopes for children. The rights discourse has become bogged down in questions of bed-time, pocket money or petty gripes about daily living rights and is hence trivialized. It is fundamentally anti-dialogical and get in the way of healthy and just ways of resolving conflicts within the context of caring relationships, building barriers between children and those who care for them. The locus of power is positioned outside the establishment with external managers, again preventing the establishment of alliances for change. In many cases the only right accorded to children in care in an increasingly punitive political culture is the right to due process as more and more of them are locked up or subject to an increasing array of correctional interventions.

THE STATE OF CARE

The trends identified above do not make state care a happy place for children or those who work with them. Despite the smoke and mirrors purveyed by the various regulatory bodies there is a conceptual fault line in attempts to provide care within neo-liberal regimes, expressed by Brannan and Moss (2003):

> [N]ew capitalism calls for individualism, instrumental rationality, flexibility, short-term engagement, deregulation and the dissolution of established relationships and practices.' Caring relationships...are predicated upon an expressive rather than instrumental relationship to others. They are based upon trust, commitment over time and a degree of predictability (202).

Cameron (2003) offers a damming indictment of what care has become: "Care as used in legislation seems to have been emptied of its potential, a dried up expression for how to manage an underclass of disadvantage" (93).

LOOKING FOR ALTERNATIVES

It is apparent from the foregoing that attempts to care for children in state care within neo-liberal regimes aren't working. What

> ...good practice that does exist does so against a backdrop of organisational and professional failure. New regulatory systems serve merely to maintain an unsatisfactory status quo in respect of public care rather than encouraging or engaging in the kind of root and branch debate that is required to move things forward (Heron and Chakrabarti 2002: 356).

Engaging with such root and branch debate requires that alternative paradigms for conceptualizing and delivering care be considered. Protective and therapeutic approaches not working (Magnusson and Baizerman 2007). I argue that rights based approaches are similarly flawed under current conditions as they have been co-opted to consumerist and child protection agendas. There are other ways of thinking about care and it is to some of these that I turn. I consider firstly what might be gleaned from reclaiming some of Scotland's distinctive tradition in respect of education and care, a tradition which resonates with European models of social pedagogy, which I go on to discuss. I then identify the dissatisfaction within social work of current ways of working and discuss attempts in some quarters to articulate a primary moral purpose for the profession as a challenge to managerialism.

A SCOTTISH TRADITION

There are persistent points of departure between Scottish approaches to social welfare and dominant Anglo-American models. There are perhaps two defining differences, one of which derives from attitudes towards education, the other relating to a philosophical predisposition to a contextual morality, which takes into account social circumstances in judging behaviours rather than more abstract and universalist principles.

With regards to the first of these differences the Reformation of 1560, which established a school in each parish, established an educational tradition in Scotland instilling a militant democracy, a critical spirit. Universal education was considered as a means to ensure social cohesion, whereas the education of the working classes in England could be considered to encourage sedition (Smout 1969).

A distinct Scottish philosophical tradition was established during the Scottish Enlightenment (Tronto 1994). The foremost writers of this period, Francis Hutcheson, Adam Smith and David Hume drew on an Aristotelian tradition, grounding moral debate firmly in the real world and embracing what might nowadays be thought of as broadly communitarian principles. The English preference was for a concern for the autonomous individual and for abstract moral principles with roots in the philosophy of Mill and Kant. Kantian ethics have been predominant in social work, contributing to the profession's preoccupation with the individual at the expense of wider social context.

Scottish approaches to education and morality came together in The Kilbrandon Report into juvenile delinquency of 1964. Kilbrandon decreed that similarities in the underlying situation of juvenile offenders … and children in need of care and protection 'far outweigh the differences', and that 'the true distinguishing factor...is their need for special measures of education and training, the normal up-bringing processes having, for whatever reason, fallen short' (1964: para. 15).

Here we have an emphasis on both social context and on the identification of education–'in its widest sense' as the preferred response to social problems. Kilbrandon sought to harness *'those natural influences for good which will assist the child's development into a mature and useful member of society'* Children's problems were best handled in the community, in partnership with parents by providing social help. The emphasis was on the *needs* of the individual child as the test for action and not simply or solely on their *deeds,* which is the case in justice oriented systems.

The Kilbrandon Report was influential in establishing Scotland's children's hearings system, a non-criminal system in which young people and their families appear before a tribunal of lay panel members drawn from the community to seek an extra judicial resolution of social problems (Smith and Whyte 2007). Despite fairly universal acclaim as a progressive and effective way of working with children in trouble, the hearings system is under threat–at one level from an increasingly correctional impulse imported from England and the US, and at another level from a rights lobby concerned that the welfare focus of the system does not adequately safeguard children's rights.

EUROPEAN MODELS OF SOCIAL PEDAGOGY

A focus on education and on upbringing is central to European approaches to caring for children. Pestalozzi was an early exponent of an educational ideal in the early 19th century. Pestalozzi's aim was to educate the whole child, including three elements–hands, heart and head, principles that remain central to current notions of social pedagogy (Petrie 2004). There was also a social dimension to the work of Pestalozzi and his followers. They were 'educators of the poor' working in special schools but also in poor rural areas. Education became linked with social development and the creation of community.

The concept of *social* pedagogy, which developed as a profession following WW2 and with some variation between countries is the model of practice applying to work with children and youth across most of Europe, is similarly concerned with ideas of community. Diesterweg, the Prussian educator who developed the concept argued that 'social pedagogy should be expressed in 'educational action by which one aims to help the poor in society (Infed 2005).' Social pedagogy aims to promote social wellbeing through broadly based socio-educational strategies, in contrast to the individualistic approaches to education favoured in an Anglo-American context. In Germany the term for a pedagogue, *erzieher*, translates to 'upbringer', resonating with Kilbrandon's identification of the centrality of idea of 'upbringing' in work with children.

Comparisons between European social pedagogues and residential care staff in the UK are stark. Across Northern Europe pedagogues undertake university level qualifications. In Denmark social pedagogy is the most popular professional training course, above even medicine and teaching. The concern of pedagogical training is to develop reflective practitioners able to work creatively and to use professional judgement rather than procedural guidance in reaching decisions about practice. Morale in practice is high; pedagogues seem to feel that they are doing a worthwhile job, again in contrast to workers in residential child care in the UK.

ANOTHER TYPE OF SOCIAL WORK

Other possibilities of reconceptualising the experience of care come from within social work itself. The managerial discourse that has dominated social work and social care over the past couple of decades is subject to increasing challenge (Moss and Petrie 2002; Meagher and Parton 2004). Critics seek to explore alternative paradigms within which practice might be framed with Webb (2006) claiming that

> the legitimacy of social work rests on exhortations that betray an ethical intent rather than a set of empirical or outcome based possibilities…the return to ethics should be a major theme that characterises social work in the late modern scenario.

There is developing interest in locating alternatives within theoretical explorations of an ethic of care (Tronto 1994; Meagher and Parton 2004). With its origins in feminist thinking an ethic of care requires a stepping in to encounters with the other rather than a stepping back into a 'rational', and objective, position where professionals distance themselves from those with whom they work by means of rules and procedures (Ricks 1992). Maegher and Parton (2004) identify the capacity of the discourse of the ethics of care to offer ways of conceiving and representing the relational dimensions of social work that are obscured by the rational-technical focus of managerialism. Barnes (2006) goes further and highlights the act of caring, which has often been devalued within the individualism of social work discourse as encouraging dependency, as being intertwined with concerns for wider social justice. Caring, she claims,

> can be important work for communities, strengthening them, enabling those least powerful to receive support and recognition, acting to resist oppression … .Care can fulfill a number of functions, including sustaining the connection between individuals at risk of exclusion and the communities in which they live and asserting the humanity and value of people who may be devalued by society (2006:142).

If caring is reclaimed as an ethical task, as the literature is beginning to point to, it needs also to be a political one. Those working with the victims of neo-liberal systems need to become confident in naming the roots of the problems encountered by children and youth rather than continually tampering with their symptoms; this merely blames the victim for their problems. Workers need to express a preferential option for the poor and to do this with love, what Freire calls *'an armed love–the fighting love of those convinced of the right and the duty to fight, to denounce and to announce* (in Darder 1998: 42). This is a broadly educational task, rather than one with roots in pathology and therapy, which has been the traditional social work response to children in state care.

CONCLUSION

Neo-liberalism offers nothing to children in state care, subject to a reductionist form of protection if identified as a victim and punishment if perceived as a villain. The need of the whole child to be brought up by caring adults is lost behind such bifurcation of needs and symptoms. At one level this might appear axiomatic; such systems by their nature create and subsequently demonise an underclass. At another level, things become rather more ambiguous. Attempts to give neo-liberalism a human face through constructs such as social inclusion fail miserably even to fulfill basic precepts of economy and effectiveness; they are both hopelessly expensive and inefficient. They are so because they fail to rise above an atavistic recourse to the principle of less eligibility. In needing to be seen to offer the poor little it offers them nothing yet spends a fortune doing so.

Other systems do not see the problems of the poor as being rooted in their own pathology but as amenable to interventions based around ideas of upbringing and of education in its widest sense. However, there is a saying that a hero will never relinquish his concubine or his horse. Politicians and indeed a majority of social work professionals and managers are heroes. They will fight to hang onto their own version of residential child care even when it is manifestly not working.

Any hope of bringing a concern for social justice for children and youth in residential child care will involve a paradigm shift, requiring that children are no longer conceptualized along the victim/villain dichotomy of neo-liberal welfare but begin to be seen as agents in their own destiny alongside those who work directly with them. Workers in turn need to recognize that caring for children and youth is a political and ethical task rather than the instrumental one it is currently conceived to be. They need to become activists, challenging the structures that cause children's difficulties rather than technicians attempting to apply spurious interventions to the manifestations of these.

REFERENCES

Bailey, R., & Brake, M. (Eds.). (1975). *Radical social work*. New York: Pantheon.

Barnes, M. (2006). *Caring and social justice*. **Basingstoke: Palgrave Macmillan.**

Bebbington, A., & Miles, J. (1989). The background of children who enter local authority care. *British Journal of Social Work, 19*(1), 349–368.

Berridge, D., & Brodie, I. (1998). *Children's homes revisited*. London: Jessica Kingsley.

Brannan, J., & Moss, P. (2003). *Rethinking children's care*. Buckingham: Open University Press.

Butler, I., & Drakeford, M. (2001). Which Blair project? Communitarianism, social authoritarianism and social work. *Journal of Social Work, 1*(1), 7–24.

Cameron, C. (2003). An historical perspective on changing child care policy. In J. Brannan & P. Moss (Eds.), *Rethinking children's care* (pp. 80–97). Buckingham: Open University Press.

Coldrey, B. (2001). The extreme end of a spectrum of violence: Physical abuse, hegemony and resistance in British residential care. *Children & Society, 15*(2), 95–106.

Dahlberg, G., & Moss, P. (2005). *Ethics and politics in early childhood education*. London: Routledge.

Darder, A. (2002). *The critical pedagogy reader*. London: Routledge/Falmer.

Ferguson, H. (2007). Abused and looked after children as 'Moral Dirt': Child abuse and institutional care in historical perspective. *Journal of Social Policy, 36*, 123–139.

Freire, P. (1974). *Pedagogy of the oppressed*. Harmondsworth: Penguin.

Lavalette, M., & Ferguson, I. (2007). *International social work and the radical tradition*. Birmingham: BASW/Venture Press.

Frost, N., Stein, M., & Mills, S. (1999). *Understanding residential child care*. London: Ashgate.

Fulcher, L., & Ainsworth, F. (2006). *Group care practice with children and young people revisited*. New York: Haworth.

Grant, C., & Gabor, P. (2006). An historical perspective on residential services for troubled and troubling youth in Canada revisited. *Relational Child and Youth Care Practice, 19*(4), 17–25.

Jackson, S. (2006). Looking after children away from home: Past and present. In E. Chase, A. Simon, & S. Jackson (Eds.), *Children and young people in and after care: A positive perspective*. London: Routledge.

Jones, C. (2007). What is to be done? In M. Lavalette & I. Ferguson (Eds.), *International social work and the radical tradition*. Birmingham: BASW/Venture Press.

Jones, C., & Novak, T. (1999). *Poverty, welfare and the disciplinary state*. London: Routledge.

Jones, K., & Fowles, A. J. (1984). *Ideas on institutions: Analyzing the literature on long-term care and custody*. London: Routledge and Kegan Paul.

Heron, G., & Chakrabarti, M. (2002). Impact of Scottish vocational qualifications on residential child care: Have they fulfilled the promise. *Social Work Education, 21*(2), 183–197.

Higham, P. (2001). Changing practice and an emerging social pedagogue paradigm in England: The role of the personal advisor. *Social Work In Europe, 8*(1), 21–31.

Humphrey, J. C. (2003). New labour and the regulatory reform of social care. *Critical Social Policy, 23*(1), 5–24.

Infed. (2007). *Johann Heinrich Pestalozzi*. Retrieved February 22, 2008, from www.infed.org/thinkers/et-pest.htm

Jackson, S. (2006). Looking after children away from home: Past and present. In E. Chase, A. Simon, S. Jackson (Eds.), *Children and young people in and after care: A positive perspective* (pp. 9–26). London: Routledge.

Jones, C., & Novak, T. (1999). *Poverty, welfare, and the disciplinary state*. London: Routledge.

Langan, M. (2002). The legacy of radical social work. In R. Adams, L. Dominelli, & M. Payne (Eds.), *Social work: Themes, issues and critical debates 2nd edition*. Hampshire: Palgrave.

Levitas, R. (1998). *The inclusive society: Social exclusion and new labour*. Basingstoke: Macmillan.

Lister, R. (2004). *Poverty*. Cambridge: Polity Press.

Magnuson, D. Barnes, F. H., & Beker, J. (1996). Human development imperatives in the organization of group care programs: A practical approach. In Beker, J. & Magnuson, D. (Eds.), *Residential education as an option for at-risk youth*. New York: Haworth Press.

McLaughlin, K. (2007). Regulation and risk in social work: The general social care council and the social care register in context. *British Journal of Social Work*, *37*(7), 1263–1277.

Meagher, K., & Parton, N. (2004). Modernising social work and the ethics of care. *Social Work and Society*, *2*(1), 10–27.

Magnusson, D., & Baizerman, R. (2007). *Work with youth in divided and contested societies*. Sense Publishers: Rotterdam/Taipei.

Magnusson, D., Barnes, F. H., & Beker, J. (2005). Human development imperatives in the organization of group care programs: A practical approach. *Residential Treatment for Children & Youth*, *13*(3), 85–97.

Moss, P., & Petrie, P. (2002). *From children's services to children's spaces*. London: Routledge/ Falmer.

Myers, C. L. (2000). *Dilemmas of children's welfare policies and practices: A critical and discursive perspective*. Retrieved July 19, 2005, from http://www.well.com/user/clmyers/children

Oliver, C. (2003). The care of the illegitimate child: The Coram experience 1900–45. In J. Brannan & P. Moss (Eds.), *Rethinking children's care*. Buckingham: Open University Press.

Parton, N. (1985). *The politics of child abuse*. London: Macmillan.

Petrie, P. (2004). *Pedagogy – A holistic, personal approach to work with children and young people across services; European models for practice, training, education and qualification*. Unpublished paper, Thomas Coram Research Unit, IoE University of London.

Pitts, J. (2005). The dismal fate of the secure estate. In D. Crimmens & I. Milligan (Eds.), *Facing forward: Residential child care in the 21st century*. Lyme Regis: Russell House.

Pollitt, C. (1990). *Managerialism and the public services*. Oxford: Blackwell.

Ricks, F. (1992). A feminist's view of caring. *Journal of Child and Youth Care*, *7*(2), 49–57.

Sachs, J., & Mellor, L. (2005). Risk anxiety, child panic and child protection: A critical examination of policies from Queensland and New South Wales. *Journal of Education Policy*, *20*(2), 131–146.

Smout, C. (1969). *History of the Scottish people*. London: Fontana.

Smith, M. (2003). Towards a professional identity and knowledge base: Is residential child care still social work? *Journal of Social Work*, *3*(2), 235–252.

Smith, M., Forrest, B., & Garland, P. (Eds.). (2005). *Secure in the knowledge*. Glasgow: University of Strathclyde.

Smith, M., & Whyte, B. (2008). Social pedagogy and social education: Reclaiming a Scottish tradition. *European Journal of Social Work*, *11*(1), 15–28.

Tronto, J. (1993). *Moral boundaries: A political argument for an ethic of care*. London: Routledge.

Webb, S. (2006). *Social work in a risk society: Social and political perspectives*. Basingstoke: Palgrave.

Webster, R. (2005). *The secret of Bryn Estyn*. Oxford: Orwell Press.

Wilkinson, R. G., & Pickett, K. E. (2007). The problems of relative deprivation: Why some societies do better than others. *Social Science and Medicine*, 65, 1965–1978.

UNICEF. (2007). *The state of the world's children*. Retrieved February 20, 2008, from www.unicef.org/ sowc07

SHANNON A. MOORE, RICHARD C. MITCHELL AND LUKE MELCHIOR

RIGHTS-BASED CRITICAL DISABILITY* STUDIES

Enabled Citizenship?

* The term disability takes multiple forms in the current literature (i.e. disAbility or (dis)Ability); however, the authors consciously choose the standard spelling 'disability' in this final chapter. From his perspective of living with the diagnosis of Duchenne muscular dystrophy and resultant severe physical disability, Luke Melchior explains: "When we use the spelling 'disability' the word is not given any valuation in my mind, it is simply a fact of my identity…however, when it is written as '(dis)Ability' or 'disABILITY' it assigns a negative valuation to my limitations by putting them in parentheses or giving my abilities a God-like quality through capitalization, suggesting my abilities are somewhat more special than those of my able-bodied counterparts".

INTRODUCTION

Extreme forms of discrimination are experienced by the more than 600 million persons living with disabilities in developed and developing countries around the world establishing a link among disability, poverty and social exclusion that is "direct and strong throughout the world" (Quinn, Degener, Bruce, Burke, Castellino, Kenna, Kilkelly, and Quinlivan 2002: 11; see also Landsdown 2005). This experience of uneven 'globality' (Schafer 2005) is further emphasized if these citizens are one of the 200 million young people living with disabilities worldwide (UNICEF 2007). Despite wide-ranging consensus regarding adversities experienced by anyone living with 'disability', as noted by one of us, the term remains highly contested and fully dependent upon one's theoretical frame of reference (e.g., medical, individual or social models). It is well established, however, that inclusive education for persons living with disabilities has an inverse relationship to poverty and a parallel relationship with citizenship, voice, social justice and access to health services (UNICEF 2007; Moore, Melchior, Davis 2008). Thus, we contend that for young people living with disabilities education attainment levels set the trajectory for patterns of inclusion and self-advocacy. Indeed, equal access to education is the foremost expression of social justice and a key to all other human rights (Tomaševski 2006). Accordingly, the aim of this chapter is to explore an alternative theoretical approach - rights-based critical disability studies - in order to move social justice in the globalized classroom closer to praxis for young people living with disabilities.

S.A. Moore and R.C. Mitchell (eds.), Power, Pedagogy and Praxis: Social Justice in the Globalized Classroom, 233–245.

Critical social pedagogues frequently argue for a post-structuralist turn towards understanding the body as site for political and cultural activity (Giroux 2003; McLaren 1998; Moore 2006; Moore, Melchior, and Davis 2008). When social justice and human rights are bridged with a standpoint of critical social pedagogy the focus shifts towards changing societal structures that support injustice in the first place (Choules 2007). As highlighted in this anthology (Mitchell and Moore; Giroux; McLaren and Jaramillo; Connolly), critical social pedagogy emerged out of the work of Paulo Friere, and emphasizes educational approaches that go against dominant discourses by raising critical consciousness and joining in solidarity with marginalized groups. It is our also our position in this chapter that critical social pedagogy will be inclusive only when educationalists respond to the active voices of persons living with disabilities (see also Bilken 2000; Choules 2007; Gabel 2002). Furthermore, this final chapter is informed by one of the authors' lived experience of disability as he uncovers nodes of social exclusion from the educational arena. A rights-based response is then articulated that reflects the social model of disability, yet not exclusively so. This rights-based discussion culminates in a comparative analysis of the UN Convention on the Rights of the Child (CRC) and the UN Convention on the Rights of Persons with Disabilities (CRPD) while suggesting pathways that transform these words into democratic and enabled forms of citizenship.

RIGHTS-BASED CRITICAL DISABILITY STUDIES

The Convention on the Rights of the Child (CRC) was approved by the General Assembly of the UN in November 1989 and the CRC asserts the inherent rights of all children. The CRC has been ratified by 192 countries. To date, the United States and Somalia are the only signatories that have not yet done so positioning the Convention as the most globally accepted human rights document in history (Mitchell 2005). Similarly, in December 2006, the General Assembly adopted the UN Convention on the Rights of Persons with Disabilities (CRPD), and received ratification from 20 member states by April 2008 enabling the Convention and its Optional Protocol to enter into international law. Although persons with disabilities are afforded the same rights under the Universal Declaration of Human Rights, this new Convention recognizes persons living with disabilities as comprising a special group in which rights are often compromised due to discrimination and lack of opportunity (UN ENABLE 2008). Moreover, critical disability discourse has altered the field by turning away from viewing barriers to inclusion within the body of the child, and towards exposing barriers in society that prevent young people from "access to basic social services, developing to their fullest potential and from enjoying her or his rights" (UNICEF 2007: 14). The drafting of the CRPD also clearly reflects the paradigm shift from medicalized versions towards social models of disability:

> It represents the culmination of a process initiated over two decades ago by the United Nations of moving from treatment of person with disabilities as 'objects' of charity, medical treatment and social protection towards viewing

> persons with disabilities as 'subjects' with rights, who are capable of claiming those rights and making decisions for their lives based on their free and informed consent, as well as being active members of society (UNICEF 2007: 11).

Dignity is a central principle of all human rights thinking and guides critical rights-based approaches with the understanding that people living with disabilities are subjects and citizens, no longer objects of concern or sympathy (Moore, Melchior, and Davis 2008). Such an approach identifies problems with accessibility and exclusion as human rights violations that are outside the physical person living with any form of disability. Through the lens of critical theory, social exclusion is then understood as a product of unequal power relations embedded within the institutions and present across contemporary societies in both developed and developing world contexts. Social, political and environmental obstacles experienced and managed by individuals experiencing disability, in the context of dominant ideologies that view disability as dependent and deficient, reveal factors implicitly taken for granted as rights for other citizens (Oliver 1998).

As affirmed in the introduction to this chapter, social exclusion and inequality remain dominant experiences for many young people living with disabilities the world over. Reinforcing these points, Lansdown (2005) confirms that the drafting of the UN Convention for People with Disabilities (CRPD) was intended to create a ground for protection from discrimination for children living with disabilities globally because the social problems faced are staggering. As Quinn et al. (2002: 11) explain:

> ...10 per cent of the world's population have a disability of one form or another. Over two thirds of them live in developing countries. Only 2 per cent of disabled children in the developing world receive any education or rehabilitation.

The recent drafting of the CRPD may bolster effective responses to inequities and discrimination described above; but social justice will only be realized if space is created for the full participation of persons living with disabilities (Bilken 1998; Gabel 2002). Landsdown reinforces these points in the context of a child's right to to full participation in society:

> Children have a body of experience and knowledge that is unique to their situation. They have views and ideas as a result of that experience. Yet, in too many countries, there is a failure or even a refusal to recognize the legitimacy of their contribution to decision-making....all people have a right to express their views when decisions are being made that directly affect their lives---and children are people too (2001: 4-7).

A participatory model was also used in the drafting of the CRPD, and consultation with children was undertaken which resulted in all provisions of the Convention applying to both adults and children alike. Furthermore, when integrated with the implementation of the CRC, the CRPD provides an international standard calling for legal accountability in domestic legislation (UNICEF 2007).

SOCIAL JUSTICE, SOCIAL EXCLUSION AND POWER RELATIONS

Social justice and rights-based discourses each have established links within disability studies (Davis 2007; Oliver 1998; Moore, Melchior, and Davis 2008). Although the term social exclusion has been criticized as too vague because of its uncertain range of contexts - including the effects of poverty and other societal interactions (Hill et al. 2004; Davis 2007) - the messages produced by such ideologies are nonetheless poignant. The shift from charity-based interventions to more holitic, rights-based policies and practices has been evident over the past two decades, and is centered on the enjoyment of all human rights without discrimination rather than arguing about specific rights such as interpreting how to understand equitable access to education (Davis 2007; Oliver 1998). As Melchior explains, the result of socially excluding those with physical, cognitive and/or mobility challenges within educational contexts may cause internalization of labels such as uneducated, unworthy, uninvolved, unemployed, unaware, or unattractive, thus increasing the likelihood of an individual being underhoused, under-funded, and experiencing early death (see also Moore, Melchior, Davis 2008).

Multiple discourses identify the need for social justice through removal of all barriers to education for students with disability, to local spaces, to leisure activities, and to employment, as well as development of macro-strategies that challenge poverty through income redistribution and approaches that promote resilience, involvement and democratic participation. This shift will be helped by a re-construction of ideas of social inclusion, children's rights and social justice as interactions and reactions to production of knowledges, to space, to power relations, to politics, and to societal change (see also McIntyre 2005). Davis (2007) illustrates these points in a study that provided paid resources for four young people with disabilities to engage with other young people with disabilities and with local decision-makers:

> These [young people's] perspectives broaden out our understanding of exclusion because they encourage us to view the different definitions of exclusion as distinct yet inseparable. They encourage us to develop a complex notion of social inclusion that also recognizes that not all issues of exclusion are experienced at any one time (131).

Projects such as this that value inclusion and emphasize participation must also take into account the diverse forms of social exclusion which will, ultimately, impact young people's participation. Indeed, "the true cost of segregation is the stigmatization and alienation of those people who would otherwise have been able and willing to take a fuller part" contends Thomas (1997: 104).

IDEOLOGIES OF DISABILITY AND INCLUSIVE EDUCATION

Much of the dominant knowledge about disability in any form has been framed by health science research on impairment and 'deficit-positivistic ideologies' says Oliver (1998). This has resulted in many young people remaining objectified within their societies rather than being recognized as competent social actors, full citizens and agents of social change (Corker and Davis 2000; Davis 2007; James and Prout 1997). The impact of these ideological and theoretical standpoints buttresses the barriers between adults in authority and young people living with disabilities while increasing the potential for institutional and familial abuses of power (Mitchell 2003; Scraton 1997). In addition, ideologies construct and re-construct adult-child power relations and newer experiences of participation, the provision of care and distribution of resources, as well as notions of risk, harm, protection and prevention (Moore, Melchior and Davis, 2008). To secure the rights of children with disabilities we need "sounder knowledge of children's lived experiences" and their unique social contexts (Childwatch International 2006: 1).

Citing Cairns (2001) and Mitchell (2000), Davis (2007) argues participatory projects should be modeled on recent action research in the UK and Canada that "put children at the centre of processes of resolution by enabling them to develop policy in partnership with service providers by creating processes of dialogue rather than consultation" (138). Davis expands the argument by linking it to the CRC and notions of children's rights.

> [A]t present we may not be well placed to develop a human rights approach to participation built of adult-child co-operation, co-dependence and collaboration. A lack of appropriate collaborative structures and relationships means that when children and young people raise issues the pace of response is slow. This suggests that we need numerous long-term and short-term ways to promote 'discursive space' between adults, children and young people. These spaces need to be established in everyday settings such as schools, community centres and leisure/entertainment spaces. They need to be structured in a way that enables participants to foster quick responses to everyday issues. These responses also need to be based on the awareness that any policy or practice will impact on different children and young people in contrasting ways (140).

This 'social model of disability' addresses the previously articulated needs for sound knowledge, and challenges the medical model and its positioning of "impairment and disability as an individual problem where the person with an impairment is viewed in terms of 'deviance', 'abnormality', 'incompetence', 'tragedy' [and] 'dysfunction' " (Corker and Davis 2000: 2). Furthermore, those writing in this discourse astutely differentiate between *impairment* and *disability, enablement* and *disablement* (MacArthur et al. 2007). Where impairment refers to functional limitations of the body, "disability is the loss or limitation of opportunities resulting from ... disabling social, environmental and attitudinal barriers rather than lack of ability" (Crow 1996: 3). Not only does the social model "dismantl[e] the traditional conception of impairment as 'personal tragedy' and the oppression [it] creates" (Crow 1996: 2), it aims to "re-construct both childhood and disability in a way that emphasizes disabled people and children as competent social actors who are an integral part of society" (Corker and Davis 2000: 2). Relating the social model to inclusive education for young people living with disabilities, Corker and Davis (2002) include an important distinction from one young person involved in their research:

> A lot of people think inclusive schooling consists of two things – lifts and ramps – wrong that's integration. Inclusive education is where people have the right attitude towards disabled young people. It is based on the social model of disability, which I think all secondary schools should teach ... I have often been the victim of other people's attitudes but I have never in my life felt myself to be a victim of cerebral palsy. When my English teacher found out how I felt about the word victim, the whole class had a discussion about it. This was good for the 30 teenagers in my class, but what about the other 1400 in my school – especially those who've called me a freak, invalid, retarded and other fantastic words (18).

Indeed, after speaking with 11-14 year old children with disabilities about their school experiences, MacArthur et al. (2007) found that their experiences of "difference" were overwhelmingly negative. Emphasizing the need for a "consistently and explicitly inclusive policy framework centered on children's rights," the authors stress the need for education that is rooted in the social model of disability. Citing Connors and Stalker (2003: 140-1), MacArthur et al. (2007) articulate how schools and children's services create special education as pedagogically distinct:

> For the professionals involved, difference seemed to be something to be removed, minimised and, in some situations, denied altogether... There did not seem to be a positive approach to difference in a number of the services disabled children encountered, some of which seemed to be working from a 'deficit' model. Nor did there seem to be any attempt among some services to educate themselves, other children, or the public in general about the value of difference (140-1).

As Canadian authors, we also find much of the domestic research in disabilities studies is understood and impacted by the medical model, so we have intentionally drawn from discourse more familiar within United Kingdom contexts, and from UN metanarratives that we argue are also rotted within this social model of disability. The strength in this integation of conceptual frameworks overcomes Canadian tendencies towards medically-biased thinking, as Mitchell (2003) has articulated:

> Where children and young people are concerned, diagnostic-free therapy ...would be viewed as radical in present-day mental health settings, or for that matter, within most service delivery structures for children presently influenced and shaped by medical-model thinking ... When considering the alternatives, it appears reasonable to adopt a moderate, culturally respectful ideology based on current theoretical and empirical understanding of how children grow through interaction within their families and the rest of society (283).

As we aim to support more thorough rights-based responses to social justice in education, we recognize that alligning with any single polarity of thought found within disability studies (i.e. the social model, the medical model or rights-based approaches) creates considerable new problems that may even lead to further exclusion. Thus, we are promoting equity and social inclusion by understanding disability from both dominant models. Articulated most clearly by an academic and disability advocate who lives with her own form of impairment, Crow (1996) recognizes the type of exclusion that results from any singular understanding of disability and supports similar notions of moderate, culturally respectful ideologies:

> We align ourselves with other civil rights movements and we have learnt much from those campaigns. But, we have one fundamental difference from other movements, which we cannot afford to ignore. There is nothing inherently unpleasant or difficult about other groups' embodiment: sexuality, sex and skin colour are neutral facts [in those contexts]. In contrast, impairment means our experiences of our bodies can be unpleasant or difficult. This does not mean our campaigns against disability are any less vital than those against heterosexism, sexism or racism; it does mean that for many disabled people personal struggle related to impairment will remain even when disabling barriers no longer exist. (Crow 1996: 4)

As Melchior has argued in the introduction, Crow also argues that although the social model has vast libratory and emancipatory potentials, those writing and researching within disability studies must not forget how people living with impairments may also be medically embodied. This argument is congruent with the transdisciplinary standpoint of critical social pedagogy in this text, and greater appreciation of the body as a site for political, cultural and social activism.

ENABLED CITIZENSHIP AND EDUCATION

The complexity of challenges impacting inclusive education for young people living with disabilities calls for more comprehensive, systemic responses that address attitudes, practices, policies and new legislative agendas. UNICEF (2007: 1) sets the tone:

> In the context of education, inclusion means the creation of barrier-free and child-focused learning environments, including for early years. It means providing appropriate supports to ensure that all children receive education in non-segregated local facilities and settings, whether formal or informal. It is framed by article 29 of the Convention on the Rights of the Child, which requires that the child's education be directed to the development of their personality, talents and mental and physical abilities to their fullest potential; to the preparation of the child for responsible life in a free society, in the spirit of understanding and tolerance.

Perhaps most importantly, inclusion involves individuals as well as institutions as this project says as much about societal attitudes as do lifts, ramps and other material supports. An inclusive education is a process by which all children, not just 'special children' have the opportunity "to grow up in an environment where diversity is the norm rather than the exception" (UNICEF 2007:1). This is an environment where everyone has multiple chances to learn, play and work together since flexibility, valuing of diversity, adaptation and necessary supports are ensured.

Still, educational systems in all nations too often reinforce social exclusion and human rights violations – many to the extreme. In response, the CRC and the CRPD are binding under international law for countries that have ratified. Moreover, these Conventions are complimentary as they articulate a more rigourous and accountable rights-based response that may also inform national legislation, provision of services, and evolved understanding towards those living with various disabilities (UNICEF 2007). At the heart of both these UN metanarratives one may hear a single fundamental assertion: to move from words to action the rights and voices of individual children are the most valuable resources (UNICEF 2007; also see White 2003).

With regard to socially inclusive principles and practices, both the CRC and CRPD are guided by organizing principles and a series of provisions that apply to all children. CRC Article 42 articulates that States must inform both children and the general public (a) of the ratification and (b) that children have not only inherent human rights but rights that are unique to young people. Such dissemination naturally invokes a commonly understood "rights-based approach" to intervening in young peoples lives – one where CRC Articles 2, 3, 6 and 12 are the organizing principles for praxis as well as the global reporting framework utilized by the UN Committee on the rights of the Child (see also Mitchell 2005). CRC Article 2 asserts that all young people have the right to be free of discrimination based on "race, colour, sex, language, religion, political or other opinion, national, ethnic or social origin, property, disability, birth or other status". The best interests of the child are to be taken into account and Article 3 states that social, legal and governmental institutions must give primary consideration to the child's quality of life when deciding upon matters of child protection. In Article 6, the CRC mandates that all children have the inherent right to life and to maximum survival and development. Finally, Article 12 affirms that all children are participatory citizens who have the right to express their views (or be represented by a third party) on issues that affect them. When these principles guide policy and practice implementation of the Convention, dignity as a basic principle of human rights is reinforced and the relevance of the remaining principles and provisions of human rights are heightened.

Building upon the CRC framework, Article 7 of the CRPD articulates human rights principles that are fundamental to all children including young people living with disabilities. CRPD echoes the principles of the CRC described above as it focuses upon non-discrimination, best interests, participation, and holistic development. All provisions of the CRPD apply to children. In addition, for both children and adults, the principles of the CRPD are expressed in Article 3 which stipulates that persons living with disabilities shall: (a) have their inherent dignity, individual autonomy, and independence (in choice and persons) respected; (b) not, in any way, be discriminated against; (c) participate fully in an inclusive society; (d) be respected and accepted for their diversity; (e) receive full opportunity; (f) have full and equal accessibility; (g) experience gender equality; (h) have, when considered as children, a right to life and identity, and their evolving capacities respected.

Furthermore, specific rights-based principles apply to education and young people living with disabilities under both the CRC and CRPD. For instance, CRC Article 28 "recognize[s] the right of the child to education" that is delivered in equal and progressive means such that it ensures: primary education is compulsory and free; secondary education is accessible and diverse in orientation; post-secondary education is made as accessible as possible; and, guidance and information are easily attainable for young people. CRC Article 28 stresses every child's right to education that is delivered "in particular with a view to contributing to the elimination of ignorance". As such, CRC Article 29 extends Article 28 by specifying the delivery of education. The provision states that education will aid in developing young people's respect for themselves and their fullest potential; fundamental human rights and freedoms; their cultural identity and values; "understanding, peace, tolerance, [and] equality"; and the natural environment.

Reflecting the joined-up, integrated and often complex nature of social problems, social inclusion and education, CRC Article 23 specifically addresses young people with disabilities, and states that they experience social inclusion when education that is:

> designed to ensure that the disabled child has effective access to and receives education, training, health care services, rehabilitation services, preparation for employment and recreation opportunities in a manner conducive to the child's achieving fullest possible social integration and individual development, including his or cultural and spiritual development (United Nations 1989).

Again, CRPD Article 24 is built upon education articles in the CRC and actually expands the foundation provided by the CRC by addressing the needs of children with complex and severe impairments. CRDP Article 24 recognizes the right to education without discrimination that is inclusive and provides equal opportunity for life-long learning (UNICEF 2007). Hence, although children and families continue to consistently experience barriers to enjoyment of their most basic human rights, the existence of the CRPD is indicative of progression towards social models of disability and provides a road map to address the challenge of meaningful social change.

Specifically, the UNICEF Innocenti Research Centre, in a recent report called "Promoting the Rights of Children with Disabilities" (2007) offers a global perspective that specifically addresses the new Convention on the Right of Persons with Disabilities and the foundation of human rights provided by the Convention on the Rights of the Child. After analyzing this report and the linkages between the CRC and CRPD it became clear that these international agreements can be synthesized further to foster implementation and realization of social inclusion in education. Such an educational environment would reflect enabled citizenship through rights-based relationships with and for *all* children (ie: an integration of CRC Articles 2, 3, 6, 12, 23, 28, 29 as well as CRPD Articles 3, 7, 24):

> OPPORTUNITY: to value and experience diversity, non-discrimination, equity and respect.
>
> FREEDOM: to contribute to decisions and make choices regarding one's own best interests on all levels of educational systems either independently or through appropriate support that affirms dignity and autonomy.
>
> ACCESS: to support and care for healthy-holistic development and to access physical environments, transportation, information, communications, technologies and education facilities that are maximizing in relation to evolving capacities.
>
> PARTICIPATION: children and young have opportunity, freedom and access (as noted above) that facilitate their democratic participation in matters that affect them as citizens by: educating others on their views, and expressing their views from a standpoint of being informed about their rights including the right to education.

The table located in Appendix A illustrates the interconnectedness between the articles of the CRPD and CRC in greater detail. It is noteworthy that the four core principles of the CRC (Articles 2, 3, 6, and 12) also emerged in correspondence to the CPRD principles in Article 3, and all CRPD provisions corresponded with at least one core CRC principle.

Additionally, in all CRPD articles CRC Article 2 (non-discrimination) was a salient dimension. This integration and analysis of the two treaties speaks to non-discrimination as a major organizing principle of both, particularly as it protects and recognizes the rights of marginalized groups. Most prominently, CRPD Article 7 specifies the rights of all young people with disabilities, and as such, the entire CRC is applicable to this provision. CRC Article 23 also specifically states that young people with disabilities "should enjoy a full and decent life, in conditions which ensure dignity, promote self-reliance and facilitate the child's active participation in the community." Indeed, this Article corresponds to 14 of 16 CRPD provisions. Further, CRC article 24 states that young people with disabilities have a right to the "highest attainment standard of health" and was relevant to 11 CRPD articles. CRC Articles 28 (the young person's right to education) and 29 (the direction or aim of that education) were similarly relevant, corresponding with 10 and eight CRPD articles, respectively including CRPD Article 24, the education provision.

FROM WORDS TO ACTION: CLOSING THOUGHTS

As Tomaševski and others in this volume declare, to move from the rhetoric contained in UN metanarratives towards full implementation and a revolutionary social action we must understand both our assets and obstacles. This begins with the honest realization that adult attitudes create many of the barriers we seek to change with and for children, and impede the evolution towards social justice and equity for all (Scraton 1997: 186). Hence one of the greatest barriers to realizing social justice within education in anyone's society is simply a new perception of full citizenship for all - including all individuals living with disabilities (see also Moore in press). Frequently, the discourse relative to rights-based potentials within UN metanarratives such as the CRC, the CRPD, the Millennium Development Goals is critiqued as untapped, and thus, unmet at levels deep enough to impact the systems that consistently violate human rights (Choules 2007; Tomaševski 2006; Moore and Mitchell 2007a, b). Nevertheless, we maintain these UN principles are congruent with the social model of disability and form a better foundation for a rights-based, critical disability discourse in which pedagogues work in solidarity alongside young people to uncover social, environmental, political and attitudinal barriers to inclusion. For educators, we have suggested taking up a critical pedagogical stance wherein the voices/participation of young people living with various disabilities are understood as the most vital resource for addressing social injustice in anyone's classroom - even those with apparently little or no voice. This approach has been illustrated by the integration of the CRC and the CRPD, and explored above under the rubrics of OPPORTUNITY, FREEDOM, ACCESS and PARTICIPATION.

Throughout this final chapter a rights-based, critical disability discussion has taken place, and a framework that integrates the Convention on the Rights of the Child with the Convention on the Rights of Persons with Disabilities has been provided to aid in this process. The salience of integrating corresponding CRC and CRPD principles and provisions - particularly in relation to education and pedagogues - reinforces the initial arguments put forth in this chapter and throught the text: the right to education can be a key that unlocks social exclusion only if and when young people first have accurate knowledge about their rights, and adults intervening in their lives create spaces for full participation of all young people. Through informed participation, young people living with disabilities may develop new skills and form productive partnerships that equip them to challenge human rights violations. Finally, we wish to emphasize solidarity with the Quinn et al. (2002: 25) declaration that:

> Disability is used not only to ***set people apart*** but also to ***keep people apart***. All points of access to the structures of everyday life – the world of education, of work, of the family or of social interaction – are established largely by reference to the dominant norm, in this instance that of the able-bodied.

For persons living with disability, the body is linked to identity politics and human rights in a manner embedded within underlying psychological, social and political constructs (Putman 2005; see also McLaren 1998), and these will continue to be re-shaped through the evolution of adult attitudes, social forces, public policy, and emerging promises of human rights. Through this chapter we have proposed and explored an alternative theoretical approach described as rights-based critical disability studies in order to move social justice in the globalized classroom towards praxis.

REFERENCES

Biklen, D. (1998). Constructing inclusion: Lessons from critical disability narratives, *International Journal of Inclusive Education*, *4*(4), 337–353.

Childwatch International Research Network. (2006). Understanding and contextualizing children's real participation, submission to the Committee on the Rights of the Child at Day of General Discussion. Retrieved September 15, 2006, from http://www.childwatch.uio.no/projects/Citizenship/Childwatch%20submission_CRC%20Day%20of%20General%20Discussion.pdf

Corker, M., & Davis, J. M. (2000). Disabled children – (Still) Invisible under the law. In J. Cooper (Ed.), *Law, rights and disability*. London: Jessica Kingsley.

Choules, K. (2007). The shifting sands of social justice discourse: From situating the problem with 'them,' to situating it with us. *The Review of Education, Pedagogy and Cultural Studies*, *29*, 461–481.

Crow, L. (1996). Including all of our lives: Renewing the social model of disability. In C. Barnes & G. Mercer (Eds.), *Exploring the divide*. Leeds: The Disability Press.

Davis, J. M. (2007). Analysing participation and social exclusion with children and young people. Lessons from practice. *The International Journal of Children's Rights*, *15*, 121–146.

Gabel, S. (2002). Some conceptual problems with critical pedagogy. *Curriculum Inquiry*, *32*(2), 177–201.

Giroux, H. (2003). *The abandoned generation: Democracy beyond the culture of fear*. New York: Palgrave Macmillan.

Hill, M., Davis, J., Prout, A., & Tisdall, K. (2004). Moving the participation agenda forward. *Children & Society*, *18*(2), 77–96.

James, A., & Prout, A. (1997). Contemporary issues in the sociological study of childhood. In A. James & A. Prout (Eds.), *Constructing and reconstructing childhood*. London: Falmer.

Lansdown, G. (2000). *Challenging Discrimination*. EURONET.

Lansdown, G. (2001). *Promoting children's participation in democratic decision making*. Florence, Italy: UNICEF Innocenti Research Centre.

Lansdown, G. (2005). A new human rights treaty for people with disabilities. *Disability News*, 8 September 2005. Children's Rights Information Network [Online]. Retrieved March 10, 2008, from http://www.crin.org/resources/infoDetail.asp?ID=6161

McIntyre, J. (2005). Working and re-working the conceptual and geographical boundaries of governance and international relations. *Systemic Practice and Action Research*, *18*(2), 173–220.

MacArthur, J., Sharp, S., Kelly, B., & Gaffney, M. (2007). Disabled children negotiating school life: Age difference and teaching practice. *The International Journal of Children's Rights*, *15*, 99–120.

McLaren, P. (1998). Schooling the postmodern body: Critical pedagogy and the politics of enfleshment. *Journal of Education*, *170*(1), 53–83.

Mitchell, R. C. (2003). Ideological reflections on the DSM-IV-R (or pay no attention to that man behind the curtain, Dorothy!). *Child and Youth Care Forum*, *32*(5), 281–298.

Mitchell, R. C. (2005). Postmodern reflections on the UNCRC: Towards utilizing Article 42 as an international compliance indicator. *The International Journal of Children's Rights*, *13*(3), 315–331.

Moore, S. A. (2006). Transdisciplinary critical multicultural pedagogy in Canadian higher education. In Dawn Zinga (Ed.), *Navigating multiculturalism* (pp. 126–139). Newcastle , UK: Cambridge Scholars Press.

Moore, S. A. (In Press). Social justice and education in a world fit for children? In J. Adele Kentel & A. Short (Eds.), *Totems and taboos risk and relevance in research on teachers and teaching*. Rotterdam: Sense Publications.

Moore, S. A., Melchior, L., & Davis, J. (2008). "Me and the 5 P's': Negotiating rights-based critical disabilities studies and social inclusion. *The International Journal of Children's Rights, 16, 249-262.*

Moore, S. A., & Mitchell, R. C. (2007a). Rights based restorative justice: Towards critical praxis with young people in conflict with the law. In A. Ang, I. Delens-Ravier, M. Delplace, C. Herman, D. Reynaert, V. Staelens, R. Steel, & M. Verheyde (Eds.), *The UN children's rights convention: Theory meets practice*. Proceedings of the International Interdisciplinary Conference on Children's Rights, 18–19 May 2006, Ghent, Belgium (pp. 50–78). Mortsel, Belgium: Intersentia. pp. 549–563.

Moore, S. A., & Mitchell, R. C. (2007b). "Herstelrecht volgens de mensenrechtenprincipes" (or "Rights-based Restorative Justice," Het Tijdschrift voor Jeugdrecht en Kinderrechten (or TJK – Flemish Journal for Youth and Children's Law) *5*(4), 251–259.

Oliver, M. (1998). Theories of disability in health practice and research. *British Medical Journal, 317*(7170), 1446–1449.

Putnam, M. (2005). Developing a framework for political disability identity. *Journal of Disability Policy Studies, 16*(3), 188–205.

Quinn, G., Degener, T., Bruce, A., Burke, C., Castellino, J., Kenna, P. , Kilkelly, U. & Quinlivan, S. (2002). *The current use and future potential of United Nations human rights instruments in the context of disability*. United Nations, New York and Geneva.

Scraton, P. (Ed.). (1997). *'Childhood' in 'Crisis'*. London: UCL Press.

Thomas, G. (1997). Inclusive schools for an inclusive society. *British Journal of Special Education, 24*(3), 103–107.

Tomaševski, K. (2006). *The State of the Right to Education Worldwide – Free or Fee 2006 Global Report*. Retrieved February 29, 2008, from http://www.katarinatomasevski.com/

United Nations. (1989). *Convention on the rights of the child*. New York: UN General Assembly.

United Nations. (2007). *Convention on the rights of persons with disabilities*. New York: UN General Assembly.

United Nations Enable. (2008). *Rights and dignity of persons with disabilities*. Retrieved March 8, 2008, from http://www.un.org/disabilities/default.asp?id=257

United Nations International Children's Fund. (2007). *Innocenti digest no. 13: Promoting the rights of children with disabilities*. Florence, Italy: Innocenti Research Centre.

White, B. (2003). *A world fit for children?–Children and youth in development studies and policy*. Paper presented on the occasion of the 51st anniversary of the Institute of Social Studies 9 October 2003, The Hague/ISS.

APPENDIX A*

Cross Referencing the Convention on the Rights of Persons with Disabilities and the Convention on the Rights of the Child

CRPD Article	CRPD Summary	CRC Article
Article 3 (a-h)	General principles of the Convention are fundamental to all provisions and to its implement-ation: respect, dignity, choice independence, non-discrimination, diversity, equal opportunity, accessibility, gender equity, respect for evolving capacity	Article 2 (non-discrimination) Article 3 (best interests) Article 5 (evolving capacities) Article 6 (maximum survival/development) Article 12 (participation) Article 23 (young people with disabilities)
Article 5	Promotes equal protection and non-discrimination for all people before the law. Provides persons with disabilities legal protection against discrimination on all grounds.	Article 2 (non-discrimination) Article 12 (participation) Article 23 (young people with disabilities) Article 42 (dissemination)
Article 6	Recognizes women and girls with disabilities as comprising a special group – subject to multiple forms of discrimination. Promotes development, advancement and empowerment for women to ensure their equal enjoyment of all human rights and freedoms.	Article 2 (non-discrimination) Article 6 (maximum survival/development) Article 12 (participation) Article 19 (neglect/abuse) Article 23 (young people with disabilities) Article 24 (access to health) Article 34 (sexual abuse)
Article 7	Ensures young people with disabilities equality and the same human rights and freedoms as with other children. Guarantees the best interests of young people with disabilities. Promotes the right of these young people to express their views in all matters that affect them, and that these views be listened to and given due weight.	All CRC Principles & Provisions
Article 8	Immediate, effective and appropriate measures shall be undertaken to: make the public aware of the rights, dignity and contributions of persons with disabilities; combat stereotypes	Article 2 (non-discrimination) Article 6 (maximum survival/development) Article 12 (participation) Article 17 (media)

	and prejudices; and promote positive perceptions of persons with disabilities leading to greater social inclusion.	Article 23 (young people with disabilities) Article 28 (education) Article 29 (direction of education) Article 42 (dissemination)
Article 9	Ensures that persons with disabilities have equal access to all services and systems that enable them to live independently and participate fully in life. Ensures that member States develop minimum standards of accessibility for persons with disabilities.	Article 2 (non-discrimination) Article 3 (best interests) Article 4 (economic, social, cultural rights) Article 6 (maximum survival/development) Article 12 (participation) Article 23 (young people with disabilities) Article 24 (health) Article 27 (standard of living)
Article 10	Guarantee that persons with disabilities enjoy their inherent right to life on an equal basis with others.	Article 2 (non-discrimination) Article 3 (best interests) Article 5 (evolving capacities) Article 6 (maximum survival/development) Article 7 (name/nationality) Article 23 (young people with disabilities) Article 24 (access to health) Article 28 (education)
Article 13	Ensures access to justice on an equal basis with others.	Article 2 (non-discrimination) Article 3 (best interests) Article 12 (participation) Article 37 (inherent dignity/humanity) Article 40 (justice)
Article 17	Ensures the physical and mental integrity of persons with disabilities will be equally protected.	Article 2 (non-discrimination) Article 3 (best interests) Article 6 (maximum survival/development) Article 12 (participation) Article 19 (neglect/abuse) Article 23 (young people with disabilities) Article 24 (access to health) Article 25 (periodic review) Article 27 (standard of living) Article 36 (exploitation)
Article 20	Promotes measures that ensure the greatest possible mobility for persons with disabilities through assistive technologies and specialist staff at affordable costs.	Article 2 (non-discrimination) Article 3 (best interests) Article 6 (maximum survival/development) Article 23 (young people with disabilities)

		Article 24 (health) Article 26 (social security) Article 27 (standard of living) Article 28 (education)
Article 23	Ensures the full and equal rights for children with disabilities. Children with disabilities shall not experience, because of their disability: separation from their parents against their will; loss of their fertility concealment, abandonment, neglect and/or segregation. Young people with disabilities and their families will be supported by early and comprehensive information and services.	Article 2 (non-discrimination) Article 3 (best interests) Article 5 (evolving capacities) Article 6 (maximum survival/development) Article 9 (separation) Article 18 (parental/guardian responsibility) Article 19 (abuse) Article 23 (young people with disabilities) Article 24 (health) Article 25 (periodic review) Article 27 (standard of living) Article 28 (education) Article 29 (direction of education)
Article 24	Ensures the right of all persons with disabilities to education that is inclusive and non-discriminatory. This education shall: develop and promote the dignity and rights of persons with disabilities to their full potential; and enable effective participation. Access to primary and secondary education shall be free and compulsory; post-secondary education shall be fully encouraged; and all levels of education will support and accommodate for all individuals as fully as possible.	Article 2 (non-discrimination) Article 3 (best interests) Article 6 (maximum survival/development) Article 12 (participation) Article 23 (young people with disabilities) Article 24 (access to health) Article 28 (education) Article 29 (direction of education) Article 31 (play) Article 42 (dissemination)
Article 25	Ensures persons with disabilities the highest attainable and non-discriminatory standard of health. Health care and services shall be: gender-sensitive, including "in the area of sexual and reproductive health and population-based public health programmes"; preventative in nature regardless of age; geographically accessible in terms of proximity; staffed by professionals who provide an equal standard of healthcare to all people, and who retain free and informed consent and promote human rights of persons with disabilities.	Article 2 (non-discrimination) Article 3 (best interests) Article 6 (maximum survival/development) Article 12 (participation) Article 18 (primary responsibility) Article 23 (young people with disabilities) Article 24 (access to health) Article 25 (periodic review) Article 27 (standard of living) Article 28 (education) Article 29 (direction of education) Article 42 (dissemination)

Article 26	Ensures that persons with disabilities shall attain maximum independence and ability; and be provided with comprehensive habilitation and rehabilitation services in the areas of health, employment and education	Article 2 (non-discrimination) Article 3 (best interests) Article 6 (maximum survival/development) Article 23 (young people with disabilities) Article 24 (access to health) Article 25 (periodic review) Article 28 (education) Article 29 (direction of education)
Article 27	Promotes that persons with disabilities have the equal right to work and gain a living. Ensures measures that prohibit discrimination in the workplace; requires workplaces to accommodate for diverse needs; and foster work experience, and career advancement and flexibility.	Article 2 (non-discrimination) Article 23 (young people with disabilities) Article 28 (education) Article 29 (direction of education) Article 32 (employment)
Article 28	Ensures persons with disabilities the right to an adequate standard of living and social protection. This includes public housing, services and assistance for disability-related needs, as well as assistance with disability-related expenses in cases of poverty	Article 2 (non-discrimination) Article 4 (social, cultural, economic rights) Article 6 (maximum survival/development) Article 23 (young people with disabilities) Article 24 (access to health) Article 27 (standard of living) Article 28 (education) Article 29 (direction of education)
Article 29	Ensures persons with disabilities equal, full and effective participation in political and public life, including right to vote, to stand for elections and to hold office.	Article 2 (non-discrimination) Article 3 (best interests) Article 12 (participation) Article 42 (dissemination)

*The Editors would like to gratefully acknowledge the contribution of Research Assistant Ms. Jaime Nikolaou in the collation of this Appendix.

BIOGRAPHIES

RICHARD C. MITCHELL

Richard is an Assistant Professor of Child and Youth Studies at Brock University, Canada. His research and scholarship focus upon local, international and transdisciplinary approaches to implementing the human rights of children and young people within political, institutional and community-based settings.

SHANNON A. MOORE

Shannon is an Assistant Professor of Child and Youth Studies at Brock University, Canada and holds a PhD in Counselling Psychology. Her scholarship emphasizes community-based implementation of UN human rights and justice instruments. This focus bridges critical theory, social justice and mental health. As a clinical counsellor she has practiced in Canada and the UK.

KATARINA TOMAŠEVSKI

This anthology is dedicated to the memory and life's work of Professor Katarina Tomaševski, deceased Oct. 4, 2006, Copenhagen - former Visiting Professor at the Law School of Peking University, former Professor of International Law and International Relations at the University of Lund, and former United Nations Special Rapporteur for Education. Tomaševski studied law at Harvard and completed her doctoral research on the theme of Terrorism and Contemporary International Law at the University of Zagreb. Her subsequent research concerned the right to food; women's and children's rights; children in prison; development aid and human rights; HIV/AIDS and human rights; and the widespread denial of the right to education. She served as Special Rapporteur for Education from 1998 to 2004 during which time she established the Right to Education Project. Tomaševski spoke many languages and lived in over a dozen countries throughout her career around the world teaching, writing and publishing widely.

HENRY GIROUX

Henry holds the Global TV Network Chair in English and Cultural Studies at McMaster University in Canada. His most recent books include: *America on the Edge*(2006); *Beyond the Spectacle of Terrorism* (2006), *Stormy Weather: Katrina and the Politics of Disposability* (2006), *The University in Chains: Confronting the Military-Industrial-Academic Complex* (2007), and *Against the Terror of Neoliberalism: Politics Beyond the Age of Greed* (2008).

JANET CONWAY

Janet is Canada Research Chair in Social Justice at Brock University where she teaches in the department of Sociology and the graduate program in Social Justice and Equity Studies. She is the author of "Praxis and Politics: Knowledge Production in Social Movements," Routledge 2006. Her current research focuses on the World Social Forum with special interest in feminist and indigenous perspectives on the anti-globalization movement.

MARY KELLETT

Mary is leading pioneer in the empowerment of children and young people as researchers and has published widely in this and associated fields. She is Director of Childhood and Youth Studies at the Open University UK where she is also Director of the Children's Research Centre and a Visiting Professorship at the Institute of Education in Qatar.

BENJAMIN WARD

Ben is a pupil at a UK primary school in Oxfordshire, and was ten years old when he undertook the research included in this text. He has an interest in environmental issues and is enthusiastic about children having a research voice.

KAREN MUNDY

Karen is an Associate Professor and Canada Research Chair, Global Governance and Educational Change, at the Ontario Institute for Studies in Education, University of Toronto. She directs the Comparative, International and Development Education Centre and its Graduate Degree Program. Her research is focused on three themes: international development cooperation in education; international organizations and global governance; educational reform in East and Southern Africa; and civil society involvement in educational policy making. She is widely published in journals in the field of comparative education, and has completed several books and monographs, including *Paradigm Lost: The Politics of Educational Reforms in Sub-Saharan Africa* (Greenwood, 2002) and *Comparative Education: Issues for Teachers* (Teachers College Press, 2008).

PETER MCLAREN

Peter is one of the leading critical pedagogists in North America, and has written and edited approximately forty books and monographs on critical pedagogy and multicultural education. His book Life in Schools: An Introduction to Critical Pedagogy in the Foundations of Education (1998) was named one of the twelve most significant writings by foreign authors in the field of educational theory, policy and practice by the Moscow School of Social and Economic Sciences.

NATHALIA E. JARAMILLO

Nathalia is an Assistant Professor of Cultural Foundations and affiliated faculty member of American Studies at Purdue University. She has authored and co-authored a number of publications in the field of critical pedagogy, socio-political critique and feminist studies. She is currently working on a co-edited text entitled "Epistemologies of Ignorance and the Study of Limits in Education" and a co-authored book, "Essays in Critical Pedagogy." Nathalia's scholarship is trans-disciplinary and she is interested in examining the connection between local spaces of transformation and broader socioeconomic and political relations characteristic of global capitalism.

TERRY WOTHERSPOON

Terry is Head and Professor of Sociology at the University of Saskatchewan. His teaching and research interests focus on relations among education, social policy, inequality, and social justice. He is the author of numerous articles and books, including *The Sociology of Education in Canada: Critical Perspectives*; *The Legacy of School for Aboriginal People: Education, Oppression, and Emancipation* (with B. Schissel) and *First Nations: Race, Class and Gender Relations* (with V. Satzewich), and a recipient of the Canadian Education Association Whitworth Award for Educational Research.

MAUREEN CONNOLLY

Maureen Connolly is a Freireian educator who translates her politics into semiotic phenomenological inquiry into stressed embodiment, institutional culture, curriculum development, movement education and narrative forms. She has a history in physical culture, education, and community service. She is a Professor at Brock University and a Canadian 3M national teaching fellow.

DAVID FANCY

David is an Assistant Professor of Dramatic Arts at Brock University in St. Catharines, Ontario. His current research, funded by a Social Sciences and Humanities Research Council of Canada (SSHRC) Grant, involves the theorization of performance from an immanentist perspective, with an emphasis on the ontology of presence.

SUSAN SPEAREY

Susan is an Associate Professor of English at Brock University in St. Catharines, Ontario. Her current research, funded by a Social Sciences and Humanities Research Council of Canada (SSHRC) grant, focuses on the ethics of readership and the function of affect in the context of literary mediations of contemporary histories of mass violence, with particular emphasis on post-apartheid South

African literature. Her collaborative research with David Fancy, funded by a Brock Chancellor's Chair for Excellence in Teaching, examines the potential applications of secular mindfulness and bodymind philosophies and practices in the university classroom, particularly in the teaching of critical theory.

WARREN LINDS

Warren is an Assistant Professor in human relations and human systems intervention at Concordia University, Montreal, Canada. He teaches undergraduate and graduate courses on diversity, small group leadership and ethical practices in human systems intervention. For the past 20 years he has been a popular theatre facilitator and community educator using 'Theatre of the oppressed' in anti-racist education programs.

LINDA GOULET

Linda is an Associate Professor in the Indigenous Education Department at First Nations University of Canada, Regina, Canada. She teaches Indigenous pedagogy, colonization, and racism and works in community programming using Forum Theatre to develop youth leadership and communities free from oppression.

MARK SMITH

Mark worked in residential school and secure accommodation settings in Scotland for almost 20 years. In 2000 he developed and delivered a Masters programme in residential child care, the first of its kind in the UK, at the University of Strathclyde. He is currently a lecturer in social work at the University of Edinburgh. He has published widely on residential child care and related areas and is working on a PhD on the nature of care in residential child care.

LUKE MELCHIOR

Luke Melchior is an Education Developer for Muscular Dystrophy Canada, and an activist in the movement for people living with disabilities in his home province of British Columbia, across Canada and internationally. Luke has collaborated with the National Film Board of Canada in the production of an autobiographical film entitled Bearing Witness ~ Luke Melchior which focused upon his lived experience of muscular dystrophy. In addition, Luke is an international keynote speaker and author in academic journal and text publications. In his words, "If things are accessible to me, they're accessible to everyone - all the resources out there, and all the people that are connected with them. And that's the route to really vibrant community, where everyone can share their gifts".

SERIES EDITOR'S BIOGRAPHIES

Michael Kompf is Professor of Education at Brock University, Canada. Interests include developmental issues for adult learners and teachers; personal construct psychology; global policies and practices in higher education; and philosophies of inquiry. Recent writing and presentations have included exploring the nature of university corporatism, higher education success rates, individual and the social implications of distance learning. A member of the International Study Association on Teachers and Teaching (isatt.org) since 1985, Michael is currently serving his fourth term as Chair.

Pam Denicolo is the Director of the Graduate School for the Social Sciences, the Director of Postgraduate and Professional Studies in the School of Pharmacy at the University of Reading and an active member of the University Committee for Postgraduate Research Studies. Her passion for supporting and developing graduate students is also demonstrated through her contributions to the UK Council for Graduate Education Executive Committee, the Society for Research into Higher Education Postgraduate Network, and other national committees and working groups which, for example, review and evaluate the national implementation of the Roberts funded generic skills training, and the concordance of UK universities with the European Code and Charter.

As a psychologist working particularly in the fields of Professional and Postgraduate Education, she has supervised more than 50 doctoral students to successful completion, examined many more, and developed and led Research Methods Programmes for social scientists in her current and previous universities. She was honoured to be appointed an Honorary Member of the Royal Pharmaceutical Society for her contributions to the education of pharmacists. Her lifelong interest in student learning, and hence teachers' teaching, led her to become an active member of the International Study Association on Teachers and Teaching (ISATT) and serving member of the Executive Committee for many years. Her research has been oriented by a commitment to understanding the way participants in learning processes construe their roles, situations and activities, through the use and development of Personal Construct Theory approaches and methods.

Printed in the United States
210630BV00005B/56/P